ASCENT
CENTER FOR TECHNICAL KNOWLEDGE

Autodesk® Vault Professional 2024
Administrator Essentials

Learning Guide
1st Edition

Published by
ASCENT Center for Technical Knowledge
630 Peter Jefferson Parkway, Suite 175
Charlottesville, VA 22911

866-527-2368

www.ascented.com

Contents

Chapter 9: Working with Items   9-1

Chapter 13: Administering Autodesk Vault Professional   13-1

Appendix A: Additional Resources   A-1

Preface

The *Autodesk® Vault Professional 2024: Administrator Essentials* guide introduces Autodesk Vault Professional 2024 to CAD administrators. The focus of this learning guide is to teach administrators how to set up and manage categories, lifecycles, revisions, file naming schemes, items, bills of materials (BOMs), and the engineering change order (ECO) process.

This guide is intended for administrators with some knowledge of Autodesk Vault Professional's data management capabilities. The hands-on practices included in this guide reinforce usage of items, BOM and ECO features, and automated workflows.

Important:

Refer to the *Course and Classroom Setup* section for installing the practice files, setting up the database, and understanding the dependencies between course practices.

Topics Covered

- Introduction to Autodesk Vault Professional

- Managing Categories

- Lifecycle Management

- Revision Management

- File Naming Schemes

- Working with Items

- Managing Change

- Working with Bills of Materials

- Administering Autodesk Vault Professional

- Reporting

- Thin Client

Prerequisites

- Access to the 2024 version of the software, to ensure compatibility with this guide. Future software updates that are released by Autodesk may include changes that are not reflected in this guide. The practices and files included with this guide might not be compatible with prior versions (e.g., 2023).

- A good working knowledge of Autodesk CAD programs and working knowledge of Autodesk Vault Basic and Autodesk Vault document management features.

Course and Classroom Setup

Classroom Environment

The courseware is intended for use in an instructor-led environment. If you plan to use the courseware on your own in a non-classroom environment, you must set up Autodesk Vault correctly. Before you set up your system, you should be aware of the following:

- Do not use a production vault for the practices. It is recommended that you set up a separate vault on a separate vault server.

- If you plan to repeat a practice, you must remove any files that were added to the vault when you previously completed the practice. It is recommended that you delete the entire vault and start again with a new vault.

- Do not attempt these practices on a production vault server until you are familiar with the procedures that are covered.

You must install and run this courseware from individual computers. You cannot run the courseware from a shared server. **DO NOT install the courseware on a computer that stores working vault data.**

Overview of Installing the Courseware

The following steps describe how to install the courseware.

1. Install Autodesk Vault Professional Client and Autodesk Vault Professional Server on each computer.

2. Install the course datasets on each computer.

3. If Autodesk Vault has been previously used on the computer, restore default settings for the user interface.

Installing Autodesk Vault

Install both Autodesk Vault Professional Client and Autodesk Vault Professional Server on each computer. See the Autodesk Vault installation help for installation instructions.

If you are using any of the following Autodesk software applications in conjunction with Autodesk Vault, they must be installed before installing Autodesk Vault.

- Autodesk Inventor

- AutoCAD

- AutoCAD Mechanical

- AutoCAD Electrical

- Autodesk Civil 3D

- Autodesk Revit

Installing the Practice Files

To install the data files for the practices:

1. Download the practice files .zip file using the link provided on the Practice Files page in the guide.

2. Unzip the .zip file to the C: drive. A *Vault Professional Admin* folder is created and contains all the files that you will need. The path for all the files should be *C:\Vault Professional Admin*.

3. The remaining files are required to restore the database. The instructions for this are detailed below.

    WARNING: The following procedure will overwrite the current datasets and file stores in your current vault. Be sure to back up any necessary vaults that might be required at a later time.

Restore the Backup

1. Click **Start>All Programs>Autodesk>Autodesk Data Management>Autodesk Data Management Server Console 2024**.

2. In the Log In dialog box:
    *   For *User Name*, enter **administrator**.
    *   Leave the *Password* field blank.
    *   Click **OK**.
    *   The Autodesk Data Management Server Console displays.

3. Select **Tools>Backup and Restore**.

4. Select **Restore**, then click **Next**.

5. In the Backup and Restore Wizard dialog box, click the browse button next to the *Select backup directory for restore:* field, navigate to the location on your local C: drive where the practice files were extracted (*C:\Vault Professional Admin*), then set the following:

- *Database data location:* **Default Restore Location**
- *File Store location:* **Original Restore Location**

6. Click **Finish**.

7. In the prompt that displays, click **Yes** (as shown below) **only if you are sure that you want to delete the current datasets**.

8. The Restore Progress dialog box displays the progress for restoring the database.

9. In the Backup and Restore Wizard dialog box, click **Close**.

10. In the Autodesk Data Management Server Console dialog box, click **File>Exit**.

In This Guide

The following highlights the key features of this guide.

Feature	Description
Practice Files	The Practice Files page includes a link to the practice files and instructions on how to download and install them. The practice files are required to complete the practices in this guide.
Chapters	A chapter consists of the following: Learning Objectives, Instructional Content, and Practices. • **Learning Objectives** define the skills you can acquire by learning the content provided in the chapter. • **Instructional Content**, which begins right after Learning Objectives, refers to the descriptive and procedural information related to various topics. Each main topic introduces a product feature, discusses various aspects of that feature, and provides step-by-step procedures on how to use that feature. Where relevant, examples, figures, helpful hints, and notes are provided. • **Practice** for a topic follows the instructional content. Practices enable you to use the software to perform a hands-on review of a topic. It is required that you download the practice files (using the link found on the Practice Files page) prior to starting the first practice.
Appendices	Appendices provide additional information to the main course content. It could be in the form of instructional content, practices, tables, projects, or skills assessment.

Practice Files

To download the practice files for this guide, use the following steps:

1. Type the URL *exactly as shown below* into the address bar of your Internet browser to access the Course File Download page.

   Note: If you are using the ebook, you do not have to type the URL. Instead, you can access the page simply by clicking the URL below.

   ## https://www.ascented.com/getfile/id/oryziasPF

   address bar of a browser

   TYPE URL HERE

2. On the Course File Download page, click the **DOWNLOAD NOW** button, as shown below, to download the .ZIP file that contains the practice files.

   DOWNLOAD NOW ▶

3. Once the download is complete, unzip the file and extract its contents.

   The recommended practice files folder location is:
   C:\Vault Professional Admin

   Note: It is recommended that you do not change the location of the practice files folder. Doing so may cause errors when completing the practices.

4. To set up the database, refer to the *Course and Classroom Setup* section.

Stay Informed!

To receive information about upcoming events, promotional offers, and complimentary webcasts, visit:

www.ASCENTed.com/updates

Introduction to Autodesk Vault Professional

This chapter provides an overview of the Autodesk® Vault Professional software, its features, functions, and benefits, and the Autodesk Vault Professional user interface.

Learning Objectives

- Describe the benefits and functionality of Autodesk Vault Professional.
- Identify the user interface elements and navigate the user Interface.

1.1 Autodesk Vault Professional Overview

In this lesson, you learn about the basic features and functionalities of Vault Professional, and its advantages as a design data management system.

With Vault Professional, you can implement an automated release and change management process with complete tracking of bills of materials (BOMs) and related design information.

Objectives

After completing this lesson, you will be able to:

- Describe Vault Professional.
- Explain the roles of Vault Professional in lifecycle management and change management.
- List some of the roles users can be assigned in Vault Professional.
- Describe Vault Professional integration with other design applications.

About Autodesk Vault Professional

Autodesk Vault Professional can use vault files as item data, making vault files available to an extended design team that can include personnel from departments outside of engineering.

Autodesk Vault Professional helps you manage your vault data by creating and tracking change orders, managing bills of materials, and working with item revisions and lifecycles to oversee files throughout the design and manufacturing process.

Benefits of Autodesk Vault Professional

When designers and engineers place their data files in a vault, Autodesk Vault Professional connects these files to item numbers that can integrate with ERP systems. Thus Autodesk Vault Professional is a gateway connecting two different parts of a company: the design/engineering team and the extended product team.

Example of How to Use Autodesk Vault Professional

With Autodesk Vault Professional, more users can connect directly to the files in the vault, assign items to these files, enable other users in a larger team to work with the items, view items using visualization files, and manage these items as they move through their lifecycle from design to manufacturing to completion.

Autodesk Vault Professional Functions

Autodesk Vault Professional automates the release management process by managing engineering changes and bills of materials. You use Autodesk Vault Professional to manage items throughout their lifecycle.

Manage Items

Function	Description
Create Items	With Autodesk Vault Professional, you can create items by assigning items to data files or by creating new items.
Delete Items	When an item has reached the end of its lifecycle and is no longer used, you can delete it from the Item Master.
Organize Items	Using the Item Master list, you can quickly search, sort, and filter items, and customize how the item list is viewed.
Add User-Defined Properties to Items	In addition to the default properties for each item, you can add user-defined properties (fields) to item records.
Where Used	You can analyze where items are used and check item dependencies before editing an item or requesting an engineering change order.
Track Item Revisions	A flexible revision numbering scheme keeps track of the history of items. You can use a predefined number of letter schemes, or use the ASME Y14.35M scheme. You can use secondary and tertiary schemes to track data with even more detail.

Bill of Materials (BOM)

Function	Description
Link Items	A BOM is built automatically when an assembly file in the vault is assigned an item.
	You can also link items together to create your own BOM that includes newly created items.
Edit BOMs	You can edit materials and quantities for any design. You can override quantities in a BOM.
Units of Measure	Autodesk Vault Professional and Autodesk® Inventor® support the same units of measure, so any units of measure used in Inventor are automatically transferred to Autodesk Vault Professional BOMs. You can also specify the base measure of items, including mass, volume, quantity, and length.
Property Mapping	You can map CAD properties in design files in Autodesk Vault to item properties. These CAD properties are carried over to corresponding items in Autodesk Vault Professional that can be used in the Item Master list and in the BOM.

Engineering Change Orders (ECOs)

Function	Description
Manage ECOs	You can create ECOs and send them to members of the team. You can also attach notes and red-lined drawings to ECOs.
	ECOs are reviewed and tracked by members of the team then can be rejected, approved, or withdrawn. The status of these ECOs is shown graphically and can be tracked to ensure that change orders are not forgotten or misplaced.
Set Up Routes	You can set up routing lists with email support. You can use these lists to ensure that the right team members are notified of changes.

Item Lifecycle

Every item is tracked with indicators that show the state of the item (Work in Progress, Released, In Review, and Obsolete). Revisions increment automatically in some cases when an item changes state. This process ensures that correct revision control is used. Generally, items are in a Work in Progress state when edited and in a Released state when released to manufacturing.

Manage Security

Users receive system access based on their departments, positions, and roles. Security features prevent inadvertent changes and enable only authorized users to access or edit data. Certain functions, such as creating new numbering schemes, mapping CAD properties to item properties, and editing users, are restricted to administrators.

Example of Linking Design Data

The design work on an ICU valve is nearing completion and released by the design team. As part of managing the valve data, you need to set up the packaged product. You add an item representing the final packaged assembly, an item representing the packaging itself, and another item representing the product specification sheet. You link these items to the assembly design data to form a BOM for all the components then release the items to manufacturing.

Based on an ECO, a new revision of the ICU valve packaged assembly has spare O-rings, and the ICU valve buttons are no longer painted.

Security and Users

You can control who has access to certain features in Autodesk Vault by assigning users different roles and permissions.

Add Users

Note: When you add a new user, you should include their email address so that they can receive automatic notification of ECOs.

As a Vault administrator, you can add, modify, and disable users from the system. You can group users with similar roles and manage permissions and roles for both groups and individual users.

You can also add users from a domain.

Specify Roles

In addition to the numerous Administrator, Content Center, and Document predefined roles, Autodesk Vault Professional has the following predefined roles: Change Order Editor (Levels 1 and 2), ERP Manager, Item Editor (Levels 1 and 2), Item Reviewer, Custom Object Consumer, Custom Object Editor (Levels 1 and 2), and Custom Object Manager (Levels 1 and 2). You can also create your own custom roles. You can do this by creating a new role, editing a role, or copying an existing role to then edit. For example, you can copy the Document Editor Level 2 role and then remove the Folder Create permission so that users cannot create their own folders within the vault. Users can be assigned roles based on their required level of access in the company.

Role-Based Permissions

Users are assigned Vault task permissions based on the role they are assigned by an administrator. Administrators can also create Access Control lists for any folder in a vault. Folder permissions such as Full Access and Read-Only can be assigned to groups or individual users.

Example

New employees join the company and require access to design data in the vault. The administrator adds new users and sets their roles based on their required access to vault and Vault Professional data. However, because the new employees are training during the first two weeks, the administrator sets their access to certain sensitive folders as read-only until they have finished training.

Integration with Other Products

The Autodesk Vault Professional software is a web services-based application. The application interfaces with files located in a vault file store and database. The file store and database were created during installation or migrated from another Autodesk Vault release.

Vault Professional integrates with the applications that produced the files in the vault. You can access the vault from the design application or open files created by these applications in Vault Professional.

Autodesk Inventor

Vault Professional integrates with Autodesk Inventor. Vault Professional reads Autodesk® Inventor® files and the relationships amongst these files. The items' type and BOM information is built on this data.

- Inventor can control BOM data. By assigning BOM structure properties to components, such as phantom or inseparable, Inventor influences how the Vault Professional application reads and builds its BOMs for those items.

- You can transfer custom properties between Inventor and Vault Professional.

- Vault Professional fully supports all units of measure used by Inventor.

AutoCAD-Based Products

Autodesk Vault Professional integrates with other design applications and reads data in AutoCAD® drawing (DWG™) files. The following list outlines how AutoCAD-based applications work with Autodesk Vault Professional.

- External references (xrefs) are added as attachments to items in Vault Professional when the parent drawings are assigned items.

- Vault Professional can read drawing files and map their properties to item properties.

- Vault Professional can read projects, drawings, and properties from Autodesk® Civil 3D® drawing files, and it can map their properties to item properties. Vault Professional also provides Autodesk Civil 3D software users with additional project management functionality by displaying a Project tree in the Prospector tab. This enables the Autodesk Civil 3D software users to safely share their drawing files and individual AEC objects with other team members.

- Vault Professional reads BOM data in AutoCAD® Mechanical drawing files. It uses this data to create BOM data and determine object types.

- If the vault is set to enforce file locking, you cannot check out a drawing from the vault unless its lifecycle state is set to Work in Progress.

Autodesk Revit

The Autodesk Vault Professional software with Revit Vault Add-in offers Autodesk Revit users with file security, version control, and multi-user support. Autodesk Vault integrates with Autodesk® Revit® Architecture, Autodesk® Revit® MEP, and Autodesk® Revit® Structure.

1.2 User Interface

Overview

This lesson describes the features of the Vault Professional user interface.

Objectives

After completing this lesson, you will be able to:

- Identify the user interface elements in Vault Professional.
- Describe the three main areas of the user interface.
- Use the main pane in Vault Professional to show a list of objects that can be files in the vault, items, or engineering change orders (ECOs).
- Navigate the user interface.

User Interface Elements

With the user interface elements in Autodesk Vault Professional, you can work quickly and efficiently with data.

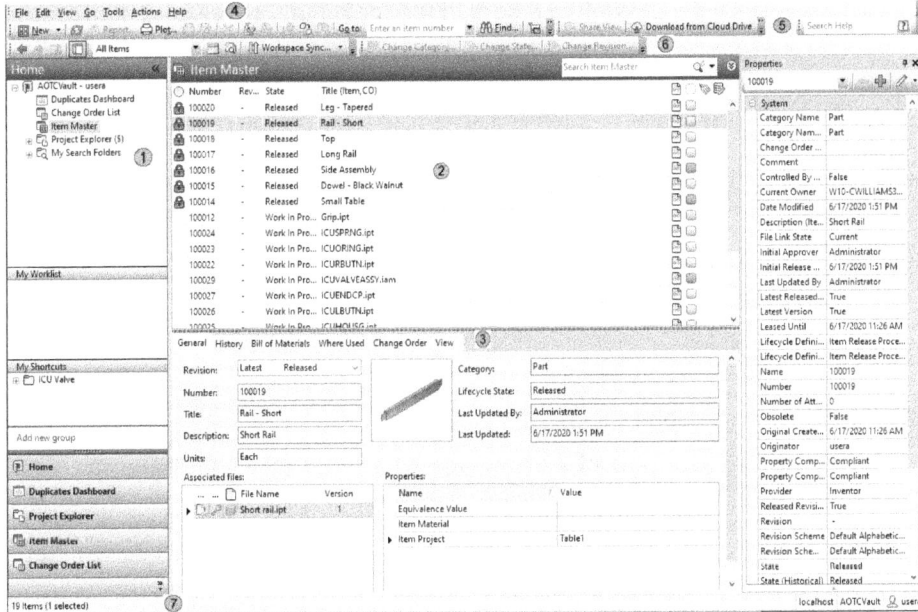

1. **Navigation pane:** Contains folders and subfolders for different environments, shortcuts for searches, and filters. The work environment (All Folders, Item Master, Change Order List, or Vault Explorer) is determined by the selection in the Navigation pane.

2. **Main pane:** Contains the primary list of data, which changes based on the current work environment. It can be a list of items, a list of files in the vault, or a list of ECOs. Depending on the type of environment, the records for these lists can be selected, previewed in more detail, and edited

3. **Preview pane:** Shows a preview of the selected record in the main pane. The different tabs are logically organized views of details of the record and change, depending on the environment.

4. **Main menu:** Contains the commands used in Vault Professional.

5. **Standard toolbar:** The Standard toolbar provides quick access to common commands depending on the environment

6. **Secondary toolbars:** An Advanced and Behavior toolbar provides quick access to other common commands depending on the environment.

7. **Status bar:** Shows information such as the number of records in the main pane, the number of records selected, the user name, and the name of the vault in which the user is logged.

Example of the Autodesk Vault Professional User Interface

In Autodesk Vault Professional, you normally begin in the Navigation pane. This pane contains one or more objects that essentially behave as folders, because they contain other objects.

When you select one of these folders, the data in the selected folder displays in the main pane. You then work in the main pane. When a record in the main pane is selected, it is previewed in the Preview pane.

About the Navigation Pane

The Navigation pane is the starting point in the Autodesk Vault Professional user interface. Use the Navigation pane to go directly to required data.

Using the main workflows, you can work efficiently with Autodesk Vault Professional and quickly locate the data you require.

Navigation Pane Areas

Screen Element	Description
Home	The upper part of the Navigation pane shows the folders you can click. These folders can be filtered so that only the Item Master or only Project Explorer is visible.
	In the following illustration, the Home view is shown, where all possible folders for navigation are visible.
	Three major work environments exist in Vault Professional:
	• Items
	• Change orders
	• Project Explorer
	By clicking the folders, you change the work environment displayed, which affects the main pane and the Preview pane
My Search Folders	In the previous illustration, saved searches are also visible.
	These saved searches are environment specific. For example, if you create a search in the Item Master for the word *Valve* then save this search, it displays under *My Search Folders*. Clicking this *Valve* folder brings up the Item Master work environment and displays the filtered items containing the word *Valve*.

Screen Element	Description
My Worklist	ECOs requiring your attention or action are listed under *My Worklist* together with the due date. Clicking the listed item brings up the Change Order List work environment with the ECO highlighted.

My Worklist
ECO-000003 (1/10/2024)

My Shortcuts	You can create group folders in the *My Shortcuts* area. You can fill these folders with shortcuts to items, documents, files in the vault, and ECO. Clicking these links takes you to the selected objects immediately.

My Shortcuts
hub_shaft_assy.iam
Trailer Hitch Ball
ICU Valve
Housing
End Cap

Add new group

Navigation Pane Buttons	Buttons in the Navigation pane, located in the lower-left corner of the main interface screen, filter the folders at the top of the Navigation pane. For example, clicking **Project Explorer** removes all folders except those displayed in Project Explorer.

Home

Duplicates Dashboard

Change Order List

Item Master

Project Explorer

Tip: Use these buttons to filter the folders saved under *My Search Folders*. In the main pane, you see the results of searches for all work environments. However, when you click a button such as **Project Explorer**, only search results for the Project Explorer environment display.

Example of the Navigation Pane

In the following illustration, **Home** is selected in the lower-left corner of the user interface. The **Item Master** is selected in the Navigation pane. The contents of this folder (Item Master) display in the main pane.

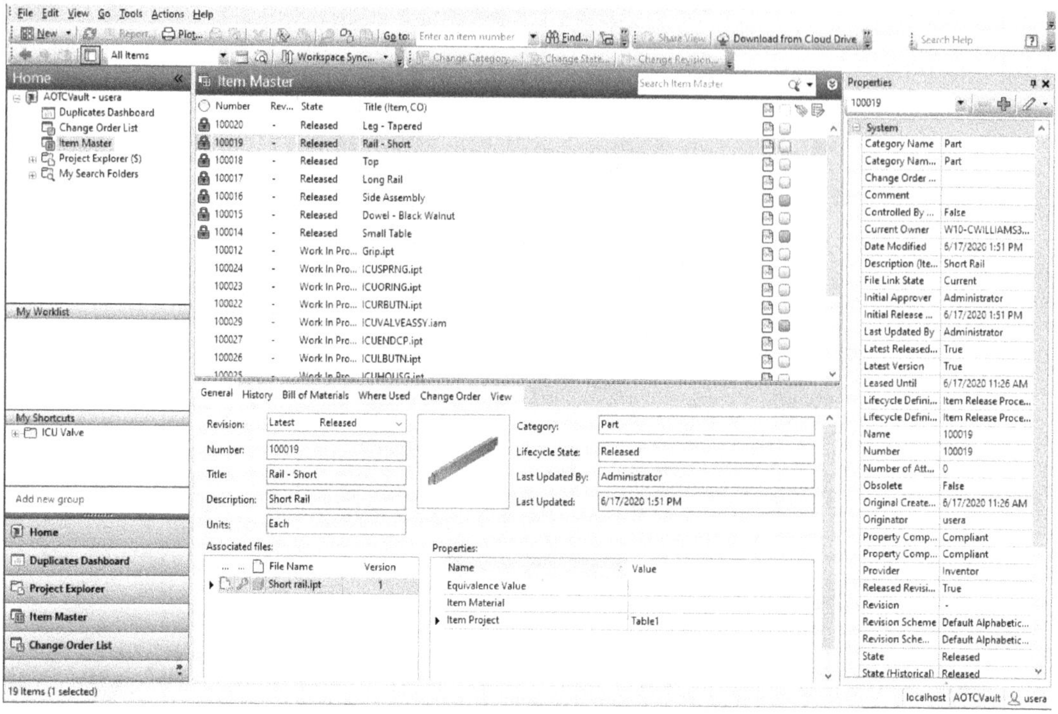

About the Main Pane

The main pane changes based on the work environment and how the view is customized. Use the main pane to sort, filter, and view records in the list.

The main pane lists records of objects. These objects can be items, files in the vault, or ECOs, based on the work environment.

You can customize the main pane to show different fields and to filter the list based on different criteria. You can also use Find to quickly search a list.

Example of the Item Master

When working with items, the main pane shows the Item Master.

	Number	Rev...	State	Title (Item,CO)
🔒	100020	-	Released	Leg - Tapered
🔒	100019	-	Released	Rail - Short
🔒	100018	-	Released	Top
🔒	100017	-	Released	Long Rail
🔒	100016	-	Released	Side Assembly
🔒	100015	-	Released	Dowel - Black Walnut
🔒	100014	-	Released	Small Table
	100012	-	Work In Pro...	Grip.ipt
	100024	-	Work In Pro...	ICUSPRNG.ipt
	100023	-	Work In Pro...	ICUORING.ipt
	100022	-	Work In Pro...	ICURBUTN.ipt
	100029	-	Work In Pro...	ICUVALVEASSY.iam
	100027	-	Work In Pro...	ICUENDCP.ipt
	100026	-	Work In Pro...	ICULBUTN.ipt

Example of the Change Order List

ECOs are listed in the Change Order List.

Change Order List — Search Change Order List

			Number	State	Title (Item,CO)	Due Date
▶			ECO-000001	Work	Adjust lubricant type	4/20/2010 6:51 PM
			ECO-000002	Open	Rework Trailer Hitch Saftey Plate	4/30/2010 7:13 AM
			ECO-000003	Approved	Remove paint from ICU Valve buttons	5/13/2010 12:00 AM

Example of Files in a Vault Folder

Files and their properties are listed when a vault folder is selected in the Navigation pane.

ICU Valve — Search ICU Valve

	Name	Version	Checked In
Folder			
	Documents		
File			
	ICU Valve Main Assembly.iam	1	4/6/2007 2:25 AM
	ICUENDCP.ipt	1	4/6/2007 2:25 AM
	ICUHOUSG.ipt	1	4/6/2007 2:25 AM
	ICULBUTN.ipt	1	4/6/2007 2:25 AM
	ICUORING.ipt	1	4/6/2007 2:25 AM
	ICURBUTN.ipt	1	4/6/2007 2:25 AM
	ICUSPRNG.ipt	1	4/6/2007 2:25 AM
	ICUVALVE.ipt	1	4/6/2007 2:25 AM
	ICUVALVEASSY.iam	1	4/6/2007 2:25 AM

About the Item Record Dialog Box

Along with the major interface panes, one of the most commonly used interface elements in Vault Professional is the Item Record dialog box. Use the Item Record dialog box to view (**Open**) or edit (**Edit**) items and their BOMs, and to attach and detach files. Items must be in the Work In Progress state in order to open them for editing. Otherwise they can be opened read-only for viewing. This feature is helpful when the item has a lot of details or when you want to view the associated files.

Using the Item Record interface, you can edit an item's properties, including the item's BOM, attach and detach files, and view change orders associated with that item.

Example of the Item Record Interface

You create a new item such as lubricant in the Item Master. In the Item Master, you double-click an item representing an assembly to open it and click **Edit** for editing. You add the lubricant item in the assembly item's BOM. When you have completed the task, you click **Save and Close** to save the changes and exit the Edit Item Record dialog box.

Organizing and Populating a Vault

In this chapter, you learn how Autodesk® Inventor® files are organized for best results with Autodesk® Vault. You then learn how to prepare existing projects and upload them to a Vault using Autodesk Autoloader.

Learning Objectives

- Describe how Inventor project, model, library, and Content Center files are organized for the best results with Vault.
- Add existing models to a vault using Autodesk Autoloader.

2.1 How Autodesk Inventor Files Are Organized

Overview

In this lesson, you learn how Autodesk Inventor project files, model files, and library files are organized for the best performance with Vault. A typical Autodesk Inventor design includes a large number of files. You can use Autodesk Autoloader to help organize your existing models before uploading them to the vault, or you can organize the files manually before you upload them. Whichever method you use, you should know how Autodesk Inventor uses the project file to find files and how regular model files and library files are organized.

The following image displays a number of designs added to a vault. The files are organized in the vault to match the local working folder structure when the files were uploaded to the vault.

Objectives

After completing this lesson, you will be able to:

- Describe how Autodesk Inventor project files work with a vault.

- Describe how Autodesk Inventor model files are organized for best results with Autodesk Vault.

- Describe how library files are organized for best results with Vault.

- Describe how Content Center files are organized for best results with Vault.

About Project Files

Autodesk Inventor uses project files to organize and locate related files. Before you upload files to a vault or try to fix resolution issues, you must learn how Autodesk Inventor uses the project file to locate the files in a design.

Project Files Defined

Autodesk Inventor uses project files to organize storage locations for related files in a design. For example, when you open an assembly in Autodesk Inventor, it looks for the component files relative to the locations specified in the project file. When you place a part from the Content Center, the generated part is stored in a folder relative to the top-level folder specified in the project file. A project file is set up to correspond with the way the files are organized in the vault.

You must create a Vault project file when you want to work with designs that will be managed using Autodesk Vault. This project file format is only available if you have Autodesk Vault installed. The Workspace, Libraries, and Content Center Files entries specify where Inventor searches for files. All paths are defined relative to a project file location.

```
Project
    Type = Vault                                    (1)
    Location = C:\AOTGVault\VaultWorkingFolder\     (2)
    Included file =
    Use Style Library = Read-Only
  + Appearance Libraries
  + Material Libraries
  - Workspace
        Workspace - .\Designs                        (3)
        Workgroup Search Paths
  - Libraries
        Library - .\Libraries                        (4)
        Frequently Used Subfolders
  - Folder Options
        Design Data (Styles, etc.) = [Default]
        Templates = [Default]
        Content Center Files = .\Content Center Files\  (5)
  + Options
  + Vault Options
```

(1) A Vault project file is required for managing designs stored in the vault.

(2) The local working folder is mapped to the root folder in the vault. All files in the design are typically located under this folder.

(3) The *Workspace* folder is the top-level folder for the models and drawings you create for all designs stored in the vault. You create subfolders under here to organize your designs.

(4) Library files in the vault are copied to folders under this local folder. Files in these folders cannot be edited.

(5) Files generated from the Content Center are stored under this folder when copied from the vault.

Autodesk Inventor uses the copy of the project file in the local working folder when you work with files you have checked out from the vault. Therefore, the paths in the project file must correspond to the way that files are organized in the local working folder. When you get files from the vault, the vault structure is reproduced in the local working folder.

Project File Location

The project file should be located one folder above all other model and library file folders. A folder beneath the project file folder holds all designs with folders for each design.

The following image displays the layout of a typical vault working folder. The project file, **Designs.ipj**, is located in the root folder (*VaultWorkingFolder*). The *Designs* folder is the workspace folder in the project file and is located under the project file. It contains folders for different designs. The *Content Center Files* and *Libraries* folders are also located under the project file but outside of the workspace folder.

Use a Single Project File

There are many ways to organize Autodesk Inventor project and model files. Some users have one project file for all designs; other users have one project file for each design. With Vault, a single project file should be used so you need to manage just one project file and do not have to switch project files when moving from one design to another.

Frequently Used Subfolders

Frequently used subfolders are shortcuts defined in the project file to give you quick access to designs and library parts in your local working folders. In the following image, a project file is displayed in the project file editor. The **Frequently Used Subfolders** entry of the project file contains paths to frequently used design and library folders.

🞕 Use Style Library = Read Only
⊞ 🞕 **Workspace**
🞕 Workgroup Search Paths
⊞ 🞕 **Libraries**
⊟ 🞕 **Frequently Used Subfolders**
🗀 Clamp - Workspace\Clamp
🗀 ICU Valve - Workspace\ICU Valve
🗀 Optic Mount - Workspace\Optic Mount
🗀 Rotary Vee - Workspace\Rotary Vee
⊞ 🞕 **Folder Options**
⊞ 🞕 **Options**
⊞ 🞕 **Vault Options**

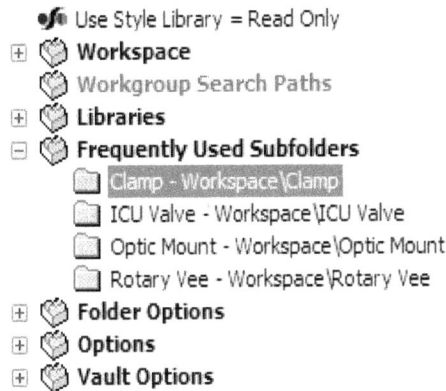

Frequently used subfolders are displayed when you browse for a file in Autodesk Inventor, making it easier to navigate to specific designs or libraries.

Mapping Project Folders

When you check in files or add new files to the vault, the files are copied from the local working folder to folders in the vault. Inventor determines where to copy the files by looking in the project file. The vault folders are specified by mapping each local search path to a vault folder.

A typical folder mapping is shown in the following image. The *Project Root* folder is where the project file is stored. In the example shown, the local *Project Root* folder is mapped to the root folder of the vault. Therefore, the project file is copied to the root of the vault, and model files will be copied to their respective folders relative to the root folder in the vault. Each library path in the project file is also mapped to a vault folder. In the following image, files in the local path named *Library* are copied to the *Libraries* folder in the vault, and files in the local *Content Center Files* path are copied to the *Content Center Files* folder in the vault.

Project Folder Mapping	✕
Mapping of local folders to the vault	

Local	Vault
🗀 Project Root	$
⧉ Content Center Files	$/Content Center Files
⧉ Library	$/Libraries

Edit...

OK   Cancel

The mapping information is stored as XML data in the project file. For example, the mapping for the *Library* folder corresponding to the previous image is displayed in the following image. The local path and the vault path are both specified.

```
<ProjectPath pathtype="Library">
    <PathName>Library</PathName> (1)
    <Path>.\Libraries</Path> (2)
    <VaultPath>$/Libraries</VaultPath> (3)
</ProjectPath>
```

(1)   Path name in project file.

(2)   Local folder path. This folder is relative to the folder containing the project file.

(3)   Corresponding vault folder path. The folder structure under this folder matches the folder structure under the local folder path.

About Model Files

There are many ways to organize model files. The method you select must be compatible with the project file and with Vault. In this section, you learn how model files are organized for the best results with Autodesk Vault.

How Inventor Model Files Are Organized

For best results, model files are organized in folders under a single project file.

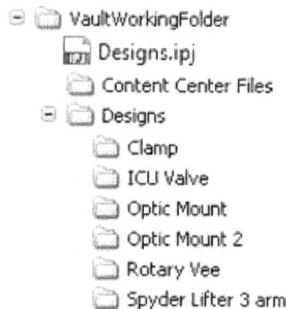

The same folder structure is used in the vault. When you retrieve files to your local working folder, they are copied to the same relative location and they open successfully in Inventor. For example, the corresponding vault is organized as shown. A single project file is located in the root of the vault.

Folders for the designs, libraries, and Content Center parts are one level below. You can further organize your files using subfolders under these top-level folders. When you get files from the vault, they are copied to the local working folder with the same structure and can be opened successfully.

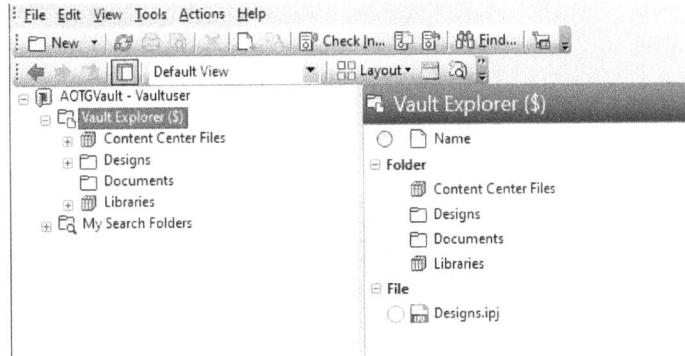

Project File Settings for Model Files

The **Workspace** path specifies the location of a top-level folder for all non-library model files. Files for different designs are stored in folders under the *Workspace* folder. If model files are saved outside of the *Workspace* folder, Autodesk Inventor will not find them.

In the project file, the workspace is set as a relative path to the folder that contains the project file.

How Common Parts Are Organized

If a part or subassembly is used in more than one design, the file should be stored in a separate folder from the designs in which the part is used, and then it should be referenced in each design. If the part or assembly rarely or never changes, the file can be stored in a library folder so that it cannot be modified by users.

The vault is used as a centralized storage area for all of your files including common parts and library parts and assemblies. Upload all of your library and common components to the vault so that Inventor users can place them in their designs using the **Place from Vault** command. The following image displays a folder named *Common Parts*, which contains parts that are included in a number of designs.

About Library Files

Library files are parts or subassemblies that do not normally change. In Autodesk Inventor, library files are treated as read-only files that are not normally versioned.

Typically, library files are used in more than one design. Common purchased components, Content Center files, and iParts are typical library components. Autodesk Inventor includes a wide selection of library parts in the Content Center libraries. You can also get library parts and assemblies from component manufacturers or create them yourself. Any file can be designated as a library file, including regular Inventor parts and assemblies and AutoCAD® drawing files. You must set up and organize library components correctly so that they work with the vault.

About Library Folders

Files that are stored in library folders in the vault are designated as library files. Library folders are similar to regular folders except that files in library folders are treated as library files and cannot be modified while stored in a library folder. Library folders must be created directly under the root of the vault, because you cannot create them under a regular folder.

Library folders use a different icon than regular folders. Note that subfolders are used to group library parts into meaningful categories. You can create any level of nested library folders to help organize the files.

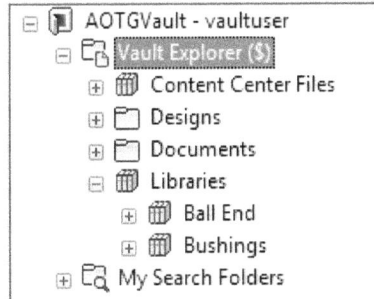

When a user retrieves a design from the vault and the design contains library files, the library files are copied into the working folder to the same relative location and folder as in the vault.

iParts in the Vault

The following image displays an iPart factory, **Heim Bushing.ipt**, in a library folder. Note that a unique icon is used to distinguish a factory from other file formats. iPart children also have unique icons.

Project Files Settings for Library Parts

When you open a model, Autodesk Inventor looks for library files in the locations specified in the project file. The following image displays a project file with a single **Libraries** path that points to the top-level *Library* folder. The library path is relative because the *Library* folder is beneath the folder containing the project file.

Importance of Relative Paths

Because all design files, including library files, are stored in the vault, all paths in a vault project file should be defined relative to the folder containing the project file. When you use relative paths, the entire local working folder structure is portable; it can be located in any location on a user's computer. If you use absolute paths to local folders such as *G:\Libraries*, or UNC names such as *\\PartServer\Libraries*, each user must have the same setup on their computer if they want to share the same project file from the vault.

About Content Center Files

Content Center files are parts that you often use in more than one design. They are similar to other library files and you need to set them up correctly to work with Autodesk Vault.

About Content Center Files and Vault

Content Center files are parts that are placed from the Content Center libraries. The Content Center libraries are databases that store definitions of parts. A part file is not created until you first place the selected part in your design. Because many designs use identical instances of a part (for example, a common fastener), you normally store the resulting part file in a common folder that is outside of your designs so that many designs can reference one copy of the library part. When you place the part from the Content Center in another model, the folder in which you store Content Center parts is checked before a new part file is created. If the part already exists, the design references the existing part instead of creating another.

When you use Autodesk Vault to manage documents for a design team, you should install the Content Center libraries with the Autodesk Data Management Server (ADMS) rather than as Inventor Desktop Content.

How Content Center Files Are Organized

As with user-defined library components, you share Content Center files between designs but you do not modify them. In the same way that you use the top-level *Libraries* folder, you specify a storage location for Content Center parts in the project file that is outside the *Designs* folder. Because you cannot modify parts generated from the Content Center, you store them in library folders in the vault. When you store a design in the vault or get versions of a design, parts placed from the Content Center act in a similar manner to other library parts.

You can organize Content Center files in many ways. However, for best results when using the vault, you should organize these files in the same way that you organize library files. The following image displays the recommended folder structure for storing Content Center files. The *Content Center Files* folder is located directly under the project file but outside of the folder where regular design files are stored.

Content Center Files in the Vault

Parts generated from the Content Center libraries are stored in the vault using the same folder structure below your working folder. When you create a part from the Content Center, the part is placed in a folder below the *Content Center Files* folder. The folder name reflects the family name of the part in the Content Center. In the vault, the local *Content Center Files* folder is mapped to a library folder one level below the root folder in the vault.

Project File Settings for Content Center Parts

In the Autodesk Inventor project file editor, the *Content Center Files* path is set to the folder that you created for the Content Center files. Because the *Content Center Files* folder is beneath the project file, the path is relative to the project file as shown in the following image. The *Content Center Files* folder should be located outside the folder specified for user-defined library components.

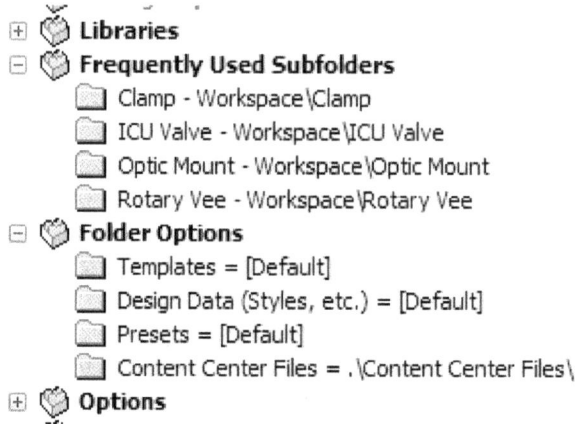

```
⊞ 🏠 Libraries
⊟ 🏠 Frequently Used Subfolders
       📁 Clamp - Workspace\Clamp
       📁 ICU Valve - Workspace\ICU Valve
       📁 Optic Mount - Workspace\Optic Mount
       📁 Rotary Vee - Workspace\Rotary Vee
⊟ 🏠 Folder Options
       📁 Templates = [Default]
       📁 Design Data (Styles, etc.) = [Default]
       📁 Presets = [Default]
       📁 Content Center Files = .\Content Center Files\
⊞ 🏠 Options
```

2.2 Adding Existing Models to a Vault

In this lesson, you learn how to prepare existing designs and add them to a vault using Autodesk Autoloader, a software that prepares, analyzes, and uploads Autodesk Inventor files to a vault. Many companies have existing Inventor designs that they need to add to the vault. You can use several methods to add your existing designs to the vault, depending on whether you want to manually prepare and upload the designs or use a more automated method such as Autodesk Autoloader.

Objectives

After completing this lesson, you will be able to:

- Prepare existing models to use Autodesk Autoloader.

- Upload models to a vault using Autodesk Autoloader.

Preparing Models

The method you use to prepare data depends on the method you use to upload data to the vault. When you use Autodesk Autoloader to upload data, there is little preparation required because Autoloader reorganizes the files for you. If Autodesk Autoloader finds problems with some file relationships, you are required to fix the problems before using Autoloader to upload the files to the vault.

Planning the Vault Structure

Before you upload existing model data, you must plan how you want to store your model files, library files, Content Center files, non-model files, and other data in the vault. If you use Autodesk Autoloader to upload your data, the software creates a single project file and the top-level vault folders for you. All that you need to create are subfolders to organize the files for each design. The structure and project file that Autoloader creates ensures that you can successfully work on your designs in Autodesk Inventor.

It is not a requirement that you have a single project file for all your designs before uploading files to a vault with Autodesk Autoloader. You can run Autoloader for each project file to upload the designs managed by the project file. It is highly recommended that you place all designs uploaded to the vault under the single vault project file created when you first upload files to a new vault using Autoloader.

Preparing Project Files

When you run Autodesk Autoloader, you select an existing folder to upload. You then select a project file associated with the designs in the selected folder and its subfolders. The selected project file is used to validate file references in the designs in the selected folder before they are uploaded to the vault. Autodesk Autoloader reads any type of project file including Single-User, Shared, Semi-Isolated, and Vault.

Autoloader uses all defined paths in the project file to determine which files to upload. Each design in the selected folder and its subfolders is examined for dependent files. Autoloader checks that all dependent files can be found in the scope of the search paths so that models correctly resolve after uploading to the vault. All dependent files are added to the list of files to upload. Because Autoloader supports all project file formats, it locates all referenced files in the *Workspace, Workgroup, Libraries,* and *Content Center Files* search paths.

Existing projects can be organized in many different ways. Because Autoloader works with one project file at a time, run Autoloader once for each project file. If you already use a single project file for all of your designs, all designs can be uploaded at once using Autoloader. If you use multiple project files, you must run Autoloader for each project file.

You do not need to convert your existing project files to a Vault-type project file before you work with Autoloader. Autoloader creates a new Vault project file for you and adds it to the vault. The new project file is ready to use, including the correct search paths and folder mappings.

Common Project File Problem

Although your existing projects can resolve correctly when you open the file in Autodesk Inventor, you might have to add additional search paths if Autodesk Autoloader cannot find files. For example, in the following image, the project file is located in the same folder as the main assembly, **Winch.iam**. The project file has *Workgroup* search paths to the *Motors* and *Hydraulics* folders, which are not located below the project file location. The project file does not contain a *Workspace* path. The main assembly opens successfully in Autodesk Inventor. However, when Autodesk Autoloader searches for files, the main assembly is not found because none of the search paths in the project file include the location of the main assembly file.

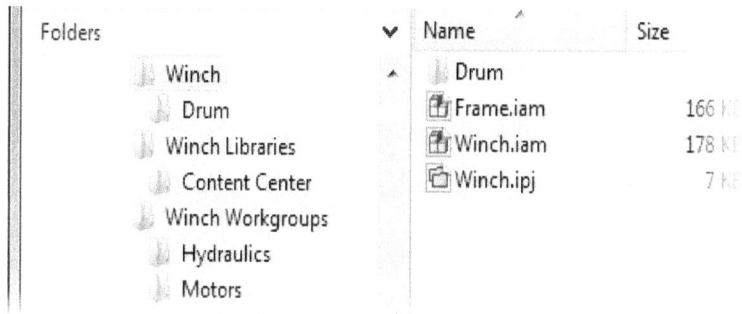

Folders		Name	Size
Winch	⌃	Drum	
Drum		Frame.iam	166 K
Winch Libraries		Winch.iam	178 K
Content Center		Winch.ipj	7 K
Winch Workgroups			
Hydraulics			
Motors			

To fix the project file, add a *Workspace* path to the existing project file, and then run Autodesk Autoloader again.

Solving File Resolution Problems

You cannot upload designs that fail to fully resolve. If Autoloader cannot find child files, you must either locate them and resolve the problem or remove the child part's reference from the parent file.

You can check your designs by opening each master assembly, drawing, and presentation file in Autodesk Inventor to ensure that all files are found. This can be a lengthy process, especially for large designs with many parent files. Alternatively, use Autodesk Autoloader to find resolution problems because it identifies just the issues that you need to resolve. Resolve the problem files and then run Autoloader again to recheck the data.

Duplicate File Names

Although you can store files with the same name in the vault, it is recommended that you use unique filenames. If files are different, they should have different names. If the same file is used in more than one model, place the file in a common folder from which you can use the file in many designs, as shown in the following image. If the file is used by many designs and is rarely or never modified, move the file to a library folder so that it is protected from unintended changes.

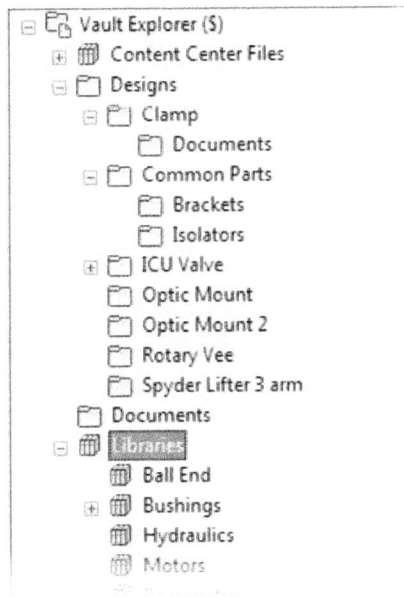

If you need to rename files, upload the files to the vault and then use the Vault renaming utility to rename the files rather than renaming the files in File Explorer and manually repairing the references. To add files with duplicate names to the vault, toggle off the **Enforce Unique File Names** setting in the vault and then add the files. In Vault, search for duplicate filenames. If the files are different, rename them. After renaming, toggle on **Enforce Unique File Names**. The option to enforce unique filenames in a vault is located on the *Files* tab in the Administration dialog box (**Tools>Administration>Vault Settings**). If using Autoloader, the **Enforce Unique File Names** option must be disabled.

Vault Settings	×
Files Visualization	
File Names Duplicates Options	
☐ Enforce Unique File Names	Find Duplicate Names

To consolidate duplicate files into one shared file, add your designs to the vault and then reorganize the files. Vault understands file relationships; therefore, you can move files without breaking links. To find where a file is used, view the *Where Used* information in Vault Explorer and record where each file is used. Delete all but one copy of the file, move the one copy from its current folder to a common folder, and then check out each dependent file and resolve the links. Use the **File Replace** operation where appropriate.

Migrating Files

If you want to migrate your design files to the latest release of Autodesk Inventor, you can migrate the files before or after you add them to the vault. To migrate files, schedule a migration task using the Task Scheduler in Inventor. The scheduled task opens all files from a local or vault folder, migrates the files, and saves them back to the same local or vault location.

You are not required to migrate Autodesk Inventor files before uploading them to the vault; however, Autoloader will not upload Inventor files older than R10 (must be migrated first) and AutoCAD files older than R14.

Uploading Models

When you have prepared your data for uploading, you use Autodesk Autoloader to upload the models to the vault. Autoloader checks file dependencies, consolidates files, creates the vault folder structure, uploads the files, and creates a vault project file. The resulting vault folder structure and project file ensure that you can successfully work with Autodesk Inventor and Vault.

How To: Upload to Vault with Autodesk Autoloader

The following steps describe how to upload an existing Autodesk Inventor design to the vault using Autodesk Autoloader.

1. Organize the folder structure of your existing designs as you want them to display in the vault.

    Project
        Type = Single User
        Location = C:\AOTGVault\Chapter9\Winch\
        Included file =
        Use Style Library = Yes
    Workspace
        Workspace - .
    Workgroup Search Paths
        Hydraulics - C:\AOTGVault\Chapter9\Winch Workgroups\Hydraulics
        Motors - C:\AOTGVault\Chapter9\Winch Workgroups\Motors
    Libraries
        Library - C:\AOTGVault\Chapter9\Winch Libraries

2. Start Autodesk Autoloader.

3. Select the top-level folder containing the designs you want to upload to the vault.

4. Select the project file that manages the files to be uploaded.

Project name	Project location
AOTGVault	C:\AOTGVault\Chapter3
✓ Winch	C:\AOTGVault\Chapter9
ManageVault	C:\AOTGVault
Designs	C:\AOTGVault\VaultWorkingFolder

5. Click **Scan** to scan all files in the project folders and confirm file relationships.

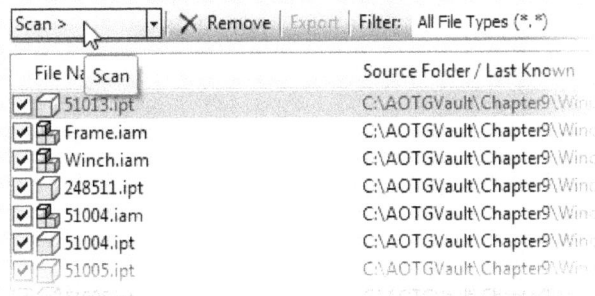

Data Scan & Report

Scan your data for problems and output a report.

Click Scan below to begin validating the file resolutions:

| Scan > | ✕ Remove | Export | Filter: All File Types (*.*) |

File Na Scan	Source Folder / Last Known
☑ 51013.ipt	C:\AOTGVault\Chapter9\Winc
☑ Frame.iam	C:\AOTGVault\Chapter9\Winc
☑ Winch.iam	C:\AOTGVault\Chapter9\Winc
☑ 248511.ipt	C:\AOTGVault\Chapter9\Winc
☑ 51004.iam	C:\AOTGVault\Chapter9\Winc
☑ 51004.ipt	C:\AOTGVault\Chapter9\Winc
☑ 51005.ipt	C:\AOTGVault\Chapter9\Winc

6. If required, fix any reported problems. Missing files and file resolution issues are reported. You are not required to abandon the Autoloader session. Open the files in their associated CAD application and repair the reported issues.

File Name	Source Folder / Last Known	Status
51013.ipt	C:\AOTGVault\Chapter9\Winch	Duplicates found
51013.ipt	C:\AOTGVault\Chapter9\Winch\Drum	Duplicates found
P31A.iam	C:\AOTGVault\Chapter9\Winch Workgroups\Motors	File resolutions not validated
Winch.iam	C:\AOTGVault\Chapter9\Winch	Issue(s) in children
Frame.iam	C:\AOTGVault\Chapter9\Winch	Successfully opened
248511.ipt	C:\AOTGVault\Chapter9\Winch\Drum	Successfully opened

7. Return to Autoloader and rescan the files. You can only proceed when all reported issues have been resolved. The problem files can also be excluded from the selection set and loaded by hand later.

8. In the drop-down list, select **Find duplicates**. This will help identify any identical files that might cause confusion later in the process.

Data Scan & Report

Scan your data for problems and output

Click Scan below to begin validating the file res

Scan > ▾	✕ Remove	Export	F
✓ Scan >			S
Find duplicates >			
✓ Grip.idw			C
✓ Grip.ipt			C
✓ Handle_Assembly.iam			C

9. Once all issues have been resolved, click **Next**.

10. Log in to the vault.

11. Map the generated folders in the vault to the corresponding folders in the existing project folder. If your project file contains multiple workgroup or library search paths, you must map each one to a corresponding folder in the vault. You can create additional vault folders below the three Autoloader-generated folders to help organize the data in the vault.

    *Note: During the mapping step, selecting to map 'Winch' to 'Products' in the vault will put 'Winch' under 'Products'. If mapping the 'Winch' folder to a 'Winch' folder in the vault, select the **Direct Mapping** option at the bottom of the Browse Vault For Folder dialog box.*

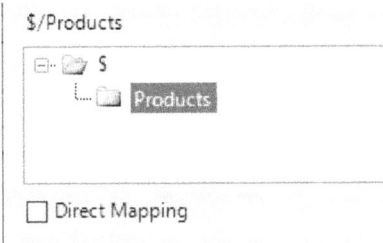

12. Click **Next**.

13. On the Copy & File Redirection Progress Page, wait until the operation is complete and click **Next**.

14. Upload the files to the vault. You can optionally generate a visualization file of each CAD file before it is uploaded to the vault. Once uploaded, the Autoloader Progress and Report page notes the report location and filename to review the details of the upload.

Autoloader Results

When you use Autoloader to upload files to a new vault, Autoloader organizes the files based on the recommended vault structure. The following image displays the results of using Autoloader to upload several designs. Autoloader creates a new Vault project file, and creates two top-level library folders, *Content Center Files* and *Libraries*, along with a single top-level *Designs* folder. The project file contains the correct search paths and folder mappings. You should not have to edit the project file unless you want to add frequently used subfolders. You can get a copy of the project file to your working folder and immediately start working with the model files.

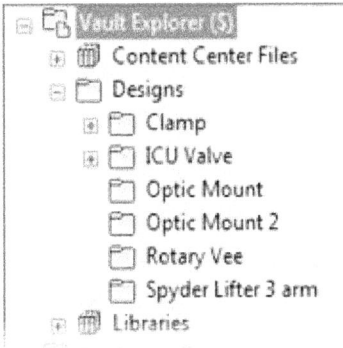

Uploading Non-Inventor Data

By default, all files in and below the selected folder are uploaded to the vault. File relationships between Autodesk Inventor documents are maintained, as are external reference relationships between DWG files. Other files, such as images, documents, and spreadsheets are also uploaded, but are not automatically attached to other documents in the vault. If required, you must manually attach them to the appropriate file after you upload the files to the vault.

In Autoloader, you can upload all files found in or below the selected folder or limit the upload to Autodesk Inventor files or DWG-based files. You can also control the upload status for each file.

Adding Visualization Files

You can also generate DWF or DWFx files for all CAD files uploaded to the vault. This can take a considerable amount of time for large datasets. You can run Autoloader multiple times with subsets filtered by file format to reduce the time for any one upload.

Another approach is to use the Task Scheduler to check out and then immediately check in all files after you have uploaded all files without DWF attachments. DWF files are created when the files are checked back in to the vault.

Practice 2a
Add Existing Projects to a Vault

In this practice, you prepare a project for uploading and then upload the design to an empty vault using Autodesk Autoloader.

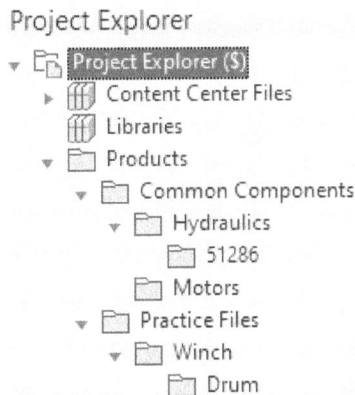

Project Explorer

- ▼ Project Explorer ($)
  - ▶ Content Center Files
  - Libraries
  - ▼ Products
    - ▼ Common Components
      - ▼ Hydraulics
        - 51286
      - Motors
    - ▼ Practice Files
      - ▼ Winch
        - Drum

The completed practice

Task 1: Add existing projects to a vault.

1. Exit Autodesk Inventor if it is running.
2. Start Autodesk Data Management Server Console.
3. Log in as **administrator**. Leave the *Password* field blank.
4. Right-click on the *Vaults* folder and select **Create**.

Autodesk Data Management Server Console

File Tools Actions Help

- W10
  - Va...
    - Create...
    - Attach...
    - AOTCVault
    - AOTCVault+Civil3D

5. In the Create Vault dialog box, for *New Vault Name*, enter **UploadVault**. Click **OK**. When the vault is created, click **OK** to close the message box.

6. Exit Autodesk Data Management Server Console.

7. In File Explorer, navigate to the folder *C:\Vault Professional Admin\Practice Files*. Right-click on **Winch.ipj** and select **Edit**. View the project file's entries for **Workgroup Search Paths**. The *Hydraulics* and *Motors* workgroup folders are located below the folder containing the project folder.

8. In the Inventor Project Editor dialog box, right-click on **Workspace** and select **Add Path**. In the location, enter **.\Winch** (a period, followed by \Winch). Press <Enter>.

Edit Project

```
📠 Project
    🏍 Type = Single User
    [ab] Location = C:\Vault Professional Admin\Practice Files\
    [📇] Included file =
    🪚 Use Style Library = Read-Write
    ⊞ 🟤 Appearance Libraries
    ⊞ 🟤 Material Libraries
  ⊟ 🔖 Workspace
        📁 Workspace - .\Winch
  ⊟ 🔖 Workgroup Search Paths
        📁 Hydraulics - .\Winch Workgroups\Hydraulics
        📁 Motors - .\Winch Workgroups\Motors
    🔖 Libraries
    🔖 Frequently Used Subfolders
  ⊞ 🔖 Folder Options
  ⊞ 🔖 Options
```

9. Click the plus sign (+) to expand **Folder Options**.

10. View the *Content Center Files* path.

```
⊟ 🔖 Folder Options
        📁 Templates = [Default]
        📁 Design Data (Styles, etc.) = [Default]
        📁 Presets = [Default]
        📁 Content Center Files = .\Winch Libraries\Content Center\
```

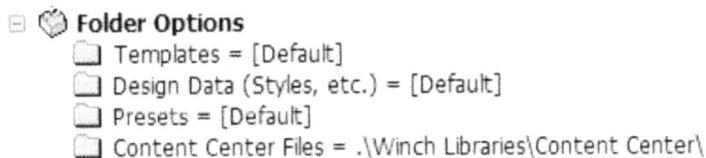

Note: If the supplied data folders were not installed to their default location, you might have to select a new path for the Content Center files.

11. Click **Save**. Click **Close** to close the Project File Editor.

Task 2: Check file dependencies.

1. Start Autodesk Autoloader from the Windows Start menu>*Autodesk Data Management* folder. On the Welcome page, click **Next**.

2. On the Select Data Source page, click **Select Folder**. Browse to and select the *C:\Vault Professional Admin\Practice Files* folder.

3. Click **OK**.

4. In the Select Project dialog box, ensure that the **Winch** project file is shown as the active project file. If not, activate it.

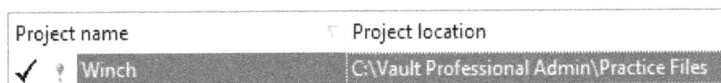

Project name	Project location
✓ 📍 Winch	C:\Vault Professional Admin\Practice Files

5. Click **OK**.

6. Click **Next**.

7. On the Data Scan & Report page, click **Scan**.

8. When the scan is complete, click **OK** to close the message box.

9. Note that **Next** is unavailable, indicating that there was a problem in one or more files. Click the *Status* column header to sort by status, and then scroll through the files and view the *Status* column.

File Name	Source Folder / Last Known	Status
☐ 51013.ipt	C:\Vault Professional Admin\Practice Files\Winch	Duplicates found
☐ 51013.ipt	C:\Vault Professional Admin\Practice Files\Winch\Drum	Duplicates found
☑ P31A.iam	C:\AOTGVault\Chapter9\Winch Workgroups\Motors	File can't be found(missing)
☑ Winch.iam	C:\Vault Professional Admin\Practice Files\Winch	Issue(s) in children

10. Under *File Name*, click **Winch.iam**. Click **>>** to expand the Autoloader dialog box, if not already expanded.

11. On the *File Dependencies* tab, scroll down to **P31A.iam**. The file resolution issue for Winch.iam is that P31A.iam cannot be found.

File Dependencies	Duplicate Files	Where Used

File Name	Status Icon	Status
⊟ Winch.iam	❌	Issue(s) in children
P31A.iam	❌	File can't be found(missing)
local.ANSI.163.750.5.ipt	✓	Successfully Opened
⊕ D-Block.iam	✓	Successfully Opened
⊕ Relief.iam	✓	Successfully Opened
⊕ 51008.iam	✓	Successfully Opened

Task 3: Solve file resolution problem.

1. Start Autodesk Inventor.

2. Ensure that **Winch.ipj** is the active project file.

3. Open **Winch.iam**.

4. In the Resolve Link dialog box, resolve the link error by selecting the **P31B.iam** file from the *Winch Workgroups\Motors* folder. Click **Open**. Click **Yes** if you are prompted to update the assembly.

5. Click **Save**. In the Save dialog box, click **Yes to All>OK**. Update the data format if prompted.

6. Close the file.

Task 4: Solve duplicate files problem.

1. Switch to Autodesk Autoloader. Click **Scan**. If you cannot restart the scan, click **Back** and **Next** again to return to the Data Scan & Report page. Click **Scan** to rescan the files. The Winch.iam file is now resolved without errors; however, the scan reports that two different **51013.ipt** files are referenced in the examined files.

File Name	Source Folder / Last Known	Status
☐ 51013.ipt	C:\Vault Professional Admin\Practice Files\Winch	Duplicates found
☐ 51013.ipt	C:\Vault Professional Admin\Practice Files\Winch\Drum	Duplicates found
☑ local ANSI 163 750 5 int	C:\AOTGVault\Chapter0\Winch Libraries\Content Center\winch	File can't be found(missing)

2. Under *File Name,* click the first **51013.ipt** row. In the details pane at the bottom of the dialog box, click the *Duplicate Files* tab. The location of each 51013.ipt file is displayed.

3. Switch to Autodesk Inventor. Open ...\Winch**Frame.iam**.

4. In the browser, select **51013:3**. On the ribbon, select the *Assemble* tab and select **Component>Replace>Replace All**.

5. In the Place Component dialog box, browse to the *Drum* folder. Select **51013.ipt**. Click **Open**.

6. Save the file. Close Frame.iam. Update the data format if prompted.

   - The original ...\Winch\51013.ipt file is no longer referenced in the assembly.

7. In File Explorer, browse to the *C:\Vault Professional Admin\Practice Files\Winch* folder. Delete **51013.ipt**.

8. Switch to Autodesk Autoloader. Scan the files again. All files are opened and resolved successfully. No duplicate files are found.

Task 5: Complete the upload.

1. Click **Next**. Log in to the vault.

   - For *User Name*, enter **administrator**.
   - Leave the *Password* blank.
   - For *Vault*, select **UploadVault**.
   - Click **OK**.

2. On the Map Vault Folders page, note that the project file's search paths are listed on the left and the new vault folders are on the right. Note that three new folders are created below the root folder in the vault.

3. Under *Resultant Vault View,* select the *Designs* folder. Click **Rename**. In the Rename Folder dialog box, enter **Products**. Click **OK** to rename the vault folder.

4. Under *Folder to Check In*, double-click **Practice Files**.

5. In the Browse Vault for Folder dialog box, select the **Products** folder. Ensure that the **Direct Mapping** checkbox is not checked.

6. Click **OK**. The workspace folder from the project file is mapped to the new folder in the vault.

7. Under *Folder to Check In*, double-click **Hydraulics**. In the Browse Vault for Folder dialog box, click **Products**. Click **New Folder**.

8. In the Create Folder dialog box, enter **Common Components**. Click **OK**.

9. In the Browse Vault for Folder dialog box, click **Common Components**. Click **OK**. A *Hydraulics* subfolder is created automatically.

10. Under *Folder to Check In,* double-click **Motors**. In the Browse Vault for Folder dialog box, click **Common Components**. Click **OK**.

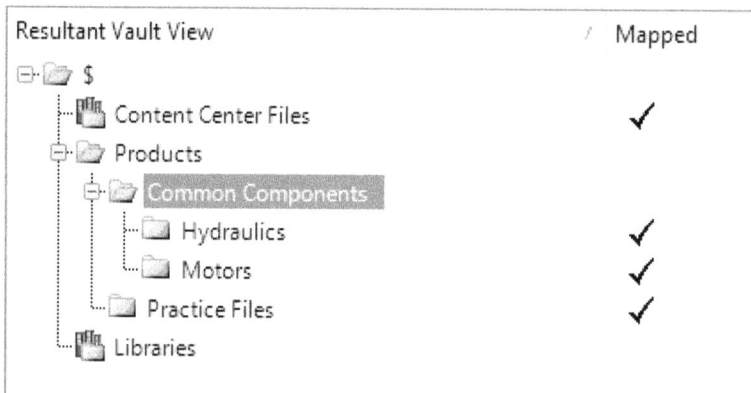

11. Click **Next**.

12. On the Copy & File Redirection Progress page, wait until the operation is complete. Click **Next**.

13. On the Specify Data Subsets page, examine the resulting structure of files in the vault.

14. Click **Upload**.

15. On the Autoloader Progress and Report page, make note of the report location and filename.

16. Click **Done**.

Task 6: Review the results.

1. Start Autodesk Vault.

   - For *User Name*, enter **administrator**.

   - Leave the *Password* blank.

   - For *Vault*, select **UploadVault**.

   - Click **OK**.

2. In the root folder of the vault, *Project Explorer ($)*, note that there is a project file named **Designs.ipj**.

3. View the contents of the other folders.

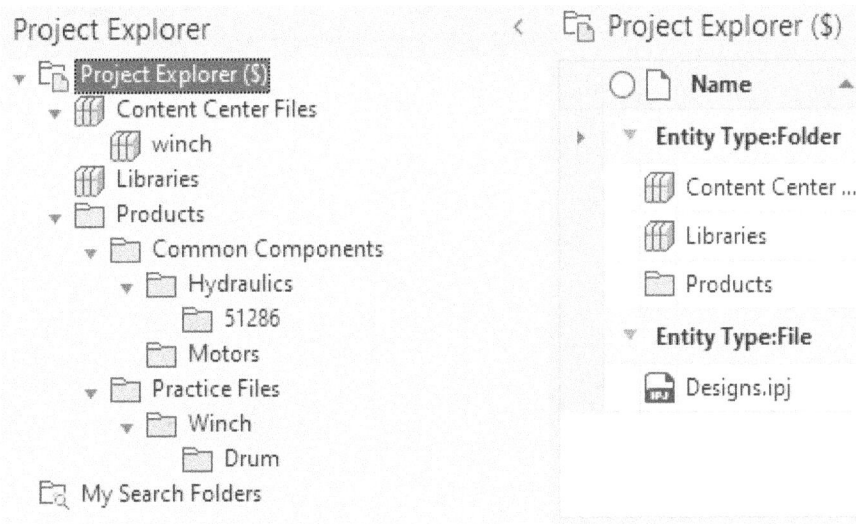

4. Exit Autodesk Vault Client.

End of practice

Managing Categories

Categories enable the grouping of documents by predetermined labels. This labeling can be set up to happen automatically during check in based on rules or a user can manually change a category.

Learning Objectives

- Change a file or folder category.
- Create and edit categories.
- Assign rules to categories.

3.1 Categories and Rules

Overview

Categories in Autodesk® Vault Professional software are a powerful method of not only classifying different types of files or folders but automatically assigning other behaviors. Combined with rules, as users add new files to the vault or migrate from Autodesk Vault, lifecycle definitions and states, revision schemes and revision levels, and specific properties can be automatically assigned to the files. This ensures a very high level of both consistency and completeness to the data.

If you have Autodesk Vault Professional software, you can also configure categories to items and custom objects.

Objectives

After completing this lesson, you will be able to:

* Understand the predefined categories.

* Change the category of a file or folder.

* Understand the basic category rules.

Categories

On one level, categories are a very simple way of grouping different files or folders based on how your company creates, uses, and manages those files or folders. A very common example is that of files created by CAD applications and those created by word processing and graphics applications. Historically and functionally, the process for creating and releasing a set of models and drawings that represent a product or component has been very different than supporting documentation such as specifications and graphics used by marketing and sales. The CAD-generated files often go through a more formal, multi-step review and change process where as the supporting documentation can be managed in a simpler 'Work In Progress' or 'Released' fashion.

Categories give you the flexibility to categorize the files or folders in a way that best suits your organization. With categories you can:

* Visually identify different types of file groupings or purposes.

* Assign one or more lifecycle states based on the category and specify the default lifecycle definition and state for a new or migrated file.

* Assign one or more revisions based on the category and specify the default revision scheme and initial revision for a new or migrated file.

* Assign a set of existing properties or metadata to the file based on the category.

Predefined File Categories

There are four preconfigured file categories shipped with Autodesk Vault. The details are listed in the following table.

Name	Glyph	Description
Base		Default category for migrated data and new files if no other rules are setup.
Engineering		Data created for design purposes. Use this for the management of CAD-based files, such as Inventor, if you are going to use multiple file categories and have more formal lifecycle management needs.
Office		General data created by word processors, spreadsheet and image files. Use this for the management of office-type files if you are going to use multiple categories.
Standard		Standard design data created by any application. Use this for the management of any file formats if you are going to only use a single category and have simpler lifecycle management needs.

The predefined categories use the following lifecycle definitions, revision schemes, and property sets.

Name	Lifecycle Definitions	Revision Schemes	Property Set
Base	• None (opt-out scheme)	• None (opt out scheme)	Biased towards Inventor file property mapped user-defined properties.
Engineering	• Flexible Release Process • Long Lead Time Release Process • None (opt out scheme)	• Standard Alphabetic Format • None (opt out scheme)	Biased towards Inventor file property mapped user-defined properties.
Office	• Simple Release Process • None (opt out scheme)	• Standard Numeric Format • None (opt out scheme)	Biased toward standard file property mapped user-defined properties.
Standard	• Basic Release Process • Simple Release Process • None (opt out scheme)	• Standard Alphabetic Format • None (opt out scheme)	Biased towards Inventor file property mapped user-defined properties.

Assigning Categories

When a file is added to the vault or a user migrates from Autodesk Vault Basic to Autodesk Vault Professional, files are automatically assigned the default category. For the default configuration this is the **Base** category. This can be changed by the Administrator.

Predefined Folder Categories

There is one preconfigured folder category shipped with Autodesk Vault. The details are listed in the following table.

Name	Glyph	Description
Folder		Default category for migrated data and new folders if no other rules are set up.

Change Category

The **Change Category** command enables the authorized user to change the current category to a new one. The file must not be a state that locks the file and the user must have the permission to change the category. For example, a file which is in a Released state cannot change category.

Changing the category of a file will apply the default lifecycle state definition and state and the default revision scheme and revision if they have not been previously assigned. If they are, changing the category will not change the current state or revision. If the file was assigned a lifecycle definition and revision scheme in the current category, changing the category will not change the lifecycle definition or revision scheme. They must be manually changed after the category change.

How To: Change Category

To change the category of a file, use the following steps.

1. Before you attempt to revise a file, you should determine whether you have permission to do so. You must be at least a Document Manager (Level 1) to revise a file. If you attempt to change the category and do not have permission to do so, you will not be informed until after you dismiss the Change Category dialog box (i.e., there is no precheck). You can have this permission as a user or by being a member of a group that has this permission. It is always best to manage permission at the group level if possible.

2. The file must not be locked. Changing the category will create a new file version and new file versions cannot be created if the file is locked. Ensure that the file is not in a 'Released' state if it has a lifecycle definition and state associated with it.

3. Select the file or group of files from the main pane that are to be changed. If you need to change a set of related files, you can use the options in the dialog box to select these for you. If the files are not related, use the <Shift> + select or <Ctrl> + select option to select the files from the list.

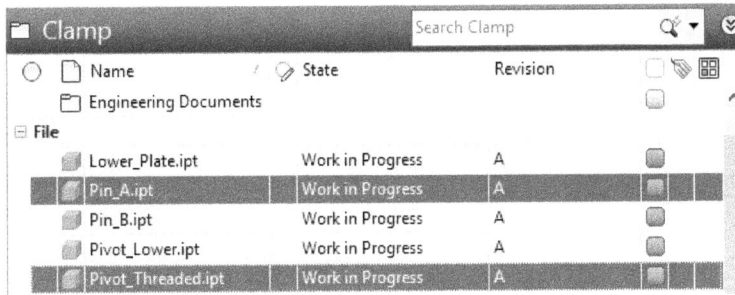

4. Select **Change Category** from the Actions menu.

*Note: You can also change categories in Autodesk Inventor by selecting **Change Category** from either the Vault tab>Control panel or from the shortcut menu in the Autodesk Vault Browser.*

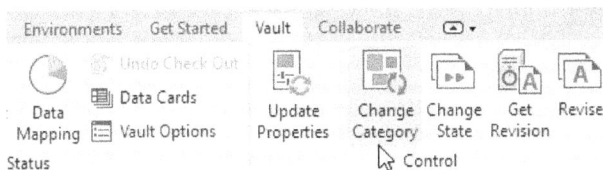

5. The Change Category dialog box displays.

6. In the *Select a new category* section, select a new category from the drop-down list. Alternatively, you can change the category in the *New Category* column for each individual file.

7. Use the View buttons to change the view to help understand file relationships.

8. Use the Parent/Child selection buttons to modify the selection.

Include Dependents   Include Parents

9. Select **Settings** to display the Settings dialog box. Here you can refine the selection of related files.

10. In the *Enter comments* area, accept the default comment, select a comment from the drop-down list (if configured), or enter a custom comment.

11. Click **OK** to complete the procedure.

Rules

Rules enable you to automatically categorize a file based on one or more file property values. This gives you the ability to assign a category to a file when it is added to the vault using Autodesk Vault explorer or the CAD add-ins.

Rules work like the Advanced Find workflow in that you can specify a list of conditions to be met based on the system, user-defined property values, or filename values of the file being added. For example:

- Assign the file to the Engineering category if the filename ends with either 'IPT', 'IAM', or 'DWG'.

- Assign the file to the Office category if the user-defined property Category contains 'document'.

- Assign the file to the Standard category if the user-defined property Title contains 'Specification'.

3.2 Managing Categories and Rules

Overview

The Administrator can create and configure categories to specify the category glyph, lifecycle definitions, revision schemes, and property sets that will be assigned when a file is assigned a category. The Administrator can also create and manage a set of rules to automatically assign a file to a category when it is added to the system.

Objectives

After completing this lesson, you will be able to:

- Edit a category.

- Add a custom category.

- Delete a category.

- Apply rules to a category.

Managing Categories

The Administrator can manage the set of categories using the Configure Categories dialog box.

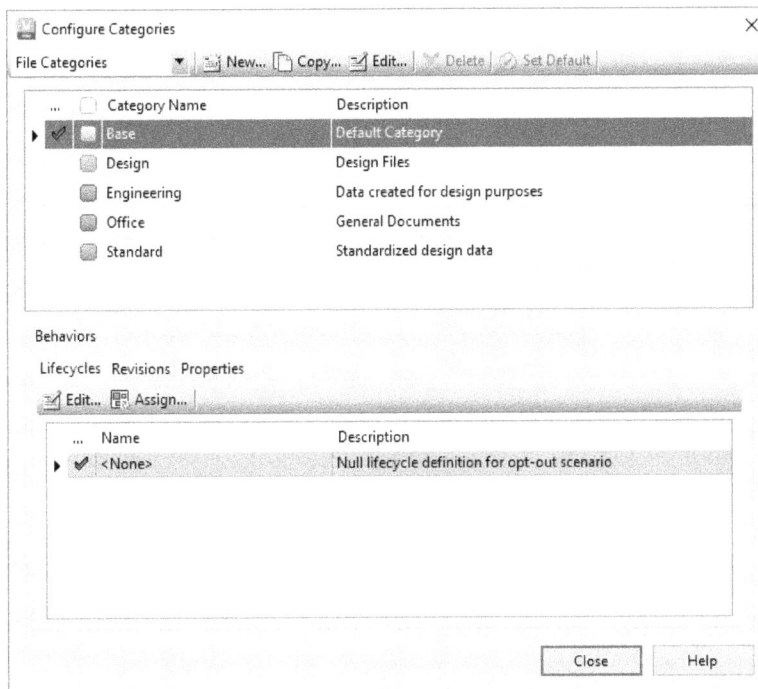

New categories can be created and existing categories can be edited. Categories that are not required and have not been used can be deleted. The category assigned to new files during migration or in the absence of any rule can be changed.

How To: Create a New Category

If the categories provided do not meet your requirements, you can create a new one by completing the following steps.

1. From the Tools menu, select **Administration>Vault Settings**.

2. Select the *Behaviors* tab and select **Categories**.

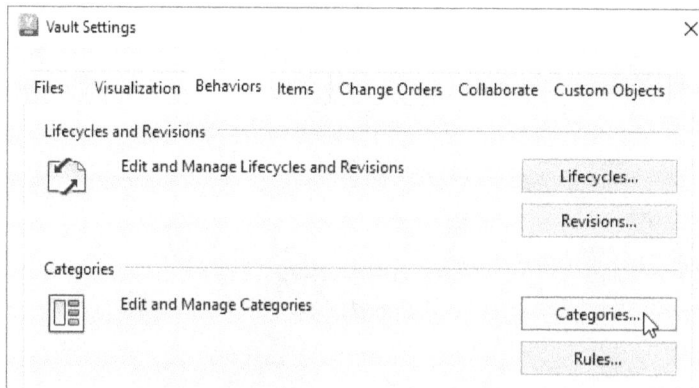

3. In the Configure Categories dialog box, select either **File Categories** or **Folder Categories** from the drop-down list and then select **New**.

   Note: If you are using Autodesk Vault Professional software, you can also create Item Categories and Custom Object Categories.

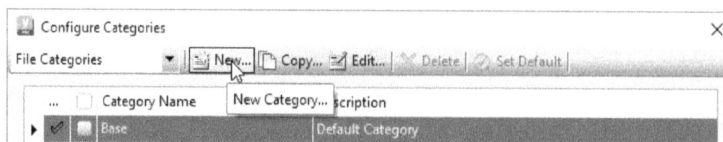

4. In the Category Edit dialog box, enter a *Name* and *Description* for your new category. Select a *Color* for the new category and click **OK**.

How To: Edit Categories

Once you have a base category defined, or for any of the existing categories, do the following to edit the category:

1. In the Tools menu, select **Administration>Vault Settings**.

2. Select the *Behaviors* tab and select **Categories**.

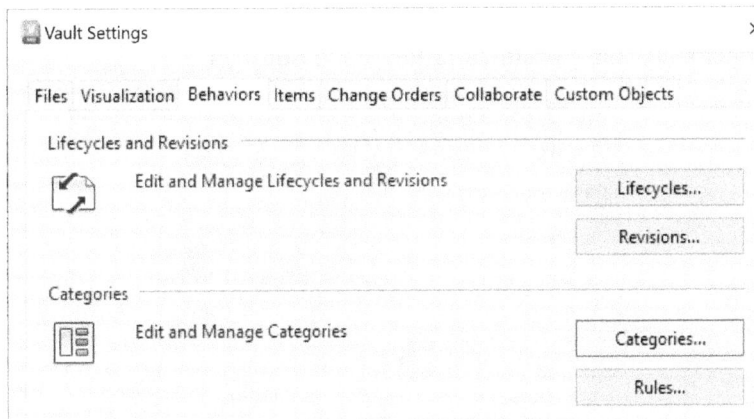

3. In the Configure Categories dialog box, select either **File Categories** or **Folder Categories** from the drop-down list, then select the category you want to edit and select **Edit**.

4. In the Category Edit dialog box, make any changes to the category and click **OK**.

How To: Apply Rules for Categories

Once you have a new category defined, or for any of the existing categories, do the following to apply a rule to the category.

1. From the Tools menu, select **Administration>Vault Settings**.

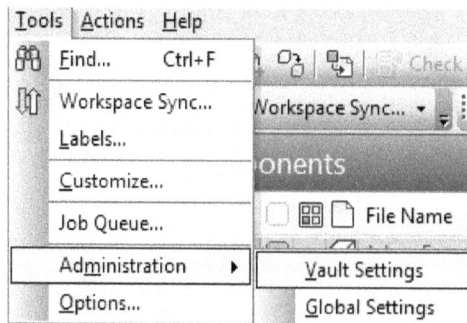

2. Select the *Behaviors* tab and select **Rules**.

3. In the Assignment Rules dialog box, select **New**.

4. You will make a rule to apply the Engineering category to all Autodesk Inventor part files. In the Edit Rule dialog box, name the rule **Inventor Parts** and select the **Engineering** category.

5. Once you click **OK**, the new Inventor Parts rule is added to the list. Select it to add the criteria, as follows:

   - *Property:* **File Name**
   - *Condition:* **ends with**
   - *Value:* **.ipt**

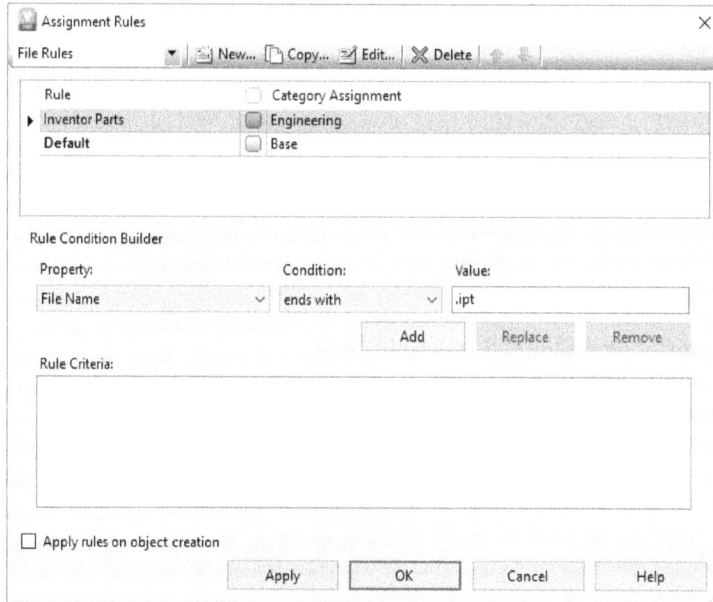

6. Click **Add** and the criteria is added automatically in the *Rule Criteria* section. Check the **Apply rules on object creation** option. Checking this box will place all new Autodesk Inventor parts in the Engineering category when they are checked in. Once this is complete, click **OK**.

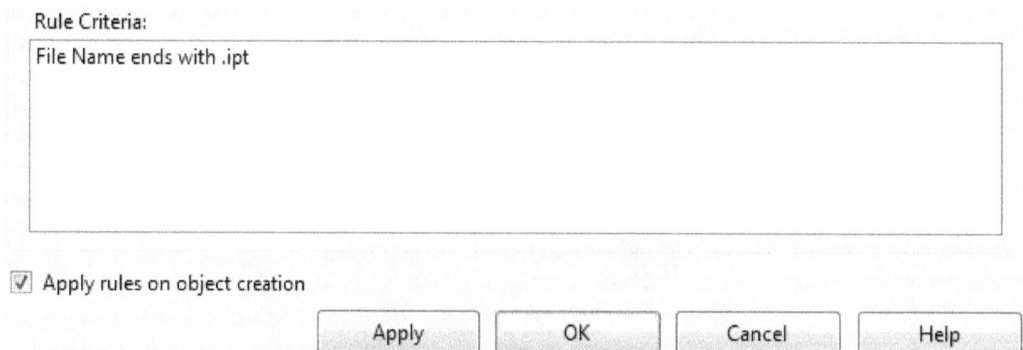

Practice 3a
Managing Categories

Use the procedures in this section to create your own category and at least one rule to apply this new category to files you can check in.

Task 1: Create categories.

1. Log in to Autodesk Vault using the following information:

   - For *User Name*, enter **administrator**.
   - Leave the *Password* field blank.
   - For *Vault*, select **AOTCVault**.

2. From the Tools menu, select **Administration>Vault Settings**.

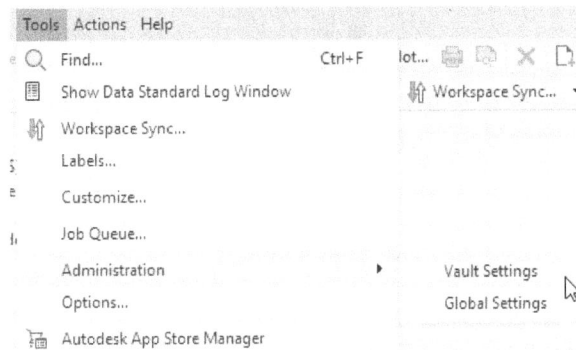

3. In the *Behaviors* tab, select **Categories**.
4. In the top left of the Configure Categories dialog box, select **File Categories**.

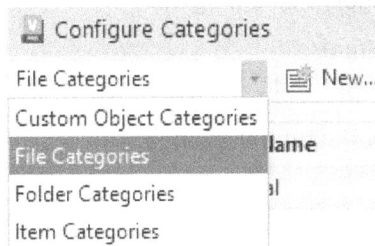

5. Click **New**. In the Category Edit dialog box:

- For *Name*, enter **Survey**.
- For *Color*, select **Green**.
- For *Description*, enter **Survey Drawings**.
- Click **OK**.

6. Click **New** again. In the Category Edit dialog box:

- For *Name*, enter **Civil**.
- For *Color*, select **Blue**.
- For *Description*, enter **Civil Drawings**.
- Click **OK**.

7. Click **New** again. In the Category Edit dialog box:

- For *Name*, enter **Architectural**.
- For *Color*, select **Purple**.
- For *Description*, enter **Architectural Drawings**.
- Click **OK**.

8. Close the Configure Categories dialog box.

Task 2: Apply rules.

1. In the *Behaviors* tab of the Vault Settings, click **Rules**.

2. In the top left of the Assignment Rules dialog box, select **File Rules**.

3. Click **New**.

4. In the Edit Rule dialog box:

    -   For *Rule Name*, enter **Survey**.

    -   For *Category Assignment*, select **Survey**.

    -   Click **OK**.

5. In the Assignment Rules dialog box, in the *Rule Condition Builder* area, do the following:

    -   For *Property*, select **File Name**.

    -   For *Condition*, select **starts with**.

    -   For *Value*, enter **V-**.

    -   Click **Add**.

6. Repeat Steps 3 to 5 to create a *Rule Name* of **Architectural** with a *Value* of **A-**, and again to create a *Rule Name* of **Civil** with a *Value* of **C-**.

Assignment Rules		

File Rules ▾   📄 New...   📋 Copy...   ✏ Edit...   ✖ Delete

Rule	☐ Category Assignment
▸ Survey	◻ Survey
Architectural	◼ Architectural
Civil	◻ Civil
Default	☐ Base

Rule Condition Builder

Property:	Condition:	Valu
File Name ▾	starts with ▾	V-

Add

Rule Criteria:

File Name starts with V-

7. Ensure the **Apply rules on object creation** option is selected.

8. Click **Apply**, then click **OK** to exit the dialog box.

9. Close all dialog boxes and exit Autodesk Vault.

End of practice

Lifecycle States

Lifecycle management refers to the process a company uses to track its products from inception through retirement. As a product is conceived, defined, designed, tested, revised, and produced, it will transit various stages that are often quite specific to a particular company.

Autodesk® Vault Professional enables lifecycle management by applying a uniform set of behaviors to project data in the lifecycle management process. Along with uniformity, Autodesk Vault Professional is a tool that enables configuration of states, transitions, and other aspects of lifecycle management so that companies can tailor the tool to best fit their processes. In this chapter, you will learn about lifecycle management, what default lifecycle definitions and states are available out-of-the-box and how to configure them or create a new lifecycle definition and set of states to meet your organization's needs. You will learn how to change the lifecycle state of a Vault object using the lifecycle definitions and states.

Learning Objectives

- Describe the default out-of-the-box lifecycle definitions and how they could be applied for different situations.
- Describe the default out-of-the-box lifecycle states and how they could be used to control data access.
- Create a new lifecycle definition and set of associated lifecycle states.
- Plan for the configuration of lifecycle definitions and associated states.
- Configure the states of a lifecycle definition.
- Apply the lifecycle definition to project data.
- Change the lifecycle state of a file.
- Understand how the lifecycle state settings affect the ability to read and modify files.

4.1 Lifecycle Definitions and States

Overview

A lifecycle definition is an engine that can be configured to automatically assign security, behaviors, and properties to Vault objects based on where the object is in the life of the design process. This functionality enables you to streamline your work environment by removing the overhead involved in managing groups of files, custom objects, or an entire project. Several lifecycle definitions are included with the "out-of-the-box" installation. These range from a simple release process where project data is either editable or locked for editing to a more complex process involving long-lead time manufacturing, the review of project data before it is released, and the ability to short cut the formal release process for simple project data changes. They are designed to fit those processes seen in many companies from small shops to large corporations.

Each of these lifecycle definitions comprise two or more lifecycle states. A lifecycle state represents a certain point in the lifecycle of vault data. Common lifecycle states include Work in Progress, Review, and Released. Lifecycle states control the ability to view and modify project data. Transitions from one state to the next control how new versions are created and other activities. There are controls for specifying required conditions before a transition can be made.

These sets of lifecycle definitions and states cover many possible processes. If one does not fit your organization, a new definition with its unique set of states can be created.

Objectives

After completing this lesson, you will be able to:

* Describe the out-of-the-box lifecycle definitions and how they could be applied for different situations.

* Describe the predefined lifecycle states and how they could be used to control project data access.

* Create a new lifecycle definition and set of associated lifecycle states.

Lifecycle Definitions

A lifecycle definition uses states to identify the state of an object in the project lifecycle. Examples of states are Work in Progress, For Review, and Released. An object moves from one state to another based on the lifecycle definition transition rules. These transition rules determine when the state change occurs, and whether the change can occur manually or automatically (or both), based on criteria determined by the administrator. The lifecycle definition also determines if any other automatic behaviors occur based on a state change.

For example, a lifecycle definition can be configured to automatically revise a file when it moves from a Work in Progress state to a Review state. Alternatively, if a user changes a folder's status to Obsolete, the lifecycle definition can automatically apply security settings to the folder so that only an administrator can modify the folder and its contents or reinstate the folder for use.

Lifecycles can be used with files, project folders, items, and custom objects.

Predefined Lifecycle Definitions

Several lifecycle definitions are included with the "out-of-the-box" installation that will assist administrators in assigning definitions to Vault content without having to create them. The lifecycle definitions are located in the Vault Settings dialog box, in the *Behaviors* tab. The following table lists the various lifecycle definitions.

Lifecycle Definition	Description
Basic Release Process	Basic manufacturing lifecycle process for release control. This definition can be used with most manufacturing project content.
Item Release Process	For use with the Vault Professional software. Basic item lifecycle process for release control. This definition can be used with all items and includes the following states: • Work in Progress • In Review • Released • Quick-Change • Obsolete
Flexible Release Process	Flexible manufacturing lifecycle process for release control. This definition includes all of the Basic Release Process states and a Quick Change state for editing released data.
Simple Release Process	A generic lifecycle process for many different types of project data. This definition consists of a Work in Progress state and a Released state.
Long Lead Time Release Process	Best suited for long lead time manufacturing projects. This definition includes a Pre-Release state indicating that the project data has been sent to manufacturing but is still in a state of change.
Long Lead Time Release Process with Change Order	Best suited for long lead time manufacturing projects directed by change orders. This definition includes the Work in Progress, Review, and Pre-Release states. The Pre-Release state indicates that a file has been sent to manufacturing but is still in a state of change. When there are no more change orders for the file, it moves to a Released state. From there, the file can return to the Pre-Release state through a Quick Change.
Design Representation Process	All PDF files created for document control are automatically assigned to the Design Representation category. A dedicated category enables administrators to manage their rules, lifecycles, and properties independent of the associated design files.
<None>	This definition enables any category to assign a null definition to opt out of using a lifecycle definition but to still retain category behavior.

Predefined Lifecycle States

The following table lists the various predefined lifecycle states.

State Name	Description
Work In Progress	Sometimes known by the abbreviation "WIP", this is the state most commonly associated with the editing of the files. The editing, and often viewing, of files in this state is usually restricted to a small group of individuals, usually in the Engineering function.
For Review	This is the state that usually precedes the release of a design to manufacturing. In this state, more users can interact with the data, but generally no editing is permitted. This state enables users to evaluate new designs and changes to existing designs, before they are re-released to manufacturing.
Released	In this state, a broad range of groups in the organization now can read the data but usually editing is not permitted or at a minimum restricted to a very small group under controlled conditions.
Obsolete	This state is associated with designs that are no longer active. The products they are associated with are no longer being manufactured or are in a maintenance state. Access to these designs is more restricted and usually no edits can be made to them.
Quick-Change	This state is common in processes where there needs to be a quick yet controlled method of updating files without going through a formal review to release process. For example, files with typographical errors but no fundamental form, fit, or function changes. Modifications are generally permitted by a very small group of people.
Pre-Release	In processes where there are a large number of files, for example large assemblies or a product, this state enables the organization to approve the design or changes to the design but not designate them as released to manufacturing. Access can be permitted to a large group, but modification is usually prohibited and the ability to move them to the Released state is also restricted.

In addition to edit ability, there is a set of rules regarding what happens to object revisions when an object is transitioned from one state to the next, who can make these transitions, and other considerations.

Considerations Using the Predefined Definitions

Each of the predefined lifecycle definitions use one or more of the default states. There are a minimum set of rules governing transitions between states and object editing or viewing in a given state. These form the basic rules of the definition and can be adequate for your organization.

It is likely that you will need to configure the lifecycle definitions and states. This could range from minor tuning to major changes in the default states. Alternatively, you might need to create your own lifecycle definitions with their associated states, transitions, rules, and actions.

Viewing Lifecycle Definitions

Viewing lifecycle definitions is an administrative task done through the Vault Settings dialog box. From the Tools menu, select **Administration>Vault Settings** and then select the *Behaviors* tab of this dialog box. The Lifecycle Definitions dialog box is accessed by selecting **Lifecycles** in the *Lifecycles and Revisions* section. From here you can choose to create new definitions, copy an existing definition, and edit or delete a definition from the Lifecycle Definitions toolbar.

Creating a New Lifecycle Definition

In some cases, it might be desirable to create a new lifecycle definition and set of states. For example, in a small organization there have been three states traditionally used to describe the files used to manufacture the product:

* Development

* Manufacturing

* Out of Production

This is a simple but effective process for the organization, and they want to use these lifecycle states rather than one of the defaults.

How To: Create a New Lifecycle Definition

Follow these steps to create a new lifecycle definition called **Company Default**:

1. In the Vault Settings dialog box, select the *Behaviors* tab, then select **Lifecycles** in the *Lifecycles and Revisions* section to display the Lifecycle Definitions dialog box.

2. In the Lifecycle Definitions dialog box, click **New** to display the Lifecycle Definition dialog box.

3. Enter a name and description for the new lifecycle definition.

4. In the Category drop-down list, select the categories you want to assign to the new lifecycle definition.

5. In the *Lifecycle Details* section, select the plus (+) to display the New Lifecycle State dialog box.

6. Enter a name and description for this state and select a color, then click **OK** to close this dialog box and return to the Lifecycle Definition dialog box.

- Note that the first state defined is assigned the default state.

7. Repeat the process for the remaining states. If a different default state is required, select the desired state and select the checkmark to set it as the default state for the lifecycle definition.

8. Reorder lifecycle states by selecting a state in the *Lifecycle Details* view and clicking the up or down arrow. The order of the lifecycle states determines the order in which they display in the Change State dialog box.

9. Click **Apply** to apply the new states for the new definition.

10. Click **OK** to close this dialog box and return the Lifecycle Definitions dialog box.

11. Before closing this dialog box, look through each tab in the right to see the default information for a given lifecycle state. Specifically, for a given state there is no lifecycle state security and every lifecycle state can transition to every other lifecycle state.

12. Click **Close** to close this dialog box and return to the Vault Settings dialog box.

Scope of Configuration

Each lifecycle definition has a set of lifecycle states. In the illustration below, you can see the states associated with the **Basic Release Process** lifecycle definition. You can see that this lifecycle definition has a lifecycle state called **Work in Progress** associated with it.

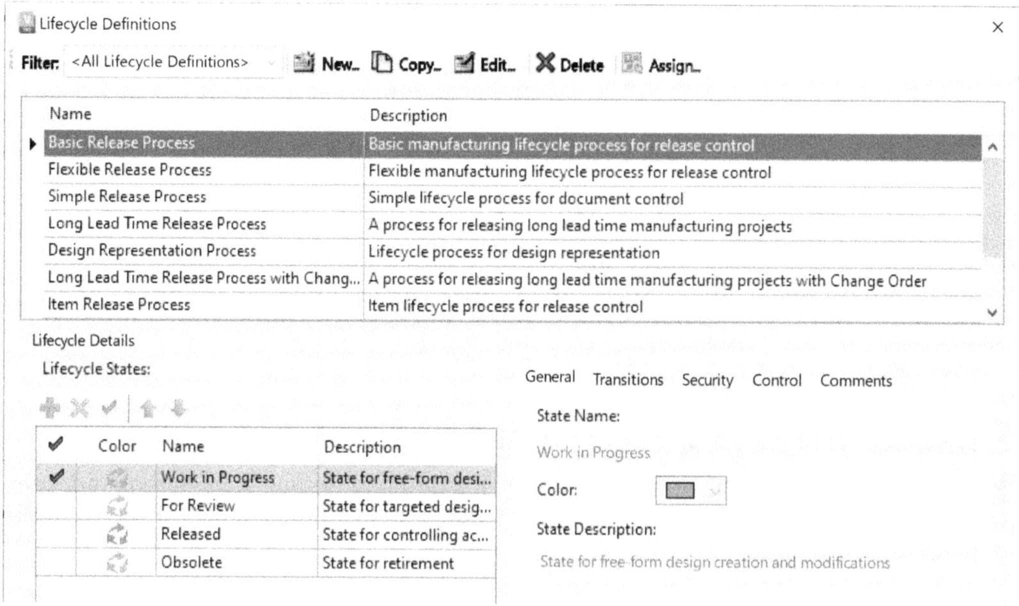

The illustration below shows the states associated with the **Flexible Release Process** lifecycle definition. This lifecycle definition also has a lifecycle state called **Work in Progress** associated with it. While they can have the same name, these are two independent lifecycle states and the rules and actions associated with the customization of one of them does not affect the other.

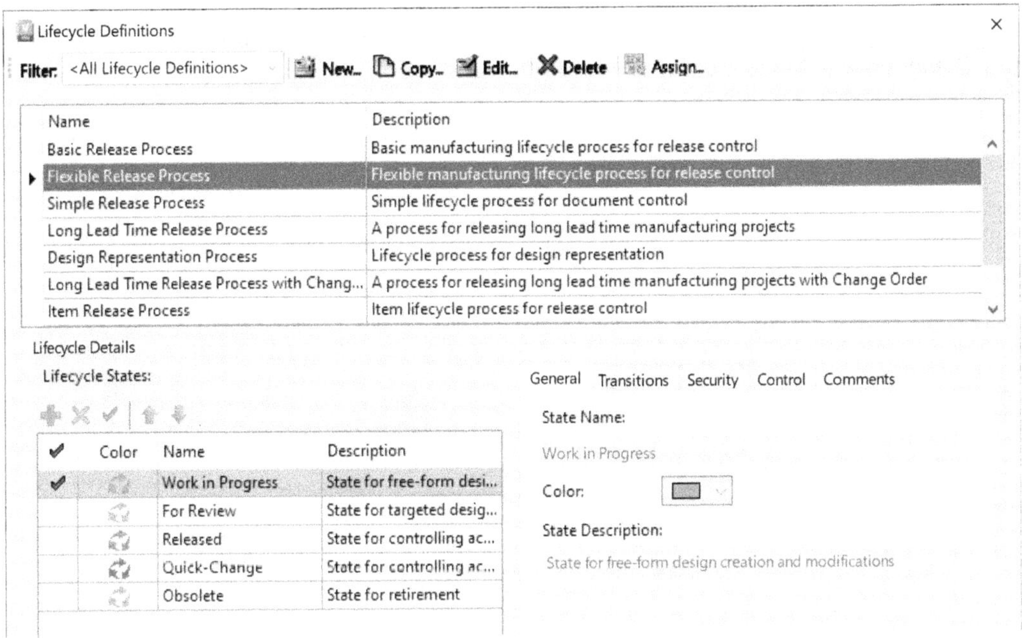

Practice 4a
Create New Lifecycle Definition

In this practice, you will create a new lifecycle definition named **Standard Process** with three states: **Development**, **Manufacturing**, and **Out of Production**.

The completed practice

1. If not already logged in, log in to Autodesk Vault using the following information:
   - For *User Name*, enter **administrator**.
   - Leave the *Password* field blank.
   - For *Vault*, select **AOTCVault**.

2. From the Tools menu, select **Administration>Vault Settings** to display the Vault Settings dialog box.

3. Select the *Behaviors* tab and then select **Lifecycles** in the *Lifecycles and Revisions* section.

4. The Lifecycles Definitions dialog box displays. In the toolbar, select **New** to display the Lifecycle Definition – 'New Definition' dialog box.

5. Do the following:
   - For *Definition Name*, enter **Standard Process**.
   - For *Description*, enter **Company Standard Process**.
   - For *Category*, leave as **None selected**.

6. In the *Lifecycle Details* section, click plus (+).

7. The New Lifecycle State dialog box opens. Do the following:
   - For *State Name*, enter **Development**.
   - For *Color*, select **Green**.
   - For *State Description*, enter **Design development**.
   - Click **OK** to return to the previous dialog box.

8. Repeat the process using the following information:
   - For *State Name*, enter **Manufacturing**.
   - For *Color*, select **Blue**.
   - For *State Description*, enter **Released designs**.

9. Repeat the process again using the following information:
   - For *State Name*, enter **Out of Production**.
   - For *Color*, select **Black**.
   - For *State Description*, enter **Archived designs**.

10. Examine the three states. Note that they display in blue text, which means they have not yet been applied.

Lifecycle States:

✔	Color	Name	Description
✔	♻	Development	Design development
	♻	Manufacturing	Released designs
	♻	Out of Production	Archived designs

Note: The next step would be to configure the three lifecycle states. This will be done in the next practice.

11. Click **Apply** to apply the three new lifecycle states, then click **OK** to dismiss the Lifecycle Definition dialog box. Note that the new lifecycle definition named **Standard Process** has been added.

Name	Description
▶ Basic Release Process	Basic manufacturing lifecycle process for release control
Flexible Release Process	Flexible manufacturing lifecycle process for release control
Simple Release Process	Simple lifecycle process for document control
Long Lead Time Release Process	A process for releasing long lead time manufacturing projects
Item Release Process	Item lifecycle process for release control
Long Lead Time Release Process with Change Order	A process for releasing long lead time manufacturing projects with Change Order
Design Representation Process	Lifecycle process for design representation
<None>	Null lifecycle definition for opt-out scenario
Standard Process	Company Standard Process

12. Click **Close** to close the dialog box and return to the Vault Settings dialog box. Click **Close** again to close this dialog box.

End of practice

4.2 Configuring Lifecycle States

Overview

The ability to define lifecycle definitions and behaviors enables you to customize your workflow environment to classify data based on their lifecycle status in the work process.

Objectives

After completing this lesson, you will be able to:

- Configure the lifecycle state to specify which users and groups can read, modify, and delete files which are in that state.
- Specify which actions should be taken when a file transitions from one lifecycle state to another.
- Specify which users and groups can transition a file from one lifecycle state to another or if the transition should be permitted by anyone.
- Specify which files versions for a given revision should be removed in a Purge operation.
- Configure the default comments added when a lifecycle state transition occurs.

Setting Up

In order to effectively configure a lifecycle definition's lifecycle states, it is critical to do some upfront planning. For example, different users can have different abilities to read or modify files in a given lifecycle state. One lifecycle state can transition to any other lifecycle state but some of these transitions might not make sense in your process and should not be permitted.

The following diagram shows an example of a lifecycle definition and the important considerations that must be planned before configuring one of the default lifecycle definitions or creating a new one.

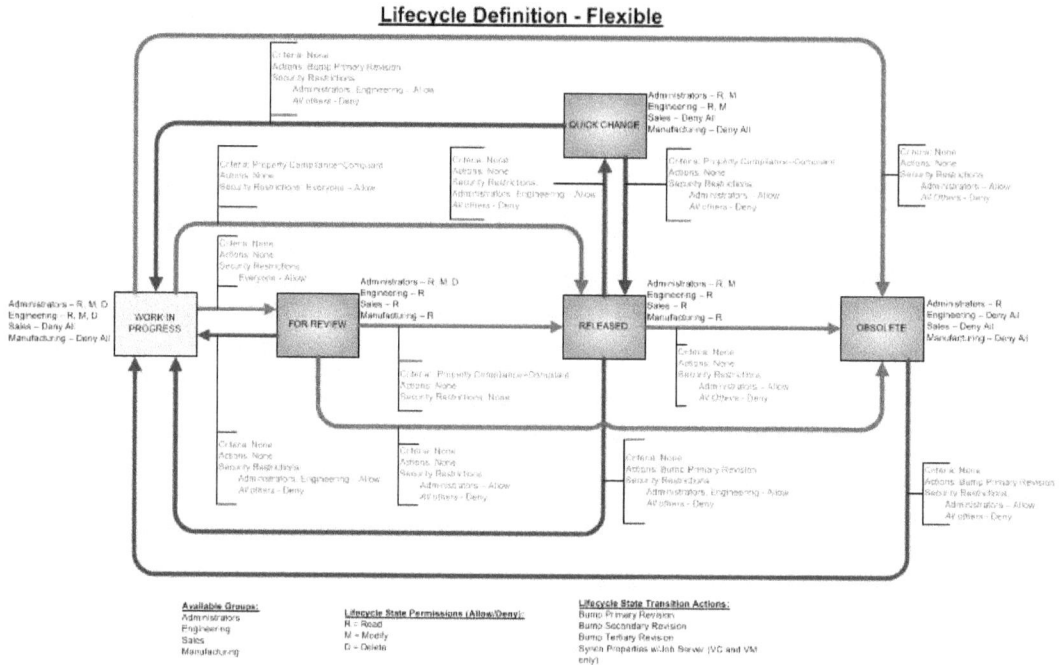

Lifecycle Definition - Flexible

Groups

It is important to think of the different groups in your organization and what access you will want them to have for files in different lifecycle states. For example, in the Work In Progress state, you probably only want the Engineering group and a few special users to be able to read or edit files. This special group of users can be administrators or department managers. In the Released state, it is common to grant access to all users but permit none, or only a small group, the ability to modify them.

Similarly, different groups of users will have different ability to transition between the lifecycle states. For example, you will likely have only a small group of users that can release a set of new or revised files to manufacturing. It is unlikely you will permit the users in the marketing or sales team to have this ability.

Access Control Lists (ACLs)

The access control list enables you to add and remove members to control who has access to certain files, folders, items, and custom objects. You can also control whether the member can only view the content, modify the content, or delete the content.

A file, folder, or custom object that does not have an access control list defined uses object-based security.

Object-based security can be overridden. An override of security means that the ACL still exists on the object but it is being overridden by a newly defined ACL. This is called an override access control list or an override ACL.

As long as an override ACL exists, the object-based security is ignored. If the user removes the override ACL, then the object-based security becomes the new security. If an override ACL is active, only members and users in the ACL list have permissions to modify the object.

General	Security	Effective Access

Security Mode:

Object-based security

☐ Override (state-based or manual)

Permissions:

Name	Read	Modify	Delete
No access control list			

Effective Security: Object-based

OK	Cancel	Help

General	Security	Effective Access

Security Mode:

Overridden security

☑ Override (state-based or manual)

Permissions:

Name	Read	Modify	Delete
Administrator	Allow	Allow	Allow
Group-Allow	Allow		Allow
Group-Deny	Allow	Deny	Deny
Group-Null	Allow	Allow	

Effective Security: Override (state-based or manual)

OK	Cancel	Help

How To: View Object Security

Examine file, folder, item, and custom object security through the context menu. You must be an administrator to view object security.

1. Right-click on a file, folder, item, or custom object in Vault and select **Details**.

2. In the Details dialog box, select the *Security* tab.

| General | Security | Effective Access |

Security Mode:

Overridden security ⌄

☑ Override (state-based or manual)

Permissions:

Name	Read	Modify	Delete
Administrator	Allow	Allow	Allow
Group-Allow	Allow		Allow
Group-Deny	Allow	Deny	Deny
Group-Null	Allow	Allow	

Effective Security: Override (state-based or manual)

| OK | Cancel | Help |

- **Security Mode:** Shows the security precedence for the selected object.

  - **Object-based security:** Security derived from the object. This is the default option and is the only option available if no other security is defined.

    Note: Items do not have object-based security.

  - **State-based security:** Security available when a state-based access control list (ACL) exists and is combined with object-based security.

  - **Overridden security:** Security available when a state-based ACL is overriding object-based security, or when the administrator sets a manual override on the object.

- **Permissions:** The ACL shows which groups and users are granted access to the selected object and their respective permissions.

- **Effective Security:** Security currently in use by the object (found at the bottom of the dialog box). In the example above, **Override (state-based or manual)** security is in effect.

3. Select the *Effective Access* tab to view user permissions for the object.

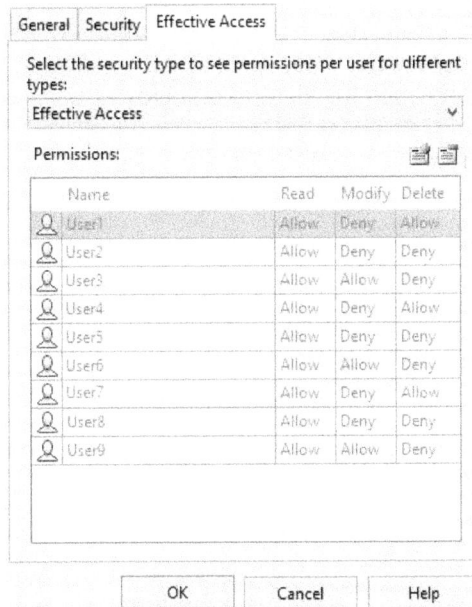

Security Type

Select a security type to see a user's effective permissions for that security mode. This is primarily useful when both object-based security and state-based security are applied, and the administrator wants to finder a user's effective permissions.

Note: Only individual user permissions can be viewed. Groups cannot be added in the Effective Access tab.

Permissions

The permissions list in the *Effective Access* tab is empty by default. Add ⊟ and remove ⊟ members from the list to view the type of access they have to the object under the selected security type. Change the security type to see how permissions are impacted.

Note: The Effective Access tab is for viewing security permissions only. Adding and removing members does not change security permissions for the object. Permission changes must be performed in the Security tab.

Configuring Lifecycle State Security

Configuring security is an important step in the configuration. By default, no security beyond that which is determined by permissions assigned to each individual object is enforced for files in a given lifecycle state, as shown in the illustration below.

For lifecycle definitions created in the 2017 software release and greater, Autodesk Vault uses a dual-gate security model that combines object security with state security. Users must have role permission and combined object and state-based permissions to access a Vault object. Administrators can control individual access to a Vault object based on organizational area or business line. For example, an administrator can ensure that a group has read, write, and delete permissions and at the same time, deny permissions to certain members of the group while in various lifecycle states.

For *Definition Security*, as shown in the following image, select one of the following options:

- **Combine with object-based security:** Any state-based security defined for individual states within this lifecycle definition combine with the object-based security set on the object. In other words, the combined security becomes the effective security for the entity.

- **Override object-based security:** Any state-based security defined for individual states within this lifecycle definition override the object-based security set on the object. In other words, state-based security becomes the effective security for the entity.

    *Note: Vaults migrated from Vault 2016 or earlier use **Override object-based security** as the default setting so that legacy (single-gate) security is maintained. However, all new vaults use **Combine with object-based security** as the default security setting, which is a dual-gate security setting. Change this setting at any time to mimic legacy (single-gate) security.*

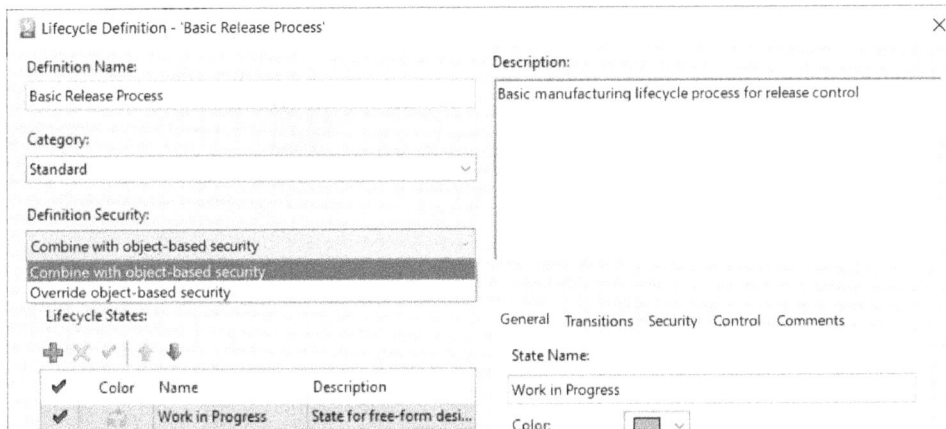

Defining State-Based Security

How To: Access Security for a Lifecycle State

1. Select **Tools>Administration>Vault Settings**.
2. In the Vault Settings dialog box, select the *Behaviors* tab and select **Lifecycles**.
3. In the Lifecycle Definitions dialog box, select the name of the lifecycle definition and click **Edit**. The selected definition name displays in the title bar.
4. Select the state for which you want to define security.
5. Select the *Security* tab to display the current security settings for that state.

How To: Disable State-Based Security

1. Click **No state-based security** if you don't want to assign security for the state. Security is determined by the permissions assigned to the object.

How To: Add a Member or Group Permission to a Lifecycle State

1. In the *Security* tab, clear the **No state-based security** checkbox if it is selected.
2. Click **Add**.
3. In the Add Members dialog box, select the member or group from the *Available Members* list and click **Add**. The selected name is moved to the *Current Members* list.

    Note: Filter the Available Members list by selecting a qualifier from the Select Members From list.

    From the *Current Members* list, select one or more members and then click **Remove** to modify the current members list.
4. Click **OK**.

How To: Edit Member or Group Permissions

1. In the Lifecycle Definition dialog box, select the state from the Lifecycle States list.

2. In the *Security* tab, select the member or group to edit.

3. In the Permissions box, enable or disable the **Allow** and **Deny** checkboxes for each permission.

Permission	Access
Read	• **Allow:** States can be viewed.
	• **Deny:** States cannot be viewed. If a member is denied read access, then they are not permitted Modify or Delete access either.
	• **None:** State cannot be viewed.
Modify	• **Allow:** States can be modified.
	• **Deny:** State cannot be modified.
	• **None:** State cannot be modified.
Delete	• **Allow:** State can be deleted
	• **Deny:** State cannot be deleted.
	• **None:** State cannot be deleted.

4. Click **OK**.

Configuring Lifecycle State Transitions

Each lifecycle state has the ability to transition to every other lifecycle state. There are several considerations dealing with the ability for a lifecycle state to be changed or transitioned to another state. These are:

*   **Criteria:** Are there property considerations governing the state transition? Criteria could also include a condition, such as not permitting a transition to In Review if the file is not associated to a change order.

*   **Actions:** What actions, if any, should be performed when making the state transition. The actions include checking that the dependent child files, dependent child folders, contained files, linked files, linked folders, or linked custom objects are released. Actions can also include incrementing revision values, synchronizing properties, and creating visualization representation files.

*   **Custom Job Types:** What custom jobs should be assigned to the transition?

*   **Security:** Which user or groups are permitted the ability to transition from one state to the next?

Each of these considerations are shown in their own tab in the Transition dialog box, as shown in the image below.

Transition Criteria

Specifying criteria is much like the Advanced Find capability. You can specify if one or more of the system or user-defined properties associated with the file meet specific criteria. If all of the criteria are met, the transition can take place. If one or more of the criteria are not met, then the user is warned and cannot make the transition until the criteria are met or the lifecycle definition is changed.

The only default criteria that are set for some of the lifecycle state transitions in the default lifecycle definitions are property compliance. A property is said to be compliant if its value meets one or more criteria itself.

For example, the property Description must have a value between 10 and 20 characters long and the property Cost must have a numeric value greater than zero. If the individual conditions are true, then the two properties are compliant. All properties that have compliance criteria must be compliant in order for the Property Compliance property to be compliant. This is a useful way of making sure that the important properties associated with a file are filled out correctly before the lifecycle state can be transitioned.

How To: Configure Transition Criteria

To configure the criteria that must be met before a file can transition into a new lifecycle state, do the following:

1. In the Vault Settings dialog box, select the *Behaviors* tab.

2. Select **Lifecycles** in the *Lifecycles and Revisions* section to display the Lifecycle Definitions dialog box.

3. Select the lifecycle definition to be customized.

4. Select **Edit** to display the Lifecycle Definition dialog box for the selected definition.

5. Select the lifecycle state from the list of *Lifecycle States* to be configured.

6. Select the *Transitions* tab to display a list of all of the lifecycle transitions for the selected lifecycle definition.

7. Select the transition to edit.

8. Select **Edit** to display the Transition dialog box.

9. Select the *Criteria* tab.

10. If required, filter which properties display based on a certain entity class using the Show drop-down list. For example, you can configure it so that only File Properties are shown in the Property drop-down list.

11. In the Property drop-down list, select the property to evaluate.

12. Specify the condition and value for that property.

13. Select **Add** to add it to the list of all properties to evaluate.

Criteria	Actions	Custom Job Types	Security

Show:

All Properties	∨

Property:		Condition:		Value:
Description	∨	is not empty	∨	

Add	Replace	Remove

Description is not empty

OK	Cancel	Help

14. Repeat the previous three steps to add additional criteria.

15. Click **OK** to dismiss this dialog box and return to the Lifecycle Definition dialog box for the selected lifecycle definition.

16. Configure the remaining transitions for the selected lifecycle state.

   Note: Every transition is shown for a given lifecycle state. For example, if you select State 1, you will find a transition from State 1 to State 2 and a transition from State 2 to State 1. Similarly, if you select State 2, you will find a transition from State 2 to State 1 and from State 1 to State 2. You only need to configure a particular state transition once. You do not need to configure it for every possible state transition. They are shown on every state transition for convenience.

17. Click **OK** to dismiss this dialog box and return to the Lifecycle Definitions dialog box.

18. Click **Close** to dismiss this dialog box and return to the Vault Settings dialog box.

Transition Actions

Actions are method of both automating process and enforcing rules associated with changing a file revision when moving from one lifecycle state to the other. When planning, some of the questions include:

- When transitioning from one state to another, is a new revision of the file created and of what kind?

- When making the transition, are there system level tasks that should be initiated?

- When transitioning to a released state, are checks on the state of the dependent children, content, or linked data required?

- If mapped property values should be synchronized by the Job Server.

- If both property values should be synchronized and visualization files updated by the Job Server.

The example in the illustration below shows the actions that are performed in a lifecycle definition where the state transition is from the Released state to the Work in Progress state. In this case the primary revision is bumped. So if the file were released at revision A, its revision would change to B when the state transition occurs. No properties would be synchronized by the Job Server and no release state checks would be performed.

How To: Configure Transition Actions

The following steps enable you to configure the actions that take place when a lifecycle state transition occurs:

1. In the Vault Settings dialog box, select the *Behaviors* tab.

2. Select **Lifecycles** in the *Lifecycles and Revisions* section to display the Lifecycle Definitions dialog box.

3. Select the lifecycle definition to be customized.

4. Select **Edit** to display the Lifecycle Definition dialog box for the selected definition.

5. Select the lifecycle state from the list of *Lifecycle States* to be configured.

6. Select the *Transitions* tab to display a list of all of the lifecycle transitions for the selected lifecycle definition.

7. Select the required state transition.

8. Select **Edit** to display the Transition dialog box.

9. Select the *Actions* tab to display the actions initiated by the selected state transition.

10. The default actions are shown. None are selected.

11. If required, select an entity class in the Filter drop-down list to show only the actions available for that entity class (e.g., select **Folders** to only see actions available for folder state transitions).

12. To specify a revision bump action, select the drop-down list to see the possible actions. Select the required action.

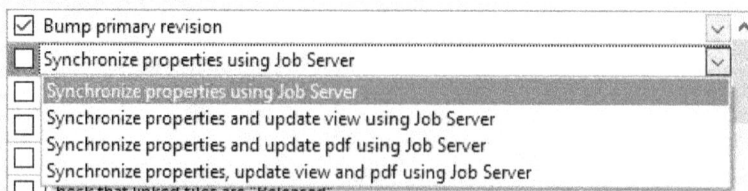

13. To specify a Job Server action, select the drop-down list to see the possible actions. Select the required action.

14. Review the final choices.

15. To specify release restrictions, select one or more of the options that check that the state of the dependent children, content, or linked data is set to released.

16. Click **OK** to dismiss this dialog box and return to the Lifecycle Definition dialog box for the selected lifecycle definition.

17. Configure the remaining transitions for the selected lifecycle state.

18. Click **OK** to dismiss this dialog box and return to the Lifecycle Definitions dialog box.

19. Click **Close** to dismiss this dialog box and return to the Vault Settings dialog box.

Transition Custom Job Types

Custom jobs can be created to automate processes during a transition. Two steps are necessary to create a custom job. First, a programmer must create the custom job and install it within the vault extensions. Then, an administrator adds it to the transition.

How To: Configure Transition Custom Job Types

The following steps enable you to associate a custom job with a state transition:

1. Click **Tools>Administration>Vault Settings**.

2. In the Vault Settings dialog box, select the *Behaviors* tab and select **Lifecycles**.

3. In the Lifecycle Definitions dialog box, select a lifecycle definition (e.g., Basic Release Process) and click **Edit**. The selected definition name displays in the title bar.

4. From the *Lifecycle States* list, select the lifecycle state to edit and then select the *Transitions* tab.

5. Select the desired transition, then click **Edit** to open the Transitions dialog box. Select the *Custom Job Types* tab.

6. Click **Add** and enter a name in the *Add to Input New Custom Job Type Name* field. Click **OK**.

Note: A typical naming convention is to add as a prefix your company name to any job types.

7. Click **OK** to exit the Transitions dialog box.

8. This custom job type will initiate whenever an object transitions through this lifecycle.

   To enable this custom job on other transitions, repeat steps 3 to 5 and specify an existing custom job type instead of creating a new custom job.

Transition Security

The last consideration for lifecycle transitions is which set of users and groups can initiate a state transition, if any is permitted to perform the state change. These are important questions for this topic:

* Does the state transition make sense for your process?

* If so, which set of users and groups can perform the transition? For example, in the default state In Review is it permitted to change the state to Obsolete? If so, who can do it? If not, then no one user or group can perform the transition.

The illustration below shows that when releasing a new design or major design change, only the **Administrator** group has the ability to initiate the transition.

How To: Configure Transition Security

The following steps enable you to specify which users and groups can initiate a state transition:

1. In the Vault Settings dialog box, select the *Behaviors* tab.

2. Select **Lifecycles** in the *Lifecycles and Revisions* section to display the Lifecycle Definitions dialog box.

3. Select the lifecycle definition to be customized.

4. Select **Edit** to display the Lifecycles Definition dialog box for the selected definition.

5. Select the lifecycle state from the list of *Lifecycle States* to be configured.

6. Select the *Transitions* tab to display a list of all of the lifecycle transitions for the selected lifecycle definition.

7. Select the required state transition.

8. Select **Edit** to display the Transition dialog box.

9. Select the *Security* tab to display the default security.

> | Criteria | Actions | Security |
>
> 🗒 Add...   🗒 Remove   ⓘ
>
> There are no security restrictions for this transition except for the permissions required by Object-based security.
> *User must have Modify permission for the object at the Object-based security level to perform a transition.*
>
> ☑ No restrictions on this transition

10. To configure security, first clear the checkbox for the **No restrictions on this transition** option.

> | Criteria | Actions | Security |
>
> 🗒 Add...   🗒 Remove   ⓘ
>
> Name   Permission
>
> In addition to the permissions defined here, the user must have Modify permission for the object at the Object-based security level to perform a transition.
>
> ☐ No restrictions on this transition

- The tab changes to enable you to specify which users and groups can perform the transition.

11. Select **Add** to display the Add Members dialog box.

12. Select the users and groups from the *Available Members* list that are granted or denied permission to perform the lifecycle change. Select **Add** to add them to the *Current Members* list.

Current Members:

	Name
▶ 👤	Engineering
👤	Manufacturing
👤	Sales
👤	Administrators

13. Click **OK** to return to the Transition dialog box with the selected members.

Note: By default, all members are permitted rights to change the file's lifecycle state. However, anyone who is not a member of a group or explicitly added as a member will be denied the ability to perform the state transition.

Criteria	Actions	Security

📑 Add... 📑 Remove

Name	Permission
Engineering	Allow
Manufacturing	Allow
Sales	Allow
Administrators	Allow

☐ No restrictions on this transition

14. For each user or group, specify if they are permitted or denied the ability to change the file's state.

Name	Permission
Engineering	Deny ▾
Manufacturing	Allow
Sales	Deny
Administrators	Allow

15. When done, review the final selections. Click **OK** to dismiss this dialog box and return to the Lifecycle Definition dialog box for this state transition.

16. Configure the remaining transitions for the selected lifecycle state.

17. Click **OK** to dismiss this dialog box and return to the Lifecycle Definitions dialog box.

18. Click **Close** to dismiss this dialog box and return to the Vault Settings dialog box.

Creating the Transition Guidelines

The illustration below shows how a tool like Microsoft Visio can be used to plan and manage the lifecycle definition's transitions.

Lifecycle Definition – Company Default

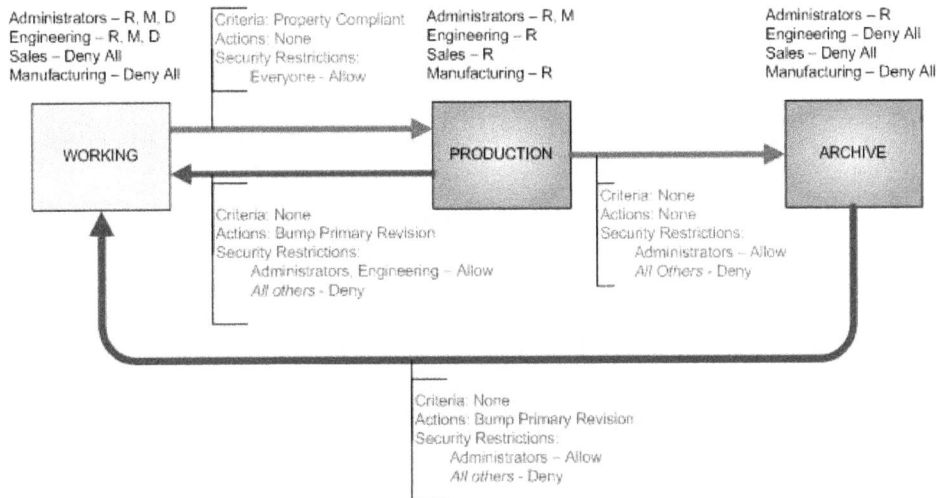

Administrators – R, M, D
Engineering – R, M, D
Sales – Deny All
Manufacturing – Deny All

Criteria: Property Compliant
Actions: None
Security Restrictions:
    Everyone - Allow

Administrators – R, M
Engineering – R
Sales – R
Manufacturing – R

Administrators – R
Engineering – Deny All
Sales – Deny All
Manufacturing – Deny All

WORKING

PRODUCTION

ARCHIVE

Criteria: None
Actions: Bump Primary Revision
Security Restrictions:
    Administrators, Engineering – Allow
    All others - Deny

Criteria: None
Actions: None
Security Restrictions:
    Administrators – Allow
    All Others - Deny

Criteria: None
Actions: Bump Primary Revision
Security Restrictions:
    Administrators – Allow
    All others - Deny

Available Groups:
Administrators
Engineering
Sales
Manufacturing

Lifecycle State Permissions (Allow/Deny):
R = Read
M = Modify
D = Delete

Lifecycle State Transition Actions:
Bump Primary Revision
Bump Secondary Revision
Bump Tertiary Revision
Synch Properties w/Job Server (VC and VM only)

Control and Comments Settings

There are two more settings that can be configured for a given lifecycle state.

Control

The *Control* setting specifies what happens during a **Purge** operation. The tab is illustrated below.

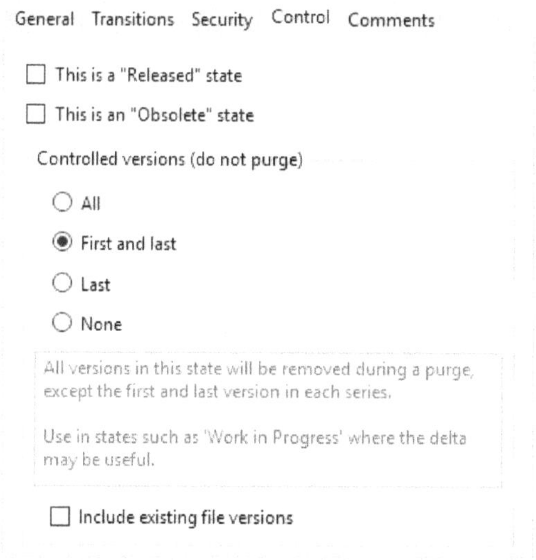

As you learned earlier, file versions are created every time you check a file in after being edited. File versions mark major milestones, for example release of a set of files representing a new product, or the subsequent major modification of one of those files for form, fit, and function purposes. For each revision, there can be many versions as files are checked out, modified, and checked in on a daily basis, a new user makes a modification to a files, etc. For the selected state, the radio buttons (**All**, **First and last**, **Last**, **None**) control which versions of a file will be kept if a purge occurs.

Comments

When an object is transitioned from one lifecycle state to another, a comment is added. The *Comments* tab controls what comment is added. The example below shows the dialog box that is presented to the user when transitioning to the For Review state.

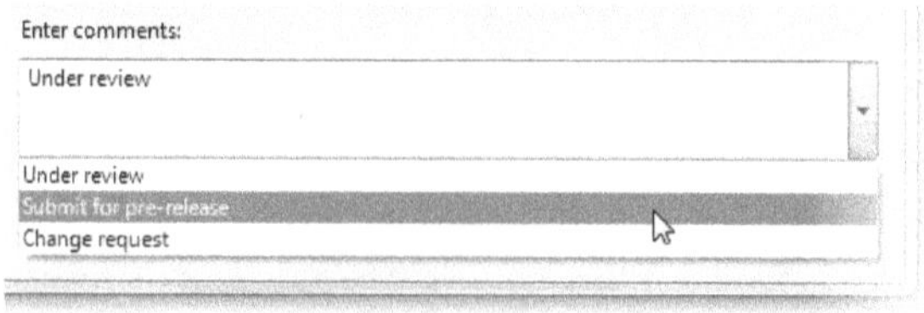

The *Comments* tab has a list of suggested text strings to use as a default. The user is free to add or replace this comment with one of their own. The illustration below shows the suggested and default comment for a state transition to For Review.

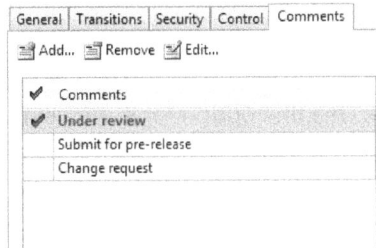

How To: Configure Control and Comments

The following steps enable you to specify which objects are removed during a purge operation and the default comment text for the state being transitioned to:

1. In the Vault Settings dialog box, select the *Behaviors* tab.

2. Select **Lifecycles** in the *Lifecycles and Revisions* section to display the Lifecycle Definitions dialog box.

3. Select the lifecycle definition to be customized.

4. Select **Edit** to display the Lifecycles Definition dialog box for the selected definition.

5. Select the lifecycle state from the list of *Lifecycle States* to be configured.

6. Select the *Control* tab to display the settings for controlled versions.

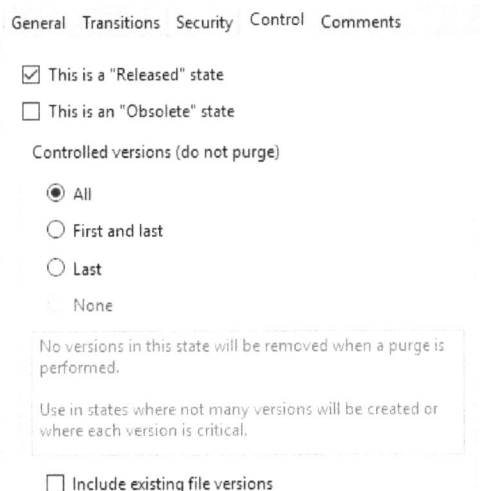

7. First, determine whether this state represents a released or obsolete condition. If it is a **"Released"** or **"Obsolete"** state, select the appropriate checkbox.

8. Determine which versions should not be purged. Select the different radio buttons to get details about each selection.

   - **All:** No versions in this state are removed when a purge is performed. This option is recommended for states where not many versions are created or where each version is critical.

   - **First and last:** All versions in this state are removed during a purge, except the first and last version in each series. Use this option for states where the changes between the first and last versions are not important.

   - **Last:** All versions in this state are removed during a purge, except the last version in each series. This option is recommended for states where a record that the file was in the state is important.

   - **None:** No version in this state will be retained after the purge has been performed.

     - **Important:** No record of the file being in this state will exist after the purge.

General Transitions Security Control Comments

☐ This is a "Released" state

☐ This is an "Obsolete" state

Controlled versions (do not purge)

○ All

○ First and last

○ Last

◉ None

> No version in this state will be retained after the purge has been performed.
>
> Warning: No record of the version being in this state will exist after the purge.

☐ Include existing file versions

9. Select the *Comments* tab to display the list of default comments (if any) prepopulated for this state.

10. Select the comment to set as default, or select **Add** to add a new comment.

11. To create a new default comment, enter the text in the *Enter comments* field. Click **OK** to close this dialog box.

12. Double-click on the new comment if one was added to make it the new default.

   * Note that you could also edit an existing comment rather than add a new one or remove a current one so it no longer displays in the drop-down list.

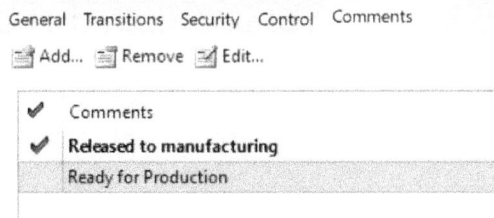

13. Configure the remaining transitions for the selected lifecycle state.

14. Click **OK** to close this dialog box and return to the Lifecycle Definitions dialog box.

15. Click **Close** to dismiss this dialog box and return to the Vault Settings dialog box.

Practice 4b
Configure Lifecycle Definition

In this practice, you will customize the Standard Process lifecycle definition that you created in *Practice 4a Create New Lifecycle Definition*.

Lifecycle Definition – Standard Process

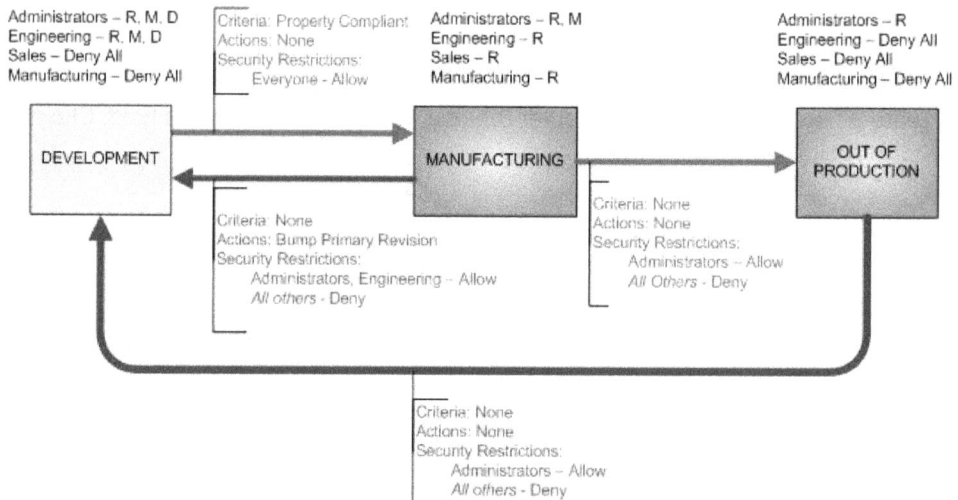

Administrators – R, M, D
Engineering – R, M, D
Sales – Deny All
Manufacturing – Deny All

Criteria: Property Compliant
Actions: None
Security Restrictions:
 Everyone - Allow

Administrators – R, M
Engineering – R
Sales – R
Manufacturing – R

Administrators – R
Engineering – Deny All
Sales – Deny All
Manufacturing – Deny All

DEVELOPMENT → MANUFACTURING → OUT OF PRODUCTION

Criteria: None
Actions: Bump Primary Revision
Security Restrictions:
 Administrators, Engineering – Allow
 All others - Deny

Criteria: None
Actions: None
Security Restrictions:
 Administrators – Allow
 All Others - Deny

Criteria: None
Actions: None
Security Restrictions:
 Administrators – Allow
 All others - Deny

Available Groups:
Administrators
Engineering
Sales
Manufacturing

Lifecycle State Permissions (Allow/Deny):
R = Read
M = Modify
D = Delete

Lifecycle State Transition Actions:
Bump Primary Revision
Bump Secondary Revision
Bump Tertiary Revision
Synch Properties w/Job Server

The completed practice

Task 1: Create groups.

1. From the Tools menu, select **Administration>Global Settings** to open the Global Settings dialog box.

2. Select **Manage Access** in the *Users and Groups* section of the *Security* tab to display the User and Group Management dialog box.

3. Create a group called **Administrators** defined with a role of **Administrator**. Select the *Groups* tab and click **New**.

4. In the New Group Profile dialog box, enter **Administrator** for the *Group Name*. Click **Roles**, select **Administrator**, and click **OK**. Click **Add** to display the Add Members dialog box.

5. Select **User A** from the *Available Members* list and select **Add** to add this to the list of *Current Members*.

6. Click **OK** to dismiss this dialog box and return to the New Group Profile dialog box.

7. Click **OK** to dismiss this dialog box and return to the User and Group Management dialog box.

8. Select **New** from the toolbar.

9. The New Group Profile dialog box opens. Do the following:

   • For *Group Name*, enter **Engineering**.

   • For *Roles*, select **Document Editor Level 2** and **Document Manager Level 2**. Click **OK**.

   • For *Vaults*, select **AOTCVault** box. Click **OK**.

10. Select **Add** to display the Add Members dialog box.

11. Select **User B** from the *Available Members* list and select **Add** to add this to the list of *Current Members*.

12. Click **OK** to dismiss this dialog box and return to the New Group Profile dialog box.

13. Click **OK** to dismiss this dialog box and return to the User and Group Management dialog box.

14. Select **New** from the toolbar.

15. The New Group Profile dialog box opens. Do the following:

   • For *Group Name*, enter **Manufacturing**.

   • For *Roles*, select **Document Editor Level 2** and **Document Manager Level 2**. Click **OK**.

   • For *Vaults*, select **AOTCVault**. Click **OK**.

16. Select **Add** to display the Add Members dialog box.

17. Select **User C** from the *Available Members* list and select **Add** to add this to the list of *Current Members*.

18. Click **OK** to dismiss this dialog box and return to the New Group Profile dialog box.

19. Click **OK** to dismiss this dialog box and return to the User and Group Management dialog box.

20. Select **New** from the toolbar.

21. The New Group Profile dialog box displays. Do the following:

   • For *Group Name*, enter **Sales**.

   • For *Roles*, select **Document Editor Level 2** and **Document Manager Level 2**. Click **OK**.

   • For *Vaults*, select **AOTCVault**. Click **OK**.

22. Select **Add** to display the Add Members dialog box.

23. Select **User D** from the *Available Members* list and select **Add** to add this to the list of *Current Members*.

24. Click **OK** to dismiss this dialog box and return to the New Group Profile dialog box.

25. Click **OK** to dismiss this dialog box and return to the User and Group Management dialog box.

...	Group Name	Members
▶	👤 Administrators	User A
	👤 Engineering	User B
	👤 Manufacturing	User C
	👤 Sales	User D

26. Select *File>Exit* to close this dialog box and return to the Global Settings dialog box.

27. Click **Close** to dismiss this dialog box.

Task 2: Configure lifecycle security.

1. From the Tools menu, select **Administration>Vault Settings** to open the Vault Settings dialog box.

2. Select the *Behaviors* tab, then select **Lifecycles** in the *Lifecycles and Revisions* section to display the Lifecycle Definitions dialog box.

3. Select the lifecycle definition **Standard Process**.

4. Select **Edit** to display the Lifecycle Definition - 'Standard Process' dialog box.

5. In the *Lifecycle Details* section, ensure that the **Development** lifecycle state is selected in the list.

✓	Color	Name	Description
✓	🔄	Development	Design development
	🔄	Manufacturing	Released designs
	🔄	Out of Production	Archived designs

6. Select the *Security* tab. By default there is no state-based security set.

General | Transitions | Security | Control | Comments

There is no security assigned to this state. Security will be determined by permissions assigned to each individual object.

☑ No state-based security

7. Clear the **No state-based security** checkbox to enable state-based security.

General | Transitions | Security | Control | Comments

Add... Remove

Name	▲	Read	Modify	Delete	Downl...

No access control list

☐ No state-based security

Options

☐ Security for associated files of items   Configure...

☐ Security for files inside folders   Configure...

8. Select **Add** to display the Add Members dialog box.

9. In the Select Members From drop-down list, select **Groups**.

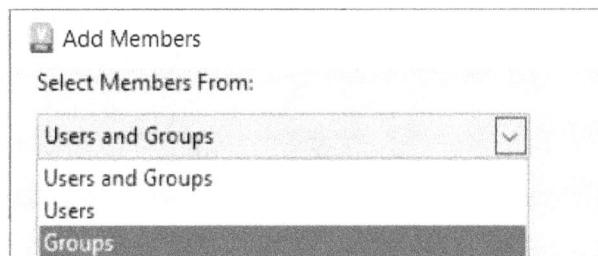

Add Members

Select Members From:

Users and Groups ▼

Users and Groups
Users
Groups

10. In the *Available Members* list, press <Ctrl> and select the **Administrators**, **Engineering**, **Manufacturing**, and **Sales** groups.

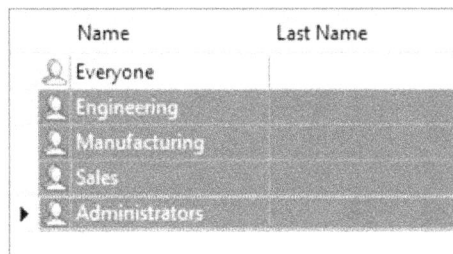

Name	Last Name
Everyone	
Engineering	
Manufacturing	
Sales	
▶ Administrators	

11. Select **Add** to add the selection to the *Current Members* list.

Current Members:

Name
▶ 👤 Engineering
👤 Manufacturing
👤 Sales
👤 Administrators

12. Click **OK** to dismiss this dialog box and return to the Lifecycle Definition dialog box.

13. Do the following for the **Development** state:

* For **Engineering**, set *Read, Modify, Delete,* and *Download* to **Allow**.
* For **Manufacturing**, set *Read, Modify, Delete,* and *Download* to **Deny**.
* For **Sales**, set *Read, Modify, Delete,* and *Download* to **Deny**.
* For **Administrators**, set *Read, Modify, Delete,* and *Download* to **Allow**.

General | Transitions | Security | Control | Comments

📑 Add... 📑 Remove

Name	Read	Modify	Delete	Download
👤 Administrator	Allow	Allow	Allow	Allow
👤 Engineering	Allow	Allow	Allow	Allow
👤 Manufacturing	Deny	Deny	Deny	Deny
👤 Sales	Deny	Deny	Deny	Deny

☐ No state-based security

Options

☐ Security for associated files of items   Configure...

☐ Security for files inside folders   Configure...

14. Select **Apply** to apply the settings to the selected lifecycle state.

15. Select the **Manufacturing** lifecycle state from the *Lifecycle States* list.

16. Clear the **No state-based security** checkbox to enable state-based security.

17. Select **Add** to display the Add Members dialog box.

18. In the Select Members From drop-down list, select **Groups**.

19. In the *Available Members* list, press <Ctrl> and select the **Administrators**, **Engineering**, **Manufacturing**, and **Sales** groups, then select **Add** and click **OK**.

20. Do the following for the **Manufacturing** state:
    - For **Engineering**, set *Read* to **Allow** and set *Modify* and *Delete* to **Deny**.
    - For **Manufacturing**, set *Read* to **Allow** and set *Modify* and *Delete* to **Deny**.
    - For **Sales**, set *Read* to **Allow** and set *Modify* and *Delete* to **Deny**.
    - For **Administrators**, set *Read* and *Modify* to **Allow** and set *Delete* to **Deny**.

General | Transitions | Security | Control | Comments

Add... Remove

Name	Read	Modify	Delete	Download
Administrator	Allow	Allow	Deny	
Engineering	Allow	Deny	Deny	
Manufacturing	Allow	Deny	Deny	
Sales	Allow	Deny	Deny	

21. Select **Apply** to apply the settings to the selected lifecycle state.
22. Do the following for the **Out of Production** state:
    - For **Engineering**, set *Read*, *Modify*, and *Delete* to **Deny**.
    - For **Manufacturing**, set *Read*, *Modify*, and *Delete* to **Deny**.
    - For **Sales**, set *Read*, *Modify*, and *Delete* to **Deny**.
    - For **Administrators**, set *Read* to **Allow** and set *Modify* and *Delete* to **Deny**.

General | Transitions | Security | Control | Comments

Add... Remove

Name	Read	Modify	Delete
Administrators	Allow	Deny	Deny
Engineering	Deny	Deny	Deny
Manufacturing	Deny	Deny	Deny
Sales	Deny	Deny	Deny

☐ No state-based security

Options
☐ Security for associated files of items   Configure...
☐ Security for files inside folders   Configure...

23. Select **Apply** to apply the settings to the selected lifecycle state.

Task 3: Configure transitions: Security.

In our example, there are three lifecycle states and six possible transitions that can occur. Some of these transitions are not permitted by anyone and will be configured first.

1. In the *Lifecycles States* list, select the **Development** state.

2. Select the *Transitions* tab to display a list of all possible transitions from and to this state.

3. Select the entry that specifies from **Development** and to **Out of Production**. Select **Edit** to display the Transition dialog box.

General | Transitions | Security | Control | Comments

Edit...

State		State
Development	⇨	Manufacturing
Development	⇨	Out of Production
Development	⇦	Manufacturing
Development	⇦	Out of Production

4. Select the *Security* tab and clear the checkbox for the **No restrictions on this transition** option.

Transition ✕

From State: To State:
Development   ⇨   Out of Production

Criteria | Actions | Custom Job Types | Security | Peer Review
Add...   Remove   ⓘ

Name   **Permission**

In addition to the permissions defined here, the user must have Modify permission for the object at the Object-based security level to perform a transition.

☐ No restrictions on this transition

OK   Cancel   Help

5. Select **Add** to display the Add Members dialog box.

6. In the Select Members From drop-down list, select **Groups**.

7. In the *Available Members* list, select **Everyone**.

8. Select **Add** to add Everyone to the list of *Current Members*.

Current Members:

Name
▶ 👤 Everyone

9. Click **OK** to dismiss this dialog box and return to the Transition dialog box.

10. The group **Everyone** has been added to the *Security* list with the default permission **Allow**. Select the default permission to open the drop-down list and select **Deny**.

Criteria | Actions | Custom Job Types | Security | Peer Review

📑 Add... 📑 Remove   (i)

Name	Permission
Everyone	Allow
	Allow
	Deny

11. Click **OK** to dismiss this dialog box and return to the Lifecycle Definition dialog box.

12. In the *Lifecycles States* list, select **Out of Production**.

13. In the *Transitions* tab, select the entry that specifies from **Out of Production** and to **Manufacturing** from the list.

General | Transitions | Security | Control | Comments

📑 Edit...

State		State
Out of Production	⇨	Development
Out of Production	⇨	Manufacturing
Out of Production	⇦	Development
Out of Production	⇦	Manufacturing

14. Select **Edit** to display the Transition dialog box.

15. Select the *Security* tab and clear the **No restrictions on this transition** checkbox.

16. Select **Add** to display the Add Members dialog box.

17. In the Select Members From drop-down list, select **Groups**.

18. In the *Available Members* list, select **Everyone**.

19. Select **Add** to add Everyone to the list of *Current Members*.

20. Click **OK** to dismiss this dialog box and return to the Transition dialog box.

21. The group **Everyone** has been added to the *Security* list with the default permission **Allow**.

22. Select the default permission to open the drop-down list and select **Deny**.

23. Click **OK** to dismiss this dialog box and return to the Lifecycle Definition dialog box.

24. In the *Lifecycles States* list, select **Development**.

25. In the *Transitions* tab, select the entry that specifies from **Manufacturing** and to **Development** from the list.

General | Transitions | Security | Control | Comments

📑 Edit...

State	State
Development	⇨ Manufacturing
Development	⇨ Out of Production
Development	⇦ Manufacturing
Development	⇦ Out of Production

26. Select **Edit** to display the Transition dialog box.

27. Select the *Security* tab and clear the **No restrictions on this transition** checkbox.

28. Select **Add** to display the Add Members dialog box.

29. In the Select Members From drop-down list, select **Groups**.

30. In the *Available Members* list, press <Ctrl> + select **Administrators**, **Engineering**, **Manufacturing**, and **Sales**.

31. Select **Add** to add the selected entries to the list of *Current Members*.

Current Members:

Name
▶ 👤 Engineering
👤 Manufacturing
👤 Sales
👤 Administrators

32. Click **OK** to dismiss this dialog box and return to the Transition dialog box.

33. The four groups have been added to the *Security* list with the default permission **Allow**. Select **Manufacturing**, then select the default permission to open the drop-down list and select **Deny**.

34. Repeat the previous step with the group **Sales**.

Name	Permission
Engineering	Allow
Manufacturing	Deny
Sales	Deny
Administrators	Allow

35. Click **OK** to dismiss this dialog box and return to the Lifecycle Definition dialog box.

36. In the *Lifecycles States* list, select **Manufacturing**.

37. In the *Transitions* tab, select entry that specifies from **Manufacturing** and to **Out of Production** from the list.

General | Transitions | Security | Control | Comments

📑 Edit...

State	State
Manufacturing	⇨ Development
Manufacturing	⇨ Out of Production
Manufacturing	⇦ Development
Manufacturing	⇦ Out of Production

38. Select **Edit** to display the Transition dialog box.

39. Select the *Security* tab and clear the **No restrictions on this transition** checkbox.

40. Select **Add** to display the Add Members dialog box.

41. In the Select Members From drop-down list, select **Groups**.

42. In the *Available Members* list, press <Ctrl> + select **Administrators, Engineering, Manufacturing**, and **Sales**.

43. Select **Add** to add the selected entries to the list of *Current Members*.

44. Click **OK** to dismiss this dialog box and return to the Transition dialog box.

45. The four groups have been added to the *Security* list with the default permission **Allow**. Select **Manufacturing**, then select the default permission to open the drop-down list and select **Deny**.

46. Repeat the previous step with the **Sales** and **Engineering** groups.

Name	Permission
Engineering	Deny
Manufacturing	Deny
Sales	Deny
Administrators	Allow

47. Click **OK** to dismiss the Transition dialog box.

Task 4: Configure states: Criteria.

In our example, there is only one state transition that has criteria. This is from Development to Manufacturing. The lifecycle state Manufacturing should still be selected in the *Lifecycle States* list.

1. In the *Transition* tab, select the from **Development** to **Manufacturing** transition.

General | Transitions | Security | Control | Comments

📝 Edit...

State		State
Manufacturing	⇨	Development
Manufacturing	⇨	Out of Production
Manufacturing	⇦	Development
Manufacturing	⇦	Out of Production

2. Select **Edit** to display the Transition dialog box. The *Criteria* tab should be displayed.

3. In the Property drop-down list, select **Property Compliance**.

4. In the Value drop-down list, select **Compliant**.

Criteria | Actions | Custom Job Types | Security | Peer Review

Show:

All Properties

Property:	Condition:	Value:
Property Compliance	is	Compliant

Compliant
Noncompliant policies
Noncompliant equivalence
Noncompliant policies and equivalence
Pending
Compliance evaluation failed

5. Select **Add** to add it to the list.

Task 5: Property configuration: Actions.

In this case, there are two state transitions that have actions. One action is from Development to Manufacturing state transition and the other is from Manufacturing to Development state transition. The Development to Manufacturing state transition should already be selected.

1. In the Transitions dialog box, select the *Actions* tab.

2. Select the checkbox next to **Check that dependent child files are "Released"**.

Criteria | Actions | Custom Job Types | Security | Peer Review
Filter:
All

☐ Bump primary revision
☐ Synchronize properties and update the selected file types using Job Server
☑ Check that dependent child files are "Released"
☐ Check that dependent child folders are "Released"
☐ Check that contained files are "Released"

3. Click **OK** to dismiss this dialog box and return to the Lifecycle Definition dialog box.

4. In the *Transitions* tab, select the from **Manufacturing** and to **Development** transition.

General | Transitions | Security | Control | Comments
Edit...

State	State
Manufacturing	⇨ Development
Manufacturing	⇨ Out of Production
Manufacturing	⇦ Development
Manufacturing	⇦ Out of Production

5. Select **Edit** to display the Transition dialog box.

6. Select the *Actions* tab.

7. Select the checkbox next to **Bump primary revision**.

Criteria | Actions | Custom Job Types | Security | Peer Review

Filter:

All ▾

☑ Bump primary revision ▾

☐ Synchronize properties and update the selected file types using Job Server ···

☐ Check that dependent child files are "Released"

8. Click **OK** to dismiss this dialog box and return to the Lifecycle Definition dialog box for the selected lifecycle definition.

Task 6: Control: Released state.

The final step is to specify that the Manufacturing state is the "Released" state. This is important to check that dependent child files with "Released" criteria know what state to enforce. The lifecycle state Manufacturing should still be selected in the *Lifecycle States* list.

1. Select the *Control* tab.

2. Select **This is a "Released" state** checkbox.

General | Transitions | Security | Control | Comments

☑ This is a "Released" state

☐ This is an "Obsolete" state

3. Select **Apply** to apply the change.

4. Click **OK** to dismiss this dialog box and return to the Vault Settings dialog box. Close all open dialog boxes.

End of practice

4.3 Changing Lifecycle States

Overview

The Change State dialog box changes the state of files, folders, items, and custom objects. Before the state is changed, the criteria, if any, are first checked. The user must have the ability to change the state and any conditions are evaluated. When the state change is performed, any actions specified are then performed. The user has the option of specifying a comment to inform others why the state was changed.

Objectives

After completing this lesson, you will be able to:

- Describe the way a Vault object's state can be changed.

- Change the state of a set of related files.

- Describe how the criteria and security can restrict lifecycle state changes.

- Understand how the new lifecycle state can impact the ability to read, modify and delete data.

Change State

There are several ways that a file can change state:

- **Adding a new file to the vault:** New files can be added to the vault using different methods: Manually adding a file, adding a file through the application add-in, migrating from Autodesk Vault to Autodesk Vault Professional and using the Autoloader to add Autodesk Inventor files. In a later lesson, you will learn how assignment rules and categories can be set up to automatically assign a lifecycle definition and default state to a file.

- **Change category:** Vault Professional enables you to create and assign files to different categories. The action of doing so can also assign a default lifecycle definition and initial state to the file. This will also be covered in a later lesson.

- **The Change State command:** This is the manual method of changing a state and is based on some significant lifecycle event like revising a set of files that represent products in production or archiving a set of deign files that is no longer in production.

Change State Command

The **Change State** command is available in three locations:

- Right-click on a file in the main pane.
- In the Actions menu.
- In the Behaviors toolbar.

This command enables the authorized user to:

- **Specify the lifecycle definition to use:** It is possible to change lifecycle definitions during a state change. This is helpful if the file needs to be managed differently. For example, your organization can manage files in the prototyping phase of product development differently from those that are in production and undergoing revision. Another example could be when one company acquires another and changes the way the company's files are lifecycle managed.

- **Specify the lifecycle state:** Once the definition is chosen, a set of valid lifecycle state transitions is presented. It is up to the user to specify which lifecycle state to change to based on the reason for making the lifecycle change.

- **Select the effected files:** Because the files can have many different relationships, it is possible to select which of the related files will also undergo the state change. This includes parent and children files and attached, library and related documentation.

- **Enter a comment:** It is important to inform other users why the change was made. The lifecycle state transition can be configured to present a list of options or the user can enter their own reason.

> ### 💡 Hint: Change State Dialog Box
>
> The Change State dialog box can change the state of files, folders, items, and custom objects. Multiple instances of any of those entity types can be acted on at one time. However, the Change State dialog box does not support more than one entity type at a time. For example, the user cannot change state on a file and folder at the same time.

How To: Change State

To change the state of a set of related files, do the following:

1. Select the file or group of files from the main pane that are to be changed. If you need to change a set of related files, you can use the options in the dialog box to select these for you. If the files are not related, use the <Shift> + select or <Ctrl> + select option to select the files from the list.

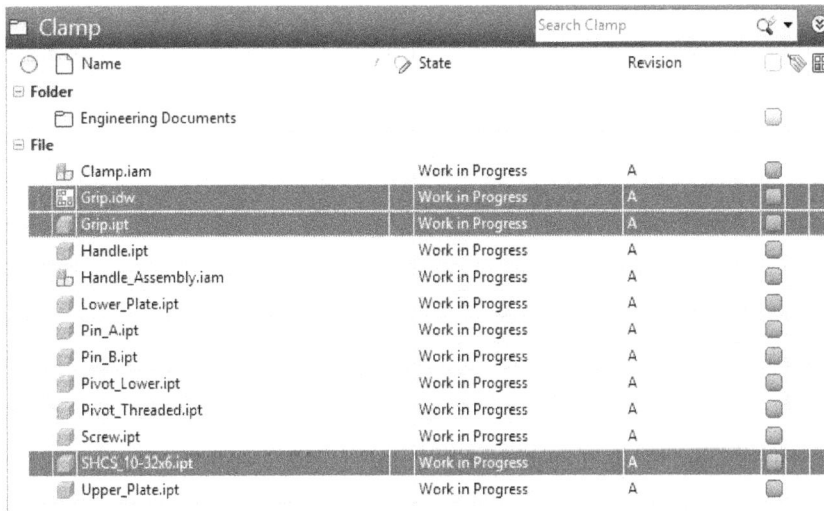

2. Select **Change State** to display the Change State dialog box.

3. In the *Select a new lifecycle state* section, select the lifecycle definition from the drop-down list.

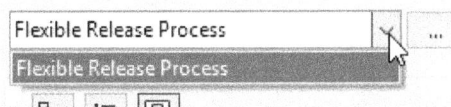

4. To select a different lifecycle definition, select the button next to the field to display the Change Lifecycle Definition dialog box. Select a different lifecycle definition, then click **OK** to dismiss this dialog box.

5. Once the definition is selected, select the state from the drop-down list.

6. When a new definition or state is chosen, the columns in the file list update to show the new selection.

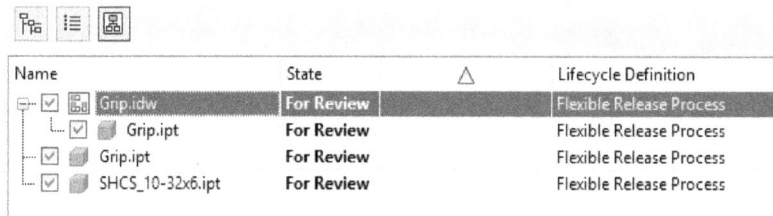

7. Use View to change the view to help understand file relationships.

8. Use the Parent/Child selection buttons to modify the selection.

Include Dependents

Include Parents

9. Select **Settings** to display the Settings dialog box. Here you can refine the selection of related files.

Settings ✕

Children (uses)
☑ Include dependents
☐ Include attachments
☐ Include library files

Parents (where used)
☐ Include parents
  ○ All parents
  ● Direct parents only

Other relationships
☑ Include related documentation

OK   Cancel   Help

Settings

10. Select the related files that will also change lifecycle state.

11. Enter a comment or select a predefined comment from the drop-down list.

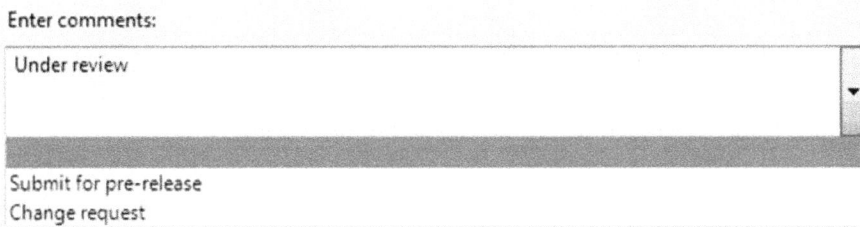

Enter comments:

Under review

Submit for pre-release
Change request

12. Click **OK** to complete the procedure.

Practice 4c
Change Lifecycle States

In this practice, you will change the state of the Table files to release them to manufacturing. You will create a new category named **Design** and assign the **Standard Process** lifecycle definition to it. In a later chapter, you will learn how categories can be used to help control your files.

Table		Search Table			
○ ☐ Name	/ ⊘ State		Revision		☐ 🏷 ⊞
⊟ **File**					
Dowel.ipt	Manufacturing		1		
leg.ipt	Manufacturing		1		
long rail.ipt	Manufacturing		1		
Short rail.ipt	Manufacturing		1		
Side.iam	Manufacturing		1		
Small Table.iam	Manufacturing		1		
Top.ipt	Manufacturing		1		

History   Uses   Where Used   Change Order   View

Number of versions:	3	(Local = Unknown)	
Number of revisions:	2	☑ Show all versions	

Thumbnail	File Name	Revision	State (Historical)
	Small Table.iam	1	Manufacturing

The completed practice

Task 1: Create a new category.

1. If not already logged in, log in to Vault using the following information:

    *   For *User Name*, enter **administrator**.
    *   Leave the *Password* field blank.
    *   For *Vault*, select **AOTCVault** from the drop-down list.

2. From the Tools menu, select **Administration>Vault Settings** to display the Vault Settings dialog box.

3. Select the *Behaviors* tab and then select **Categories** in the *Categories* section to display the Configure Categories dialog box.

4. Select **File Categories** from the drop-down list.

5. Select **New** in the toolbar to display the Category Edit dialog box.

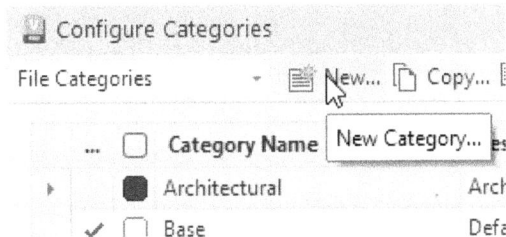

6. In the Category Edit dialog box, enter the following information:

    *   For *Name*, enter **Design**.
    *   In the *Color* drop-down list, choose **Orange** as shown below.
    *   For *Description*, enter **Design Files**.
    *   Ensure that the **Available** checkbox is selected.

7. Click **OK** to return to the Configure Categories dialog box.

8. Ensure that the new **Design** category is selected in the list.

9. In the *Behaviors* section of the Configure Categories dialog box, select the *Lifecycles* tab.

10. In the toolbar, select **Assign**.

11. The Assign Category – Design dialog box displays.

12. In the *All Lifecycle Definitions* list, select **Standard Process**.

13. Select **Add** to add it to the *Assigned Lifecycle Definitions* list.

14. Double-click on the **Standard Process** entry to make it the default lifecycle definition to use for the Design category.

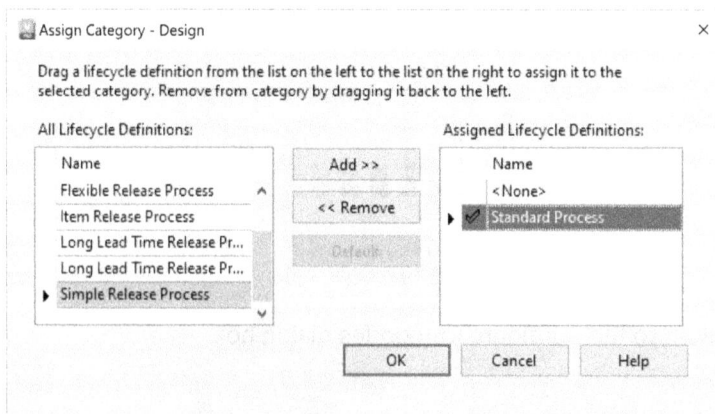

15. Click **OK** to dismiss this dialog box and return to the Configure Categories dialog box.

16. Select the *Revisions* tab in the *Behaviors* section.

17. Select **Assign** to display the Assign Category – Design dialog box.

18. In the *All Revision Schemes* list, select **Standard Numeric Format**.

19. Select **Add** to add it to the *Assigned Revision Schemes* list.

20. Double-click on the new entry to make it the default.

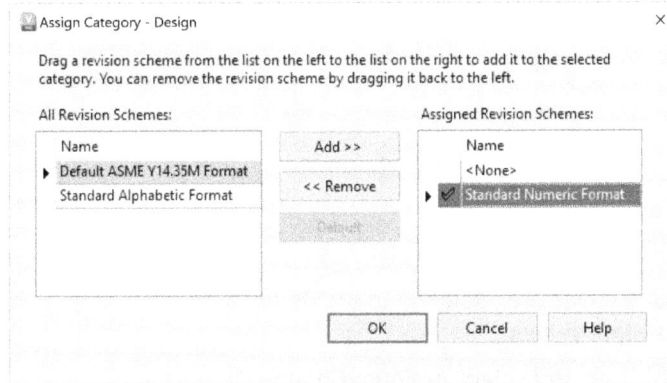

21. Click **OK** to close the dialog box and return to the Configure Categories dialog box.

22. Click **Close** to dismiss this dialog box and return to the Vault Settings dialog box. Click **Close** to dismiss this dialog box and return to Vault.

23. Log out of Autodesk Vault.

Task 2: Change category.

1. Log in to Autodesk Vault using the following information:

- For *User Name*, enter **usera**.
- For *Password*, enter **vault**.
- For *Vault*, select **AOTCVault** from the drop-down list.

2. In the Navigation pane, expand the *Project Explorer ($)* folder and then expand the *Designs* folder. Double-click on the *Table* folder to display the table assemblies and parts in the main pane.

- Note that all of the files are assigned to the **Base** category during the migration and have no *Revision* or *State* values.

3. Select **Small Table.iam** and select **Actions>Change Category**.

4. In the dialog box, select **Design** from the Select a new category drop-down list.

5. All of the children for the table should also be selected. If not, select **Include Dependents** in the row of buttons below the file list.

6. In the *Enter comments* text box, enter the comment **Design files**. Review the dialog box entries. Click **OK** to finish the Change Category workflow.

7. Return to the main pane and review the file list.

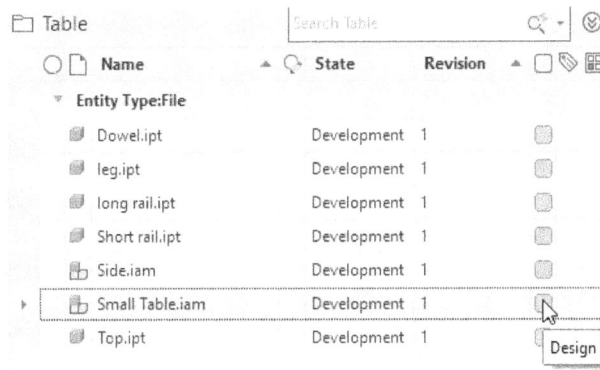

- The Category glyph is now set to **Design**.
- The Design category specifies the default lifecycle state for the files to be **Development**, which you can see in the *State* column.
- The rules for changing to the Development lifecycle state specify the revision be bumped based on the primary revision with the Standard Numeric Revision scheme. The first value in this revision scheme's sequence is 1, which you can see in the *Revision* column.
- Because a new file version is created when a new revision is made, the files are all at version 2.

8. Log out of Autodesk Vault.

9. Log in to Autodesk Vault using the following information:

   - For *User Name*, enter **userd**.

   - For *Password*, enter **vault**.

   - For *Vault*, select **AOTCVault** from the drop-down list.

10. In the Navigation pane, expand the *Project Explorer ($)* folder and then expand the *Designs* folder.

11. Select the *Table* folder. Note that the files are not displayed. In the Development lifecycle definition state, the Sales group (which userd is a member of) has no Read, Modify, or Delete permissions.

12. Log out of Vault.

13. Log in to Autodesk Vault using the following information:

   - For *User Name*, enter **userb**.

   - For *Password*, enter **vault**.

   - For *Vault*, select **AOTCVault** from the drop-down list.

14. In the Navigation pane, expand the *Project Explorer ($)* folder and then expand the *Designs* folder.

15. Select the *Table* folder. Since userb is part of the Engineering group, and this group has Read permission in the Development state, the files display.

Task 3: Change lifecycle state.

1. Select **Small Table.iam**.

2. In the Behaviors toolbar, select **Change State**.

3. The Change State – 'Small Table.iam' dialog box displays. Ensure that only the main assembly Small Table.iam is checked, as shown below.

4. In the *Select a new lifecycle state* field, in the right side drop-down list, select **Manufacturing**.

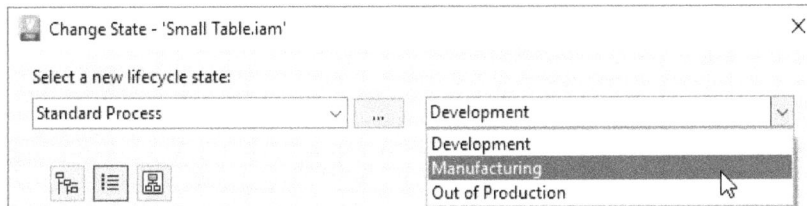

5. In the *Enter comments* field, enter the comment **Release to production**.

> Enter comments:
>
> Release to production
>
> OK

6. Click **OK** to finish the lifecycle state change.

7. An error message displays. Select **Details** to see the complete error message.

> ⬛ Can't change state   ✕
>
> ❌ One or more files can't change to the specified state due to errors or restrictions.
>
> List of affected objects: Print Preview
>
> | Affected Object ▲ | Restriction |
> | --- | --- |
> | Small Table.iam | Revision 1 of Dowel.ipt is not released. |
> | Small Table.iam | Revision 1 of Side.iam is not released. |
> | Small Table.iam | Revision 1 of long rail.ipt is not released. |
> | Small Table.iam | Revision 1 of Top.ipt is not released. |
>
> Close   Details <<

- In the Control setting for the Manufacturing state, you specified that the state was a released state. In the transition from Development to Manufacturing lifecycle state change, you set the criteria that 'Check that dependent child files are released'. So you must first release the children. To do this, select all the children in the Change State - 'Small Table.iam' dialog box.

8. Repeat Step 1 to 6. In the Change State dialog box, include dependents to set the new state to Manufacturing for all children as well.

Change State - 'Small Table.iam' ✕

Select a new lifecycle state:

Standard Process ▾ [...] |Manufacturing| ▾

✓		Name	Next State	⚠ Next Lifecycle Definition
☑		Small Table.iam	*Manufacturing*	Standard Process
☑		Dowel.ipt	*Manufacturing*	Standard Process
☑		Side.iam	*Manufacturing*	Standard Process
☑		long rail.ipt	*Manufacturing*	Standard Process
☑		Top.ipt	*Manufacturing*	Standard Process
☑		Short rail.ipt	*Manufacturing*	Standard Process
☑		leg.ipt	*Manufacturing*	Standard Process

7 objects / 1514 KB

Enter comments:

[OK] [Cancel] [Help]

9. Review the results.

📁 Table [Search Table] 🔍 ▾ ⊗

◯		Name	▲ ↻ State	Revision	▲		⊞
	▼	**Entity Type:File**					
🔒		Dowel.ipt	Manufacturing	1			
🔒		leg.ipt	Manufacturing	1			
🔒		long rail.ipt	Manufacturing	1			
🔒		Short rail.ipt	Manufacturing	1			
🔒		Side.iam	Manufacturing	1			
🔒		Small Table.iam	Manufacturing	1			
🔒			Manufacturing	1			

No local file
Locked

- The files are locked and cannot be edited.
- The lifecycle state is now set to **Manufacturing**.
- The state change did not create a new revision or version for any of the files.

10. Log out of Autodesk Vault.

11. Log in to Autodesk Vault using the following information:

- For *User Name*, enter **usera**.
- For *Password*, enter **vault**.
- For *Vault*, select **AOTCVault** in the drop-down list.

12. In the Navigation pane, expand the *Project Explorer ($)* folder and then expand the *Designs* folder. Select the *Table* folder.

13. Review the files.

🗀 Table			Search Table			
○ 🗋 **Name**	▲ ↻ **State**		**Revision**	▲	🏷	▦
▼ **Entity Type:File**						
🗋 Dowel.ipt	Manufacturing		1			
🗋 leg.ipt	Manufacturing		1			
🗋 long rail.ipt	Manufacturing		1			
🗋 Short rail.ipt	Manufacturing		1			
🗋 Side.iam	Manufacturing		1			
▶ 🗋 Small Table.iam	Manufacturing		1			
🗋 Top.ipt	Manufacturing		1			

History | Uses | Where Used | Change Order | View | CAD BOM | Datasheet

Number of versions: 3 (Local = Unknown)

Number of revisions: 2 ☑ Show all versions

Thumbnail	File Name	Revision	State (Historical)
▶	Small Table.iam	1	Manufacturing

- The files do not show as being locked. This is because usera is part of the Administrators group, which has Modify permission in the Manufacturing (Released) state. This enables the Administrators to make minor changes to the files without taking them out of production.

End of practice

Revision Management

Products have defined lifecycles from inception through production. Product development and enhancement introduces changes to the product files. These changes must be tracked and managed to provide a complete history of the changes and modifications as the product develops. Revision management provides consistency throughout the product lifecycle by applying a common definition and behavior to files in a vault.

Learning Objectives

- Describe the difference between a revision and a version and why both are important.
- Explain what revision schemes and revision scheme formats are.
- Know the details of the default revision schemes and revision scheme formats supplied with the Autodesk® Vault Professional software.
- Know how to modify an existing revision scheme.
- Create new revision scheme.
- Describe the different ways a file or item can be revised.
- Explain the concepts of revision controlled documents and describe what released biased means.
- Understand how the concept of released biased revisions gives the designer increased flexibility in the design process.
- Use the **Change State** command to automatically revise a group of files or items.
- Use the **Change Revision** command to manually revise a file or item.

5.1 Revisions and Versions

Overview

Revision management is functionality available in Vault Professional that enables a user to label a significant change or set of changes to a document and its related files. The label itself is the revision and the collection of files affected in that revision are considered a revision level. A revision level can be retrieved later so that a document and the version of the related files associated with that particular revision are preserved.

Objectives

After completing this lesson, you will be able to:

- Describe what a version is and why they are useful.

- Describe what a revision is and why they are useful.

- Describe the relationships between revisions and versions.

Concept

When editing documents in a vault, the changes are saved as versions history on the server using the default file settings. The history has little information that can be used to identify significant events.

The engineering industry has standards used for labeling significant changes to data. This is typically called the document revision. The revision is usually marked with one or more characters, and the document is given a new character string for any significant changes that are done after the document has been released.

The Revision Management feature provides the ability to mark any point in time as a significant change to a document and its related files. A revision level of a document can be retrieved along with the correct revision level of any related documents. When used in combination with lifecycles, a revision level is created automatically during predefined events. The revision will also be marked as 'Released' when the document is placed into certain lifecycle states identified as released states. During open and download procedures, the user can choose to retrieve released or non-released revisions of the document and its related files.

Definition: Version

A version is an iteration of a document and its meta-data that has been committed to the system.

Autodesk Vault is designed to help you manage different versions of a file. You can get a previous version or revert to a previous version.

Definition: Revision

A revision is a collection of file versions rolled up into one object that displays to the user. After a revision is created, document edits are contained in that revision until a new revision is created. This means that as changes are made and committed to the system, the user sees no change to the revision label.

For example, a document is created and assigned the revision level "A". As the user makes changes and those versions are committed, the revision label remains "A". Only when the user performs a revision bumping action will a new revision be created. One way to do this is by using the **Change Revision** command to iterate the revision. This will cause a new revision of the document to be created with the label "B". Any subsequent edits would then be collected in revision "B". The illustration shows the results for a CAD file that is revised four times, a new revision B is created and then revised four more times. The underlined version is the latest version for a given revision.

> *Note: When you create a new revision of a file, a version of the file is also created. The last file version 4 for revision A in the illustration is the same as the first file version 5 for revision B.*

Once the revision objects have been created, any revision can be downloaded or opened. When a revision is downloaded, only one version in that revision is used to represent the revision. If lifecycles are not used, then that version is always the latest version in that revision.

In general, it is up to the user to create a new revision of a file (or set of files) when some milestone is met. As part of a lifecycle transition, actions can be setup to automatically increment the revision based on a set of lifecycle state rules.

For the case of a lifecycle state change, the most common example is when a file that represents a part or component that is being manufactured needs to be changed to address form, fit, or function, problems. In this example, revision A represents the manufactured part before the change is made and revision B represents the revised revision. However, revisions can be used to signify any notable event where it is important to keep a history of the files and its metadata at that point in time.

You can manually create a new revision using the **Change Revision** command. The command enables you to specify the next revision from a specified revision definition and add a comment as to the nature of the revision.

The revision definition is a formula that will automatically calculate the next revision character in a sequence.

The next image shows the effect of changing the lifecycle state of the file. The lifecycle rules, as you saw in the last lesson, can be defined to 'bump' (create) a new revision for certain state changes.

For both manual and lifecycle-based revision changes, a set of revision schemes with associated revision scheme formats are used to specify the next character or set of characters in the next revision.

Default Revision Schemes and Scheme Formats

Definition of Terms

The following table defines the terms for revision schemes.

Term	Description
Revision Scheme	A formula used to calculate the initial revision characters for a file and the subsequent revision characters as that file is revised.
Revision Scheme Format	A defined sequence of characters used to create a revision scheme.
Revision Scheme Format Type	Enables multiple levels of incrementing a revision. The three types are: • Primary Scheme Format • Secondary Scheme Format • Tertiary Scheme Format
Delimiter	A single character that separates the revision scheme format types.

There are three default revision scheme formats, ten delimiter characters, and four default revisions scheme definitions included with Autodesk Vault Professional.

Default Revision Scheme Formats

Autodesk Vault Professional has three predefined revision scheme formats. A format simply specifies the progression of characters as a revision is bumped. They are listed in the following table.

Name	Description
Alphabetic	Only alphabetic characters[1] are permitted in the primary format. The first revision is A.
Numeric	Only numeric characters[2] are permitted in the primary format. The first revision is 1.
Default ASME Y14.35M	Only alphabetic characters with some characters omitted[3] are permitted in the primary format. The first revision is '-'.

Notes:

1. Alphabetic formats include alphabetic characters starting at A through Z and then AA through ZZ.

2. Numeric formats include the numeric sequence from 1 to 99.

3. Default ASME Y14.35M formats include alphabetic characters starting at A through Y and then AA through YY, excluding any character or combination of characters containing the following letters: I, O, Q, S, X, and Z, as these could be confused with numbers.

For example, as the primary revision is bumped for the Alphabetic sequence, the progression is A, B, C, D....

For a Numeric format, the progression is 1, 2, 3, 4, 5....

Default Revision Scheme Definitions

From these three default revision scheme formats, four different revisions schemes are provided.

Name	Delimiter	Primary	Secondary	Tertiary
Standard Alphabetic	Period (.)	Alphabetic	Numeric	Numeric
Standard Numeric	Period (.)	Numeric	Numeric	Numeric
Default ASME Y14.35M	Period (.)	Default ASME Y14.35M	Numeric	Numeric
None	Null Revision Scheme for opt out scenario			

These revision schemes and revision scheme formats are designed to cover a wide range of the revision practices in industry. If either a format or scheme does not meet your needs, new ones can be created.

5.2 Creating and Modifying Revision Schemes

Overview

The Autodesk Vault Professional software comes with multiple revisions schemes. These represent common revision practices found in a cross section of the manufacturing industry. They can be used with or without modification.

It is possible to modify one of the provided schemes to adapt it to your environment. In some cases, a new revision scheme needs to be created.

Objectives

After completing this lesson, you will be able to:

- Create a new revision scheme.

- Create a new revision scheme format.

- Modify an existing revision scheme.

Revision Scheme and Revision Formats

A revision scheme is defined by two basic entities: the delimiter and the revision scheme format. For every revision scheme, there are three revision scheme formats separated by two delimiters. Revision scheme formats can be different but you can only use one type of delimiter per revision scheme.

Delimiter

This is a character that separates the three revision scheme formats. The permitted characters for delimiters are:

- Single quote (')

- Hyphen (-)

- Double quote (")

- Comma (,)

- Period (.)

- Forward slash (/)

- Colon (:)

- Semi-colon (;)

- Back slash (\)

- Underscore (_).

Revision Scheme Format

As discussed earlier, these can be alphabetic or numeric sequences. There must be three revision scheme formats for every revision scheme:

- Primary Format

- Secondary Format

- Tertiary Format

Building a Revision Sequence

The example below shows how the delimiter and the three revision scheme formats are used to build a complete revision scheme.

<Primary Format><Delimiter><Secondary Format><Delimiter><Tertiary Format>

Several examples of revision sequences are shown below using different delimiters and different alphabetic and numeric revision scheme formats.

A, A.1, A.1.1, A.1.2, B...

1, 1/A, 1/B, 1/B/1, 1/B/2, 2...

A, A-A-1, A-A-2, A-B, C...

Note: An organization can use secondary or tertiary formats if they desire, but they must be used in conjunction with a primary format. For each revision scheme, all three formats must be present.

Creating a New Revision Scheme

Creating a new revision scheme involves importing a simple text file that has all of the possible characters for the primary revision scheme format. For example, the primary revision scheme format looks like the following sequence:

R1, R1, R3 ...

This is not one of the supplied formats so one will need to be created.

How To: Create a New Revision Scheme and Format Using Import

The following steps show how a new revision scheme is created:

1. In a plain text editor like Microsoft Notepad, create a file where each row represents a revision character. The first row will be the first character in the sequence, the second row the second character in the sequence and so on.

    Note: You will need to enter as many rows as you expect to use when creating different revisions. If you get to the last character in the sequence then the bump primary revision command will start incrementing the secondary revision and so on with the tertiary until all possible characters are used. This is not likely to happen unless you build all three formats with very few characters.

2. Save this file on your local file system.

3. Return to Autodesk Vault Professional logging in as an Administrator. Open the Vault Settings dialog box and go to the *Behaviors* tab.

4. Select **Revisions** to open the Revision Schemes Definitions dialog box.

5. In the toolbar, click **Import**.

6. The Import Revision Scheme Definition dialog box displays.

7. Select the button next to the *Name* field and browse to the file you created. Select the file from the file browser.

8. The scheme represented by the values in the file is created. By default, the secondary and tertiary formats are set to the numeric format.

9. The default name used is the same as the filename. This should be changed to reflect the true name of the new sequence.

10. In the Delimiter drop-down list, select the delimiter to use.

11. Enter a *Description* and leave the *Category* field blank.

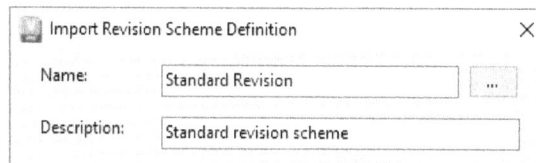

12. Click **OK** to dismiss this dialog box and return to the Revision Scheme Definitions dialog box.

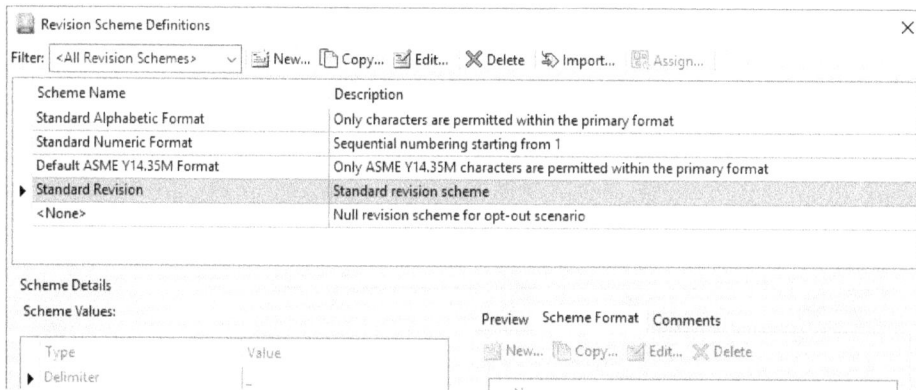

13. Review the new revision scheme. Note the default values for the secondary and tertiary formats. If this is acceptable, click **Close** to dismiss this dialog box.

14. To change the secondary or tertiary formats, select **Edit** from the toolbar.

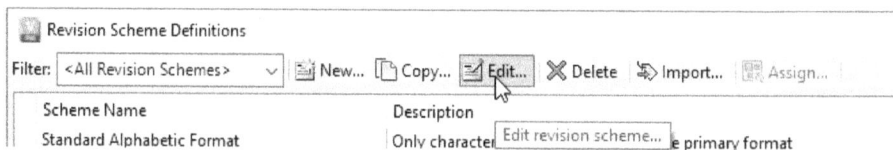

15. The Revision Scheme Definition dialog box for the selected sequence displays.

16. In the *Scheme Values* list, select the scheme you want to change. Note that you could also change the primary value at this point.

17. Review the examples of the new revision sequence in the *Preview* tab.

Note: In the process of creating a new revision scheme, a revision scheme format was also created. You can use this new revision scheme format in other custom revision schemes you might need.

18. Click **OK** to close the dialog box and return to the Revision Scheme Definitions dialog box.

19. Click **Close** to return to the Vault Settings dialog box.

Modifying an Existing Revision Scheme

In some cases, modifying an existing revision scheme will enable it to conform to your existing practices or process design.

How To: Modify an Existing Revision Scheme

The following steps show an example of how an existing revision scheme can be modified:

1. In the Vault Settings dialog box, select the *Behaviors* tab.

2. Select **Revisions** in the *Lifecycles and Revisions* section to display the Revision Scheme Definitions dialog box.

3. Select **Edit** in the toolbar.

Revision Scheme Definitions	✕

Filter: `<All Revision Schemes>` ✏ New... 📋 Copy... ✅ Edit... ✖ Delete 🔄 Import... 📋 Assign...

Scheme Name	Description
Standard Alphabetic Format	Only characters Edit revision scheme... primary format
Standard Numeric Format	Sequential numbering starting from 1
Default ASME Y14.35M Format	Only ASME Y14.35M characters are permitted within the primary format
▶ Standard Revision	Standard revision scheme
<None>	Null revision scheme for opt-out scenario

4. The Revision Scheme Definition dialog box for the selected revision scheme displays.

Revision Scheme Definition - 'Standard Revision' ✕

Definition Name:

Standard Revision

Category:

None selected ⌄

Description:

Standard revision scheme

Scheme Details

Scheme Values:

Type	Value
Delimiter	-
Primary Scheme Format	Standard Revision ⌄
Secondary Scheme Format	Numeric
Tertiary Scheme Format	Numeric

Preview   Scheme Format   Comments

Revision primary sequence values:

Rev A
Rev B
Rev C
Rev D
Rev E
Rev F
Rev G
Rev H

Example Revision Formats

Delimiter Character: -
Primary: Rev A
Secondary: Rev A-1
Tertiary: Rev A-1-1

OK   Cancel   Help

5. Change the *Definition Name*, *Category*, and *Description* to better reflect the purpose for this scheme.

Definition Name:

Company Standard

Category:

Design, Office, Assembly, Document, Electrical, Electrica... ▾

Description:

To be used for all standard processes

6. In the *Scheme Details* section, select the *Value* column for the **Delimiter** and select a new value in the drop-down list.

Type	Value
Delimiter	. ▾
Primary Scheme Format	
Secondary Scheme Format	
Tertiary Scheme Format	

7. In the *Scheme Details* section, select the *Value* column for the revision scheme format that you want to change and select the new value.

Scheme Values:

Type	Value
Delimiter	-
I Primary Scheme Format	Numeric
Secondary Scheme Format	Alphabetic
Tertiary Scheme Format	Default ASME Y14.35M
	Numeric

Scheme Values:

Type	Value
Delimiter	-
Primary Scheme Format	Numeric
✎ Secondary Scheme Format	Numeric
Tertiary Scheme Format	Alphabetic
	Default ASME Y14.35M

8. At any point, you can see an example of the changes in the *Preview* tab.

Revision primary sequence values:

```
1
2
3
4
5
6
7
8
```

Example Revision Formats

Delimiter Character:	-
Primary:	1
Secondary:	1-A
Tertiary:	1-A-1

9. To create a new scheme format to use in this scheme or any other schemes, select the *Scheme Format* tab and select **New**.

Preview Scheme Format Comments

☐ New... ☐ Copy... ☑ Edit... ✖ Delete

Nar New...
▶ Alphabetic
Numeric

10. In the List Scheme Format dialog box, you can either enter and arrange the values manually or select the button next to the *Scheme Format Name* field to import a list of values from a plain text (.TXT) file. Click **OK** when done to add the new format to the list.

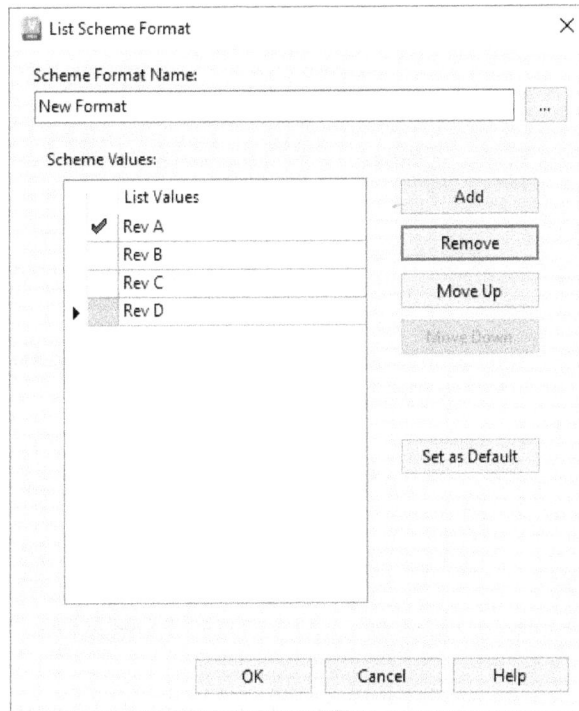

11. In the *Comments* tab, you can create one or more comments that will display in the Revise dialog box.

12. Select **Add** to add a new comment in the Comment for dialog box. Click **OK** to dismiss this dialog box and add the new entry to the list.

13. Remove any unwanted comments by first selecting the comment and then selecting **Remove**.

- Now when the file is revised, the Revision Definition displays in the list of revised files and the comment displays in the *Enter comments* text box.

14. Click **OK** to dismiss the Revision Scheme Definition dialog box for this revision scheme.

15. Select **Close** to dismiss the Revision Scheme Definitions dialog box and return to the Vault Settings dialog box.

Practice 5a
Create a Revision Scheme

In this practice, you will create a new revision sequence. The primary revision scheme will be imported from a file. The secondary and tertiary formats along with the delimiter will be configured from the supplied formats. The method used will be a variation on the one shown in the procedure.

The completed practice

Task 1: Create the file.

1. Start Microsoft Notepad to create an empty text file.
2. Enter **Rev A** in the first line.

3. Enter nine more lines, each time incrementing the letter. For example, the second line should read **Rev B**.

4. Save the file on your desktop with the name **Revision File.txt**.

```
Revision File.txt - Notepad

File   Edit   Format   View   Help
Rev A
Rev B
Rev C
Rev D
Rev E
Rev F
Rev G
Rev H
Rev I
Rev J
```

Task 2: Create the revision scheme.

1. Log in to Autodesk Vault using the following information:

   - For *User Name*, enter **administrator**.
   - Leave the *Password* field blank.
   - For *Vault*, select **AOTCVault** from the drop-down list.

2. From the Tools menu, select **Administration>Vault Settings**.

3. In the *Behaviors* tab, select **Revisions** to display the Revisions Scheme Definitions dialog box. Click **New**.

```
Revision Scheme Definitions

Filter:  <All Revision Schemes>      ▼    📄 New...   📄 Copy...   📄 Edit...

   Scheme Name                                    Description
                                                  New revision scheme...
 ▶  Default Alphabetic Format

    Default ASME Y14.35M Format
```

4. In the Revision Scheme Definition dialog box, do the following:

  - For the *Definition Name*, enter **Standard Revision**.

  - For the *Description*, enter **Standard revision scheme**.

  - Leave the *Category* drop-down list as **None selected**.

5. In the *Scheme Details* section, select the **Delimiter** line and then select the *Value* field to display the drop-down list. At the bottom of the list, select the underscore (_).

6. Select the **Primary Scheme Format** line.

7. In the tab section, select the *Scheme Format* tab.

8. Select **New** to display the List Scheme Format dialog box.

9. Select the button next to the *Scheme Format Name* to display an Open dialog box. Browse to the file you created at the beginning of the practice and select **Open** to return to the List Scheme Format dialog box.

10. Click **Add** to add a new line to the list.

11. Enter **Rev K**. Move it to the bottom of the list.

I...	List Values
✔	Rev A
	Rev B
	Rev C
	Rev D
	Rev E
	Rev F
	Rev G
	Rev H
	Rev I
	Rev J
I	Rev K

12. In the *Scheme Format Name* field, change the name to **Standard Primary Format**.

List Scheme Format ✕

Scheme Format Name:
Standard Primary Format

13. Click **OK** to dismiss this dialog box and return to the Revision Scheme Definition dialog box.

14. Select the *Value* field for the **Primary Scheme Format** and select the new format.

Type	Value
Delimiter	_
Primary Scheme Format	Numeric
Secondary Scheme Format	Alphabetic
Tertiary Scheme Format	ASME Y14.35M
	Default Alphabetic
	Default Numeric
	Numeric
	Standard Primary Format

15. For the **Secondary Scheme Format**, select the *Value* field to display the drop-down list. Select **Alphabetic**.

16. For the **Tertiary Scheme Format**, select the *Value* field to display the drop-down list. Select **Numeric**.

17. Select the *Preview* tab to preview a sample revision character display.

> Preview | Scheme Format | Comments
>
> Revision primary sequence values:
>
> Rev A
> Rev B
> Rev C
> Rev D
> Rev E
> Rev F
> Rev G
> Rev H
> Rev K
>
> Example Revision Formats
>   Delimiter Character: _
>
>   Primary: Rev A
>
>   Secondary: Rev A_A
>
>   Tertiary: Rev A_A_1

18. Select the *Comments* tab and then click **Add** to display the Comment for 'Standard Revision' dialog box. Enter the text **New Revision**.

> Comment for 'Standard Revision'
>
> Enter comments:
>
> New Revision|

19. Click **OK** to dismiss the dialog box and return to the Revision Scheme Definition dialog box.

20. Click **OK** to dismiss this dialog box and return to the Revision Scheme Definitions dialog box that shows all of the schemes.

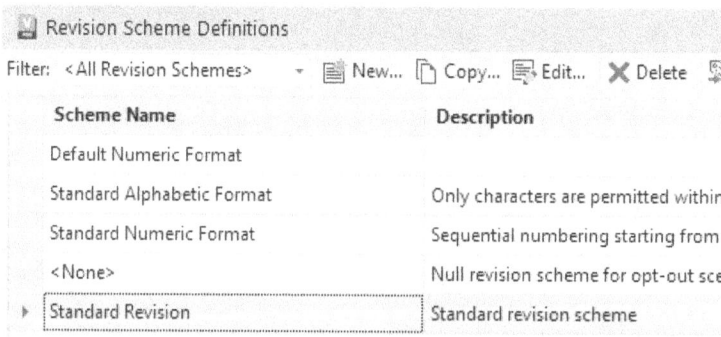

> Revision Scheme Definitions
>
> Filter: <All Revision Schemes> ▾ 📄 New... 📋 Copy... 📝 Edit... ✖ Delete 🔁
>
> | Scheme Name | Description |
> | --- | --- |
> | Default Numeric Format | |
> | Standard Alphabetic Format | Only characters are permitted within |
> | Standard Numeric Format | Sequential numbering starting from |
> | <None> | Null revision scheme for opt-out scel |
> | Standard Revision | Standard revision scheme |

21. Click **Close** to dismiss this dialog box and return to the Vault Settings dialog box.

End of practice

5.3 Revising Files

Overview

The document revision management system in the Autodesk Vault Professional software is very flexible. There are several ways in which a file or item can be revised.

Revisions enable you to label a significant milestone or change to a file or item and all related files. The collection of files affected in a revision are considered a revision level, stored as part of the revision label you assign. A revision level can be stored and retrieved, ensuring that a document, item, and related files associated with that particular revision are preserved.

Objectives

After completing this lesson, you will be able to:

- Describe the different ways a file or item can be revised.

- Explain the concepts of revision controlled documents and describe what released biased means.

- Understand how the concept of released biased revisions gives the designer increased flexibility in the design process.

- Use the **Change Revision** command to manually revise a file or item.

Revision Controlled Documents

When using documents that are related to each other, such as an assembly and its referenced components, a relationship is created between the specific revisions of those documents. When an assembly is checked into a vault, the revision of each of its components is recorded so that when that revision is recalled, each related document is retrieved using the recorded revision.

Editing a Referenced File Without Creating a New Revision

If a document references other files and those files are edited without bumping the revision, the referencing document will consume the edits. For example:

1. Revision A of an assembly references revision B of a part.

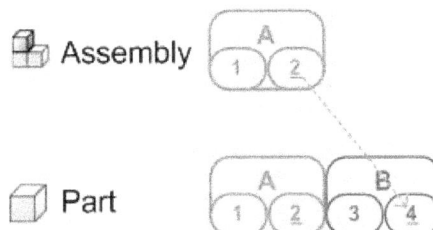

2. Changes are made to revision B of the part after revision A of the assembly has been checked in.

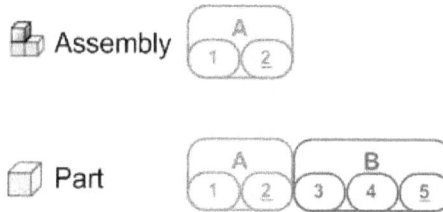

3. The changes to revision B of the part will show in revision A of the assembly when it is next checked out or opened.

Editing a Referenced File After Creating a New Revision

If a document references other files and a new revision is created for one of those files, the referencing document still maintains a relationship with the original revision. For example:

1. Revision A of an assembly references revision B of a part.

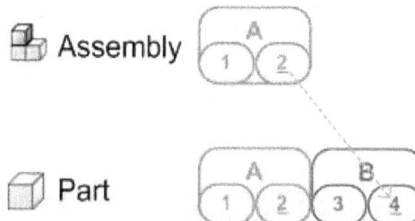

2. A new revision of the part is created and labeled C.
3. Edits are made to revision C of the part.

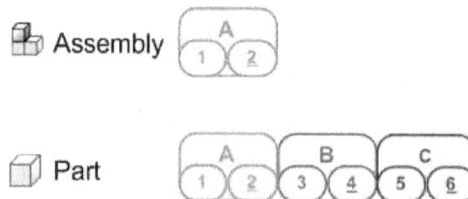

4. The changes to revision C of the part will show in revision A of the assembly if the Revision in the Get/Check Out dialog box for the assembly is set to **Latest**.

Revisions and Lifecycles

Using revisions and lifecycles together provides significantly more flexibility than revisions alone can provide. For example, a given revision of a component can be edited and released out of context of any referencing assemblies, and the released changes will be used when the assembly is opened.

What Does It Mean When a Revision Is Marked as Released?

When a version in a revision is marked as released, it is given priority over newer versions and will represent the revision. This prioritization is known as a released bias and is an option that can be toggled off in several of the dialog boxes.

Note: Versions marked as released can never be purged from the system and can only be deleted by an administrator.

What Does Released Biased Mean?

Released biased is an option in several of the dialog boxes indicating that released data should take priority over non-released data. This will help to ensure that new, non-released revisions of parts are not consumed unintentionally. This option can be toggled off.

Note: Released bias is enabled by default.

Example 1: Released Biased Options

In the following illustration, Assembly1.iam is in a Released state at Revision A. It uses two parts. Part1.ipt is in a Work in Progress state at Revision C. Part2.ipt is in a Released state at Revision A.

				File Name	Revision	Version	State		Comment
▶ 🔒			☐	Assembly1.iam	A	3	Released		Released at Rev A
△			☐	Part1.ipt	C	8	Work in Progress		edited at C
🔒			☐	Part2.ipt	A	3	Released		Released at Rev A

The *Uses* tab of Assembly1.aim is shown in the next illustration.

| History | Uses | Where Used | Change Order | View |

| Latest | Released | ▼ |

Released Biased
Use released data for related files when available.

File Name	/	Revision				
▶ ⊟ Assembly1.iam		A	3	Released	Released at Rev A	
Part1.ipt		B	6	Released	Released at rev B	
Part2.ipt		A	3	Released	Released at Rev A	

By default, the view is Released Biased. The Released revision of Part1.ipt is shown. In the next illustration, the **Released Biased** option is toggled off.

History	Uses	Where Used	Change Order	View

Latest   Released   ▼ 🔲

Non-Released Biased
Use newer edits for related files.

File Name	/	Revision			Comment	Cre
▶ ⊟ 🔲 Assembly1.iam		A	3	Released	Released at Rev A	Ad
🔲 Part1.ipt		C	8	Work in Progress	edited at C	Ad
🔲 Part2.ipt		A	3	Released	Released at Rev A	Ad

In this case, the *Uses* tab shows that the assembly uses the Work in Progress Revision C of Part1.ipt.

Example 2: Released Biased Option in Inventor

Using the parts shown in the previous example, a new Assembly2.iam file is created in the Autodesk Inventor software. The **Place From Vault** command is used to place an instance of Part1.ipt in the new assembly.

File name:	Part1.ipt
Files of type:	Component Files (*.ipt; *.iam)
Revision:	Latest Work in Progress

Non-Released Biased
Use newer edits for related files.

The default in Autodesk Inventor is to use **Non-Released Biased** revisions. If the part were placed and the assembly checked in, the results in the *Uses* tab of Assembly2.iam will be as shown in the illustration below.

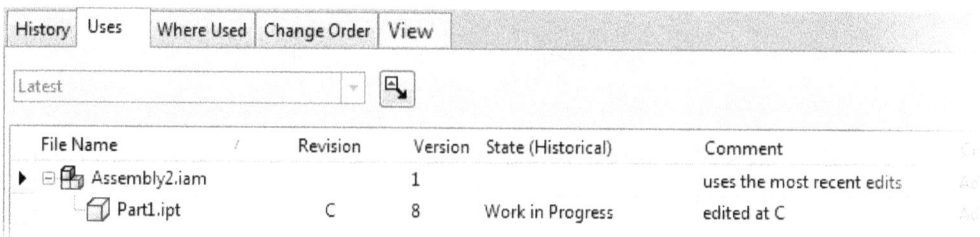

History	Uses	Where Used	Change Order	View

Latest   🔲

File Name	/	Revision	Version	State (Historical)	Comment	C
▶ ⊟ 🔲 Assembly2.iam			1		uses the most recent edits	A
🔲 Part1.ipt		C	8	Work in Progress	edited at C	A

Another Assembly3.iam file is created. The **Place From Vault** command opens the Select From Vault dialog box. This time, the user specifies to use the Released version of Part1.ipt. Note the **Released Biased** indicator now shows that the released data will be used.

When this new assembly is checked in, the *Uses* tab shows that the Released revision of Part1.ipt is used.

What Does Leading Mean When Referring to a Version or Revision?

The leading version is always the latest version of a file, even if Released Bias is enabled. The leading revision is always the latest version of the latest revision of a file, even if Released Bias is enabled.

Change Revision Command

The **Change Revision** command is used to manually create a new revision of a file or item and is available in the Actions menu.

Note: You can also change the revision in the Autodesk Inventor software by selecting Revise in the Vault tab>Control panel or in the shortcut menu in the Autodesk Vault Browser.

How To: Revise a File or Item

To create a file revision using the **Change Revision** command, do the following:

1. Select the file or group of files from the main pane that are to be changed. If you need to change a set of related files, you can use the options in the dialog box to select these for you. If the files are not related, use the <Shift> + select or <Ctrl> + select option to select the files from the list.

2. Select **Change Revision** in the Actions menu.
3. The Change Revision dialog box displays with the selected file(s).

Note: You can also specify that the value of a user-defined property can be used to create the next revision. In a later lesson, you will learn how you can map a file property value to a user-defined value. This is especially useful when the authoring application controls the revision. For example, you might want to use the Autodesk Inventor Rev Number file property to control the revision.

4. The dialog box indicates that the **Latest (Non-Released Biased)** revision will be copied to the new revision. In the Select next revision drop-down list, indicate which revision scheme format type (**Primary**, **Secondary**, or **Tertiary**) will be used to determine the next revision.

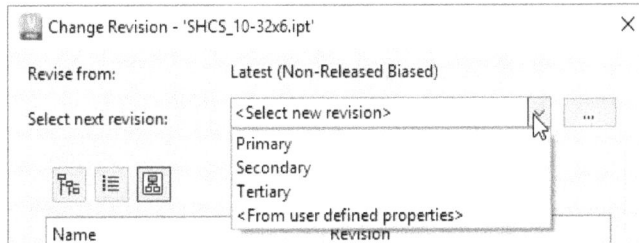

5. To change the revision scheme definition to use to generate the next revision, select the button next to the drop-down list to display the Change Revision Definition dialog box. Select the new revision scheme definition from the list. Click **OK** to dismiss the dialog box and return to the Change Revision dialog box.

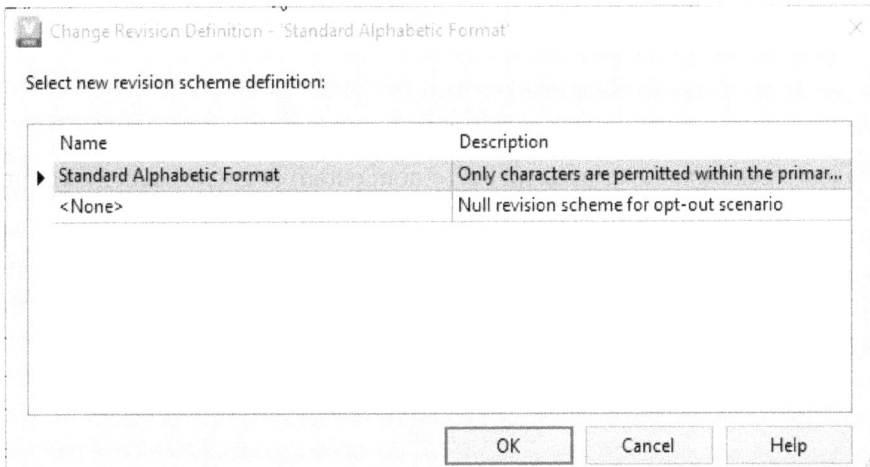

6. Use the View buttons to change the view to help understand file relationships.

7. Use the Parent/Child selection buttons to modify the selection.

8. Select **Settings** to display the Settings dialog box. Here you can refine the selection of related files.

9. Select a comment from the drop-down list (if configured) or enter a custom comment.

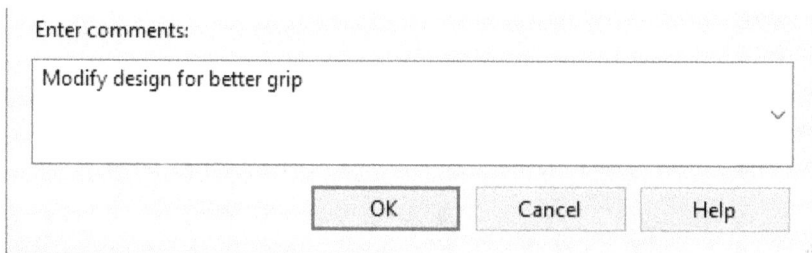

10. Click **OK** to complete the procedure.

Roll Back the Lifecycle State of a File

Return a file or files to a previous lifecycle state with the **Roll Back Lifecycle State Change** command.

When a file is rolled back, it:

* returns to the file version associated with the rolled-back state.

* returns to the security, lifecycle definition, and revision scheme associated with the rolled-back state.

* retains any property definitions associated with the current version.

The current version of the file is deleted when the file is rolled back to a previous state.

Rules for Rolling Back a File Lifecycle State

The lifecycle of a file can be rolled back if:

* the file is currently checked in.

* no parent versions consume the current child version that you want to roll back.

* the previous lifecycle state has not been deleted.

* the file is not in <null> definition.

* there is no label on the current version of the file.

* the administrator has not enabled the **Restrict File and Item Lifecycle State Changes to Change Orders** option.

How To: Roll Back a File's Lifecycle State

You must be a Document Manager Level 2 or Administrator to roll back a file's lifecycle state.

1. Select one or more files in the main view and select **Actions>Roll Back Lifecycle State Change**.

2. A dialog box displays describing to which state the file will be rolled back. Click **Continue** to complete the lifecycle state rollback.

Managing Properties

Streamline your vault environment by managing property values for easier indexing and searching. Use the mapping feature to automatically update property values based on other file input, establishing property constraints to ensure that values meet your specifications.

Learning Objectives

- Understand the difference between system-defined properties and user-defined properties.
- Manage user-defined properties (create new, edit, add, or remove properties).
- Work with the Properties Grid in Autodesk® Vault and edit property values.
- Configure property constraints.
- Map properties.

6.1 System-Defined Properties vs. User-Defined Properties

Overview

Properties are attributes associated with a file. Autodesk Vault recognizes two types of property definitions: system-defined properties and user-defined properties (UDPs). System-defined properties are those properties that are derived from the vault. Autodesk Vault has a global set of properties that are applied to files in the vault. User-defined properties are created by using the administrative tools.

Objectives

After completing this lesson, you will be able to:

- Differentiate between system-defined properties and user-defined properties.

- Create, delete, and edit user-defined properties.

- Administrate system-defined properties in Vault Property Administration.

Terms, Data Types, and Attributes

Before working with properties, it is important to become familiar with the terms, data types, and attributes associated with the Autodesk Vault properties system.

The following table contains terms commonly used with properties.

Term	Definition
Associations	Attribute that determines whether the property is associated with a file, folder, item, or change order.
Compliant	The status of a property that meets all property policies and equivalence evaluations.
Data Type	The type of data accepted for the property value. This type can be text, number, Boolean, or date.
Database Property	Any property in the database, either user-defined or system.
Entity	An entity is the system class with which a file can be associated. Entities are files, items, or change orders.
Equivalent	The status of a mapped property when its value matches the source value.
File Property	A property associated with a file.
Mapped Property	A property from which the propriety being defined gets its value. For example, a UDP can get its value from several different file properties. A file property can get its value from a system property.

Term	Definition
Mapping	A set of relationships between the property being defined and a property from which it receives its value. There can be multiple mappings for a given property definition.
Master	The property from which a mapped property gets its value. The master property writes its value to the subordinate property.
Non-compliant	The status of a property when it has failed to meet one or more property policies or its equivalence evaluation.
Non-equivalent	The status of a mapped property when its value does not match the source value.
Property Definition	All attributes and constraints about the property including its name, data type, initial value, mapping, minimum and maximum values, case values, in-use value, and basic search value.
	The name used in the GUI (graphical user interface) to identify the property.
Property Name	The name used in the GUI (graphical user interface) to identify the property.
Property Policy	Depending on the data type, the property policy specifies certain constraints that must be met. The constraints can include a value range, a value type, or a value format must be met. For example, a property policy can be described as follows: the property must have a value and that value must be in the range of 1 to 10.
	When a property fails to meet its property policies, it is considered non-compliant.
Property Value	The literal content of a property attribute for a specific file version.
Override	Determines whether the property value is overridden by the policy defined by its category.
Subordinate	The mapped property that receives its value from the master property.
System-Defined Property	A property in the database created by the system, which is then assigned to a file.
User-Defined Property (UDP)	A property in the database created by an administrator. The property can be applied to a file when it is added to a vault.

Every property value has a data type that determines how that value is read and processed.

Data Type Name	Description
Boolean	True or False
Date Type	Can be a specific date or date range expressed by a beginning and end date
Number	Numbers only
Text	Letters, numbers, and punctuation

Properties have attributes that determine how the property is described and the constraints for its value.

Attribute Name	Description
Basic Search	A constraint that determines whether or not the property should be included in basic searches.
Case Sensitivity	A constraint that applies to text data types. This constraint can be set to none, UPPER CASE, lower case, Name Case, or Sentence case.
Enforce List of Values	A constraint that determines whether the property must have a value from a list.
Initial Value	An attribute that specifies the initial property value when one is not specified.
	Note the initial values are best used with write mappings. If an initial value is set on a regular read mapping, that read mapping has higher priority and will overwrite the initial value. The only case in which an initial value will not be overwritten by a read mapping is if the value it maps to is blank.
List Values	Displays the List Type dialog box from which you can enter and order values for a list. At least one item must display in the list.
Minimum Length	The minimum number of characters a property value can have.
Maximum Length	The maximum number of characters a property value can have.
Requires Value	A constraint which determines whether the property must have a value to be compliant.
State	The state of a property definition specifies whether it is enabled or disabled in the vault. A disabled property is not displayed or searched and cannot be used to store a value for a given file.
Usage	Indicates the number of files currently using the property. Use this information to determine which properties are used more than others, to help decide which properties can be removed from the vault.

The main view in the vault client has a *Property Compliance* column that lists various status icons. The icons in this column indicate whether a property associated with the file is compliant, non-compliant, pending, or has failed the equivalence evaluation.

Icon	Value	Definition
No icon	Compliant	All properties meet policy requirements and equivalence.
	Non-compliant	One or more properties do not meet property policy requirements or equivalence.
		Hover the cursor over the icon to learn more about why one or more properties failed compliance.
	Not calculated	There has been a change to one or more properties but equivalence and policy have not been verified yet.

Icon	Value	Definition
🕓	Pending	Properties are currently being evaluated for equivalence.
⊗	Evaluation failed	The equivalence evaluation failed. This is a rare situation and can result when the processor enters an evaluation loop. **Note:** In the Find dialog box, an evaluation failed value is added. This enables you to search for any files for which the evaluation failed.

Introduction to the Property Definitions Dialog Box

When files are checked into the vault, only the properties that are set enabled are automatically extracted and indexed by default. All the extracted properties being tracked by the vault can be managed using the Property Definitions dialog box. The Property Definitions dialog box lists:

Property Name — The name of the property as it displays in the interface. The display name can be edited by the vault administrator.

Data Type — The type of data represented by the property. The data types are: text, number, date, and Boolean.

Usage — Indicates the number of files currently using the property. Use this information to determine which properties are used more than others, to help decide which properties can be removed from the vault.

State — Indicates whether or not the property is enabled for indexing and visible to the user.

- **Enabled:** If a property is set to **Enabled**, the property is indexed and extracted from files when they are added or checked into the vault.
- **Disabled:** If a property is set to **Disabled**, it is not indexed and it is not extracted from files when they are added or checked in to the vault. Administrators can clean up unwanted properties by marking them **Disabled**.

Associations — Lists the entity class that can use the property. Classes are files, folders, items, change orders, and custom objects.

Folder Categories — If the property is associated with a folder category, the category name displays. Category values will override property values if the property **Override** attribute is enabled.

File Categories — If the property is associated with a file category, the category name displays. Category values will override property values if the property **Override** attribute is enabled.

Item Categories — If the property is associated with an item category, the category name displays. Category values will override property values if the property **Override** attribute is enabled.

Basic Search	Indicates if a string property is searched when using the basic search feature. The possible values are:

- **Searched:** The property is included in the basic search.
- **Not Searched:** The property is excluded from the basic search.
- **Not Allowed:** The property is not a string value and therefore cannot be included in the basic search.

Important: When a new user-defined property is created, it does not have to be associated with any categories. However, even if the property is associated with an entity (e.g., file, folder, change order, item, or custom object), if it is not associated with any categories, it will not display in the properties grid for that entity.

When migrating an existing vault database, all existing properties set to **Enabled** are migrated. However, any new properties default to **Disabled**. To improve indexing performance, all properties without mappings are not created unless specified by the administrator.

How To: Rename a Property

The display name of a property can be edited to make it more meaningful. Both system-defined and user-defined names can be changed by selecting Edit in the Property Definitions dialog box.

1. Select **Tools>Administration>Vault Settings**.
2. In the Vault Settings dialog box, select the Behaviors tab.
3. In the Properties section, select **Properties**. The Property Definition dialog box opens. Here you can rename the selected Property by using the command Edit.

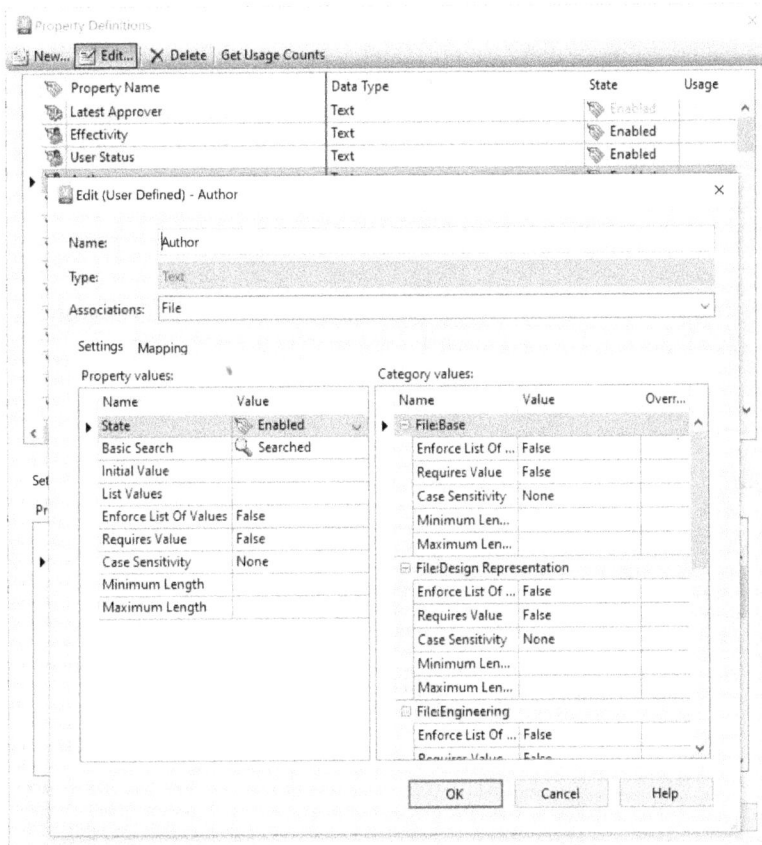

Change the State

The state of a property determines whether or not the property is included in the vault index.

You specify which properties to include in the vault by setting the state to **Enabled**. Marking properties as **Disabled** lets administrators remove unused properties from view.

When a property is not in use, it is no longer associated with any files and it is removed from the index. This makes searching more efficient overall because there are fewer properties. You cannot search on a property that is not in use. You cannot display an unused property as a column in a grid. You cannot map properties to unused file properties. Unused properties can be re-associated with files by changing the state back to **Enabled** and then using the server console to re-index the properties.

Examining Usage Count

The usage count of a property tells you how prevalent the property is throughout the vault. The number in the *Usage* column is the number of files with which the property is associated. The usage count of a property tells you how many files have a value associated with them for this property. You will find the command in the menu pane of Property Definitions dialog box.

Specifying Searchable Properties

The Basic Search setting for a property determines whether or not that file property is available for searching when a basic search is performed. The Basic Search setting applies only to the basic search and not to searches using the query builder or the Find dialog box. Only string type file properties can be set to Searched.

String type file properties that are set to Searched are available for the basic search. Properties set to Not Searched are not currently available for the basic search. By setting unused file properties to Not Searched, you can increase search performance. Properties set to Not Allowed are not string type properties and are not available for the basic search. A property set to Not Allowed cannot be changed to any other setting.

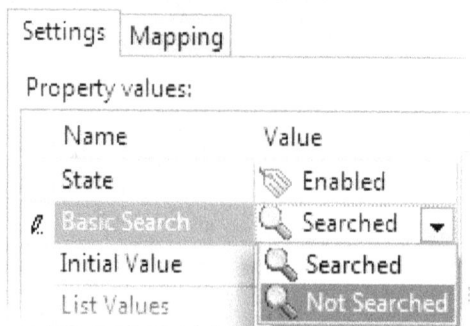

When the state of a property is set to **Disabled**, the basic search setting is automatically set to **Not Searched**. If that property is later set to **Enabled**, the basic search setting remains **Not Searched**. In order for the property to be available for searching, the administrator must manually set the property to **Searched**.

Initial Value

The *Initial Value* is applied once when the property is initially associated with an object. The initial value is only applied in the absence of a user-supplied or a mapped value.

The initial association occurs in three circumstances: 1) object is created (e.g., adding a file or creating an item); 2) assignment to a category that automatically attaches the property; and 3) manual property attachment.

There are two types of initial value: **static** and **mapped**. The static value is a fixed value and can be any value that is valid for the selected data type. An initial mapped value copies the value from a file or BOM property.

Initial values should NOT be used on properties where all regular mappings read the value from a file or BOM. A blank value in the mapped file or BOM field takes precedence over the initial value. This can appear as if the initial value is not applied when in fact the mapped value of 'blank' takes precedence.

List Values

Properties of type *Text* and *Number* can provide a list of values for user selection and searching. The administrator can add or remove values from the list at any time. Removal of a value from the list does not remove the value from any property where that value has been applied. When specifying the value for this property, the user can choose from the list of values. Entering values that are not on the list is permitted. If this property is mapped to read a value from a file or BOM, the imported value is not required to be on the list.

Enforce List Values

When enabled, the **Enforce List Values** option provides a warning symbol adjacent to this property if the value is not on the list. When a value is in violation of this policy, the default configuration for lifecycle transitions will not permit for a file or item to be released.

Add or Remove a User-Defined Property

A user-defined property (UDP) can be added to a file or removed from a file. When a new version of the file is created, the change to the property assignment is shown. You must have administrative access to perform these tasks. To use the **Add or Remove Property** command, you cannot have the file checked out for edit.

How To: Add or Remove a Property

1. From the main file list, select one or more files.
2. Select **Actions>Add or Remove Property**.
3. In the Add or Remove Property dialog box, select the property from the *Property* list.

4. For the *Action* value of the property, select **Add** or **Remove** from the drop-down list.

    *   **Add:** The property is added to the selected file or files using the default value. If the property is already assigned to a selected file, no action is taken for that file.
    *   **Remove:** The property is removed from the selected file or files. If the property is not assigned to a selected file, no action is taken for that file.

    Note: If a property is assigned by means of a category, it cannot be removed from a file.

5. Click **OK**.

    Note: If any restrictions occur with a selected file, the property is neither added nor removed and an error message displays.

Practice 6a
Create a New User-Defined Property

In this practice, you will create a new user-defined property (UDP). After the new property is created, you will edit some settings and finally add this property to a selection of files.

Task 1: Create a new UDP.

1.   From the Tools menu, select **Administration>Vault Settings**.

2.   In the Vault Settings dialog box, select the *Behaviors* tab and select **Properties**.

3. In the Property Definitions dialog box, click **New**.

4. In the New Property dialog box, enter **MyNewProperty**.

5. In the *Type* list, select the **Text** property type.

6. Assign the UDP to one or more categories of your choice by selecting the category checkboxes in the *Associations* drop-down list. Categories can be preselected in this list based on the filter previously selected in the Property Definitions dialog box. You can select or clear categories as required. Click **Close**, then click **OK** to return to the Property Definitions dialog box. Click **Close** again to return to the Vault Settings dialog box.

Task 2: Edit the new property.

1. In the Vault Settings dialog box, select the *Behaviors* tab and select **Properties**.
2. In the Properties Definitions dialog box, select **MyNewProperty** and select **Edit**.

3. Rename your new property (e.g., change from **MyNewProperty** to **MyEditedProperty**).
4. Modify some other settings like Basic Search, Category values, etc.
5. Click **OK** to save the changes, then click **Close** twice to close the open dialog boxes.

Task 3: Add/remove properties to files.

1. Select one or more non-released files you want to add the new property to.
2. Select **Actions>Add or Remove Property**.
3. In the Add or Remove Property dialog box, search for the new property named **MyEditedProperty**.
4. In the *Action* column, you can select **Add** or **Remove** to add and remove properties.

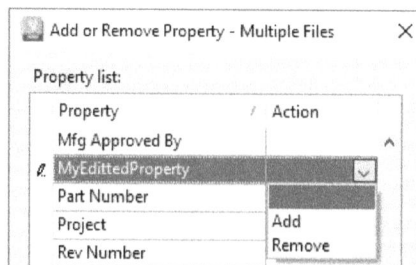

5. Click **OK** to confirm and save these settings.

End of practice

6.2 The Properties Grid

You can customize the files in the vault by creating, adding, and removing properties, and modifying property values. The Properties grid lists all properties for a selected file. The tab for the Properties grid displays at the bottom of the right pane when a file is selected from the file list.

Properties are separated based on whether they are system-defined or user-defined. Collapse or expand each group to review the properties for those definitions.

The Properties grid displays the name and value of each property associated with the selected file. You can configure the Properties grid to show only certain properties

Note: System-defined property values cannot be modified. You can only modify values of user-defined properties.

Hide/Restore Properties

To hide and restore properties from the grid, there are two buttons in the upper-right corner in grid.

How To: Hide/Restore Properties from the Properties Grid

1. Select a property that should disappear from the grid list. By clicking on the minus symbol (Hide Properties), the property is hidden and can be restored by clicking the plus symbol (Restore Properties).

2. A Property Filter dialog box opens. Select the property you want to restore and select **Restore Selected Properties**.

3. All selected properties are restored and available in the grid.

- You can make selections on one or more properties and hide/restore them by one click. Conform to the Windows shortcut standards (press <Shift> or <Ctrl> for selection).

Edit Properties from the Grid

User-defined properties in a vault can be edited using the Property Editing wizard. The wizard enables you to select any number of files, regardless of type, and edit their properties. The selected files are checked out, the properties are updated, and then the files are checked back in to the vault.

> *Note: You must be assigned the role of either Editor or Administrator to perform this action. Contact your vault administrator to verify your role. The files must also be checked in and unlocked.*

Files can be selected from the main pane, the Properties grid, or while in the property editor to have properties edited. You can select multiple files at once to edit properties. For example, you can select an Inventor assembly and all of its children from the *Uses* tab and then use the Property Editing wizard to edit all the properties for the entire design.

For Autodesk Inventor files, including Inventor .DWG files, and Microsoft Office documents, all user-defined properties are available for editing. If a property is missing a value, you can fill it in and it will be added to the file. If the file does not contain the property as a predefined object, then a custom property can be created containing the value.

Note: If using Autodesk Vault Professional, items and change orders can also be selected along with other files for editing their properties in a heterogeneous view.

How To: Edit Properties from the Properties Grid

1. Select multiple files (e.g., Autodesk Inventor .IPT files) and open the Properties grid.

2. Select the property (or multiple properties) you want to edit.

3. Selecting the **Edit Selected Properties** command to open the Property Edit dialog box, which enable you to edit the selected properties of the selected files.

4. You can edit the properties, then confirm the changes by clicking **OK**.

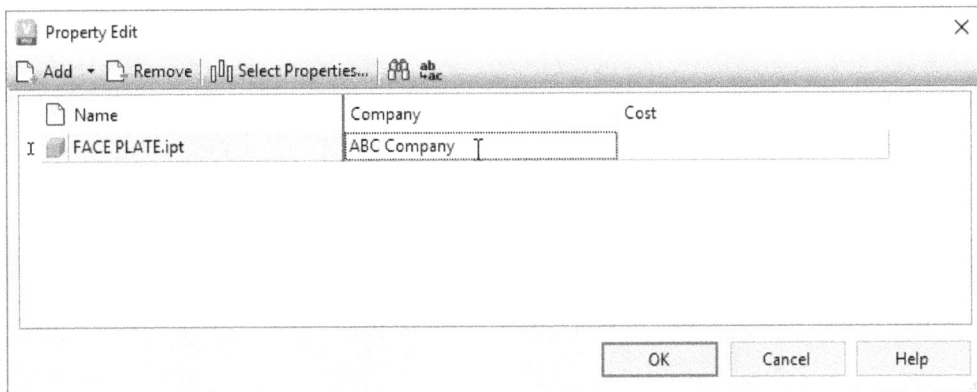

5. The property values are saved and you will get a confirmation dialog box with the results.

Property	Success	Original Value	New Value	Reason
▶ ⊟ Name: FACE PLATE.ipt				
Company	☑		ABC Company	Successfully updated
Cost	☑		5	Successfully updated
File Property: Comp...	☑		ABC Company	Successfully updated from Vault File property 'Company'
File Property: Cost	☑		5	Successfully updated from Vault File property 'Cost'

Property Edit Results ✕

Report... Send To Vault...

Close   Help

6.3 Mapping Properties

Overview

Powerful tools and options make it easy for administrators to map their file and item user-defined properties (UDPs) in a flexible and user-friendly way.

Objectives

After completing this lesson, you will be able to:

*   Map properties
*   Set mapping priorities

Mapping Priority

Mapping priority determines the order in which properties are written to a file. If more than one property writes to a particular file, the highest ranking property takes precedence.

You can map properties to a user-defined property so that values from the master file, such as a file property, are written to the subordinate UDP.

Importing and Exporting Values Between Vault and File Properties

There are two ways in which a file property value is added to the vault:

*   Certain file property definitions come with the client and are already included in the vault.
*   Adding a file to the vault only captures the values based on the existing mappings. In the case of a mapping that writes to the file, it will only write if the file property field exists, or if the write setting is set to 'create' for a custom property. Otherwise, only property definitions already defined in the vault will be created for the file to reduce extraneous property definitions or duplicates.

Mapping

To create a property mapping, the administrator must first choose which object group is to be mapped. In the image below, this is specified under the first column titled *Entity*. The available choices are based on the value of the *Associations* field. Several content providers are included, but in most cases it is best to leave the selection on **All Files (*.*)**. Vault will automatically select the most appropriate content provider based on the file format. Next, select a file that contains the property or BOM field to be mapped. The image below shows the file properties available for mapping in the file **manifold_block.ipt**.

The *Type* column shows the data type of the source property. Mapping can be done across data types. However, there are special considerations that are detailed in the next section. The mapping direction by default will choose bi-directional unless the file or BOM property does not support the input of values. When this occurs, the mapping option will be limited to **Read only**. Read-only mappings should be used sparingly because any UDP that contains only read-only mappings cannot be modified in Vault.

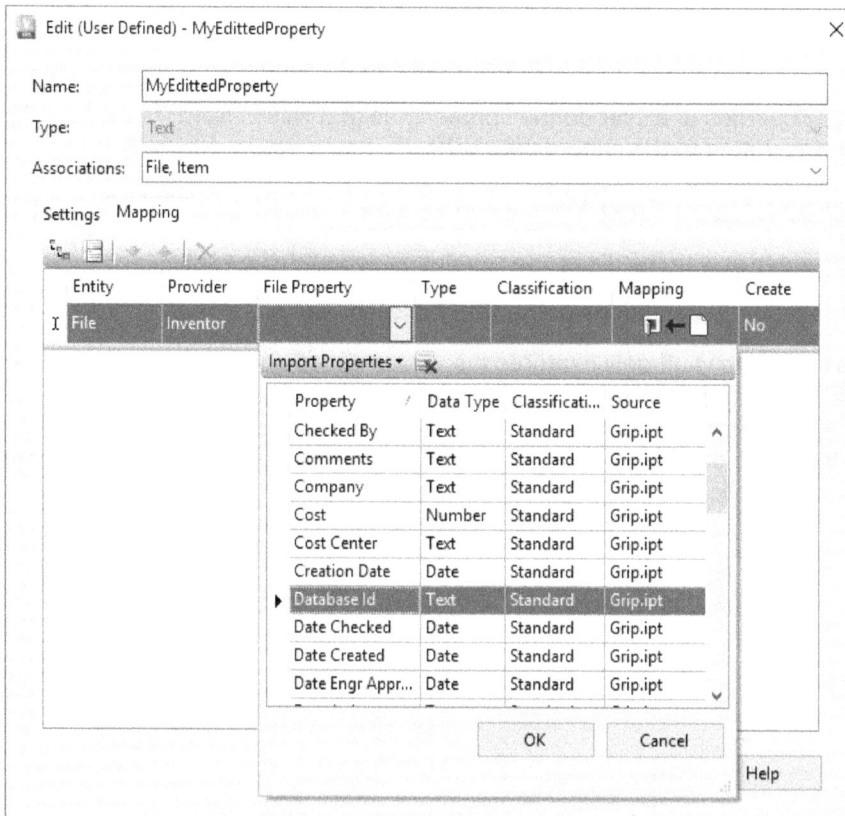

Mapping Across Data Types

There are four property types: **Text**, **Number**, **Boolean**, and **Date**. The following matrix defines valid property mappings.

Source Property (File or BOM)

		Text	Number	Boolean	Date
	Text	Yes	Yes(2)	Yes(1)	Yes(2)
	Number	Yes(2)	Yes	Yes	No
	Boolean	Yes(1)	Yes	Yes	No
UDP	Date	Yes(2)	No	No	Yes

Whenever a mapping is created between two different property types, there is the possibility of incompatibility. The onus is on the user to input valid values. If an invalid value is entered, in most cases the equivalence will flag the property as non-equivalent. The exceptions are listed below.

1. **Mapping Boolean with Text:** The supported valid text values are: Yes/No, True/False and 1/0. These values are localized. A string like 'Autodesk' entered in a Text property cannot be transferred to a Boolean property. This property mapping would be flagged as not equivalent.

2. **Mapping Text with Number or Text with Date:** Works well when all clients and the server are in the same language-locale. With mixed locales, values can convert in a manner that is not intuitive and can produce an undesirable result. Therefore, mapping Text with Number or Text with Date is only recommended when the server and all clients are working in the same locale.

Create Option

The **Create** option applies to write mappings. If the file property does not exist when a value is pushed to the file, the administrator can choose whether the file property is created or not.

The **Create** option has another function that is not obvious. When enabled, the equivalence calculation will consider the absence of the property definition in the file as a blank value and compare it against the value of the UDP in Vault. When the **Create** option is disabled, equivalence will be set to 'Good' when the mapped property definition does not exist in the file.

Example: I have two departments in my organization that both create .DWG files but they use different file properties to represent the same information. The R&D department uses the file property **DwgNum**. The Tooling department uses the file property **DrwNo**. I want to manage all drawings from both groups in a single Vault and with one **Drawing Number** UDP. The correct configuration is to create bidirectional mappings and set the **Create** option to **Off** for both mappings. The result is that a modification of the Drawing Number UDP will write its value back to whichever property exists and it will not create an extra property.

Mapping AutoCAD Block Attributes

Autodesk AutoCAD® block attribute mapping requires configuration on the ADMS. Select **Index Block Attributes** from the Tools menu in Autodesk Data Management Server Console. Enter the AutoCAD block names from which to extract attributes. Note that the block names are case sensitive. After this is done, it is possible to map a UDP to an attribute using the mapping process described above. Configured mappings enable the system to read and/or write values between the UDP and the attribute.

Usage of attribute mapping is intended for single instances of a block or when all block instances have the same attribute values. It is not possible for multiple block instances to be mapped to separate UDPs. Many companies have one instance of a title block in a given .DWG files. Occasionally, there are companies that use multiple instances of a title block in a single file. In these cases, the attributes often share the same values. An example is a drawing file that contains three borders of different size. Each border uses the same title block with attributes.

The attributes for *Customer Name*, *Engineer*, *Project Number*, etc. will share the same value for all instances. Such attributes that share the same value can be mapped to a UDP. Attributes like *Border Size* will have a unique value for each block instance. Therefore, *Border Size* should not be mapped to a UDP in Vault.

AutoCAD Mechanical

Autodesk AutoCAD Mechanical (ACM) supports three distinct sets of properties, all of which can be mapped to Vault UDPs. The three ACM property sets are file, assembly, and component. See the ACM documentation for details about the intended use and differences between these properties.

Vault file properties can map to ACM file properties and Vault item properties can map to ACM assembly and component properties.

It should also be noted that ACM assembly and file properties having the same name should not be mapped to the same Vault UDP.

AutoCAD Electrical

Autodesk AutoCAD Electrical (ACE) supports both file and BOM properties. ACE BOM properties can be mapped to Item properties. ACE uses properties located in .DWGs, .WDPs, and associated databases. ACE properties are exposed to Vault in four ways:

- Ordinary DWG™ file properties and block attributes can be mapped to Vault File objects. The majority of these mappings support bi-directional mapping. Creation of these mappings is described in the Mapping section of this document.

- WDP properties support mapping to Item properties. They also support bi-directional mapping. Creating a mapping with WDP properties requires the AutoCAD Electrical Content Source Provider. The provider is specified in the second column of the image at the right. This provider is automatically set when a file of type **.WDP** is selected under the *File Property* column. If an associated .WDL file has been created, both the line number and the alternate property name will automatically display in the list for selection. You can select the line number or the alternate display name to create the mapping. All WDL properties will display in the list of selectable properties; it does not matter if a value is present.

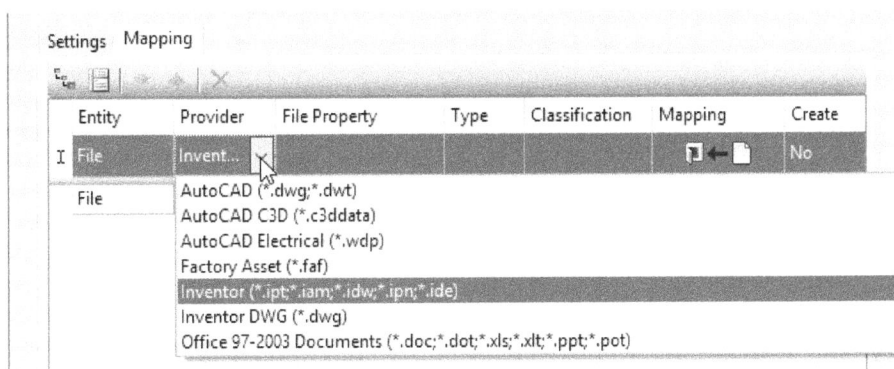

- Component BOM properties can be mapped to Item properties. This includes properties such as *Catalog Number, Component Name, Component Type, Electrical Type, Equivalence Value, Manufacturer*, etc.

  - To create a mapping to a component BOM property, create a new UDP and associate it to Items. Then, in the *Mapping* tab, create a new mapping, ensuring that the first column *Entity* is set to **Item**. Under the *File Property* column, browse and select any file that contains the property to which you will create the mapping. Some properties require that a value exist or the property is not available for selection in the list.

  - **Reminder:** When creating new properties it is best to associate them to a category, which will automatically associate them to the files and/or items where the property should display. If this is not done, the property will have to be manually associated to the file or item.

- Reference Designator properties, when mapped, will display in Vault as optional data on an Item BOM. There are eighteen Reference Designator properties available: INST, LOC, TAG, DESC1...3, RATING1...12. These properties can be mapped to an Item BOM using the DWG content source provider.

  - To create a mapping to a Reference Designator, create a new UDP and associate it to Reference Designator. Then, in the *Mapping* tab, create a new mapping, ensure that the first column *Entity* is set to **Reference Designator**. Under the *File Property* column, select the DWG containing the Reference Designator to which the mapping needs to be created. All Reference Designators are available for selection in the list without requiring a value.

Practice 6b
Map Properties

In this practice, you will learn how to map your newly created user-defined property.

Task 1: Create a user-defined property and map it with a file property.

1. From the Tool menu, select **Administration>Vault Settings**.

2. In the Vault Settings dialog box, select the *Behaviors* tab and select **Properties**.

3. As the customer is working with SAP, the file property *Part Number* should be mapped with a new user-defined property called **SAP-ID**. Therefore, create a new UDP with name **SAP-ID**. Ensure that your *Type* is set to **Number**.

Name:	SAP-ID
Type:	Number
Associations:	File

4. Select the *Mapping* tab.

5. Click in the * **Click here to add a new mapping** field.

Settings | Mapping

Entity	Provider	File Property	Type	Classification	Mapping	Create
*		Click here to add a new mapping				

6. Select the entity type for this property mapping.

7. Click in the blank field under *Provider* and select **Other Files**.

8. Click in the field under *File Property* and select **Import Properties**.

Settings | Mapping

Entity	Provider	File Property	Type
✎ File	Other Files		

Import Properties ▾ ☰ₓ

Import From Vault ⁞ Cl

Import From File

9. Select whether you want to import properties from a file in the vault or from a source file.

10. In the Select File dialog box, locate the file from which you want to import. Click **Open**.

11. The Import Properties list is updated with the properties available for import from the specified source.

12. Click **OK** to save the imported property list and create the mapping.

13. Click the (Clear Properties list) icon at any time to remove all imported properties.

14. In the *Mapping* tab, click **OK** to commit all changes and return to the Edit Property dialog box.

Task 2: Edit mapping priorities.

Properties at the top of the list take precedence over those lower on the list. You can reorganize the list using the Move Up and Move Down arrow icons in the *Mapping* tab.

1. In the *Mapping* tab, select the property that you want to prioritize, and click the **Move Up** or **Move Down** arrow icons as required to change mapping priority.

   Note: A subordinate property is a property that receives its values from other properties that are mapped to it. The mapped properties (the master properties) write values to the subordinate property.

2. Click **OK** to commit all changes and return to the Property Definitions dialog box.

End of practice

Automatic File Naming in Autodesk Vault Professional

The **Automatic File Naming** feature lets you configure how files and items are named when they are added to the vault. You can select from two existing schemes, Mapped and Sequential, or you can create custom numbering schemes using one or more parameters. In this chapter, you will learn how to use and configure automatic file numbering schemes.

Learning Objective

*   Create, edit, and delete custom numbering schemes that automatically create a filename or number on save.

7.1 Creating Custom Numbering Schemes

Overview

In the Autodesk® Vault Professional software, it is possible to assign a numbering scheme that gives the ability to apply an automatic file naming or numbering on save from a new file created from a template inside of Autodesk® Inventor® or AutoCAD®.

Objectives

After completing this lesson, you will be able to:

- Define several different numbering schemes in the Administration panel.

- Set a default numbering scheme.

- Understand the different field types for numbering schemes.

- Delete an existing numbering scheme.

- Create a file from Inventor or AutoCAD and automatically save it with the defined numbering scheme/file naming.

Define Numbering Schemes

You can select from several existing schemes (Mapped, Sequential, ECO) or you can create custom numbering schemes using one or more parameters.

Mapped	Numbers are generated based on the user-defined properties mapped to the file or item in the Map Properties dialog box.
Sequential	Numbers are generated sequentially. This is the default number scheme and cannot be edited or deleted.
ECO (if using Autodesk Vault Professional)	Change order names are generated based on a defined fixed text, a delimiter, and an auto-generated number.
Custom	Numbers are generated based on a custom design. This feature provides the flexibility to create a numbering scheme where the number carries information about the file.

How To: Define the Numbering Schemes for Auto File Naming

1. From the Tools menu, select **Administration>Vault Settings**.

2. In the Vault Settings dialog box, click the *Behaviors* tab.

3. In the *Numbering* section, select **Define**.

Numbering Field Essentials

Each separate part in a file number is called a field. There are six basic fields:

	Example	Description
Autogenerated	1001, 1002, 1003	Creates a sequential file number automatically each time a file is created. No user input is required.
Delimiter	-	A single character, such as a dash that separates each field.
FixedText	2004	Use this for a value you do not want changed and want to have in each file number.
FreeText	prototype	Creates a free form field so users can enter additional information.
PredefinedList	blue, yellow, green	Provides a list of choices to the user each time a file is created.
Workgroup Label	WG1	The workgroup ID for the workgroup in which the number is generated.

Numbering Generator

There are three types of number generators:

Simple Number Generator	It produces numbers based on the other information provided in the numbering scheme.
Centralized Number Generator	It avoids duplicated generated number at the same time in a replicated environment.
Custom Generator	User-specified numbering generators configured on the Vault server.

General numbering scheme rules:

- Only one auto-generated field per numbering scheme sequence is allowed.

- A user-defined numbering scheme can only be edited or deleted when it is not in use. That is, the user-defined numbering scheme has not been used or all the objects using it have been deleted.

- The sequential numbering scheme cannot be edited or deleted.

Defining File Fields

The field type selected in the Add Field dialog box determines the available field settings. The default choice is **Auto-generated sequence**.

Auto-generated Field Settings

- Use the *Name* text box to give a name to the auto-generated field.
- The *Length* determines the number of characters of the *Range* field, and must be a positive value.
- The *Range* specifies the beginning and end of the auto generated number.

  Note: The lower limit must be less than the upper limit.

- *Step Size* controls how the auto-generated number is incremented.

Delimiter

- The value **must be a character**. The delimiter is used to separate fields.

Fixed Text

- Use the *Name* text box to give a name to the fixed text field.
- The value entered in the *Fixed Text* field always displays in the file number and cannot be modified by the user.

Free Text

- Use the *Name* text box to give a name to the free text field.
- *Max Length* controls the maximum number of characters permitted for this field.
- **Max Length required** forces user to enter the number of characters specified in the *Max Length* field. The number length cannot be over 50.

Predefined List

- Use the *Name* text box to give a name to the predefined list field.
- Specify a list of values in the *Code* field. You can optionally enter a description for each of the values.
- Use **Move up** and **Move down** to change the order of the values.
- Use **Delete** to remove a value.

Workgroup Label

- Selecting this option automatically assigns the workgroup label as a fixed value in the numbering scheme.

Preview and Edit Numbering Schemes

The New Numbering Scheme dialog box and the Edit Numbering Scheme dialog box enable you to review and edit a numbering scheme.

- The name displays in the *Name* field. The name of the numbering scheme cannot be modified.

- The *Preview* field displays all fields defined. A field requiring user input displays as a question mark (?). Auto-generated fields display as a pound sign (#).

- The *Number of Digits* field shows the maximum possible file number length.

- The **Append workgroup label** checkbox lets you add the workgroup label to the file or item name. This label is useful in differentiating files between workgroups.

- Use **Move Up** and **Move Down** to change the order of the values.

- Use **Edit**, **Delete**, and **Add** to perform their respective operations.

- Force letters to uppercase by selecting the **Force to uppercase** checkbox.

How To: Delete an Existing Numbering Scheme in Vault

1. Open the Numbering Scheme dialog box using **Tools>Vault Settings>Behaviors tab>Numbering section>Define**.

2. Now you can view all defined numbering schemes in Vault. To delete, select the numbering scheme you want to delete permanently from the system and click **Delete**.

Name	Type	Active	Default	Preview	
NewNumberingScheme	File	☑	☐	######-USA?-??????-WG1	Edit...
▶ Sequential	File	☐	☐	######	New...
					Delete

(Numbering Schemes dialog box, File selected)

3. A dialog box opens to confirm the deletion. Click **OK** to delete the scheme permanently.

💡 Hint: General Numbering Scheme Rules

- Only one auto-generated field per numbering scheme sequence is permitted.

- A user-defined numbering scheme can only be edited or deleted when it is not in use. That is, the user-defined numbering scheme has not been used or all the files using it have been deleted.

- The sequential numbering scheme cannot be edited or deleted.

Practice 7a
Define a Custom Numbering Scheme

In this practice, you will learn how to use numbering schemes. You will manage existing numbering schemes, create and edit new ones, and finally delete the created scheme.

Task 1: Manage numbering schemes.

1. From the Tools menu, select **Administration>Vault Settings**.

2. In the Vault Settings dialog box, select the *Behaviors* tab.

3. In the *Numbering* section, select **Define**.

4. The Numbering Schemes dialog box lists the available numbering schemes. The default numbering scheme is indicated with a checkmark. You can also create new schemes, edit existing schemes, and set the default scheme.

5. Select whether you want to view **File**, **Item**, **Change Order**, or **All numbering schemes** from the Filter drop-down list.

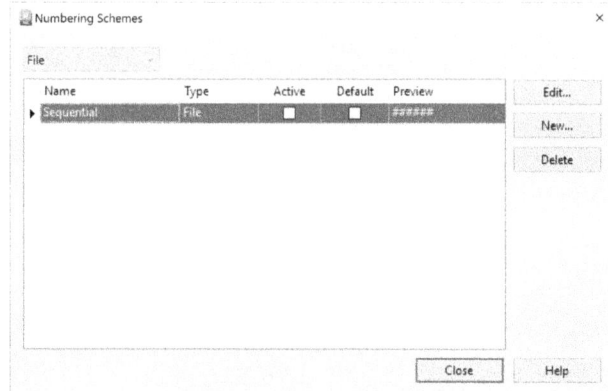

Task 2: Create a new numbering scheme.

1. Click **New**.

2. In the New Numbering Scheme dialog box, enter the scheme name.

3. Click **New** to add fields for the numbering scheme.

Add Field   ✕

Field Type:
- ⦿ Auto-generated sequence
- ○ Delimiter
- ○ Fixed text
- ○ Free text
- ○ Pre-defined list
- ○ Workgroup label

Auto-generated Field Settings

Name:

Length:

Range: --

Step Size: 1

☑ Zero-pad auto-generated sequence

4. In the Add Field dialog box, select one of the following field types:

Auto-generated sequence

- Enter a name for the auto-generated field.
- Specify the length for the range. The length must be a positive number.
- Enter the starting and ending value for the range.
- Enter the step size. The *Step Size* value must be at least 1.
- The auto-generated sequence is zero-padded by default. To remove zero-padding, clear the checkbox. An example of zero-padded numbers is 000001, 000002, 000003.

Auto-generated Field Settings

Name:	Sequence
Length:	6
Range:	000001 -- 999999
Step Size:	1

☑ Zero-pad auto-generated sequence

Delimiter

- Enter the delimiter value. It must be a character, such as a dash (-), used to separate fields.

Delimiter Field Settings

Delimiter Value:	-

Fixed text

- Enter a name for the fixed text field.
- The value entered in the *Fixed Text* field is a constant and cannot be edited. The value cannot exceed 50 characters.

Fixed Text Field Settings

Name:	Location
Fixed Text:	USA

Free text

- Enter a name for the free text field.
- Enter the maximum length of the field.
- Select the **Max length required** checkbox to fix the length of the field to the value specified in the *Max Length* field.

Free Text Field Settings

Name:	My free text
Default Value:	ADSK
Max Length:	4

☑ Max length required

Predefined list

- Enter a name for the free predefined list field.
- Enter a value in the *Code* field. You can optionally enter a *Description* for each of the values.
- To change the order of the entries, highlight a value, and then click **Move up** or **Move down**.
- To delete an entry, highlight a value and click **Delete**.

Predefined List Field Settings

Name: Pre-defined List

Enter code list:

Is Default	Code	Description	
✔	MyCode	Internal Codeword	Delete
			Move up
			Move down
			Set as Default

Workgroup label

*   This option automatically assigns the workgroup ID to the number. The workgroup ID is based on the workgroup in which the number is generated.

> ◉ Workgroup label
>
> Workgroup label Settings
>
> Workgroup label: WG1

The new Numbering Scheme dialog box should now look similar to following picture (here you can see that two more delimiters were created to separate the values). You can use **Move Up** and **Move Down** to change the order.

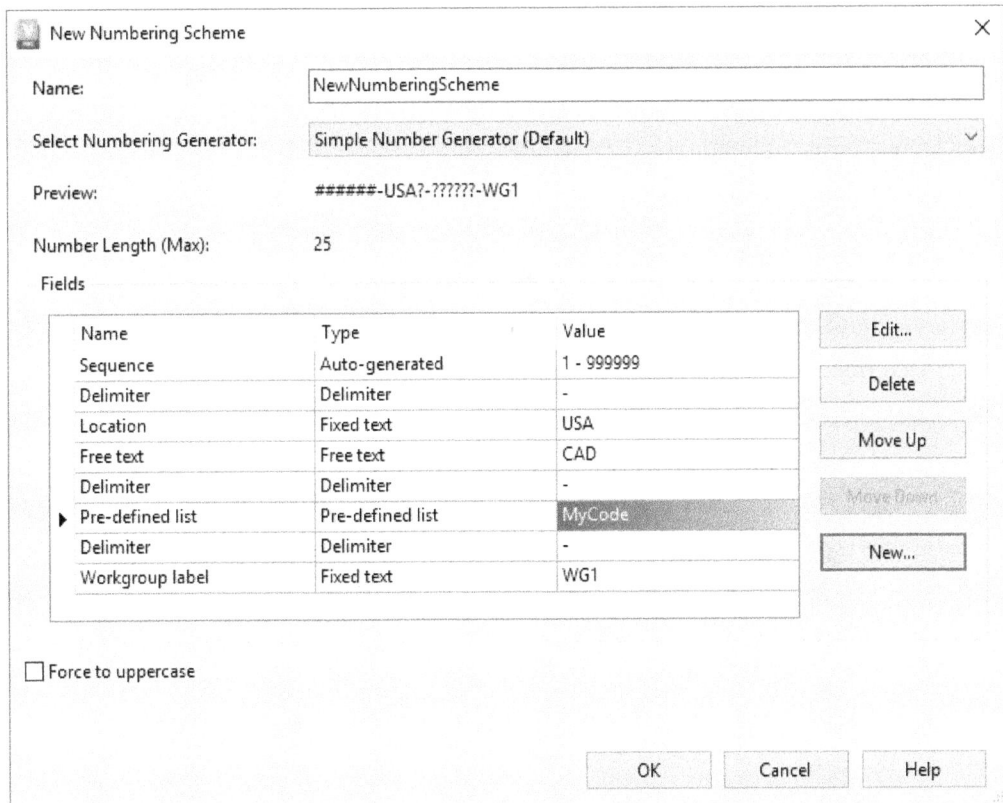

New Numbering Scheme			✕
Name:	NewNumberingScheme		
Select Numbering Generator:	Simple Number Generator (Default)		⌄
Preview:	######-USA?-??????-WG1		
Number Length (Max):	25		

Fields

Name	Type	Value	
Sequence	Auto-generated	1 - 999999	Edit...
Delimiter	Delimiter	-	Delete
Location	Fixed text	USA	
Free text	Free text	CAD	Move Up
Delimiter	Delimiter	-	
▸ Pre-defined list	Pre-defined list	MyCode	Move Down
Delimiter	Delimiter	-	New...
Workgroup label	Fixed text	WG1	

☐ Force to uppercase

OK	Cancel	Help

5. Click **OK**.

    The New Numbering Scheme dialog box displays a preview of the settings defined in the Add/Edit dialog box.

6. To change the settings, click **Edit**. To delete, click **Delete**. To add another numbering scheme, click **New**.

7. To display text in all capital letters, select the **Force to uppercase** checkbox.

8. Click **OK**.

Task 3: Edit an existing numbering scheme.

Only numbering schemes that have not been used by a file can be edited, with the exception that in-use schemes can have their ranges increased.

1. Select a numbering scheme from the list.

2. Click **Edit**.

3. In the Edit Numbering Scheme dialog box, change the values for the selected numbering scheme.

4. Click **OK**.

Task 4: Set the default numbering scheme.

1. Select a numbering scheme from the list.

2. Click the **Default** checkbox.

Task 5: Delete a numbering scheme.

Only schemes that are not in use can be deleted.

1. Select a numbering scheme from the list.

2. Click **Delete**.

   Note: *You cannot delete a default scheme. Select another scheme to be the default before deleting it.*

End of practice

Practice 7b
Create a New Autodesk Inventor File Numbering Scheme

In this practice, you will create a new Autodesk Inventor part and save it from within the Autodesk Inventor software to the Autodesk Vault software. The new part will be created with the new numbering scheme you create.

Task 1: Create your own number scheme.

1. Go through the steps explained in *Practice 7a: Define a Custom Numbering Scheme* to create your own numbering scheme that works for you.

2. After you are done, ensure that your new numbering scheme is set to **Active** and **Default**.

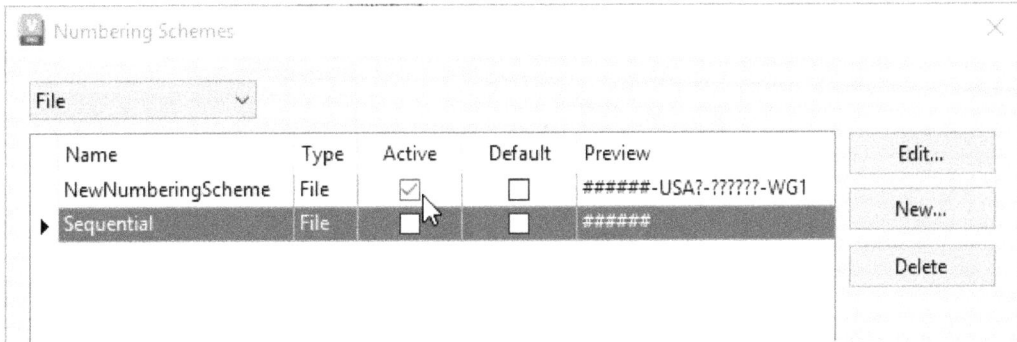

Task 2: Create an Inventor component and save it to Vault.

1. Open Autodesk Inventor and create a new simple component (e.g., a plate).

2. After you have finished your work on the component, ensure that you are connected to the right Vault. Select the *Vault* tab and log in to the **AOTCVault** vault as **administrator**.

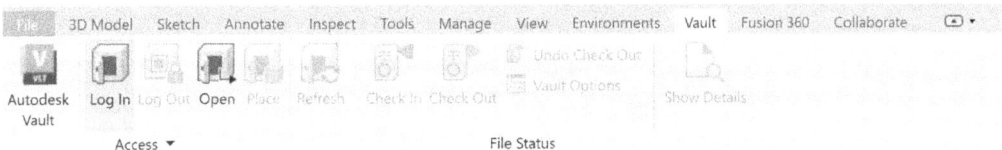

3. Save your component. When clicking **Save** in Inventor, the Generate File Number dialog box opens automatically and asks you to confirm the new numbering scheme.

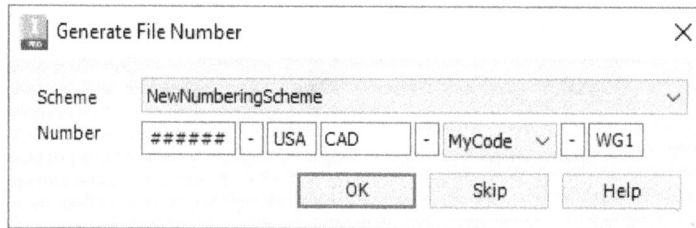

4. Click **OK** to confirm the numbering scheme.

5. The component is saved to your folder structure.

6. Open the Vault Browser in Autodesk Inventor and select the component you just created.

7. Right-click to open the context menu and click **Check In** to check the component into Vault. You can edit the comment in the confirmation dialog before you click **OK** to finish this task.

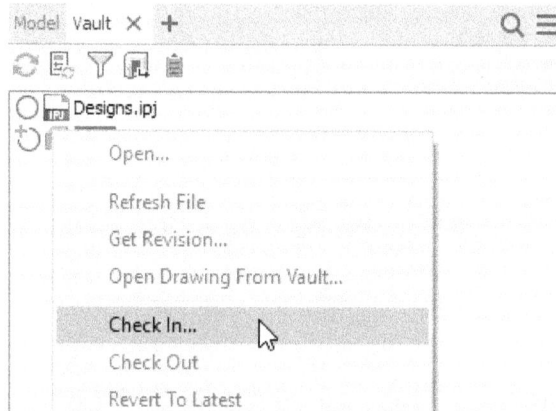

8. Your newly created component is saved to Autodesk Vault with the new numbering scheme.

⊟ **File**

    000001-USACAD-MyCode-WG1.ipt

End of practice

Autodesk Inventor In-CAD Data Management

You can manage and evaluate your vault file data from within the Autodesk® Inventor® software by using the **Data Cards** and **Data Mapping** features. Data Cards lets you examine pertinent vault details about a model and modify property information for individual or multiple files. Data Mapping lets you generate report data for a model and publish the results as a chart. You can also map the report results onto the open model to better evaluate your design.

Both of these features give you an advantage in understanding and managing your design without ever having to leave the Autodesk Inventor software.

In this chapter, you learn how to view data cards, modify properties using data cards, generate reports, and map report data to your model.

Learning Objectives

- Enable and access both data card views.
- Build and navigate a data card deck, isolate a card, and remove a card from a card deck.
- Edit properties and track changes with data cards.
- Generate a report based on an open model.
- Map data in a report to the open model.

8.1 Working with Data Cards

Overview

Data cards provide convenient summaries of the metadata assigned to a file or group of files through a single point of access. With data cards, you can determine a file's vault status, see a thumbnail of the file, and review and modify property information without leaving the Inventor application.

In this lesson, you learn how to enable the **Data Cards** feature and view file properties in fingertip view and full data card view. You also learn how to build and manage a card deck, and use single or multiple data cards to manage file properties.

Objectives

After completing this lesson, you will be able to:

- Enable the **Data Cards** feature and view file properties.

- Switch between fingertip view and full data card view.

- Build and navigate a data card deck, including locating the Home card in a deck.

- Isolate and remove a data card from a data card deck.

- Modify component properties using data cards.

About Data Card Views

Data cards let you view pertinent vault details and properties for specified files. This insight into the statuses and properties of your model files makes it easier to manage the files throughout the lifecycle of the model.

Whenever a part is selected on the CAD canvas or in the Model or Vault browser list, the part is highlighted on the canvas and in the list, and the data card automatically updates to show the relevant information for that part.

Data cards can be displayed in two different ways: the fingertip view and the full data card view.

Access the Data Cards feature by clicking **Data Cards** in the Autodesk Vault ribbon.

Fingertip View

The fingertip view is the default view for Data Cards. This view is a collapsed, read-only version of the full data card.

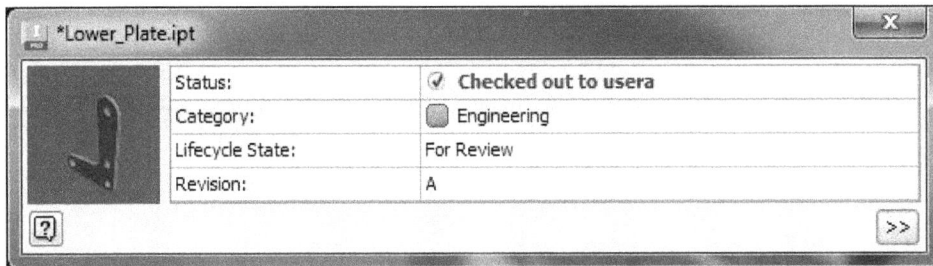

When a file is selected and the **Data Cards** feature enabled, the fingertip displays the following information:

*   Thumbnail

*   Component name

*   Status

*   Category

*   Lifecycle State

*   Revision

Click **>>** (Expand) to switch from fingertip view to full data card view.

Full Data Card View

The fingertip can be expanded into a full data card, which displays all of the information in the fingertip view and certain property information. The CAD administrator can determine which properties display in the Configure Data Card dialog box, which is accessed through the Vault Settings dialog box in the Autodesk Vault client.

The tasks you can perform with the data card depend on whether the data card is in read-only mode or edit mode.

Read-Only Mode

The read-only mode is the default mode for viewing the full data card. This mode enables you to compare selected files and to filter the property values based on your needs.

When a data card opens for a selected file or when a **Refresh** command is performed, the values for the properties are grabbed from the server and displayed. A pending icon displays next to the property name when the retrieval is in process. The pending icon disappears once the value is received for that property.

Edit Mode

The property grid can be changed to edit mode by clicking **Edit**. When in edit mode, the file is automatically checked out of the vault and you can edit the displayed property values. When you are finished editing, the new values are written to the local file and to the server file. These edits are made permanent when the file is checked into the vault. All actions performed on an individual card affect only the component associated with the card.

Example of Using a Data Card to Examine File Information

You just found out that one of the parts you are working with in your model has been set from Released back to Work in Progress. You need to find out who last checked in the part so that you can talk to that person about the changes they made.

You select the part in the model and then click **Data Cards** to enable the fingertip view for that part. You can see the lifecycle state is set to Work in Progress and that a revision bump has occurred, but you still need to know which engineer last made changes. You click the **>>** (Expand) button and discover that it was your colleague Tim Smith who altered the part. Now you can talk to him about why the part was returned to Work in Progress.

How To: Enable Data Cards

1. Click **Data Cards** in the Autodesk Vault ribbon. The data card for the selected file displays in fingertip view.

How To: View Fingertip Information

1. Enable data cards by clicking **Data Cards** in the Autodesk Vault ribbon. The data card window displays.

2. Select a part in the model. The data card grid updates automatically to show the part's filename, a thumbnail, revision, state, category, and vault status.

How To: View Full Data Card Information

1. Click **>>** (Expand) in the lower right-hand corner of the data card to switch between the fingertip view and the full data card view. The data card expands to display the properties. Some properties will show a pending icon until the value is retrieved from the server.

   Note: Property information displayed on the data card is determined by the administrator in the Configure Data Card dialog box in the Autodesk Vault client.

2. Click the tabs at the bottom of the grid to see additional properties.

Understanding Data Card Decks

Multiple data cards can be retrieved to create a card deck. You can specify the scope of the card deck by selecting individual files or an entire open model. A card deck contains one data card for each file specified in the scope and a Home card which lists the data cards in the card deck.

Data Card Deck Controls

At the top of the card deck, a toolbar has been provided for navigating and managing the data cards in the card deck. These commands enable you to retrieve the data cards for a model or a specified group of files and place them into a deck, refresh the data card values, remove a card from the deck, and isolate a card from the deck. There are also navigation buttons that enable you to move through the deck to the data card you want to review.

The following table defines each of the icons located in the data card navigation toolbar.

Icon	Command	Definition
Get CAD Selection / Get CAD Selection / Get Entire Model	**Get Data Cards (Get CAD Files or Get Entire Model)**	Retrieves either the selected CAD files or all the files in the open model and creates a card deck. Whichever Get Data Cards command is used last remains displayed.
	Refresh	If a single data card displays; the property values for that card are retrieved from the server.
		If the Summary card is selected, the property values for all data cards defined by the current Get command are retrieved from the server.
	Remove Card	Removes the current card or selected cards from the deck.
	Isolate On	Toggles on Isolation mode for the selected card or cards. Only the files for the selected data cards remain displayed and all other files in the card deck are rendered transparent on the canvas.
	Isolate Off	Toggles off Isolation mode for the selected card or cards. All files that were transparent when Isolate was toggled on, are displayed again.
	Select in CAD	Sends the current card selection to the CAD environment as a selection set.
	Clear CAD Selection	Clears the current CAD selection set.

Icon	Command	Definition
	First	Goes to the first card in the card deck (also referred to as the Home card).
	Back	Goes back one card in the deck.
	Next	Goes to the next card in the deck.
	Home	Goes to the Home card.
	Last	Goes to the last card in the deck.

Building a Data Card Deck

You can create a deck of data cards for faster referencing of properties and vault status information. Data cards are gathered from the open model or from a selection set and placed into a card deck. A Home card is added as a summary card of the card deck contents.

How To: Build a Data Card Deck

1. Enable the data cards feature by selecting **Data Cards** in the Autodesk Vault ribbon.
2. Select a model or selection set in Inventor.
3. Click **>>** (Expand) at the bottom of the data card to expand the data card from fingertip view to full view.
4. In the data card deck control toolbar, click the **Get** drop-down arrow and select either **Get CAD Selection** or **Get Entire Model**.
5. The data is retrieved from the vault. Depending on the size of the deck being created, the updates might take some time. You can continue working until all property values have been retrieved.
6. When all the data is retrieved, the Home card displays and the navigation controls on the data card deck toolbar are activated.

Removing Data Cards from a Card Deck

Refine your card deck by removing a data card or group of data cards from the card deck.

How To: Remove an Individual Data Card from a Card Deck

1. Select the data card you want to remove from the card deck.
2. Right-click and select **Remove Card**. The card is removed from the card deck.

How To: Remove Multiple Data Cards from a Card Deck

1. Click the **Home** button to go to the Home card in the card deck.

2. Select the data cards that you want to remove from the card deck from the data card list.

3. Right-click and select **Remove Card**. The cards are removed from the card deck.

Home Card

The Home card displays the list of the files in the card deck and their property attributes. The property values that display depend on whether a single data card, multiple data cards, or no data cards are selected from the data card list.

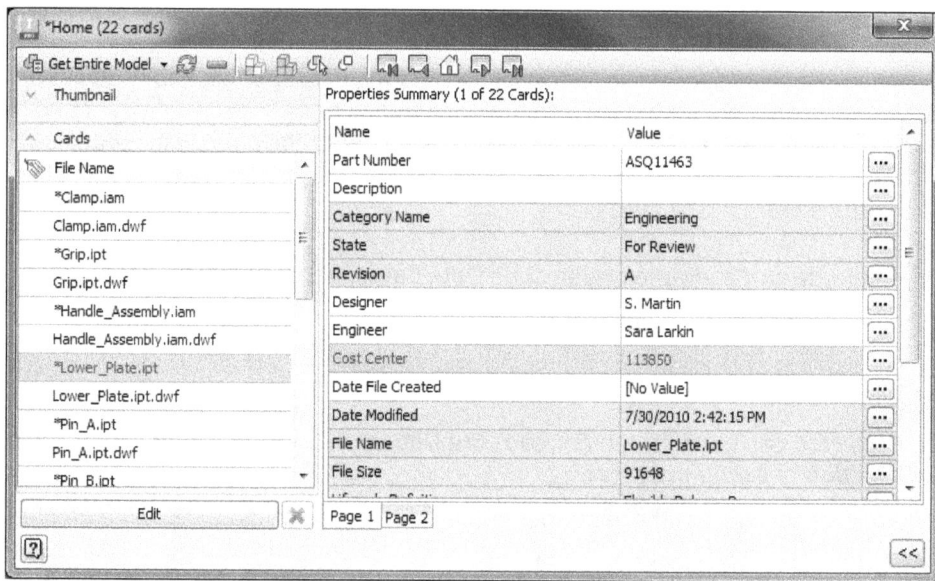

Home Card with 1 File Selected

Home Card Display Rules

- If a single data card is selected, then the property values for that data card display on the Home card.

- If multiple data cards are selected, then the property values shared across the selected data cards display. If the values differ, then the word **VARIES** displays.

- If no data cards are selected in the data card list, then all the property values shared across the entire deck display. If the values differ, then the word **VARIES** displays.

You can make edits with individual data cards or use the Home card to make bulk edits throughout the entire card deck. When making bulk edits for properties with different values throughout the deck, a value collector is used to list the different values associated with that property.

At the top of the Home card, the number of cards in the deck and the number of cards selected for comparison display.

Isolation Mode

Sometimes, in models with many parts, it is necessary to isolate a part for easier examination. The isolation feature enables you to distinguish specified parts in a model. Select the data card(s) for the part(s) that you want to view and click **Isolate On** from the data card deck controls. The selected parts remain visible on the CAD canvas while all other parts in the card deck become transparent.

Click **Isolate Off** from the data card deck controls to make all parts on the CAD canvas visible again.

Isolating Parts in Autodesk Inventor

You can isolate a part or parts for easier examination by enabling the Isolation feature.

How To: Toggle Isolation On

1. Click **Home** in the data card deck toolbar to go to the Home card.
2. Select the data cards for the parts that you want to isolate on the CAD canvas.
3. Click **Isolate On** in the data card deck toolbar. The parts remain viewable on the CAD canvas and all other parts with unselected data cards in the card deck become transparent.

- Click **Isolate Off** in the data card deck toolbar to make all parts on the CAD canvas visible again.

Editing Properties with Data Cards

Properties can be edited on both the full data card and in a card deck. Changes with data cards can only be made when the data card is in edit mode. Click **Edit** to begin changing property values.

Files must be checked out before changing anything. If any files in the card deck are not checked out or if a data card is not available for editing, you will receive a message asking you to check out the files or to remove any invalid cards from the card deck. When a property is edited, click **Save** to commit the changes. An asterisk displays beside the filename to indicate that the data card has been modified.

> *Note: Autodesk Vault operations are disabled when a data card is in edit mode.*

Modified files must be checked back into the vault for the changes to become permanent. If you attempt to close the card deck or to change the data card view while a modified file is checked out, you will be prompted to check the file in or discard your changes before proceeding.

Tracking Edits

Since edits are not immediately permanent, you can track edits and review them before checking the modified files into the vault. If a property has been modified, an asterisk (*) displays beside the filename on the data card and beside the filenames in the data list on the home card if you are using a card deck.

Additionally, the font changes for property values that have been modified.

The following table explains the different text effects and their significance.

Text	Meaning	Edit
Normal font	Same as original value (no change)	The value is the same as the original value or has been reset before checking the file back in.
Normal font with gray background	Read-only	The property cannot be altered even in edit mode.
Strikethrough font	Deleted value	The original value was deleted. When the file is checked back into the vault, this value is blank.
Blue font	Edited value	The original value has changed but the file has not been checked back into the vault to commit the change.

Undoing Changes

During the editing process, you can choose to undo a single property change or to undo all changes as long as the current changes have not been committed.

Right-click on the property on the data card to open a context menu. Select **Revert** to reset the selected property to its original value. Select **Revert Selected Files** to reset the properties of the selected files to their original values.

Compliance Rules

Compliance is a key component in managing properties. When a property is non-compliant, a red exclamation icon is inserted into the value field on the data card. On the Home card, a non-compliant icon displays beside the filename to let you know that one of the properties for that file is non-compliant.

Hover the cursor over the exclamation icon to see a tooltip describing the reason why the property is not compliant. Since some data cards contain multiple tabs of properties, the icon will also display on the tab to indicate if there is a non-compliant property not displayed on the data card. There is also a tab that shows all non-compliant properties in one list.

In the illustration below, the *Cost Center* value for Lower_Plate.ipt is not compliant because it requires a minimum of six characters and only five have been entered.

How To: Edit a Single Data Card

1. Go to the data card for which you want to change a property value.

2. Click **Edit** to enter edit mode. Properties that cannot be edited are disabled.

3. Locate the property you want to change. Use the tabs at the bottom of the values grid to navigate through all available properties.

4. Enter a new value in the property field.
    OR
    Right-click on the field and select **Undo** in the context menu to undo any previous changes.

    Note: Changes made to property values are not permanent until the affected files are checked back into the vault. If you attempt to resize the data card or close the data card feature, you will be prompted to check in changed files first.

5. Click **Apply** to commit the changes. An asterisk (*) displays beside the name of the data card to indicate that it has been modified.

How To: Edit Properties for Multiple Data Cards

1. Go to the Home card.

2. Click **Edit**. Properties that cannot be edited are disabled.

3. Select the data cards in the data card list for which you want to edit property values. Alternatively, clear all selections to change values from the whole deck.

4. Locate the property that you want to change. Use the tabs at the bottom of the values grid to navigate through all available properties.

   Note: Changes to the property value affect all cards selected or the entire card deck if no cards are selected.

5. Enter a new value in the property field. If the field has a value of **VARIES**, select a value from the list or enter a new one.

6. Click **Apply** to commit the changes. An asterisk (*) displays beside the name of the data card to indicate that it has been modified.

Working with Value Collectors

The value collector is a dialog box that lists the different values associated with a particular property. The values listed are collected from the data cards selected on the Home card or the entire deck if no cards are selected. The value collector contains a *Value* column with the list of property values and a *Usage* column that displays how many data cards share that particular value. Value collectors can be accessed from the Home card or from a single data card.

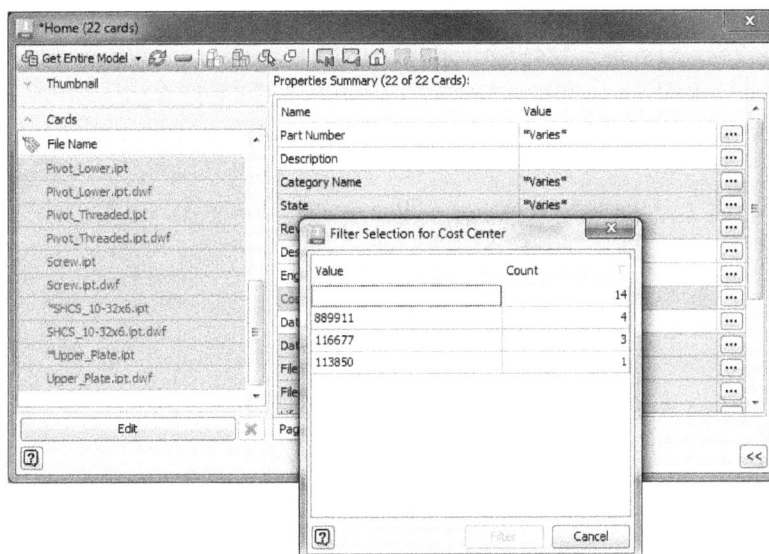

Using a Value Collector with the Home Card

In a card deck, the same properties are repeated for each card. If the selection of data cards shares the same value for that property, then that value displays next to the property name on the Home card. However, if the property values differ, then the word **VARIES** displays next to the property. Properties with a value of VARIES display with a small ellipsis icon (...). Click the icon to access the value collector.

You can filter property values for review in read-only mode or change them in edit mode.

Read-Only Mode

In read-only mode, you can filter values collected. Select a value in the value collector and click **Filter** to select the cards in the card list that contain that property value.

> **Note:** *The file associated with a data card must be checked out before editing any properties.*

For example, the value collector for the *Cost Center* property lists all of the values for *Cost Center* in the deck. If you select **324657** from the collector and click **OK**, the five cards with **324657** as the value for *Cost Center* are selected in the card list.

This process can be repeated for additional properties, enabling you to refine the data card selection each time.

In edit mode, you can change the values for a file associated with a particular data card or make bulk changes to all cards associated with that value.

The value collector has both a *Values* and a *Count* column. However, unlike read-only mode, an editing field at the top of the value collector enables you to adjust values for the data cards that use that property.

For example, the value collector for the *Cost Center* property lists all of the values for *Cost Center* in the deck. If you select **889911** in the collector, **889911** displays for editing at the top of the dialog box. The value can then be cleared or modified. Click **Save** to commit any changes.

Using a Value Collector with a Single Data Card

On a single data card, the properties are the same as those on every other card in the deck. However, only the property values for the selected data card display. A small ellipsis icon (...) displays next to each property. Click the icon to access the value collector.

Read-Only Mode

In read-only mode, the value collector displays a list of available values in the card deck. These values do not impact the card.

Edit Mode

In edit mode, the value collector displays a list of available values in the card deck. A value can be selected from the list and applied to the file associated with the current data card.

Using a Value Collector to Filter Property Values (Read-Only)

How To: Use a Value Collector to Filter Property Values from the Home Card

1. Go to the Home card. Ensure that you are in read-only mode. (**Edit** should be visible.)

2. Select the data cards in the data card list for which you want to collect property values. Alternatively, clear all selections to collect values from the whole deck.

3. Click the ellipsis (...) next to the property value you want to review. The icon is only available for properties displaying a value of **VARIES**.

4. In the Filter Selection dialog box, select the value you want to use to filter your data card selection. The data card list is updated to display only those data cards containing that property value.

5. Continue filtering the data card selection using other properties, if required.

How To: Use a Value Collector to Filter Property Values from a Single Data Card

1. Select a data card in the card deck to review its property values.

2. Ensure that the card deck is in read-only mode. (**Edit** should be visible.)

3. Click the ellipsis (...) next to the property value you want to review. A list of values that already exist in the card deck for that property displays.

Using a Value Collector to Edit Property Values

Note: The file associated with a data card must be checked out before editing any properties.

How To: Use a Value Collector to Edit Property Values from the Home Card

1. Go to the Home card.

2. Click **Edit**.

3. Select the data cards in the data card list for which you want to collect property values. Alternatively, clear all selections to collect values from the whole deck.

4. Click the ellipsis (...) next to the property value you want to change. The icon is only available for properties displaying a value of **VARIES**.

5. In the Edit Value dialog box, select a new value for the selected property from the *Values* list or enter a value in the editing field.

6. Any changes made to a value affect all data cards using that property value. Refer to the *Usage* column for the number of data cards affected. If required, refine your data card selection using the steps described in the *Read-Only* section above before continuing.

    Note: Changes made to property values are not permanent until the affected files are checked back in to the vault. If you attempt to resize the data card or close the data card feature, you will be prompted to check in changed files first.

7. Click **Save** to commit the changes and close the Edit Value dialog box. An asterisk (*) displays beside the name of the data card to indicate that it has been modified.

How To: Use a Value Collector to Edit Property Values from a Single Data Card

1. Select a data card in the card deck for which you want to edit property values.

2. Click **Edit**.

3. Click the ellipsis (...) next to the property value you want to change.

4. A list of values that already exist in the card deck for that property displays.

5. Select a new value for the selected property from the *Values* list or enter a value in the editing field. Click **Save** to commit the changes and close the Edit Value dialog box. An asterisk (*) displays beside the name of the data card to indicate that it has been modified.

Managing the Data Card Layout

Administrators can streamline property management with data cards by customizing the data card layout. In the Configure Data Card dialog box in the Vault Settings of the client, administrators can determine how many pages a data card uses and which properties display.

Select **Tools>Administration>Vault Settings>***Behaviors* **tab** and click **Data Card** to access the Configure Data Card dialog box.

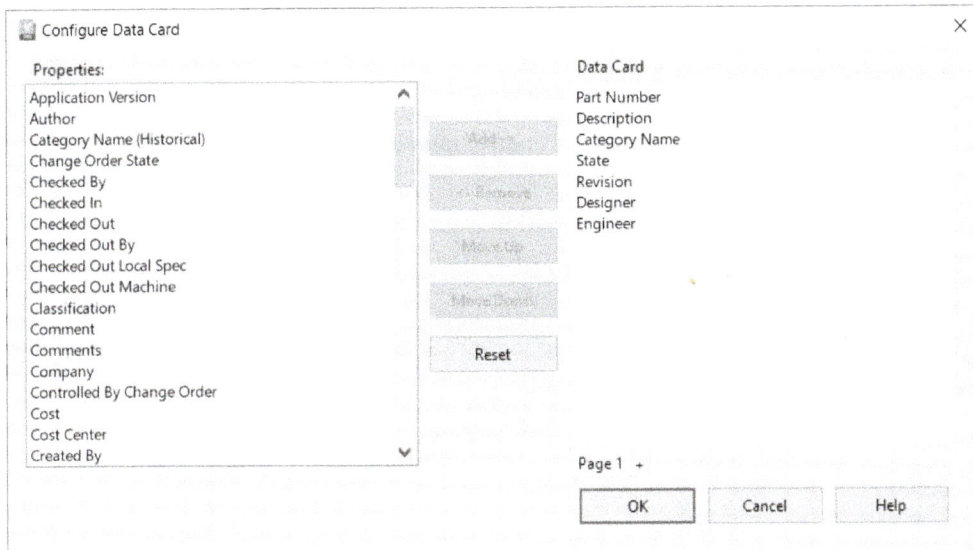

You can manage tabs and determine which properties are available for the CAD user to modify in the Configure Data Card dialog box. A properties list displays all of the properties that can be added to the selected tab. A property can be added to a single tab only once. Several different tabs, however, can list the same property.

Actions	Description
Add	Select one or more properties from the properties list and click **Add** to include them in the selected data card tab.
Remove	Select a property already assigned to a tab and click **Remove** to delete it from that tab.
Move Up	Moves a property up in the selected tab.
Move Down	Moves a property down in the selected tab.
Reset	Returns the current tab to the last layout.
Rename tab	Double-click on the tab to rename it.
Add new tab	Click the small tab with a plus sign (+) to add a new tab to the data card. By default, the tabs are numbered sequentially.
Delete a tab	Click the X in the selected tab to delete the tab itself.
OK	Saves the changes to the data card layout and closes the dialog box.

How To: Configure the Data Card Layout

1. Select **Tools>Administration>Vault Settings>Behaviors tab**. Click **Data Card**.
2. In the Configure Data Card dialog box, select one or more properties from the properties list and click **Add** to add them to the selected tab.
   - Select a property and click **Remove** at any time to refine the properties in the selected tabs.
3. If required, click **Move Up** or **Move Down** to reorganize the properties in the tab, as required.
4. Double-click on the selected tab and rename it.
5. Click the + tab to create a new tab.
6. Click the X tab to delete a tab.
7. When finished, click **OK** to save your settings and close the dialog box.
8. Click **Reset** at any time to restore the dialog box to the last saved layout.

Practice 8a
Manage a Card Deck

In this practice, you create a custom data card deck for a design.

Task 1: Create a card deck.

1. Start Autodesk Vault. Log in using the following information:

    *   For *User Name*, enter **administrator**.
    *   Leave the *Password* field blank.
    *   For *Vault*, select **Data Card and Mapping Vault**.

2. In the Navigation pane, click **Project Explorer ($)**.

3. Click **Find** in the toolbar.

4. In the Find dialog box, search for **Clamp.iam**.

5. Right-click on **Clamp.iam** and select **Open** to launch it in the Autodesk Inventor software. Select **Yes** to checking out the file and select the Data Cards and Data Mapping Exercise project file.

6. Log in to Vault as **administrator**, if required.

7. In the Autodesk Vault ribbon, click **Data Cards**.

8. The fingertip view of the data card for the clamp displays.

9. Click the **>>** (Expand) button on the fingertip view to switch to full data card view.

10. Note that the title says Home and that there is only 1 card in the deck, as shown below. Now you will add data cards for referenced parts.

11. At the top of the full data card view, click **Get Entire Model** from the drop-down list in the toolbar.

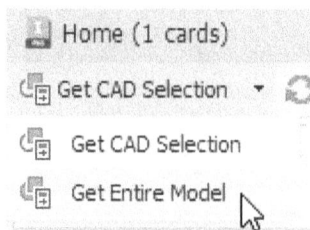

- Data cards for all of the design components are retrieved.

Task 2: Edit properties for a single data card.

You now have a card deck consisting of data cards for all of the components in the Clamp.iam design. Note that one of the cards has a non-compliant icon next to it.

1. Click the **Lower_Plate.ipt** name in the card list to go directly to that card.

∧ Cards	Part Ih
... **File Name**	Descri
Handle_Assembly.iam.dwf	Categ
Lower_Plate.ipt	State
Lower_Plate.ipt.dwf	Revisi
Pin_A.ipt	Desigr
Pin_A.ipt.dwf	Engine

2. The *Cost Center* property for the Lower_Plate.ipt does not comply with property policy. In this case, the minimum character length for *Cost Center* is six characters.

3. Click **Edit** to enter editing mode.

4. Click the ellipsis (...) in the *Value* field for *Cost Center*.

5. The Edit Value for Cost Center dialog box opens. Note that only one card is using the **11385** cost center but no other cards in the deck are using a cost center. You will fix this in a few steps.

Edit Value for Cost Center	✕
11385	✕
Value	**Count** ▾
11385	1

⑦   Save   Cancel

6. Enter **113850** in the entry field at the top of the dialog box and click **Save**.

7. The *Cost Center* value has been updated. Note that the new value is in bold blue in the data card field. This means that the value has been changed but it has not been applied yet.

8. Click **Apply** on the data card to commit the change. A Property Edit Result dialog box displays whether the change was a success. Click **Close** to exit this dialog box.

Property	Success	Original Value	New Value	Reason
▼ Name: Lower_Plate.ipt				
Cost Center	☑	11385	113850	New property value saved to vault.
Cost Center	☑	11385	113850	Property updated successfully in local file.

Property Edit Result ✕

Close   Help

9. Click **Home** in the data card toolbar to return to the Home card in the card deck. Note that the compliance error has been resolved.

10. Double-click on the **Upper_Plate.ipt** file in the card list to go directly to that card.

11. Since this part is from the same cost center as the Lower_Plate.ipt, ensure that this card is updated as well. To do so, click **Edit**.

12. Click the ellipsis (...) beside the *Cost Center* value.

13. All available values are listed or you can enter one manually. Since you know that this part shares the same cost center as the previous part, simply double-click on the **113850** value and it enters that same value in the entry field.

14. Click **Save** to close the dialog box.

15. Click **Apply** on the Upper_Plate.ipt data card to commit the changes.

16. Click **Close** in the Property Edit Result dialog box.

17. Click **Home** to return to the Home card.

Task 3: Edit properties for multiple data cards.

Pin_A.ipt, Pin_B.ipt, and Grip.ipt all share the same cost center but it's different from the one you just did. Rather than edit them one at a time, you can make a mass edit from the Home card.

1. Select **Grip.ipt**, **Pin_A.ipt**, and **Pin_B.ipt** in the data cards list by holding <Ctrl> as you click on the filenames.

2. Click **Edit** in the Home card.

3. Click the ellipsis (...) next to the value for *Cost Center*.

4. In the Edit Value for Cost Center dialog box, enter **116677** and click **Save**.

5. Click **Apply** to commit the changes.

6. The Property Edit Result dialog box shows the multiple changes and whether they were saved to the server successfully.

Property	Success	Original Value	New Value	Reason
Name: Grip.ipt				
Cost Center	☑		116677	New property value saved to vault.
Cost Center	☑		116677	Property updated successfully in local file.
Name: Pin_A.ipt				
Cost Center	☑		116677	New property value saved to vault.
Cost Center	☑		116677	Property updated successfully in local file.
Name: Pin_B.ipt				
Cost Center	☑		116677	New property value saved to vault.
Cost Center	☑		116677	Property updated successfully in local file.

Property Edit Result ✕

[Close] [Help]

7. Click **Close** to exit the dialog box.

8. In the Home card, select all of the cards in the card list. Note that the *Cost Center* says **VARIES**. This means that more than one value exists for *Cost Center* in the selected group of cards.

9. Click the ellipsis (...) to review the different values for *Cost Center* in the deck. Note that the *Count* column indicates how many cards share each value.

10. Double-click the value that is blank and click **Filter**.

11. The data cards with the empty (blank) value are automatically highlighted in the Home card list.

12. Click **Edit**.

13. Click the ellipsis (...) beside the *Cost Center* value.

14. Enter **889921** in the Edit Value for Cost Center dialog box and click **Save**.

15. Click **Apply** to commit the changes.

16. Click **Close** in the Property Edit Result dialog box. All *Cost Center* values are now updated.

End of practice

8.2 Data Mapping and Report Generation

Overview

The **Data Mapping** feature enables you to easily assess important business data for your model. Report data is mapped on to the model to provide visual output of the correlation between report results and the open model. Mapping the report to the model colors the model to match the corresponding chart elements. The entire chart can be mapped onto the model, or you can choose which chart elements to map.

Use data mapping to visually evaluate your design.

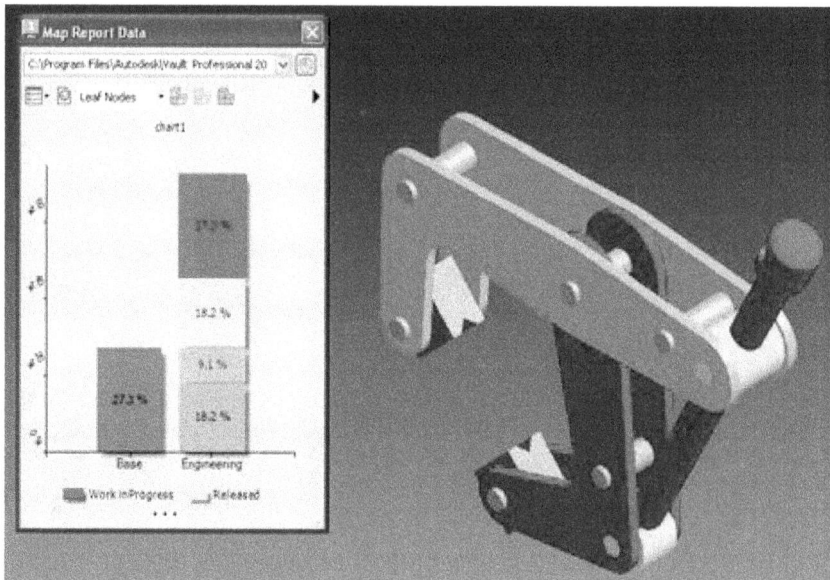

Objectives

After completing this lesson, you will be able to:

* Map your data onto a model.

* Generate a report based on your data mapping results.

* Manage chart elements.

* Configure the color assignments for your reports.

Introduction to the Data Mapping

Data mapping is a useful tool for viewing different levels of data in a model. However, because the model hierarchy can be mapped at different levels, it is important to know from where the data is being collected to accurately interpret the results. Additionally, you should also know how file attachments affect the report results.

> **Note:** *Data Mapping is not available in sketch mode.*

Enabling Data Mapping

Data mapping must be enabled before you can generate reports or map any model data for review. In the Autodesk Vault ribbon, click **Data Mapping** to launch the Map Report Data dialog box.

File Attachments

A report is generated using all of the files in the current model, including attachments. As a result, the chart might not have a 1:1 correlation with the files displayed in the canvas.

For example, a pie chart slice can indicate that a large percentage of files are currently in the Work in Progress (WIP) state. However, when mapping the data onto the model, only a small number of files are color coded to the WIP slice. This difference in display is because the slice is taking into account the attached files and the part files, but only the part files display on canvas. You can view the full report to see a complete list of files that make up a pie slice.

Mapping Report Data to the Model Hierarchy

When a report is generated, the reporting system evaluates the files without knowledge of their relationships. The resulting chart represents actual flat data. Since a model has several levels to it, you have the option of mapping your data as three different levels to better understand the report data. This versatility enables you to examine model data at the parts level, the assemblies' level, and the first children level. By examining all three levels, you will have the most complete picture of the report results.

Leaf Node Mapping

Leaf node mapping is the most granular view of the model. Only parts in assemblies are mapped. This level is used most often early in a project to see where components are in the development process.

All Assemblies Mapping

All assemblies mapping provides a perspective of the report results as they relate to the assembly level and first level parts. The color of an assembly determines the color of its parts but subassemblies are assigned their own colors.

First Level Children Mapping

First level children mapping is the least granular view. All parts and assemblies within each first level child are given the same color as the first level child.

Mapping Your Data

The Map Report Data dialog box contains several features that enable you to generate reports, map report results, and manage chart elements. The Map Report Data dialog box turns opaque when the mouse moves over it and transparent when the mouse moves away. The chart legend can be toggled on or off to further reduce the size of the dialog box and conserve canvas space.

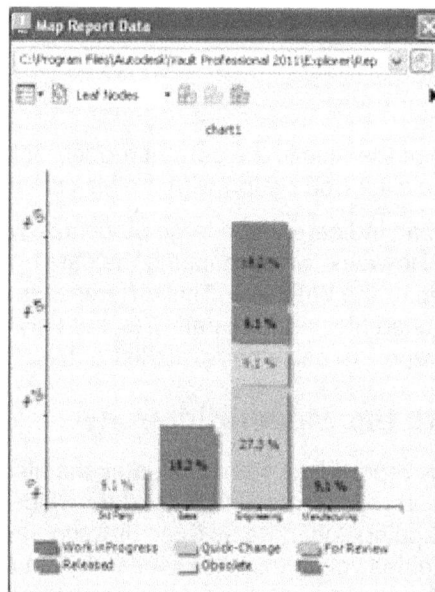

When the Map Report Data dialog box first opens, only the **Report Template** menu and the **Generate Report** button are enabled. All other controls are disabled until a report is generated.

Since the Map Report Data dialog box is document-based, each document can have its own dialog box.

Understanding the Map Report Dialog Box

The following table describes each of the features available in the Map Report Data dialog box.

	Feature	Description
no icon	**Report Template menu**	The report template drop-down list contains a list of the most recently used templates and the options for opening an existing template from either a local folder or the vault.
		Note: Opening a template from the vault checks that file out of the vault. The file is checked in after it is saved.
	Generate Report	Creates a report based on the selected template. Click the button again to refresh report results after making changes.
	Display Options	Enables or disables chart labels and the chart legend.
	View Full Report	Displays the full report in a report viewer.
Leaf Nodes ▾	**Mapping Method menu**	Enables you to select which of the three mapping methods to use when mapping chart data or isolating files. The three options are: leaf nodes, all assemblies, and first level children.
	Apply Color Mapping	Assigns the chart element colors to the corresponding model components based on the selected mapping method.
		This button is a toggle and can be clicked again to toggle off color assignments.
	Apply Isolation	Dims the files that are not represented by the chart elements and leaves the selected chart data mapped on the screen at full visibility. The data is isolated based on the current mapping method.
		This button is a toggle and can be clicked again to toggle off isolation and restore all files to full visibility.
	Clear Color Mapping or Isolation	Updates the current mapping and isolation display if any changes are made to the chart element selection.
		Note: If new data is added to the vault, the report must be regenerated. This button does not re-run the report.
▶	**Chart Selector**	Enables you to select which chart to use for data mapping if more than one chart exists for the template.
		If data is currently mapped when a new chart is selected, the data is cleared. Click Data Mapping to map the data from the new chart.

	Feature	Description
	Chart element context menu	Enables you to select and manage chart elements for custom data mapping. Access the menu by right-clicking on any of the elements in the.
		By default, all chart elements are mapped to the model.
	Chart Legend	Displays the chart elements and associated color map data graph assignments in a colorful graph.

How To: Map Report Data

After generating a report, you can map the results onto the open model in Inventor.

1. Generate a report. See the previous section for more information on generating a report.
2. Once the report is generated, select one of the three mapping methods.
3. Click **Map Report**. The model is colored relative to the report displayed in the data map control.

    Note: The report is generated using all of the files in the current model, including attachments. The resulting chart might not have a 1:1 correlation with the files displayed in the canvas. View the full report to see a complete list of files that make up the pie slice.

Creating Reports for Your Model

The reporting feature, when used in conjunction with data mapping, lets you map report data to the canvas for visual overview of a model's status and development. This information makes it easier to track designs and projects throughout their lifecycles. You can generate reports of model data based on any of the templates supplied with the client. The report feature is accessed from the Data Mapping dialog box.

AUTODESK.

System File Properties by Category Report

Folder Name   :
Generated By   :
Date   : 7/15/2015 4:52:05 PM
Search Root   :
Search Conditions   :

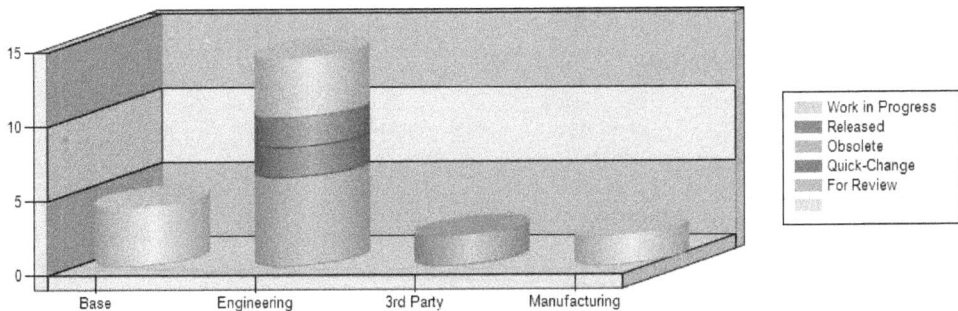

Report Templates

Several report templates are provided with the Autodesk Vault client. These report templates contain a color palette for a chart, but the templates do not specify which color is assigned to which chart element. You can specify how chart elements are color coded when you use the data mapping feature. Color coding chart elements enables quick, repeatable viewing of model data.

You can assign standard color mapping in the Assign Color dialog box in the Autodesk Vault client. Access the dialog by selecting **Tools>Administration>Vault Settings**. Select the *Behaviors* tab and then select **Define** under *Report Management*.

> *Note: Refer to the chapter on Reporting for more information on working with report templates.*

Report Charts

The in-CAD report feature can display data in four different charts:

- Pie chart
- Doughnut chart
- Column chart
- Stacked column chart

> *Note: If a report contains a chart type not supported by the in-CAD report control, the chart is not displayed on the CAD canvas. The report can be viewed outside the application with a report viewer.*

How To: View the Full Report

In addition to mapping the data from the report onto the Inventor model, you can view the complete report including any tables and additional layout and formatting.

Click Generate Report

Select a Template

Once report is generated, click View Full Report

1. Enable report control by clicking **Data Mapping** in the Autodesk Vault ribbon. The Map Report Data dialog box displays.

2. In the Map Report Data dialog box, select a report template from the drop-down list, or open a new template from a local folder or the vault.

3. Click the **Generate Report** icon. A progress bar displays with the status of the report. Depending on the size of your model, this process can take a few minutes. You can continue to work while the report is being generated.

   • Once the report has been generated, the report chart displays in the data mapping control.

4. Click the **View Full Report** icon to display the full report.

Managing Chart Elements

The ability to manipulate chart elements makes it easier to customize how you view your report data when it is mapped. The chart control enables you to override chart colors, create a selection set of files in Inventor based on chart elements and the mapped components, and retrieve a data card deck for the mapped components through a convenient context menu.

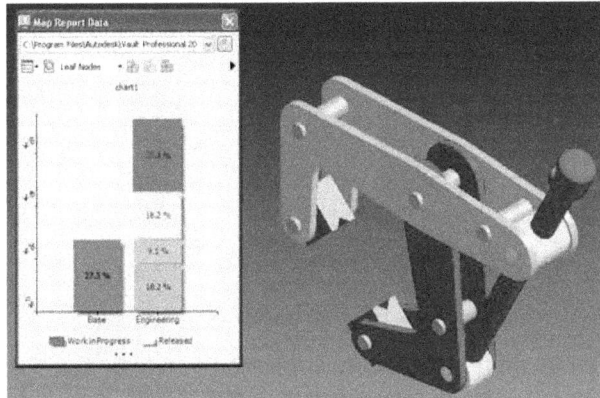

Selecting Chart Elements

When you map report data, all chart elements are mapped to the model by default. However, you can select individual chart elements in the report and map only those elements. Additionally, you can manipulate the way the data displays on the open model.

There are three ways to select chart elements. Once the chart elements are selected, use the context menu to customize how the data is mapped or viewed.

* Click a single element in the chart to select it. The element is outlined in red.

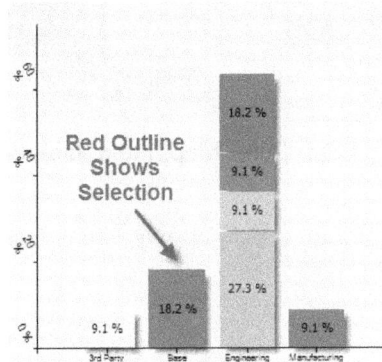

- Hold <Ctrl> and click multiple chart elements to select multiple chart elements and act on those elements using the context menu.

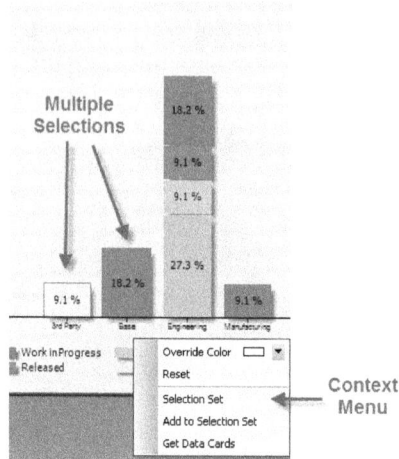

- Double-click on different chart elements to separate them from the chart. When **Map Data** is toggled on or the data mapping is refreshed, the selected pieces are mapped on the model.

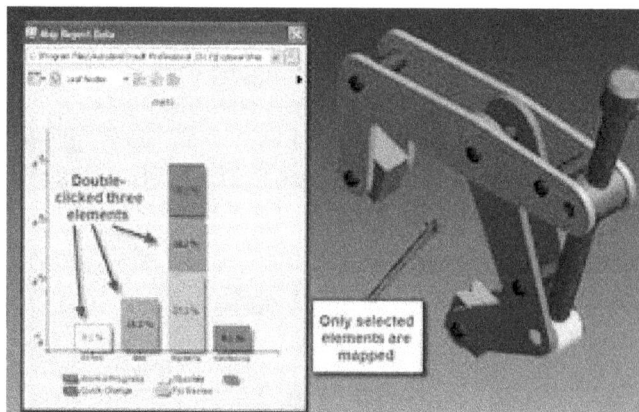

- Once a selection is made, click **Clear Color Mapping** or **Isolation** to update the data mapping or to update the isolation.

Note: Changes to element selection and color overrides are not mapped onto the model until you update the mapping.

Chart Context Menu

A context menu provides additional options for manipulating mapped data and customizing the view.

Command	Definition
Override Color	Enables you to specify a different color for a chart element.
Reset	Removes a color override.
Selection Set	Creates a selection set from the components corresponding to the selected chart elements. The corresponding components are selected in the browser and the canvas.
Add to Selection Set	Includes the components corresponding to the chart element to the current selection set.
Get Data Cards	Retrieves data cards for each of the currently mapped components.

Managing Data Mapping Reports

The report management feature enables the administrator to assign colors to values in a report template. When the template is used by the report generation feature in the CAD application, the colors are automatically assigned to their associated values. The administrator can also remove unused or outdated values from the report template.

When a report is generated that returns a value for which a color has not yet been assigned, the report control will assign a color to the new value from a predetermined list of colors and write back the report template a name and value pair for the new color. The new value and default color assignment display in the Assign Color dialog box, where the administrator can update the template by assigning a color to this new value.

The Assign Color Dialog Box

When a template is opened in the Assign Color dialog box, the chart elements contained in the template are listed along with the currently assigned color for each element. If the template contains more than one chart, the chart elements are grouped by chart.

Templates can be opened from a local folder or from Autodesk Vault. The *Value* column will be populated with the names of chart elements only if a report has already been generated. If no report has been generated, the fields in the *Value* column are blank.

By default, the Assign Color dialog box displays a default palette of eight colors. Unless specified in the template, the colors are assigned to chart elements in this order:

- Grey
- Red
- Orange
- Yellow
- Light Green
- Cyan
- Blue
- Violet

You can enter the exact chart element name in the *Value* field and then select a color to assign that color to the chart element. Remember to save the template to commit the changes.

How To: Manage Report Templates

1. From the Tools menu, select **Administration>Vault Settings**.
2. In the Vault Settings dialog box, select the *Behaviors* tab.
3. Select **Define** under *Report Management* to open the Assign Color dialog box.
4. From the File menu, open a report template from either the vault or a local folder.

   Note: If the template is stored in the vault and the administrator has write-permission on the current file, the template is checked out of the vault.

5. If the template does not contain any custom color properties, the default color palette displays. If the custom color properties have already been added to the template, the value names are extracted and displayed with their assigned color in the dialog box. Any new values without an assigned color display with the next available color in the default list.
6. Do one of the following:
   - Specify a new color assignment for an existing property by selecting a new color in the *Color* field.
   - Enter the exact value name for a new property in the *Value* field.
   - Select a color to assign to the property from the *Color* field.
7. Select **File>Save** to commit the changes. If the template was checked out of the vault, it is checked back in after being saved.

Practice 8b
Map Your Data

In this practice, you learn to generate a report based on your model's data and map report data to the open model.

Task 1: Create a full report.

1. If required, start Autodesk Vault. Log in using the following information:
   - For *User Name*, enter **administrator**.
   - Leave the *Password* field blank.
   - For *Vault*, select **Data Card and Mapping Vault**.
2. In the Navigation pane, click **Project Explorer ($)**.
3. Click **Find** in the toolbar.
4. In the Find dialog box, search for **Clamp.iam**.
5. Right-click on **Clamp.iam** and select **Open** to launch it in Autodesk Inventor.

6. In the Autodesk Vault ribbon, click **Data Mapping**.

7. The Map Report Data dialog box opens. Select **Open Local Template** from the Select Report Template drop-down list.

8. Navigate to *C:\Program Files\Autodesk\Vault Client edition\Explorer\Report Templates* and select the **File By Category.rdlc** report template.

   Note: If you receive a warning indicating the template is read-only, a workaround is to check in the File By Category.rdlc template file to the vault and use the Open from Vault command instead of Open Local Template.

9. Click **Open**.

10. In the Map Report Data dialog box, click **Generate Report**.

11. A bar graph report displays in the Map Report Data dialog box. The graph shows a percentage breakdown of files in each category based on state. The available states in the example below are Work in Progress, Quick-Change, For Review, Released, Obsolete, or no state.

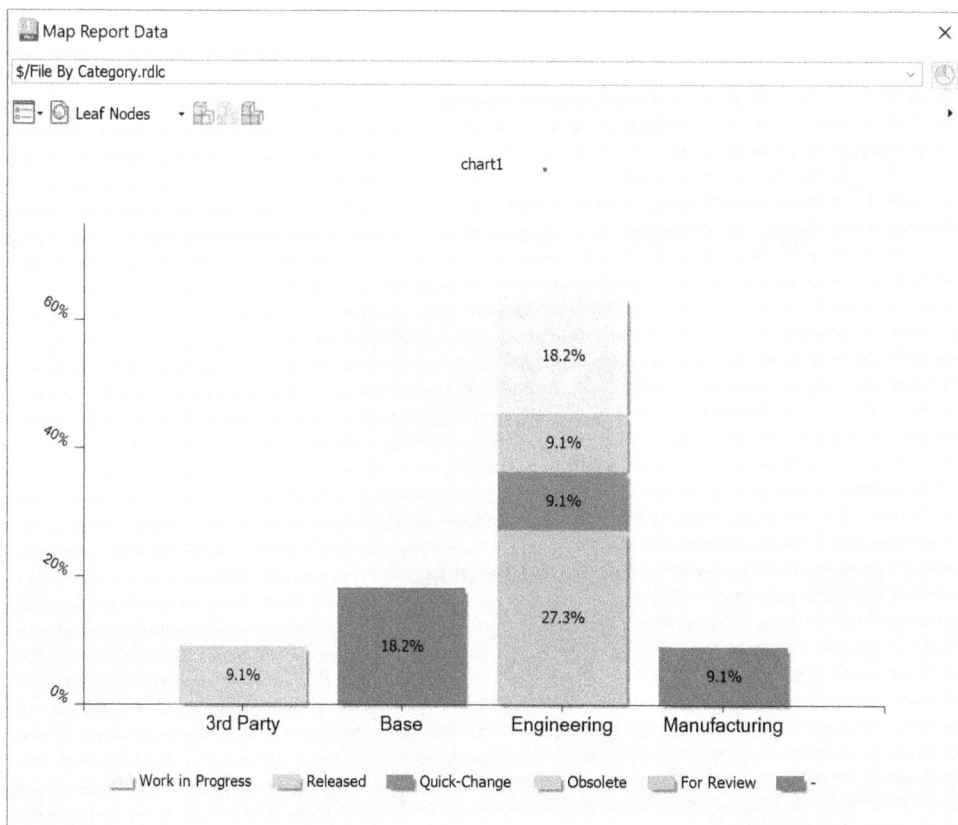

12. Click **View Full Report** to see the report in printable format.

The report automatically launches in Microsoft Viewer.

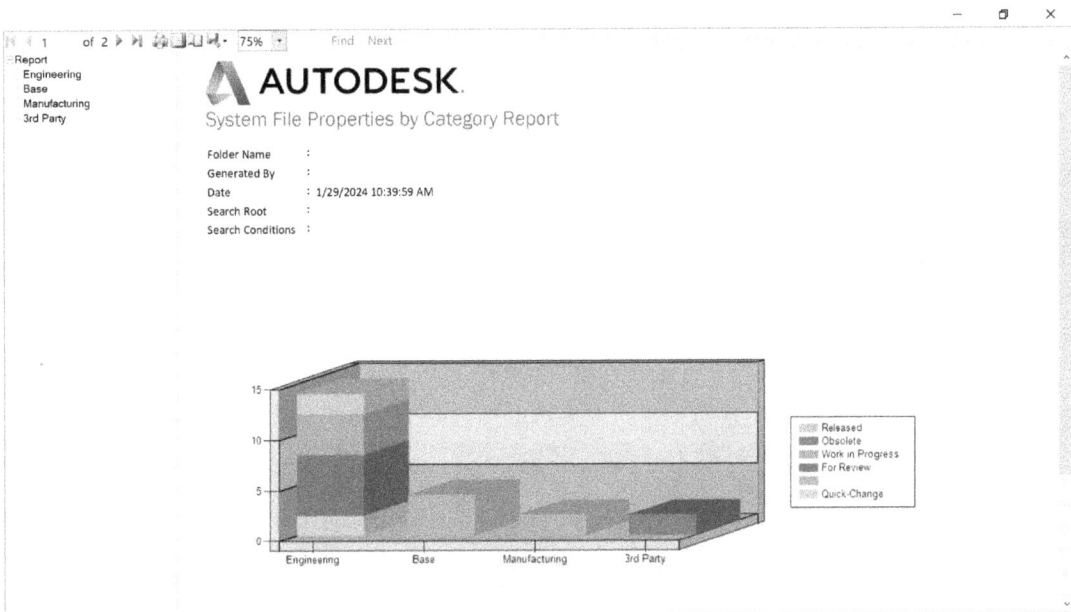

13. Click **Export** and select **PDF** to save the file to a local folder as a PDF. The file can then be emailed or stored in a vault.

Task 2: Map report data to the model.

It can be useful to view the report data on the model for an easier understanding of the state of the design.

1. Go to the Map Report Data dialog box that is still open from the previous task. If you closed the dialog box, simply click **Data Mapping** and generate the report once more.

2. Click **Apply Color Mapping** to map the report data to the model in its entirety.

- By examining the model and referencing the Map Report legend, you can determine the state of each component. For example, the Lower_Plate.ipt is in the For Review state.

3. In the Map Report Data dialog box, double-click on the **For Review** section of the Engineering bar.

4. In the Map Report Data toolbar, click **Apply Isolation** to show only the For Review pieces in the model.

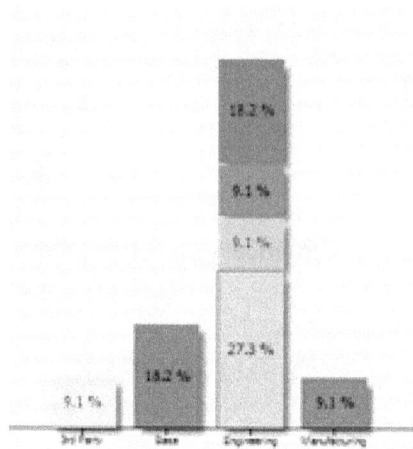

5. Examine the components in the Released and Quick-Change states. In the Map Report Data dialog box, double-click on the **Released** and **Quick-Change** pieces as well.

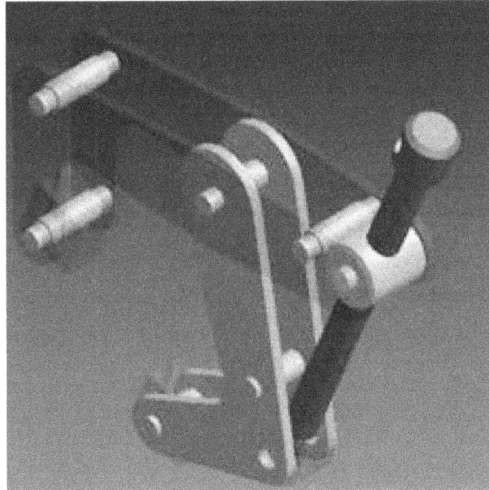

- The components are mapped on the model and all other components are transparent.

End of practice

8.3 Sheet Set Manager Integration

Overview

Autodesk Vault Professional integrates with the AutoCAD Sheet Set Manager (SSM) for supported AutoCAD products. This integration enables you to add, access, and modify the sheet sets to Vault. You can also access and modify sheet sets in a collaborative environment. In addition, users can rely on up-to-date Vault status on sheet drawings in Sheet Set Manager.

Vault also supports all sheet set functionality, including property management, plotting, and publishing tasks. In Vault Explorer, you can use search capabilities to find sheets and sheet sets based on properties inside the sheet set manager. Sheets are represented as files in the Vault which gives you the relationship between sheets and associated drawings.

Once you start working on a sheet set in a Vault environment, there are some changes to how certain Sheet Set commands work.

Objectives

After completing this lesson, you will be able to:

*   Understand how to work on a sheet set with Autodesk Vault.

Resave All Sheets

When you work on a sheet set with Vault, you are working in a collaborative environment. When you resave all sheets, note the following differences:

- When working in a shared sandbox environment, you can **Resave All** as long as none of the sheets/files involved is currently checked out by other users. The **Resave All** command gets aborted if there are files that cannot be checked out and, therefore, saved. A file might not be available for check out if it is currently checked out to another user or if vault constraints restrict access to the file.

- When working in a non-shared sandbox environment, you can **Resave All** even if some of the files are checked out by other users. You get a list of files that are not available for saving when the sheet set command is completed.

Remove Sheet or Sheet Subset

When you remove a sheet or subset from a vaulted sheet set, its equivalent vaulted copy is NOT removed automatically. As a result, if you were to reuse the same sheet or sheet subset name, you are informed that the files already exist in the Vault.

> *Note: Historical references from sheets or sheet set files are lost when they are removed with Vault Explorer.*

If the removed sheet or sheet subset files are expired or redundant, you can remove them via Vault Explorer.

Move, Rename, and Copy Design in the Vault Client

Move, **Rename**, and **Copy Design** changes made in the Vault Client are ignored when you open the edited sheet set in SSM.

Working with Items

This chapter describes how to create and manage items in Autodesk® Vault Professional. You can assign items to CAD files in the vault or create new items for products not specifically modeled in CAD.

Items are used to represent the design data, but a large collection of items can be difficult to manage in the vault. By using customized views and filters, you can sort or filter the item list based on item properties to manage the items effectively.

Learning Objectives

- Create, modify, and delete items, use filters to view items, and add and remove file attachments.
- Create, modify, and delete custom views, use filters to view items, and find items.
- Work with default item properties and user-defined properties, including item numbers.
- Export item data.

9.1 Creating Items

Overview

In this lesson, you learn how to create, modify, and delete items, use filters to view items, and add and remove file attachments.

Use items to help manage your vault data and make that data available to the extended design team.

Objectives

After completing this lesson, you will be able to:

- Create items by assigning items to selected design data from Autodesk Vault.

- Work with the Item Master.

- Assign items to files in a vault, and create new items from scratch.

- Attach engineering documents such as specifications, design and product data sheets, and regulatory documents to items.

- Use automatic attachments to expedite assigning items to files in the vault.

About Items

Working with items is a crucial part of automating the data management process and maintaining control of your design data. When a new design is added to the vault, each part or assembly can be assigned an item so it can be clearly identified.

You create items by assigning them to design data from the vault or by creating a new item directly in the Item Master.

Definition of Items

Items represent physical elements that a company uses to produce the products it manufactures. Common items include parts and assemblies, documents, consumable goods such as grease, paint, fluids, and lubricants, and even artwork. Some items are purchased while others are manufactured by the company.

An item is identified by a unique identifier (the item number). This number is used to identify the item in change orders, product lists, bills of materials, and ERP systems.

	Number	Revision	State	Title (Item,CO)	
	100019	-	Released	Long Rail	

Example of Assigning Items

As part of a new design, a new part is added to the vault. You assign an item to the part. The new item has a unique item number, which can be as simple as a six number sequence (Part 100352) or a complex set of text and numbers (Part RD-100-0152).

This item number normally follows company standards and is used to help identify the item. The application uses this number to track the item through its lifecycle.

Item Master

To manage and track the lifecycle of items used in product development, users are required to access a list of items where they can preview, create, modify, and delete items as required. The Item Master is where this list of items is found.

About the Item Master

The Item Master contains a complete list of all items in the Vault. These items usually represent design data in the vault. Items in the Item Master are identified by unique identifiers (item numbers). Each item has a number of system and user-defined properties.

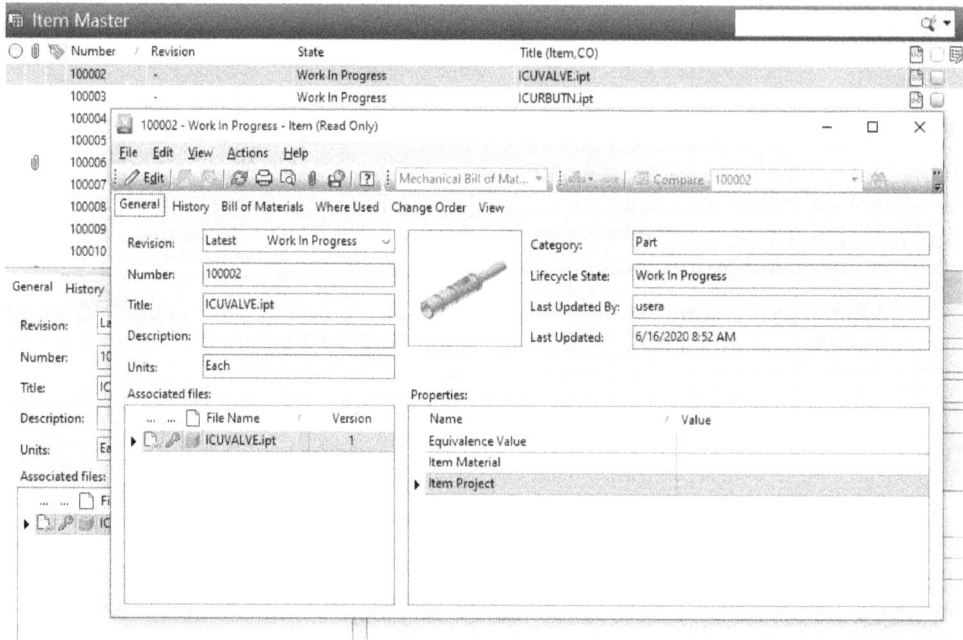

Using the Item Master

Using the Item Master, you can:

- List all items in the system and define custom views to filter the list.

- Add or remove columns (fields) in the list, change column order and width, and sort by any column.

- Group items by column headings.

- Preview comments automatically.

- Go to a specific item.

- Find an item or items, and optionally save the search.

- Change column text alignment.

- Create new items.

- Edit items.

- Preview items in the Preview pane.

Example of the Item Master

As new designs are added to the vault and assigned items, the Item Master list grows.

	Number	Re...	State	Title (Item,CO)
🔒	100015	-	Released	Dowel - Black Walnut
	100012	-	Work In Pr...	Grip.ipt
	100031	-	Work In Pr...	ICU Button Paint
	100030	-	Work In Pr...	ICU O-Ring Lubricant
	100028	-	Work In Pr...	ICU Valve Main Assembly.iam
	100027	-	Work In Pr...	ICUENDCP.ipt
	100025	-	Work In Pr...	ICUHOUSG.ipt
	100026	-	Work In Pr...	ICULBUTN.ipt
	100023	-	Work In Pr...	ICUORING.ipt
	100022	-	Work In Pr...	ICURBUTN.ipt

Item Master — Search Item Master

Creating Items

Typically when you create items you assign them to data files in the vault. In some cases, you need to create an item that is not modeled in the design. Examples include purchased items or items that are typically not modeled such as lubricants, paint, artwork, or packaging. You can include these items in the Item Master by creating new items. Another example would be when you follow a "BOM first" workflow. You create a list of items in the Item Master based on what you know about the BOM structure and then fill it in with CAD data at a later time.

Items can be created in the following ways:

- Use the **New Item** command in the Item Master to create an item from scratch.

- Assign an item to a file using the **Assign Item** command.

- Drag and drop files into the *Item Master* tab.

- Drag and drop files into the **Item Master** node in the browser.

If an item is in read-only mode, you can use **File>Save As** to copy the item's properties, BOM rows, and attachments to a new item. The new item is automatically added to the Item Master and opened in read-only mode. Note that file links are not copied to the new item. For this reason, CAD rows are copied over as manual rows.

How To: Create New Items

The following steps describe how to create new items using the **New Item** command.

1. Select **Item Master**.
2. In the Standard toolbar, click **New**.
3. If the administrator has granted you permission to assign item categories, select a category and click **OK** to continue to the new item record.

4. Review the item properties. If required, add or change the units and add a title and description.

5. Click **Save and Close**. The new item is created. Note that you can change item numbers using **Actions>Change Number**.

How To: Assign Items to Files in Vault

The following steps describe how to assign items to files in Vault Professional using the **Assign/Update Item** command. Note that with Inventor files, only models should be assigned items. Inventor drawings will automatically be associated to items via their relationship to the models. AutoCAD drawings can be assigned items, as they do not make use of model files.

1. Ensure that all files to which you want to assign an item are checked in to the vault.

2. Select **Project Explorer**.

3. In the main pane, right-click on one or more files and select **Assign/Update Item**. A new item is created for each of the files selected and for the related files.

4. If you assign an item to a single file, the item record automatically opens for editing. Begin making changes, if required.

5. If you select multiple files and assign an item, an item icon displays in the *Item* column. However, you must right-click on a file and select **Open Item** to view the item record. Select **Edit** on the item record toolbar to begin editing. **Note:** Item numbering is automatically applied based on the default numbering scheme. However, if the numbering scheme requires user input, the Item Number dialog box opens. Enter the required values and click **OK** to continue.

6. Click **Save and Close** when you are finished.

7. The item master is updated with the new items. If items were assigned to Autodesk Inventor assembly files, any associated drawing (.IDW) and presentation (.IPN) files are linked to the items. If items were assigned to Inventor part files, the associated drawing (.IDW) files are linked to the items.

   Note: When you assign an item to an assembly file, all parts and subassemblies in that assembly must have items assigned as well. Items are assigned automatically to all the required files if they do not have items assigned already.

Attaching and Detaching Files

When you create an item from a file in the vault, the vault file is automatically attached to the item. You can manually attach additional supporting files such as documents or images. You can add attachments such as drawings for a purchased part, product specification sheets, assembly instructions, regulatory documents, material safety data sheets, rendered images of the product, and so on.

You attach and detach files by editing items. By default, the latest version of an attached file displays when an item is updated.

File attachment links are represented in three ways: a primary associated file (displays a blue key), a secondary association (displays a gray key), or a general/automatic attachment (no key shown).

In some cases, you might want to maintain a specific version of an attached file by pinning the attached file. When pinned, the version of the file specified when the file was originally attached remains when the file or item is updated. This is useful in legacy data where an older part might be specified by a previous version of a now updated specification.

How To: Manage File Attachments

The following steps describe how to attach files to items or detach files from items.

1. Right-click on an item and select **Attachments**. The current attachments for the item display in the Attachments dialog box.

2. To manually attach files, click **Attach** and browse to the location of the file or click **Search** to find files in the vault. Select one or more files and click **Open**. The most recent version of the attached file displays in the Attachments dialog box. An additional method to attach files to an item is to open an item and change to edit mode, then drag and drop a file from Vault into the item's attachments window. **Note:** The item must be in a Work in Progress state to modify attachments.

3. Modify the way an **Item Update** operates on the attached files. By default, attached files update to the most recent version each time the item is updated. You can pin a particular version of the file to the item so that it references that version instead of the newest version during item updates.

4. Select the *Version Number* field and select the version of the file you want to pin from the drop-down list.

5. Select the **Pin** checkbox to pin the file to the specified version. During an update, the file version specified at the time of attachment remains attached to the item and the item is updated with the most current information from that file version.

6. To detach a file, select the file and click **Detach**.

7. Click **OK** to save your changes and close the dialog box.

Automatic Attachments

Some files are associated automatically with the primary associated file when it is promoted to an item.

Definition of Automatic Attachments

When you add CAD files to a vault, the relationships and links between files are maintained. For example, the links between an assembly file and its part and subassembly files are maintained by the vault. These linked files are automatically promoted to items when the assembly is promoted. In a similar way, cross-reference links between drawings in AutoCAD®, AutoCAD® Mechanical, AutoCAD® Electrical, or Autodesk® Civil 3D® are also maintained in Vault.

Example of Automatic Attachments

An Inventor drawing is created from an Inventor part, and both are checked in to the vault. In Project Explorer, the two files are visible.

After assigning an item to the Grip.ipt part, the Grip.idw file also shows a link to an item in Project Explorer.

After assigning an item to the Grip.ipt part, the item also shows a link to both the files in the *Associated files* list on the *General* tab. Note that the key icon indicates the item's primary associated file.

Practice 9a
Assign Items to Vault Files

In this practice, you create a custom view for Vault, assign an item to a part and an assembly, and attach files to an item.

The completed practice

Task 1: Create a custom view.

1. Start Autodesk Vault Professional. Log in using the following information:
   - For *User Name*, enter **administrator**.
   - Leave the *Password* field blank.
   - For *Vault*, select **AOTCVault**.
2. In the Navigation pane, click **Home** and expand **AOTCVault**. Expand **Project Explorer**.

3. Navigate to the *Designs\ICU Valve* folder.

4. In the Advanced toolbar, select **Define custom views** from the toolbar drop-down list.

5. In the Manage Custom Views dialog box, do the following:

   - Click **New**.
   - Under *View Name*, enter **Thumbnails**.
   - Click **OK**.

6. In the Manage Custom Views dialog box, select the **Thumbnails** view. Click **Modify**.

7. Click **Fields**.

8. In the Customize Fields dialog box, do the following:

   - In the Select available fields from drop-down list, select **Any**.
   - In the *Available fields* list, multi-select **Attachments**, **Checked In**, **Created By**, and **Thumbnail**. Click **Add**.

- Under *Show these fields in this order*, select **Thumbnail**. Click **Move Up** until Thumbnail displays above Name. Order the fields as shown in the following image.

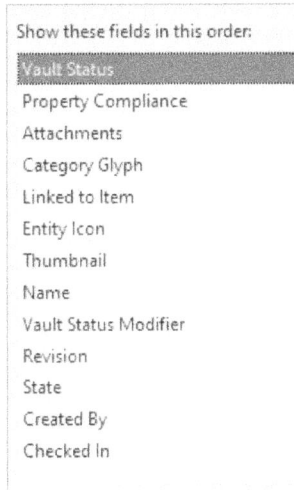

- Click **OK**.

9. Click **Close** twice to close the other dialog boxes. The main pane displays thumbnails (generated from the visualization files) of the files.

10. To adjust the size of the thumbnails, resize the *Thumbnail* column.

Task 2: Assign an item.

1. In the Advanced toolbar, click **Default View** from the toolbar drop-down list.

2. In the main pane, right-click on **ICUVALVE.ipt**.
3. Select **Assign/Update Item**.

4. The item is created for ICUVALVE.ipt, displaying the *General* tab information.

5. In the toolbar, click **Save and Close** to save the item and close the window.

6. In the main window, place the pointer on the item icon located in the last grid column. The Go to Item tooltip displays.

7. Hold <Ctrl> and click the item icon to display the item. Note the tabs in the Preview pane.

8. Under Home, click **Designs\ICU Valve**.

9. In the main pane, drag **ICU Valve Main Assembly.iam** onto the Item Master node in the Navigation pane. A new Item is created for the assembly.

10. In the toolbar, click **Save and Close**.

11. An item icon displays next to all files in the *ICU Valve* folder.

- Note that when you assign an item to an assembly file, it automatically assigns items to all subassemblies and parts used in the assembly. Without these extra items, the bill of materials is incomplete.

12. Under Home, select **Item Master**. If required, in the Advanced toolbar drop-down list, select **All Items**. The list is updated with the new items.

Task 3: Attach files to an item.

1. In the Item Master window, select **ICU Valve Main Assembly.iam**.

2. In the Preview pane, select the *General* tab. Only one file is associated with the item in the main assembly.

3. In the Item Master, double-click **ICU Valve Main Assembly.iam**.

4. Click **Edit** to edit the item.

5. In the toolbar, click **Attachments**.

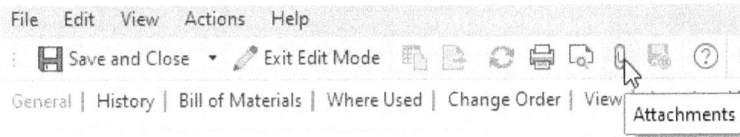

6. In the Attachments dialog box, click **Attach**.

7. Navigate to the *Designs\ICU Valve\Documents* folder. Select **ICU Valve Rendering.png** and click **Open**.

8. In the Attachments dialog box, click **OK**. The attached files are listed under the associated files.

9. In the toolbar, click **Save and Close**.

End of practice

Practice 9b
Create New Items

In this practice, you will create new items to represent physical objects not modeled in the vault.

	Number	Revision	State	Title (Item,CO)			
○	**Number**	**Revision**	**State**	**Title (Item,CO)**			
	100009	-	Work In Progress	ICUSPRNG.ipt		☐	
	100008	-	Work In Progress	ICURBUTN.ipt		☐	
	100007	-	Work In Progress	ICUVALVEASSY.iam		☑	
	100006	-	Work In Progress	ICUENDCP.ipt		☐	
	100005	-	Work In Progress	ICULBUTN.ipt		☐	
	100004	-	Work In Progress	ICUHOUSG.ipt		☐	
	100003	-	Work In Progress	ICU Valve Main Assembly.iam		☑	
	100002	-	Work In Progress	ICUVALVE.ipt		☐	
▸	100011	-	Work In Progress	O-Ring Lubricant		☑	

Item Master · Search Item Master

General | History | Bill of Materials | Where Used | Change Order | View | Associated Files | Datasheet

Revision: Latest   Work In Progress

Number: 100011

Title: O-Ring Lubricant

Description:

Units: Millimeter

Category: Purchased

Lifecycle State: Work In Progress

Last Updated By: Administrator

Last Updated: 12/21/2023 12:04 PM

Associated files:

... ... ☐	**File Name**	**Version**
▸ ⬗	ICU Valve Spec...	1

Properties:

Name	▲ **Value**
Equivalence Value	
▸ Item Project	

The completed practice

1. Start Autodesk Vault Professional. Log in using the following information:

   - For *User Name*, enter **administrator**.
   - Leave the *Password* field blank.
   - For *Vault*, select **AOTCVault**.

2. Under Home, click **Item Master**.

3. Right-click on **Item Master** and select **New Item**.

4. In the New Item – Select Category dialog box, select **Purchased** and click **OK**.

5. In the Edit Item dialog box, do the following:

    *   For *Title*, enter **O-Ring Lubricant.**
    *   For *Units*, select **Milliliter**.
    *   Click **Save and Close**.

6. The new item displays in the Item Master.

7. In the Item Master, right-click on the **O-Ring Lubricant** and select **Attachments**.

8. In the Attachments dialog box, click **Attach**.

9. Navigate to the *Designs\ICU Valve\Documents* folder. Select **ICU Valve Specification Sheet - Grease.doc** and click **Open**.

10. In the document row, in the Pinned icon column, select the checkbox.

11. Click **OK**.

End of practice

9.2 Working with Items

Overview

In this lesson, you learn how to create, modify, and delete customized views, use filters to view items, and work with item properties. You can also export items for use with other applications or to create reports.

You can use items to index and manage products in manufacturing. You also use items in the creation of bills of materials (BOMs) in Autodesk Vault Professional and in tracking change orders.

			Number	Revision	State	Title (Item,CO)
▶			100020	-	Work In Progress	ICUVALVE.ipt
			100021	-	Work In Progress	ICU O Ring Lubricant
			100022	-	Work In Progress	ICU Button Paint
			100023	-	Work In Progress	ICU Valve Main Assembly.iam
			100024	-	Work In Progress	ICULBUTN.ipt
			100025	-	Work In Progress	ICUHOUSG.ipt
			100026	-	Work In Progress	ICUSPRNG.ipt
			100027	-	Work In Progress	ICUENDCP.ipt
			100028	-	Work In Progress	ICURBUTN.ipt
			100029	-	Work In Progress	ICUORING.ipt
			100030	-	Work In Progress	ICUVALVEASSY.iam

Objectives

After completing this lesson, you will be able to:

- View specific items and files attached to the item.

- Use the *Where Used* tab to show item dependencies in the vault.

- Define custom filters to view and work with items.

- Use the Item Master to view, search, and filter items.

- Find items using **Go To**, shortcuts, and saved searches.

Using the Item Preview Pane to View Items

The extended design team requires access to design data. Because many team members outside the engineering team do not use CAD, items cannot be viewed directly in the native CAD application.

Visualization files are the main tools used for viewing items. Visualization files can be of different file formats but the most common are DWF and DWFx files. Visualization files can be published automatically when files are checked in to the vault, thereby making viewing items in the vault easier and faster. With 3D visualization files, users can pan, zoom, and orbit 3D Autodesk Inventor models. Individual components in an assembly can be shown, hidden, or isolated. With 2D visualization files, users can print and view drawings and mark them up to provide feedback.

Use the *View* tab in the Preview pane to view an item's associated vault files.

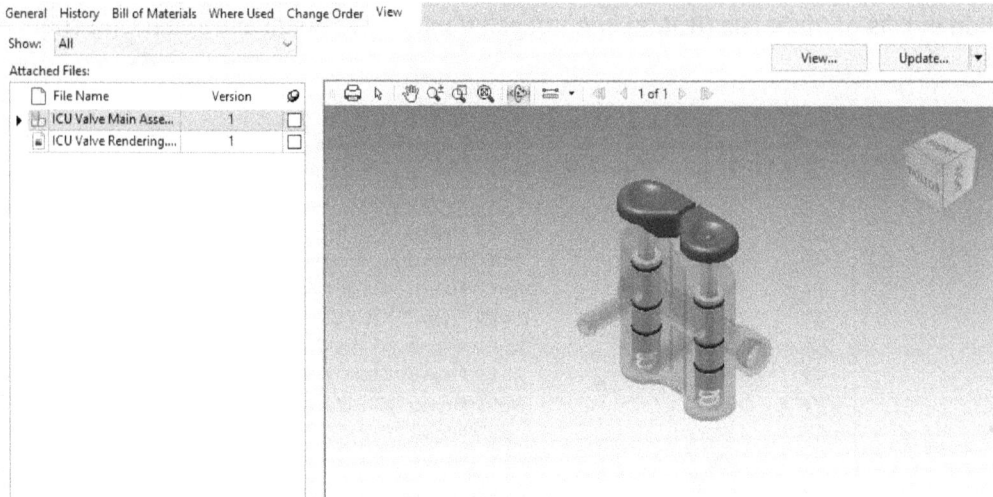

Viewing Revision History

You can view revisions on the *History* tab. Vault Professional provides thumbnail images of the different revisions to the file.

Thumbnail	Number	Version	Revision	State (Historical)	Title (Item,CO)	Category Name	Units
	100026	5	-	Work In Progress	ICULBUTN.ipt	Part	Each
	100-10006	4	-	Work In Progress	ICULBUTN.ipt		Each
	100008	3	-	Work In Progress	ICULBUTN.ipt		Each

How To: View an Item

The following steps describe how to view an item's associated files:

1. In the Item Master window, select the item.
2. In the Preview pane, click the *View* tab.
3. Select the file in the *Attached Files* list.

How To: View Data in a Separate Dialog Box

The following steps describe how to view data that opens in a separate dialog box:

1. In the Item Master window, select the item.
2. In the Preview pane, click the *View* tab.
3. Select the file in the *Attached Files* list and click on the thumbnail to display the file in the Preview pane.
4. Click **View** to open the file in a separate window.
5. Click **Maximize** in the upper-right corner to view in full screen mode.

Using the Where Used Tab

With the *Where Used* tab in the Preview pane, you can analyze where items are included in the vault. By detecting dependencies before making changes, you can avoid costly mistakes.

Example of Using the Where Used Tab

In the following illustration, the *Where Used* tab shows that the **ICUVALVE** part is used in the **ICUVALVEASSY** assembly. In turn, the assembly is used in the **ICU Valve Main Assembly** file. The part is used directly in one assembly (it has one direct parent) and is used in a total of two assemblies (total number of parents).

Define Custom Filters to View Items

The number of items in the system can grow quite rapidly, and finding items in the list can be difficult. Many methods are available to filter the item list. By default, a custom view is already applied to the Item Master, which shows the items that have been updated in the last seven days. The default custom view displays in the Advanced toolbar.

It is strongly recommended that you create custom views to filter your data. Customizing helps speed up the display of item lists because only filtered item data is retrieved from the server rather than the entire item list.

How To: Define a Custom Filter in the Item Master

The following steps describe how to define a custom filter in the Item Master:

1. In the Item Master list, right-click on the heading of a column and select **Customize View**.

2. In the Customize View dialog box, select **Custom Filters**.

3. In the Custom Filters dialog box, select an item property, condition, and value required.

4. Click **Add**.

5. If required, select additional properties, conditions, and values then add them to the criteria list.

6. Click **OK**. The Item Master list is filtered. A small filter symbol displays on the right side of the Item Master title bar.

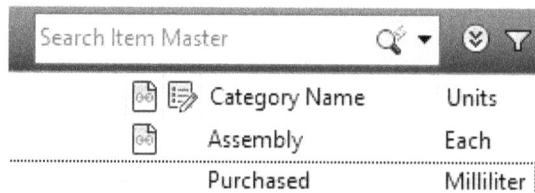

Note: If the Item Master list is not displaying items you expect to see, check the filter settings and ensure that it is displaying the required content.

How To: Save Custom Views

The following steps describe how to save custom views:

1. In the Advanced toolbar, from the Views list, select **Define custom views**.

2. In the Manage Custom Views dialog box, click **New**.
3. In the Create Custom View dialog box, enter the required view name. Click **OK**.

    Note: If a custom filter already exists (the filter icon displays on the Item Master title bar), then you might not want to edit the filter again. Skip the next four steps.

4. Click **Modify**.
5. In the Customize View dialog box, select **Custom Filters**.
6. In the Customize Filters dialog box, add the filter criteria.
7. Click **OK** to exit the Custom Filters dialog box. Click **Close** to exit the Customize View dialog box.
8. Click **Close** to exit the Manage Custom Views dialog box.

How To: Manage Custom Views

The following steps describe how to manage custom views:

1. In the Advanced toolbar, from the Views list, select **Define custom views**.
2. In the Manage Custom Views dialog box, select the required view name.

    Note: You cannot rename or delete the default custom views (e.g., All Items, Last 7 Days, etc.). Although not recommended, it is possible to add additional custom filter criteria to these two custom views.

3. Click **Modify**, **Copy**, **Rename**, or **Delete**, as required.
4. Close all dialog boxes.

    Note: Use the Custom View list in the Advanced toolbar to switch between custom views.

How To: Clear Custom Filters

The following steps describe how to clear custom filters:

1. In the Item Master window title bar, right-click on **Custom Filter Applied**.

2. Select **Clear Custom Filters**.

How To: Enable Filtering by Column

The following steps describe how to enable filtering by column:

1. On the right side of the column heading, click the **Column Filter** icon.

    Note: *Hover over the column you want to filter and the Column Filter icon will appear in the top right of the column.*

2. Select either the *Values* tab or *Text Filters* tab.

3. To create a filter from column values, in the *Values* tab, select checkboxes next to the files whose data you would like displayed. Click **Close** when finished.

4. To create a filter using text filters, in the *Text Filters* tab, select an operator from the drop-down list. Click **Close** when finished.

5. To create a custom filter, select the *Text Filters* tab and select **Custom Filter**, then define criteria.

Customize Column Display in the Item Master

Columns in the Item Master list represent item properties. Many item properties are available, and you can filter the number of columns (properties) displayed in the list.

In this procedure, you customize the Item Master view by working with the list columns.

How To: Remove Columns in the Item Master

The following steps describe how to remove a column in the list:

1. In the Item Master list, right-click on the column header you want to remove.
2. Select **Remove This Column**.

How To: Add, Remove, and Rearrange Columns in the Item Master

The following steps describe how to add, remove, and reorder columns:

1. In the Item Master list, right-click on a column header and select **Customize View**.
2. In the Customize View dialog box, click **Fields**.
3. In the Customize Fields dialog box, add and remove fields as required.
4. Customize the order of the fields by moving them up and down the list.

   Note: If you want to customize only the order of the fields (columns), drag the column headers to rearrange them in the Item Master list.

How To: Group Items by Column Header

The following steps describe how to group items by column header:

1. In the Advanced toolbar, click **Group By Box**.

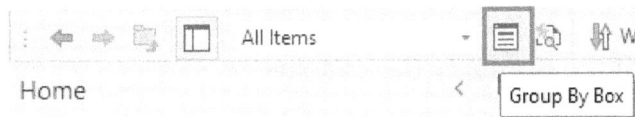

2. In the Item Master, drag a column header to the location indicated. The items in the list are automatically listed in groups based on the column header value. In the following illustration, the items are grouped by state.

Grouping by column header value can be useful when you work on a number of projects.

- Add a project name property to each item in the Item Master.
- Customize the view to show the item project field, then group the items by this field.

How To: Toggle Off the Group By Box Display

The following steps describe how to toggle off the Group By Box display:

1. In the Advanced toolbar, ensure that **Group By Box** is selected.
2. Drag the column header back to the header row.
3. In the Advanced toolbar, click **Group By Box** to disable the utility.

Find Items

In this procedure, you find items by using the item number, using shortcuts, and searching for items.

Search Tips

* Use **Go To** and go directly to an item.
* Use **My Shortcuts** to go to items.
* Search for items using **Find**.

How To: Go to a Specific Item by Item Number

The following steps describe how to go to a specific item by item number:

1. In the toolbar, click in the *Go to* box.

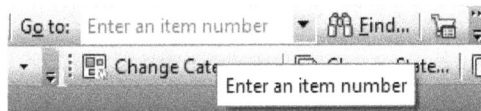

2. Enter an item number and press <Enter>.

How To: Create and Use Shortcuts to Navigate in the Item Master

The following steps describe how to create and use shortcuts to navigate in the Item Master:

1. In the Item Master, drag an item to the My Shortcuts window in the Navigation pane.

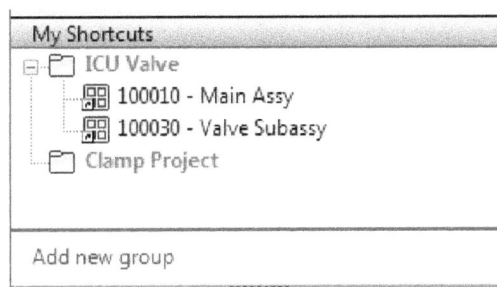

2. Under My Shortcuts, you can also add new groups (folders) to organize the shortcuts.
3. To go to an item, click the item shortcut.

How To: Search Items

The following steps describe how to search for an item or items and how to save the search:

1. In the search box, enter the search text.

2. Click **Search**. The items containing the search string display.
3. To save the search, do the following:

    *   In the search bar, click **Show search options** menu.
    *   Click **Save Search**.
    *   Enter a search name and click **OK**.

    *   The saved search displays in the Navigation pane under *My Search Folders*.

Practice 9c
Work with Items

In this practice, you will create shortcuts and a saved search for the project. You will also learn how to link the ICU Button Paint item to the ICU buttons, how to delete items, and how to export the Item Master view.

🔳 Item Master

◯ Number	Revision	State	Title (Item,CO)
100011	-	Work In Progress	O-Ring Lubricant
100010	-	Work In Progress	ICUORING.ipt
100009	-	Work In Progress	ICUSPRNG.ipt
100008	-	Work In Progress	ICURBUTN.ipt
100007	-	Work In Progress	ICUVALVEASSY.iam
100006	-	Work In Progress	ICUENDCP.ipt
100005	-	Work In Progress	ICULBUTN.ipt
100004	-	Work In Progress	ICUHOUSG.ipt
▸ 100003	-	Work In Progress	ICU Valve Main Assembly.iam
100002	-	Work In Progress	ICUVALVE.ipt
100012	-	Work In Progress	ICU Button Paint

General | History | Bill of Materials | Where Used | Change Order | View | Associated Files | Datasheet

Latest   Work In Progress ▾   Today   Multi-Level ▾   All Rows ▾

Number	Row Order	▲ Position Number	Quantity	Title (Item,CO)	Revision
▸ ▾ 🔳 100003	-		-	ICU Valve Main Assembly.iam	-
🔳 100004	1	1	1 Each	ICUHOUSG.ipt	-
🔳 100006	2	2	1 Each	ICUENDCP.ipt	-
▾ 🔳 100005	3	3	1 Each	ICULBUTN.ipt	-
🔳 100012	3.1		1 Milliliter	ICU Button Paint	-
▾ 🔳 100008	4	4	1 Each	ICURBUTN.ipt	-
🔳 100012	4.1		1 Milliliter	ICU Button Paint	-
▾ 🔳 100007	5	5	2 Each	ICUVALVEASSY.iam	-
🔳 100002	5.1	1	1 Each	ICUVALVE.ipt	-
🔳 100010	5.2	2	3 Each	ICUORING.ipt	-
🔳 100009	5.3	3	1 Each	ICUSPRNG.ipt	-

The completed practice

Task 1: Create shortcuts.

1. Start Autodesk Vault Professional. Log in using the following information:

    - For *User Name*, enter **usera**.
    - For *Password*, enter **vault**.
    - For *Vault*, select **AOTCVault**.

2. Under *Saved Shortcuts*, right-click and select **New Group**.

3. Enter **ICU Valve**. Press <Enter>.

4. Under Home, select **Item Master**. In the Item Master, drag the **ICU Valve Main Assembly.iam** item to the *ICU Valve* shortcut group.

5. Expand the *ICU Valve* shortcut group.

6. Right-click on the shortcut to the **ICU Valve Main Assembly.iam** item and select **Rename**.

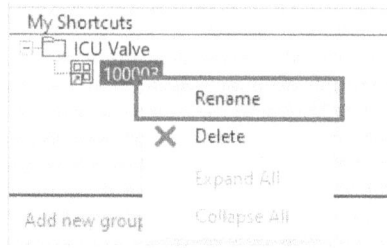

7. Enter **- Main Assembly** after the item number.

8. Press <Enter>. Note that your item number might differ than the one shown in the image below.

9. In the standard toolbar, click **Find**.

10. On the *Basic* tab, for the search text, enter ***BUTN** and press <Enter>.

11. Select **File>Save Search**.

12. In the Save Search dialog box, for *Search Name*, enter **Buttons**. Click **OK**. The saved search displays under *My Search Folders*.

13. Close the Find dialog box.

Task 2: Link items.

1. Under Home, right-click on **Item Master** and select **New Item**.

2. In the New Item – Select Category dialog box, select **Purchased** and click **OK**.

3. In the Edit Item dialog box, do the following:

   - For *Title*, enter **ICU Button Paint**.

   - For *Description*, enter **Paint**.

   - Set *Units* to **Milliliter**.

   - Click **Save and Close**.

4. Under *My Search Folders*, click **Buttons**.

5. Right-click on the **ICURBUTN** item and click **Update** to edit it.

6. Select the *Bill of Materials* tab.

7. Right-click on the row and select **Add Row>From Existing Item**.

General | History | Bill of Materials | Where Used | Change Order | View | Asso

Latest   Work In Progress   ▾   Today   Multi-Lev

	Number	Row Order ▲	Position Number	Quantity
▸	⊞ 100008	-	-	-

     Turn Row On
     Turn Row Off
     Add Row   ▸   From Existing Item...
     Remove Row   From New Item

8. In the Find dialog box, select the *Basic* tab if it is not selected already. Do the following:

   - For the search text, enter **Paint**.
   - Click **Find Now**.
   - Select the row displayed.
   - Click **OK**.
   - The ICU Button Paint item is linked to the ICURBUTN.ipt item.

General | History | Bill of Materials | Where Used | Change Order | View | A

Latest   Work In Progress   ▾   Today   Multi·

	Number	Row Order ▲	Position Number	Quantity
▸ ▾	⊞ 100008	-	-	-
	⊞ 100012	1		1 Milliliter

9. Click **Save and Close**. Repeat the previous steps to link the **ICU Button Paint** item to the **Left button (ICULBUTN.ipt)** item.

10. In the *ICU Valve* shortcut group, click the shortcut to the **Main Assembly**.

11. In the Preview pane, click the *Bill of Materials* tab. Verify that the **ICU Button Paint** item is listed twice, under the ICU buttons.

General | History | Bill of Materials | Where Used | Change Order | View

Latest   Work In Progress   ▾   Today   Multi-Level   ▾   All Rows

Number	Row Or... ▲	Position Number	Quantity	Title (Item,CO)
▶ ▼ 100003	-	-	-	ICU Valve Main Assembly.iam
100004	1	1	1 Each	ICUHOUSG.ipt
100006	2	2	1 Each	ICUENDCP.ipt
▼ 100005	3	3	1 Each	ICULBUTN.ipt
1...	3.1		*1 Milliliter*	ICU Button Paint
▼ 100008	4	4	1 Each	ICURBUTN.ipt
1...	4.1		*1 Milliliter*	ICU Button Paint
▶ 100007	5	5	2 Each	ICUVALVEASSY.iam

Task 3: Delete items.

1. In the Item Master, right-click on the **O-Ring Lubricant** item and select **Change State**.

2. In the Select Lifecycle dialog box, select **Obsolete**.

3. Click **OK**.

4. In the Item Master, right-click on the **O-Ring Lubricant** item again and select **Delete**.

   Note: You can delete an item only if its lifecycle state is set to Obsolete.

5. Click **Yes** to confirm the item deletion.

End of practice

9.3 Item Properties

Overview

In this lesson, you will learn how to use item properties to search for and sort items, organize items, and filter the Item Master list. You use item properties to manage items.

Number	Revision	State	Title (Item,CO)	Category Name	Item Project	
100020	-	Work In Progress	ICURBUTN.ipt	Part	ICUV1	
100021	-	Work In Progress	ICUORING.ipt	Part	ICUV1	
100022	-	Work In Progress	ICUVALVEASSY.iam	Assembly	ICUV1	
100023	-	Work In Progress	ICUVALVE.ipt	Part	ICUV1	
100024	-	Work In Progress	ICU O-Ring Lubricant	Purchased	ICUV1	
100025	-	Work In Progress	ICU Button Paint	Purchased	ICUV1	
100026	-	Work In Progress	ICU Valve Main Assembly.iam	Assembly	ICUV1	
100027	-	Work In Progress	ICULBUTN.ipt	Part	ICUV1	
100028	-	Work In Progress	ICUHOUSG.ipt	Part	ICUV1	
100029	-	Work In Progress	ICUSPRNG.ipt	Part	ICUV1	
100030	-	Work In Progress	ICUENDCP.ipt	Part	ICUV1	

Objectives

After completing this lesson, you will be able to:

* Describe default item properties.

* Describe the use of revisions.

Default Item Properties

By default, each item has several properties that store and manage its number, revision, lifecycle, and other associated data.

Definition of Default Item Properties

Items have properties that apply to all items by default, called system properties. In some cases, the properties are marked (Item, CO) to denote that they are unique to items and change orders.

The following list describes the main properties that display on the *General* tab:

Property Name	Description	Comment or Example
Number	Unique item identifier	Normally a numerical sequence
Category	Categorization of the item.	"Part," "assembly," or "purchased"
Title	Brief description of item or change order	Up to 128 characters
Description	Secondary description of item or change order	Up to 128 characters
Units	Quantity	Select from a list
Lifecycle State	Item lifecycle state	"Work in Progress" or "Released"
Revision	Item revision	String or character
Last Updated By	Name of user who last updated item	Read-only, assigned by system
Last Updated	Date the item was last updated	Read-only, assigned by system

Example of Specifying Default Item Properties

When an item is assigned to a file, the item is given a number of default properties.

The new item has a unique item number, which can be as simple as a six- number sequence (Part 100010) or as complex as a set of text sequences (Part BRD-200-0012). You can change the item number after it is assigned if required. The *Title* and *Description* can be used to help distinguish the item later on. The *Units* are specific to the item – for the most part the unit is 'each' but for consumables, it can specify how much (volume, weight, etc.) of the item is used in the product.

The final set of properties is controlled by the system. The *Lifecycle State* designates the position in the product development process. You can change the lifecycle state to Released, signifying it is ready for production, or Work in Progress, denoting that it is being edited. As designs evolve, they are given *Revisions* to denote major milestones in a product development lifecycle. For example, a part can be released to manufacturing at Revision A, but later be modified based on warranty reports to Revision B to correct a defect noted by customers. The updates are tagged with the user that last updated the item (*Last Updated By*) and the time the update was done (*Last Updated*).

User-Defined Item Properties

In addition to the system properties, there are a number of predefined user-defined properties that are assigned to items as they are created. These are based on common file properties associated with the different authoring applications. For example, the property *Material* (designating what property the item is made of) can be set from a file property in Autodesk Inventor.

Additionally, you might want to specify some properties that are unique to your company. For example, you can have different *Business Units* that produce designs that you might want to identify or search on.

Best Practices for Working with User-Defined Properties

The administrator can define additional item properties to add company-specific properties to items. You can use these properties to help arrange or find items in the vault.

It is recommended that:

- You attach user-defined properties to items or remove them from items in the vault. Properties are created and managed by the administrator using the Property Definitions dialog box (found under **Tools>Administration>Vault Settings>Behaviors>Properties**).

- The administrator maps item properties to read values from CAD files in the vault if possible. For example, the property *Material* (designating what material the item is made of) can be set from a file property in Autodesk Inventor.

- You begin all user-defined properties with Item (or an acceptable prefix), as shown in the following illustration. This will avoid confusion with properties in the vault or in another application. You can also scroll to the right to view the *Association* column, which displays the entity class of the property.

Example of Using a User-Defined Item Property

You create an *Item Project* property value for a predefined item user-defined property so that you can sort by that property or use it to search for items.

You can ask the administrator to map the user-defined item property to properties in the vault files.

- You can attach or detach properties per item by right-clicking in the *Properties* field and selecting **Add or Remove Property**.

- You can edit the properties of more than one item at a time by selecting multiple items and then selecting **Edit Properties** (<Ctrl>+<E>).

Inventor Instance Properties

You can also assign properties to individual component instances. Instance properties work the same way as item property occurrences within the Vault bill of materials (BOM). Items with the same part number are grouped by the instance property value. If no instance properties exist, the BOM works as in the previous releases.

Item Numbering Schemes

All items have unique item numbers that you can use to identify and track the items in different operations. These item numbers are assigned based on a numbering scheme that is created by the administrator.

Guidelines for Item Numbers

There are two predefined numbering schemes shipped with Vault Professional. It is recommended that you use customized numbering schemes created by the administrator.

The two predefined schemes are shipped with the software by default.

- **Sequential numbering:** This scheme creates item numbers in sequence and is the default. This is a simple numbering scheme that starts with 100001 and goes to 999999.

- **Mapped numbering:** This scheme is selected automatically when a file property is mapped to the item number. You can choose the numbering scheme when you add new items to the vault. It can be any value up to 50 characters long.

Custom Numbering Schemes

If you choose to use a custom numbering scheme, the scheme can follow company standards or use any identifier. It is recommended that you make this identifier as simple as possible. A six-digit numbering scheme starting with 100000 is ideal.

Example of Using Item Numbers

The following illustration shows the use of a custom sequential scheme. Note that parts, assemblies, and purchased items are numbered from 100033 to 100043.

Number	Revision	State	Title (Item,CO)	Category Name	Units
100033	A	Work In Progress	ICUVALVE.ipt	Part	Each
100034	B	Released	ICU O Ring Lubricant	Purchased	Milliliter
100035	B	Released	ICU Button Paint	Purchased	Milliliter
100036	A	Work In Progress	ICU Valve Main Assembly.iam	Assembly	Each
100037	B	Released	ICULBUTN	Part	Each
100038	A	Released	ICUHOUSG.ipt	Part	Each
100039	A	Released	ICUSPRNG.ipt	Part	Each
100040	A	Released	ICUENDCP.ipt	Part	Each
100041	C	Work In Progress	ICURBUTN	Part	Each
100042	A	Work In Progress	ICUORING.ipt	Part	Each
100043	A	Work In Progress	ICUVALVEASSY.iam	Assembly	Each

Numbering schemes can include such things as company initials, a type sequence, a numeric sequence, and a manufacturing process code, as in BRD-PRT-10051-P. However, a scheme like this might be needlessly complex and require too much work to set up and use.

It is recommended that you start the item numbering with a digit other than zero since some spreadsheets eliminate the leading zeros when data is imported.

For example, the following illustration shows the use of the sequential scheme. Note that parts, assemblies, and purchased items are numbered from 000012 to 000022.

Number	Revision	State	Title (Item, CO)	Category Name	Units
000012	A	Work In Progress	ICUVALVE.ipt	Part	Each
000013	C	Work In Progress	ICU O Ring Lubricant	Purchased	Milliliter
000014	C	Work In Progress	ICU Button Paint	Purchased	Milliliter
000015	A	Work In Progress	ICU Valve Main Assembly.iam	Assembly	Each
000016	C	Work In Progress	ICULBUTN	Part	Each
000017	B	Work In Progress	ICUHOUSG.ipt	Part	Each
000018	B	Work In Progress	ICUSPRNG.ipt	Part	Each
000019	B	Work In Progress	ICUENDCP.ipt	Part	Each
000020	C	Work In Progress	ICURBUTN	Part	Each
000021	A	Work In Progress	ICUORING.ipt	Part	Each
000022	A	Work In Progress	ICUVALVEASSY.iam	Assembly	Each

This is poor practice. Many software programs such as spreadsheets import the item numbers without the leading zeros, so item number "000020" displays as "20", which might be undesirable when creating a report.

How To: Change Item Numbers

1. Right-click on one or more items in the Item Master or BOM view and select **Change Number**.

2. Select a numbering scheme from the drop-down list. **Use Property Mapping** uses mapped properties to generate the item number.

3. If a field requires user input, enter text as required.

4. Click **Precheck** to verify the new item number. Make any changes, if required.

5. If more than one item is in the list and you want to remove one, select the item and click **Remove**.

6. Click **OK** to accept the new item number.

Practice 9d
Work with Item Properties

In this practice, you add a new item with user-defined properties, link the item to the ICU valve assembly, display the user-defined property in the Item Master view, add a customized view for the current project, change the item project property, group the Item Master list by project, customize the view by box, and renumber items.

Number	Revision	State	Title (Item,CO)	Item Project
100021	-	Work In Progress	ICU Valve Main Assembly.iam	ICUV1
100022	-	Work In Progress	ICUVALVE.ipt	ICUV1
100023	-	Work In Progress	ICU O-Ring Lubricant	ICUV1
100024	-	Work In Progress	ICU Button Paint	ICUV1
100025	-	Work In Progress	ICUSPRNG.ipt	ICUV1
100026	-	Work In Progress	ICUORING.ipt	ICUV1
100027	-	Work In Progress	ICURBUTN.ipt	ICUV1
100028	-	Work In Progress	ICUVALVEASSY.iam	ICUV1
100029	-	Work In Progress	ICUENDCP.ipt	ICUV1
100030	-	Work In Progress	ICULBUTN.ipt	ICUV1
100031	-	Work In Progress	ICUHOUSG.ipt	ICUV1

The completed practice

Task 1: Add a new item.

1. If not already started, start Autodesk Vault Professional. Log in using the following information:

    *   For *User Name*, enter **usera**.

    *   For *Password*, enter **vault**.

    *   For *Vault*, select **AOTCVault**.

2. Under Home, click **Item Master** to display items for the ICU valve. Right-click on **Item Master** and select **New Item**.

3. In the New item – Select Category dialog box, select **Purchased** and click **OK**.

4. In the Edit Item dialog box:

   - For *Title*, enter **ICU O-Ring Lubricant**.
   - For *Description*, enter **Grease for subassembly**.
   - For *Units*, select **Milliliter**.

5. Under *Properties*, if the *Item Project* user- defined item is visible, skip to Step 8.

6. Under *Properties*, right-click under **Name** and select **Add or Remove Property**.

7. In the Add or Remove Property dialog box:

   - Select **Item Project**.
   - Select **Add** from the Action drop-down list.
   - Click **OK**.

8. Under *Properties*, click the *Value* field next to **Item Project**. Enter **ICUV1**.

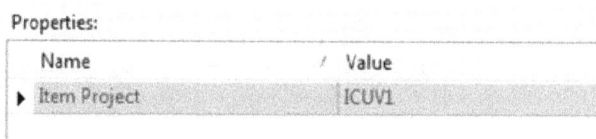

9. In the standard toolbar, click **Attachments**. Click **Yes** to save.

10. In the Attachments dialog box, click **Attach**.

11. Navigate to the *Designs\ICU Valve\Documents* folder.

    - Select **ICU Valve Specification Sheet - Grease.doc**.
    - Click **Open**.
    - Click **OK**.

12. Close the Item dialog box. The new item displays in the Item Master list.

Task 2: Link item to the assembly.

1. Double-click the **ICUVALVEASSY.iam** item to open it.

2. In the standard toolbar, click **Edit**.

3. Select the *Bill of Materials* tab. Right-click on the top row and select **Add Row>From Existing Item**.

4. In the Find dialog box, click the *Basic* tab if it is not selected already.

5. Enter **Grease** as the search text. Click **Find Now**.

6. Select the row displayed. Click **OK**. The ICU O-Ring Lubricant item is now linked to the ICUVALVEASSY.iam item. (Your item numbers might be different.)

7. Click **Save and Close**.

Task 3: Display the user-defined property.

1. In the Advanced toolbar, select **All Items** from the Custom Views list.

2. In the Advanced toolbar, select **Define Custom Views** from the Custom Views list.

3. In the Manage Custom Views dialog box, click **New**.

4. In the Create Custom View dialog box, for *View Name*, enter **Listing by Project**. Click **OK**.

5. Select **Listing by Project** and click **Modify**.

6. In the Customize View dialog box, click **Fields**.

7. In the Customize Fields dialog box, for *Select available fields from*, select **Items** from the list.

8. In the *Available fields* list, select **Item Project**.

9. Click **Add** to add **Item Project** to the list on the right after **Title (Item, CO)**.

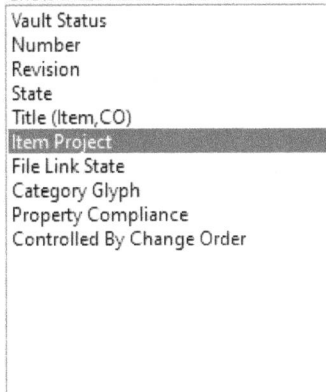

10. Click **OK**.

11. Close the remaining dialog boxes.

12. The Item Master list now shows the *Item Project* column.

   Note: The new customized view you just created lists all items in the Item Master. Because this list can be very long, you create another custom view that is based on it, but that adds a custom filter to search for "ICUV1" in the Item Project property.

Task 4: Add a customized view.

1. In the Advanced toolbar, select **Define Custom Views** from the Custom Views list.

2. In the Manage Custom Views dialog box, with **Listing by Project** selected, click **Copy**.

3. In the Create Custom View dialog box, for *View Name*, enter **ICU Valve 1 Project**. Click **OK**.

4. With **ICU Valve 1 Project** selected, click **Modify**.

5. Click **Custom Filters**.

6. In the Custom Filters dialog box, do the following:

   • For *Property*, select **Item Project**.

   • For *Condition*, select **contains**.

   • For *Value*, enter **ICUV1**.

   • Click **Add**.

   • Click **OK** to close the Custom Filters dialog box.

7. Close the remaining dialog boxes.

8. In the Advanced toolbar, select **ICU Valve 1 Project** from the Custom Views list. Only one item, the **ICU O-Ring Lubricant** you added, displays because none of the other ICU Valve items have **ICUV1** in the *Item Project* property.

Task 5: Change Item Project property.

1. In the Advanced toolbar, select **Listing by Project** from the Custom Views list.

2. In the Item Master, double-click the **ICUVALVE.ipt** item. Click **Edit**.

3. Under *Properties*, click the value next to *Item Project*. Enter **ICUV1** and click **Save and Close**.

4. Select all ICU Valve Items and then click the **Edit Properties** icon in the Properties pane to edit multiple properties at the same time. Repeat the previous three steps for all of the items belonging to the ICU valve.

5. Under Home, expand **Project Explorer**, **Designs**, and **Table**.

6. In the Table list, right-click on **Small Table.iam** and select **Assign/Update Item**.

7. Click **Save and Close**.

8. Under Home, click **Item Master**.

9. Edit each of the seven items belonging to the Table project, and enter **Table1** in the *Item Project* property.

10. In the Advanced toolbar, for Custom Views, select **ICU Valve 1 Project** from the list. Only the ICUV1 project items display.

11. For practice, add a new custom view called **Table 1 Project**, which is based on the ICU Valve1 project, by searching for the **Table1** *Item Project* using the custom filters.

Task 6: Group the listing by project.

1. In the Advanced toolbar, select **Listing by Project** from the Custom Views list.

2. In the Item Master, right-click on the *Item Project* header and select **Group by This Field**.

3. From the View menu, select **Refresh**.

4. In the Advanced toolbar, click **Group By Box** to toggle it off. The listed items are grouped and boxed by project. You can expand or collapse each project as you work.

💡 Hint: Group by Box View

The Group by Box view does not display as expected for items that are used in more than one project. For example, an item that is used in the Table1 and ICUV1 projects might have an *Item Project* property of "ICUV1, Table1." This shared item lists correctly using the ICU Valve 1 Project custom view and the Table 1 custom view, but does not list correctly under the Group by Box Listing by Project View.

Task 7: Renumber items.

1. In the Advanced toolbar, from the Custom Views list, select **ICU Valve 1 Project**. Make a note of which items are assemblies and which are purchased.

   Note: You can add the Category Name column to your view to make it easier to see which are assemblies and which are purchased.

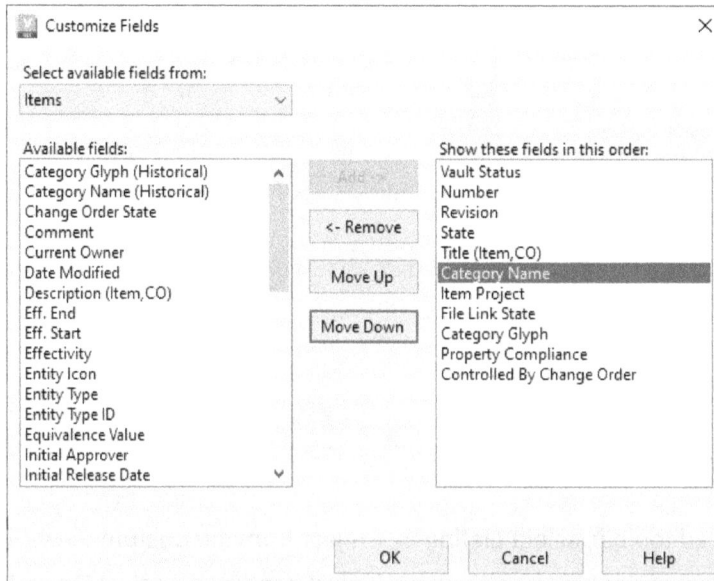

2. In Item Master, do the following:

   - Select the first item in the list.
   - Press <Shift> and select the last item in the list.
   - Right-click anywhere over the selected items and select **Change Number**.

3. In the Change Item Number dialog box, from the *Select a Numbering Scheme* list, select **AOTC-Complex**.

4. In the Change Item Number dialog box, do the following:

   - For *Type*, select **200** to change the assembly item numbers.
   - For *Type*, select **300** to change the purchased item numbers.
   - For *Type*, select **100** to change the part item numbers.

5. Click **OK**. The new item numbering scheme displays in the Item Master.

Number	Revision	State	Title (Item,CO)
200-10001	-	Work In Progress	ICU Valve Main Assembly.iam
100-10001	-	Work In Progress	ICUVALVE.ipt
300-10001	-	Work In Progress	ICU O-Ring Lubricant
300-10002	-	Work In Progress	ICU Button Paint
100-10002	-	Work In Progress	ICUSPRNG.ipt
100-10003	-	Work In Progress	ICUORING.ipt
100-10004	-	Work In Progress	ICURBUTN.ipt
200-10002	-	Work In Progress	ICUVALVEASSY.iam
100-10005	-	Work In Progress	ICUENDCP.ipt
100-10006	-	Work In Progress	ICULBUTN.ipt
100-10007	-	Work In Progress	ICUHOUSG.ipt

6. In the Advanced toolbar, select **All Items** from the Custom Views list.

7. In the Advanced toolbar, select **ICU Valve 1 Project** from the Custom Views list.

8. In Item Master, do the following:

   - Select the first item in the list.
   - Press <Shift> and select the last item in the list.
   - Right-click anywhere over the selected items and select **Change Number**.

9. In the Change Item Number dialog box, from the *Select a Numbering Scheme* list, select **AOTC-Numeric**. Click **OK**. Note that the item numbers differ from the ones at the start of the practice. To avoid confusion, old item numbers are not reused.

End of practice

9.4 Exporting Items

Overview

Other data management and analysis applications are often used along with Autodesk Vault Professional. You can export Vault Professional item properties in a range of file formats to provide engineering and product data to other applications.

Objective

After completing this lesson, you will be able to:

* Export item data.

Export Items from Vault Professional

You can export item data from Autodesk Vault Professional to a variety of file formats.

How To: Export Items

The following steps describe how to export items to a file:

1. Log in to Autodesk Vault Professional as a user assigned the ERP Manager role.
2. In the Item Master, select all the items to export. It might be useful to filter the items or export from a saved search to restrict the items to those required.
3. Select **File>Export Items**.
4. Select the **Released and Obsolete items only** checkbox to only show items in this state.
5. Items that are checked are exported. If you do not want to export an item that is checked, toggle off the checkbox next to that item.

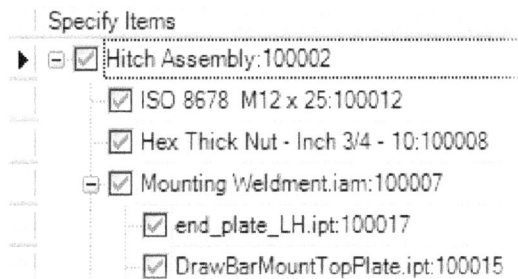

Note: If you export an assembly, its child components are automatically selected for export.

6. Click **Next**.

7. On the Specify File pane, under *File types*, click **CSV (Comma Separated Values .CSV)**.

File types:

CSV (Comma Separated Values .CSV)
TDL (Tab Separated Values .TXT)
Design Web Format (DWF)
XML

8. Under *BOM Indicator*, click **Level numbers**.

   Note: If you select Parent Item for the BOM indicator, each exported item, other than the top-level items, includes the item number of its parent item.

The exported file includes a numeric indicator of the hierarchical position of the file in the item structure. For example, if the first subassembly was assigned Level 1, the first child part in the subassembly is assigned Level 1.1, the second part 1.2, and so on.

	A	B	C	D
1	Level	Number	Title (Item,CO)	Quan
2	1	100002	Hitch Assembly	
3	1.1	100012	ISO 8678 M12 x 25	
4	1.2	100008	Hex Thick Nut - Inch 3/4 - 10	
5	1.3	100007	Mounting Weldment.iam	
6	1.3.1	100017	end_plate_LH.ipt	
7	1.3.2	100015	DrawBarMountTopPlate.ipt	
8				

9. Click **Browse**. Browse to your export folder. Enter the filename. Click **Save**.

10. Click **Next**. On the Specify Attributes pane, drag field names from the *Attributes* list to the *Export file* list. To remove a field from the *Export file* list, drag it outside the list. Click **Clear Mapping** to remove all fields except **Level**.

    Note: If you select Level Numbers as the BOM indicator, you must include the Number attribute in the Export File list.

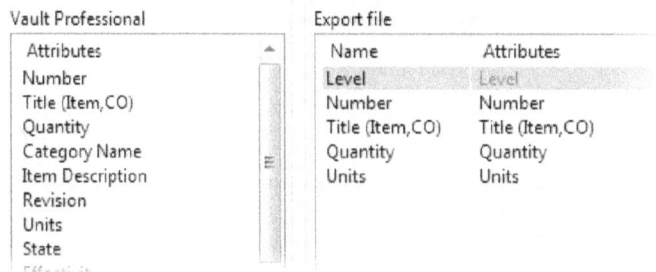

Vault Professional

Attributes
Number
Title (Item,CO)
Quantity
Category Name
Item Description
Revision
Units
State
Effectivity

Export file

Name	Attributes
Level	Level
Number	Number
Title (Item,CO)	Title (Item,CO)
Quantity	Quantity
Units	Units

11. Click **Export**. An export summary displays. On the Summary pane, you can print the report or distribute it by email.

12. Click **Finish**. The exported file is available for import into an ERP system or other software. An example CSV export file is shown in the following illustration.

```
Level,Number,Title,Quantity,Units,R
1,100002,Hitch Assembly,1,Each, - ,
1.1,100012,ISO 8678 M12 x 25,4,Eac
1.2,100008,Hex Thick Nut - Inch 3/4
1.3,100007,Mounting weldment.iam,1.
1.3.1,100017,end_plate_LH.ipt,1,Eac
1.3.2,100015,DrawBarMountTopPlate.i
1.3.3,100013,ANSI AISC 2x2x 1/4 - 1
1.3.4,100016,end_plate_RH.ipt,1,Eac
```

Practice 9e
Export Items from Vault Professional

In this practice, you change an assembly and its components to a Released lifecycle state, then export properties of the items to a .CSV file.

1. Start Autodesk Vault Professional. Log in using the following information:

   - For *User Name*, enter **administrator**.
   - Leave the *Password* field blank.
   - For *Vault*, select **AOTCVault**.

   Note: To export items, you must be logged in as a user with at least ERP Manager role permissions.

2. Under Home, click **Item Master** to display the list of items in the vault.

3. In the Advanced toolbar, select **Assembly Items** from the Custom Views list.

4. In the main pane, right-click on the **Small Table assembly item** and select **Change State**.

5. In the Select Lifecycle dialog box, click **Released**. Ensure that **Include dependents** is selected in the Change State dialog box and click **OK**.

   Select a new lifecycle state:

   | Item Release Process | ▼ | ... | | Released | ▼ |

   - The lifecycle state of the table assembly and each of its components is set to Released.

6. In the main pane, select the **Small Table** assembly item.

7. Click **File>Export Items**.

8. For Specify File, do the following:

   - Click **Next**.
   - Select **CSV**.
   - Browse to the Desktop folder.
   - For *File Name*, enter **Small Table Items**.
   - Click **Save**.
   - Click **Next**.
   - Drag a few field names from the Vault Professional list to the Export file list.
   - Click **Export**.

9. Click **Finish** and open the file in Microsoft Excel and review the data.

End of practice

Creating Reports

Autodesk® Vault Professional software provide the ability to generate formatted reports representing data contained in a vault. You can generate reports for files, items, and change orders, and organize the report based on specific properties. For example, a report can display files grouped by a category, show the distribution of lifecycle states across a model, and summarize currently open change orders, or show the distribution of lifecycle states across a model. Reports can display the data in a variety of ways, including charts, tables, and data sheets. You can also format data using dozens of predefined operators.

In this chapter, you learn how to create and modify report templates so that you can customize Vault reports that contain information relevant to your business, in a format that suits your needs.

Learning Objectives

- Create reports from an advanced search and configure how the data displays.
- Identify the different out-of-the box report templates and the information they are formatted to display.
- Create new report templates using the Autodesk Template Utility (for advanced users).
- Create project reports, also known as folder reports or folder dashboards.

10.1 Creating Reports

Overview

In this lesson, you learn how to create a report from an advanced search and configure how the report data displays.

Use search reports to illustrate details about files stored in the vault by using charts, tables, and data sheets.

Objectives

After completing this lesson, you will be able to:

- Create reports from an advanced search.
- Understand how to use each of the out-of-the box templates included with Autodesk Vault Professional.
- Configure how the report data displays

About Reports

Working with reports is a way of illustrating file details for those who do not have direct access to the vault. Reports can be organized to suit the needs of your business and to illustrate certain file details.

Search options specified in the Advanced Find dialog box determine which vault objects display in a report. The properties displayed in the report and the report layout are specified in a report template file that is selected during the report generation. Through the report template, you have complete control of the report content, layout, and format.

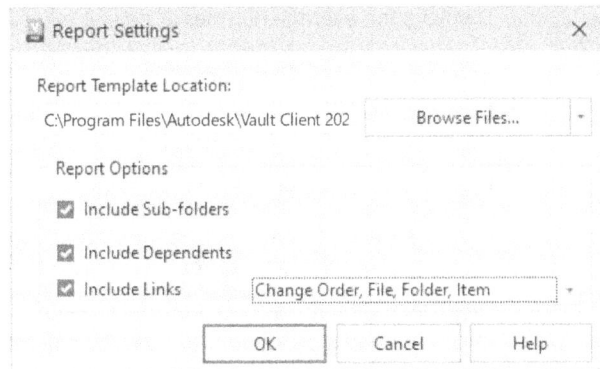

You generate reports by creating an advanced search with specified parameters and then clicking **Report**. After selecting a template for the report, the information displays in a window for viewing.

You can also generate and view reports from the *Reports* tab, built into the Preview pane of a folder. These reports are known as folder reports or vault project reports and are based on data contained in the selected folder. You can also include data from subfolders, dependents, and links in these reports.

Example of Creating a Report

A report must be generated to determine which files in a vault have been released for manufacturing. You create an advanced search with the condition that the search return files only with the lifecycle state of released. Once the search is complete, you generate a report and choose the template that shows the details of each file listed. Once the report is generated, you save a copy to the vault and email a copy to the project manager for review.

Report Templates

Report descriptions for Autodesk Vault reports are contained in RDLC files stored on the Vault client machine. These report description files are referred to as report templates. Autodesk Vault report templates are fully RDLC compliant, but Autodesk Vault requires certain naming conventions in the <DataSet> section of the template for integrating Vault data into the report.

A report template authoring utility is installed with the vault client to help you create simple client report definition files (.RDLC) for storing search data. This utility provides only a raw template structure for categorization purposes. A more sophisticated template authoring tool is required for custom visual layouts.

Pre-existing Report Templates

When the Autodesk Vault Client is installed, several pre-existing report templates are provided. The following table describes some of these templates:

Template Name	Description
ECO Average Close Rate	Displays the average number of days it takes to close an ECO.
ECO By State	Displays the ECOs in groups based on ECO state.
ECO Detail	Displays the ECO Number, Change Order Properties, State, Due Date, and submission information without table formatting.
ECO Status Created on Month	Displays the number of ECOs per State.
ECO Table	Displays the ECO Number, Change Order Properties, State, Due Date, and submission information in table format.
File by Category	Displays the filename, revision, state, comments, and check-in information in a pie-chart organized by category.
File Detail	Displays the filename, revision, state, check-in information, and comments without table formatting.
File Table	Displays the filename, revision, state, check-in information, and comments in a table format.
File Transmittal	Displays the filename, revision, state, vault folder location, and date the version was created for each file.
File by Lifecycle State	Displays the filename, revision, state, comments, and check-in information in a graph by lifecycle state.
File Checked Out By	Displays checked out information in a graph.
Item By State	Displays the item information in groups based on state.
Item Detail	Displays the item name, revision, state, type, units, modification information, compliance status, and description without table formatting.
Item Table	Displays the item name, revision, state, type, units, modification information, compliance status, and description in a table.
Project Dashboard	Displays project data in graphical format, including graphs for Lifecycle State Distribution by Category, Category Distribution, Lifecycle State Distribution, and Checked-Out Files Distribution by Users.

Template Name	Description
Vault Professional In-CAD	Displays check out information, lifecycle state, category, designer, and other In-CAD data displayed in pie-charts.
BOM - First-Level	Displays the BOM First Level details.
BOM - Multi-Level	Displays the BOM Multi-Level details.
BOM - Parts-Only	Displays the BOM Parts Only details.

Microsoft Report Viewer

Autodesk Vault uses the Microsoft Report Viewer to generate and display reports. Microsoft Report Viewer contains a full-featured, highly customizable reporting engine to display reports for SQL Server Reporting Services. However, the report viewer can also be run in "local mode" - enabling applications like Vault to provide data for report rendering without requiring the overhead of SQL Server Reporting Services. Autodesk Vault runs the report viewer in local mode. Report descriptions for Vault reports are contained in RDLC files stored on the Vault client machine.

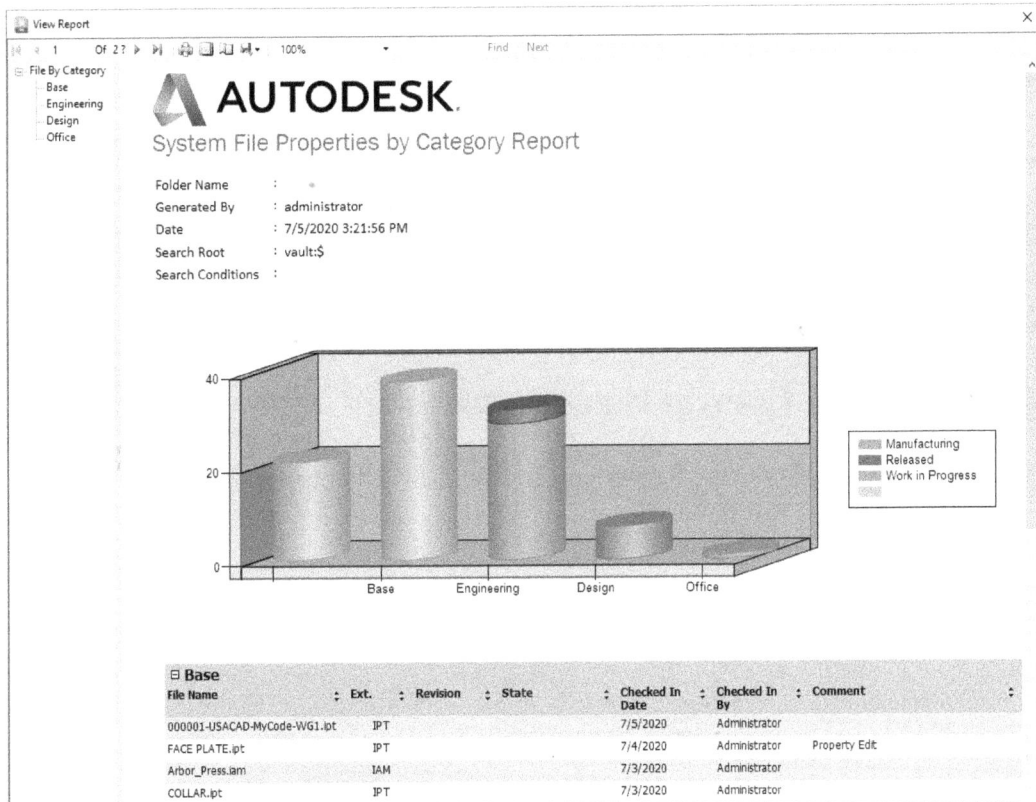

Creating Search Reports

To create a search report, you must be familiar with how to generate searches with conditions. Familiarize yourself with the template you intend to use before creating the search. Once you understand which file properties will be displayed, you can specify search conditions to return the required vault objects for the report.

Report templates can be stored in a local folder or in a vault. During installation, the pre-existing report templates are placed in a local folder at *C:\Program Files\Autodesk\Vault <edition> <year>\ Explorer\Report Templates*.

How To: Create a New Report

The following steps describe how to create a new search report:

1. Click **Find**. The Find dialog box displays.

2. Select the *Basic* tab or the *Advanced* tab depending on the type of criteria for which you want to search.

3. Specify the search criteria for this report.

4. Click **Report**. The Select Report Template dialog box displays.

5. Enter the path of a template that you would like to use or click **Browse** to navigate to the required template. The last selected report template displays by default.

6. Click **OK** to generate a report. If none of the search criteria is set to **ask me later**, the report is created and displayed automatically.

7. If any of the criteria has a value set to **ask me later**, the Specify Search Values dialog box displays. Specify the search values for the listed properties and click **OK**. The Select Report Template dialog box displays.

8. Click **OK** to generate and view the report. The report automatically displays in Microsoft Report Viewer.

9. In Microsoft Report Viewer, click **Page Setup** to configure printing preferences and to print the report.

10. To export the report, click the **Export** icon and select whether to export the report as an Excel file, a PDF file, or a Word file.

Creating Autodesk Vault Project Reports

To create a vault project report, also known as a folder report, ensure that all objects (files, subfolders, items, or change orders) or links to the objects that are being reported on are in one project folder.

How To: Create a Vault Project Report

The following steps describe how to create a vault project report:

1. Select a project folder in the main pane.

2. Select the *Reports* tab in the Preview pane and select **Configure**.

3. In the Report Settings dialog box, select **Browse Files** to navigate to the required template. The last selected report template displays by default.

4. Select the required report template and click **Open**.

5. Select one or more report options if required.

6. Click **OK** to generate and view the report. The report automatically displays in the Preview pane.

Practice 10a
Create a Search Report

In this practice, you create a search report using a pre-existing template and save the report to Autodesk Vault.

AUTODESK.

System Item Properties Report

Folder Name   :
Generated By   : administrator
Date   : 1/29/2024 12:40:45 PM
Search Conditions : State contains Work In Progress

Item Number	REV	State	Title	Type	Units	Last Modified	By
100030	-	Work In Progress	ICUVALVE.ipt		Each	1/29/2024	User A
100029	-	Work In Progress	ICU Valve Main Assembly.iam		Each	1/29/2024	User A
100028	-	Work In Progress	ICUHOUSG.ipt		Each	1/29/2024	User A
100027	-	Work In Progress	ICULBUTN.ipt		Each	1/29/2024	User A
100026	-	Work In Progress	ICUENDCP.ipt		Each	1/29/2024	User A
100025	-	Work In Progress	ICUVALVEASSY.iam		Each	1/29/2024	User A
100024	-	Work In Progress	ICURBUTN.ipt		Each	1/29/2024	User A
100023	-	Work In Progress	ICUORING.ipt		Each	1/29/2024	User A
100022	-	Work In Progress	ICUSPRNG.ipt		Each	1/29/2024	User A
100021	-	Work In Progress	ICU Button Paint		Milliliter	1/29/2024	User A
100020	-	Work In Progress	ICO O-Ring Lubricant		Milliliter	1/29/2024	User A

The completed practice

Task 1: Create a search report.

1. Start Autodesk Vault. Log in using the following information:

    • For *User Name*, enter **administrator**.

    • Leave the *Password* field blank.

    • For *Vault*, select **AOTCVault**.

2. In the Navigation pane, click **Project Explorer ($)**.

3. Click **Find** in the toolbar.

4. In the Find dialog box, select the *Advanced* tab.

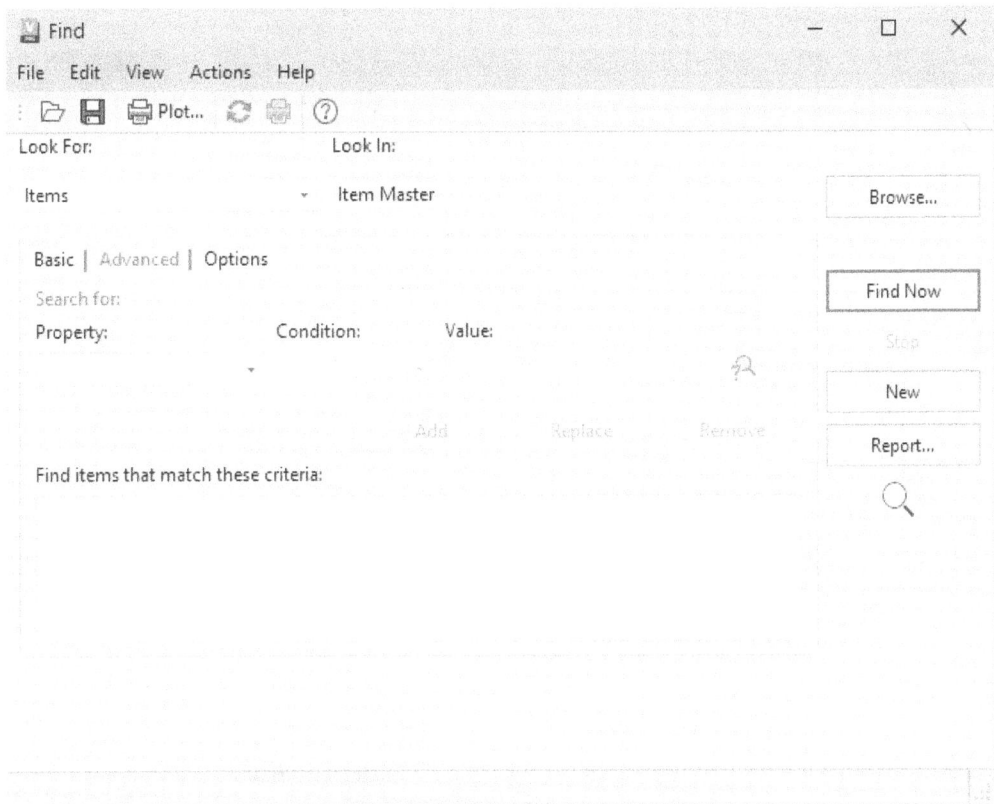

5. In the *Advanced* tab, do the following:

- Select **State** from the *Property* drop-down list.
- Select **contains** from the *Condition* drop-down list.
- Enter **Work in Progress** in the *Value* field.
- Click **Add**.

6. Click **Find Now**. All of the files in a Work in Progress state are listed.

Name	Revision	State
Pivot_Lower.ipt	A	Work in Progress
Pin_B.ipt	A	Work in Progress
Arbor_Frame.ipt	A	Work in Progress
ICU Valve Main Assembly.iam	A	Work in Progress
ICUVALVEASSY.iam	A	Work in Progress
ICUVALVE.ipt	A	Work in Progress
ICUSPRNG.ipt	A	Work in Progress

7. Click **Report**.

8. In the Select Report Template dialog box, do the following:

   - Click the ellipsis (...) button.
   - Select **Item Table.rdlc**.
   - Click **Open**.

9. Click **OK** in the Select Report template dialog box. The report is generated and immediately launched in Microsoft Report Viewer.

Task 2: Create a second search report.

1. In the Navigation pane, select **Home**.

2. Select the Item Master list. Alternatively, you can click **Item Master**.

3. Click **Find** in the toolbar.

4. In the Find dialog box, select the *Advanced* tab.

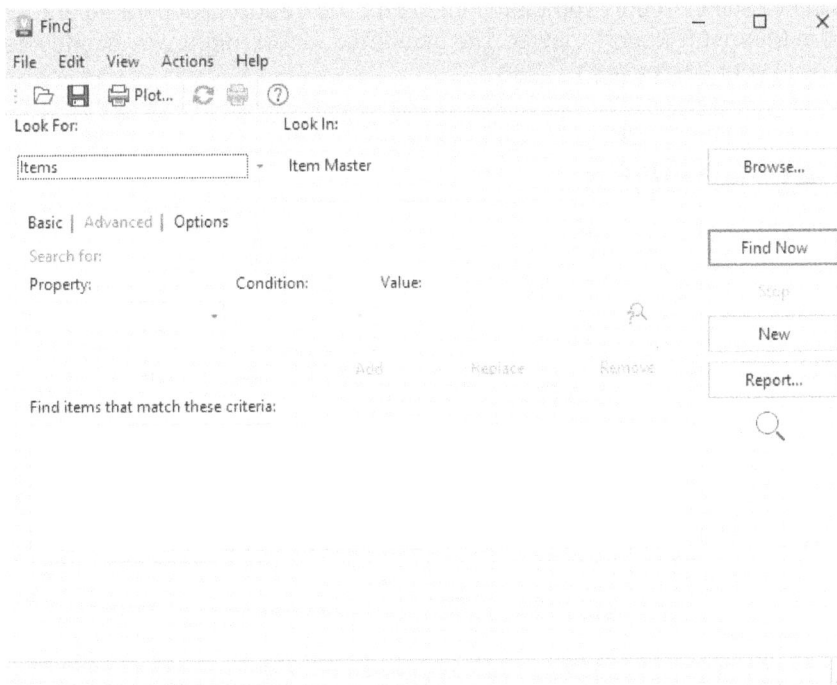

5. On the *Advanced* tab, do the following:

   - Select **State** from the *Property* drop-down list.
   - Select **does not contain** from the *Condition* drop-down list.
   - Enter **Obsolete** in the *Value* field.
   - Click **Add**.

Find items that match these criteria:

State does not contain Obsolete

6. Click **Find Now**. All of the items that are not in an Obsolete state are listed in the report.

7. Click **Report**.

8. In the Select Report Template dialog box, do the following:

   - Click the ellipsis (...) button.
   - Select **Item Table.rdlc**.
   - Click **Open**.

9. Click **OK** in the Select Report Template dialog box. The report is generated and immediately launched in Microsoft Report Viewer. The generated report might vary slightly depending on the files in your database.

10. Click **Export** in the View Report toolbar.

11. Select **PDF** as the format in which you will save the report.

12. In the Save As dialog box, navigate to the desktop.

13. Name the report and click **Save** to store it on your desktop.

14. Close the View Report and Find dialog boxes.

Task 3: Create a Vault project report.

1. Select **Project Explorer**.

2. Right-click on **Project Explorer ($)** and select **New Folder**.

3. Create a new folder called **Projects**.

4. Right-click on **Projects** and select **New Folder** to create a new folder called **10-A-555**. Click **OK**.

New Folder	×
Folder:	10-A-555
Category:	Folder

OK   Cancel   Help

5. Select **Designs\TrailerHitch**.

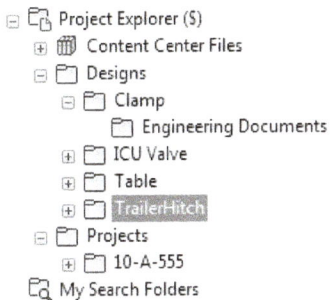

```
Project Explorer (S)
    Content Center Files
    Designs
        Clamp
            Engineering Documents
        ICU Valve
        Table
        TrailerHitch
    Projects
        10-A-555
    My Search Folders
```

6. Select all of the folder's files using <Ctrl>+<A>.

7. In the Edit menu, select **Copy**.

8. Navigate to the *10-A-555* project folder.

9. In the Edit menu, select **Paste as link**.

10. Select **Item Master**.

11. Select all of the items using <Ctrl>+<A>.

12. In the Edit menu, select **Copy**.

13. Navigate to the *10-A-555* project folder.

14. In the Edit menu, select **Paste as link**.

15. In the main pane, select the **10-A-555** project folder.

16. In the *Reports* tab of the Preview pane, select **Configure**.

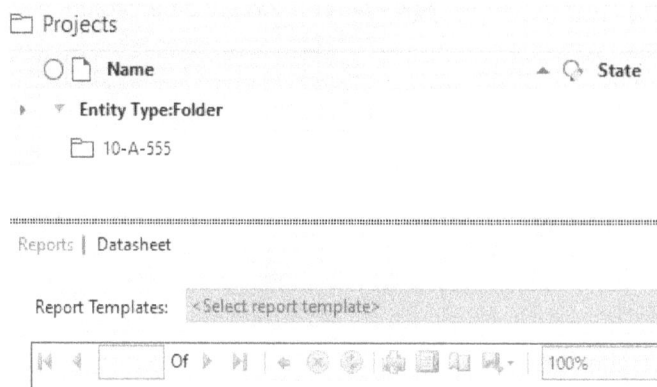

17. In the Report Settings dialog box, ensure all *Report Options* are selected and click **Browse Files**.

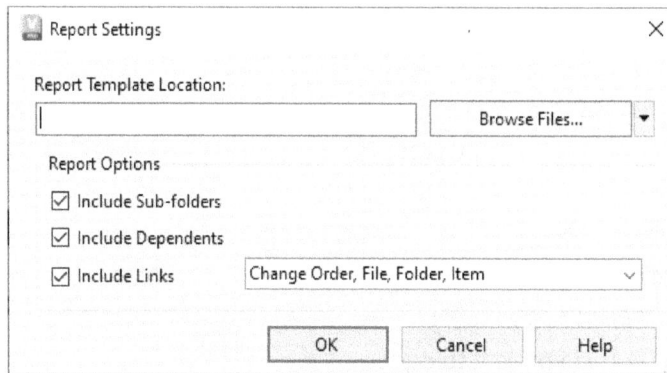

18. Select the **Project Dashboard.rdlc** template and click **Open**.

19. Click **OK**. The report is automatically displayed in the Preview pane. The generated report might vary slightly depending on the files in your database.

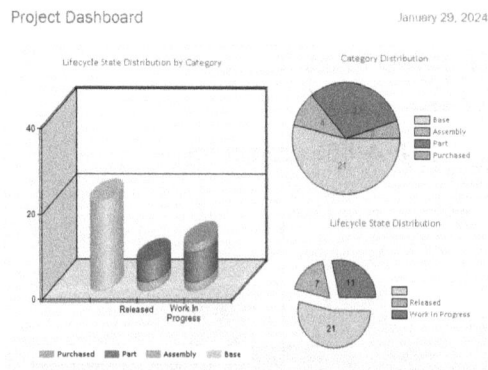

End of practice

10.2 Creating Custom Report Templates

Overview

In this lesson, you learn how to create and modify custom report templates using the Autodesk Report Template Utility and Microsoft Visual Studio.

Note: The Autodesk Report Template Utility is intended for advanced users who are familiar with XML and RDLC authoring applications. You must have Microsoft Visual Studio installed to complete this lesson.

Use custom report templates to illustrate your vault data in a way that suits your business needs.

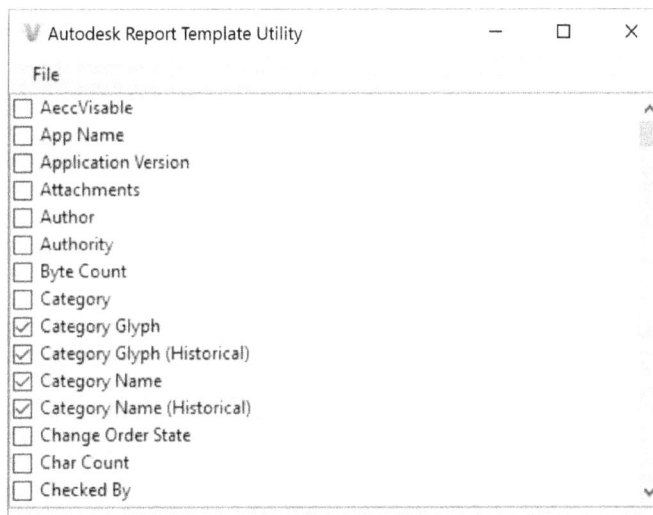

Objectives

After completing this lesson, you will be able to:

* Log in to the Autodesk Report Template Utility.

* Create and modify custom report templates.

Introduction to the Autodesk Report Template Utility

The Autodesk Report Template Utility is a software used to create an initial RDLC report template that contains all of the required Vault data binding information, but no formatting. You can open the RDLC file created by the Autodesk Report Template Utility in Visual Studio to specify the layout and formatting.

The **ReportTemplateAuthoritingUtility.exe** file is located in the *C:\Program Files\Autodesk\ <Autodesk Vault edition> <year>\Explorer* folder, where <Autodesk Vault edition> is the name of the Autodesk Vault edition you are using (such as Autodesk Vault Professional) and <year> is the release year.

Report Template Authoring

Report Viewer uses the Microsoft-proposed standard Report Definition Language (RDL) to describe the format of the report. RDL is an XML schema that can contain:

- Formatting descriptions for tables, charts, images, headers, footers, and so on

- Data field definitions

- Report parameters

There are two types of RDL files supported by Report Viewer – one each for the server and local report processing mode. Vault uses the local processing mode, so you will be using the local types of RDL file – which, by convention, is stored in files with the .RDLC extension. RDL and RDLC files have the same XML schema, but RDLC files do not contain database connection information since the client application (in this case Vault) provides the data.

Although RDLC files contain XML, no knowledge of XML is required to create and edit them.

How To: Access the Autodesk Report Template Utility

The following steps describe how to access the Autodesk Report Template Utility:

1. Open File Explorer.

2. Navigate to the *C:\Program Files\Autodesk\<Autodesk Vault edition><year>\Explorer* folder, where <Audodesk Vault edition> is the name of the Autodesk Vault edition you are using (such as Autodesk Vault Professional) and <year> is the release year.

> 💡 **Hint: Editing RDL Files**
>
> Detailed information on the editing of RDL files is outside the scope of this lesson, but Microsoft provides a good overview here: http://msdn.microsoft.com/en-us/library/ms159267.aspx, and a tutorial here: http://msdn.microsoft.com/en-us/library/ms167305.aspx.
>
> There are also a number of books available on the subject of SQL Server Reporting Services that have sections covering RDLC report template creation and editing.

Creating a New Report Template

You create a new report template in three steps:

1. Create a preliminary template in the Autodesk Report Template Utility with the properties you want to show in the report

2. Customize the template layout using Microsoft Visual Studio.

3. Test the template by generating a sample report.

Example of Using the Autodesk Report Template Utility

Your manager asks you to print a comprehensive report about files in all existing projects that have been released. She requests that the report include the file's state, revision ID, originator, and relative project. With these properties in mind, you open the Autodesk Report Template Utility and generate a preliminary template that meets your manager's criteria.

Then, using Microsoft Visual Studio, you modify the layout of the template to show the files in a bar chart based on project. Afterward, you create a search that returns all released files across all projects and then run the report using the newly created template.

How To: Create a Preliminary Report Template

The following steps describe how to create a custom report template:

1. Open File Explorer.

2. Navigate to the *C:\Program Files\Autodesk\<Autodesk Vault edition><year>\Explorer* folder, where <Audodesk Vault edition> is the name of the Autodesk Vault edition you are using (such as Autodesk Vault Professional) and <year> is the release year.

3. Launch the **ReportTemplateAuthoringUtility.exe** file. The Login dialog box displays.

---

4. Enter your login data and click **OK**. The Autodesk Report Template Utility dialog box displays.

5. Select **File>New**.

6. Select the type of report template that you want to create from the Report Type drop-down list.

7. Select the report properties that you want to include in your report template from the *Report Properties* list.

8. Select **File>Save As**. The Save Template dialog box displays.

9. Navigate to the local folder or vault folder where you want the report template file to be saved and enter a filename in the *File name* field.

10. Click **Save** to save the file.

    Note: The report template is blank as the Autodesk Report Template Utility did not add any layout or format information to the RDLC file.

How To: Customize the Layout of a New Report Template

The following steps describe how to create a custom report template:

1. Open Visual Studio and load the RDLC file you created using the Autodesk Report Template Utility.

2. Add controls from the toolbox to the report template.

3. Once a control is placed in a report template, the control can be configured to display the value of a Vault property. Right-click on the control and select **Expression** in the context menu. In the Expression dialog box, select **Fields** from the *Category* list. Double-click on a property name to fill in the expression text box. Click **OK**.

The field expression is now associated with the report control. When the report is generated, this control will be filled with the specified property for each Vault object processed.

4. Save the template as an .RDLC file.

How To: Test the Report Template in Vault

1. Without exiting Visual Studio, start Vault and then run a report.
2. Specify the newly created template in the Report Template dialog box.
3. View the results.
4. Modify the template in Visual Studio, as required.
5. Save the template.
6. Repeat, as required.

Including Non-Property Vault Data in a Report

There is information relevant to a report that is not stored as properties in Autodesk Vault. To display this information in a report, a number of RDL-defined parameters must be supplied with values by the Vault prior to report processing. This process enables the template author to place and format these values in a report.

The following report parameters are supplied with values by Vault:

Template Parameter Name	Value
Vault_UserName	The name of the Vault user who generated the report.
Vault_VaultName	The name of the vault that provided data for the report. This is the vault that the user who generates the report is logged into.
Vault_SearchRoot	The name of the folder(s) specified in the Look in control located in the Find dialog box in Autodesk Vault.
Vault_LatestVersionOnly	The state of the **Find latest versions only** checkbox in the *Options* tab of the Find dialog box in Autodesk Vault.
Vault_SearchSubFolders	The state of the **Search Subfolders** checkbox in the *Options* tab of the Find dialog box in Autodesk Vault.
Vault_SearchFileContent	The state of the **Search file content** checkbox in the *Basic* tab of the Find dialog box in Autodesk Vault.
Vault_SearchConditions	A string representation of the search conditions specified in the *Advanced* tab of the Find dialog box in Autodesk Vault.

Creating Reports with Non-Property Vault Data

To use one or more of these parameters in your report, create a parameter of the same name in your template by loading the template in Visual Studio, right-clicking outside of the report template, and selecting **Report Parameters**.

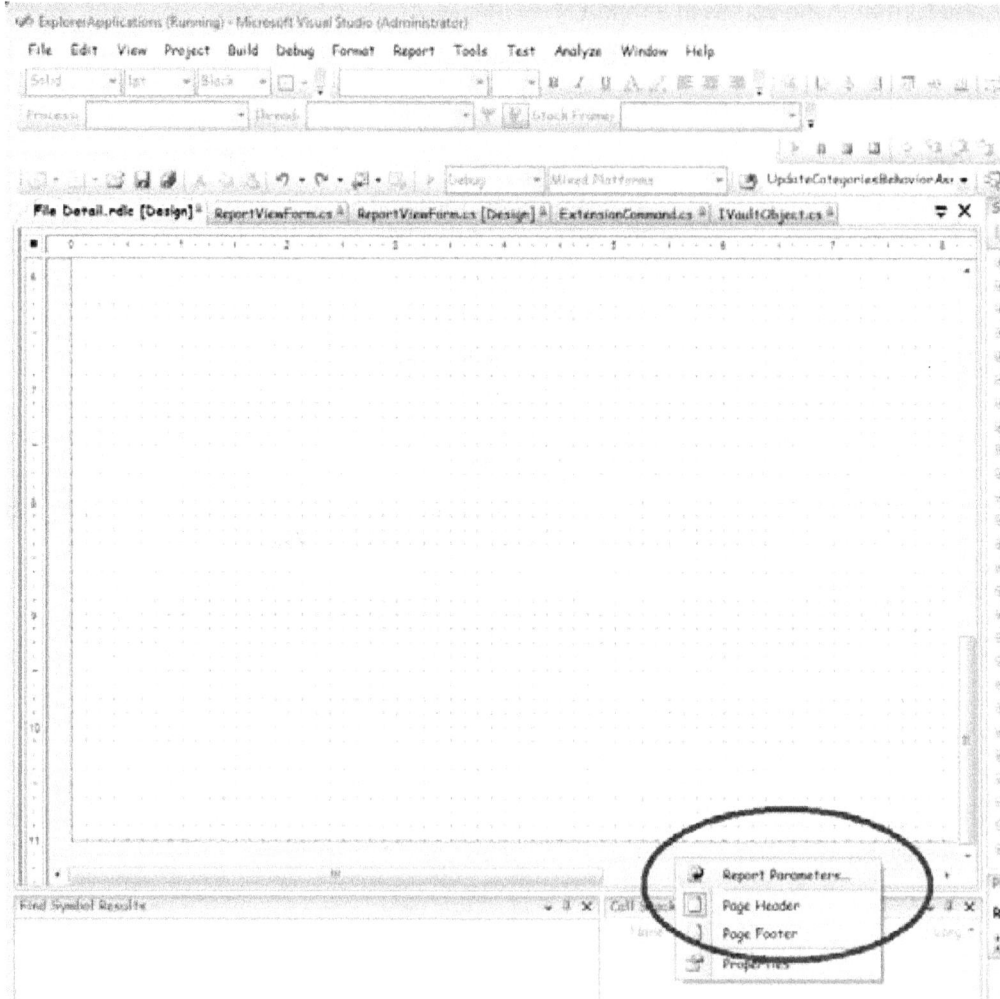

In the Report Parameters dialog box, you specify the parameters you want to include in your report. If you specify any of the reserved report parameter names listed above, the Vault reporting engine will supply a value for that parameter at runtime. Reserved parameter names must be spelled exactly as displayed in the table for the report engine to find them. Parameter names are case sensitive. The remainder of the fields in the Report Parameters dialog box can retain their default values as shown in the example below.

Placing a parameter value in a report is similar to placing property values: right-click on a control and then select **Expression** in the context menu. In the Expression dialog box, double-click on a property name to specify that the parameter value to be used for this control.

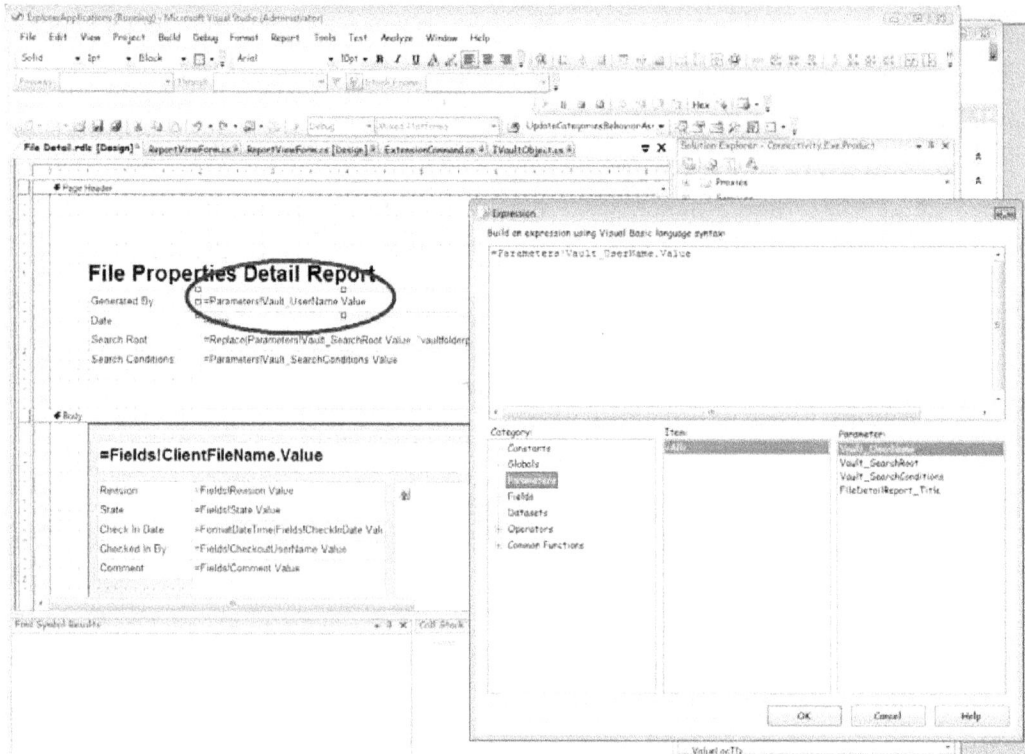

You can use parameter values in expressions just like field value. All of the sample templates included with Vault do parameter formatting in this way.

Managing Change

Vault Professional provides control over how new designs or design changes are released, eliminating the issues commonly involved with manual processes. Creating a change order enables you to describe the changes to a design and manage the progression of that change order as it is reviewed, approved, or rejected.

Learning Objectives

- Create and change item lifecycles manually.
- Create and approve change orders.

11.1 Revision Control

Overview

In this lesson, you learn how to use revision control to manually control lifecycle states and how different workflows affect revision control.

In design and manufacturing, a part can go through many design iterations. Lifecycle states control the revisions of a part or assembly in this process.

Objectives

After completing this lesson, you will be able to:

- Define item lifecycle states.
- Control lifecycle states.
- Manually change lifecycle states.

© 2024 Autodesk, Inc.

Item Lifecycle States

To manage design data, you must control the various stages from design to manufacturing. To do this, you mark an item using one of the lifecycle states.

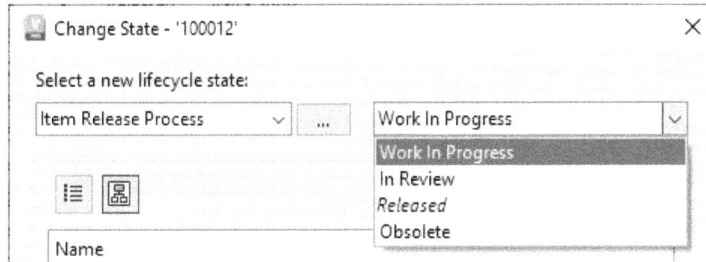

Definition of Lifecycle States

Note: The actual names of the lifecycle states can be changed to reflect those used in your organization. This will be covered in a later lesson.

The lifecycle state of an item indicates where it is in the design and manufacturing process. The following table describes the default states:

Lifecycle State	Description
Work in Progress	The item is available for editing. Files associated with the item can be checked out and edited. The item can be updated to the latest file versions. New items are automatically assigned Work in Progress status.
In Review	The item is being reviewed prior to release to production. The item and its associated files cannot be edited or updated.
Released	The item is available for production. The item cannot be edited or updated.
Obsolete	The item is no longer used in production and cannot be updated. Items in the Obsolete state can be deleted.

Manually Changing a State

To change a state, right-click on the item in the Item Master and select **Change State**. The Change State dialog box displays the states available based on the current state of the item.

In the following illustration, the item is set to **Work in Progress**. You can select **In Review**, **Released**, or **Obsolete**.

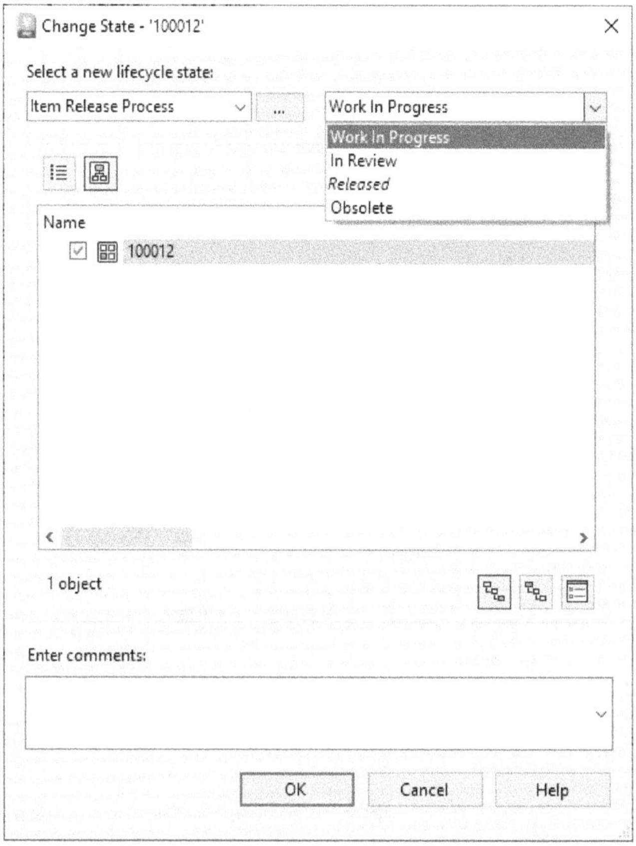

Example of a Manual State Change

The design team has determined that a part is ready for manufacturing. During the design phase, the part has a Work in Progress (WIP) lifecycle state. You set the lifecycle state to Released to indicate that the part is ready for manufacturing and distribution.

Revisions and Lifecycle State

By default, when you change an item's state from Released to WIP, the revision automatically bumps using the primary revision bump action.

The following state changes do not bump the revision status of an item:

- WIP to Obsolete
- WIP to Released
- WIP to In Review
- Released to Obsolete
- In Review to Obsolete

- In Review to Released
- In Review to WIP
- Obsolete to In Review
- Obsolete to WIP

Note: Depending on your company's configuration, not all of these state changes will be available.

Revision Formats

A user with an administrator or Item Editor (Level 2) role sets the revision sequence and can either specify one of the formats shown in the following illustration or create a custom revision scheme.

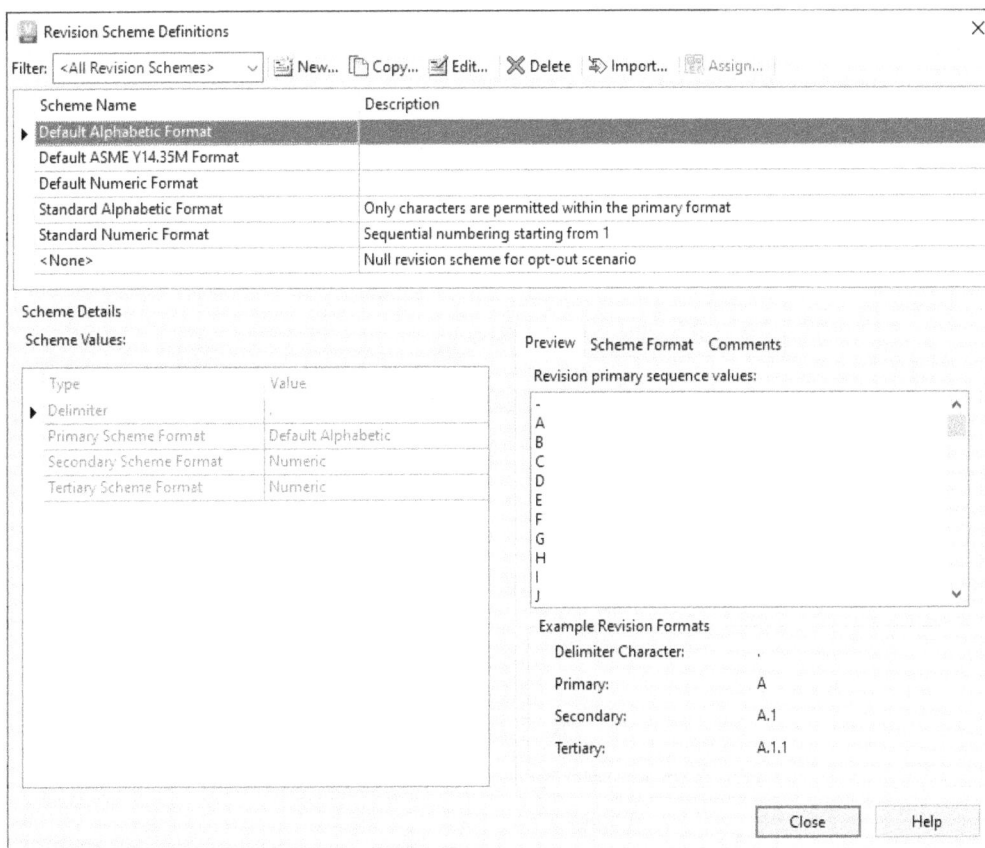

Examples of the revision format display in the *Preview* tab of the Revision Scheme Definitions dialog box.

Practice 11a
Change Lifecycle States Manually

In this practice, you create an item and manually change the lifecycle state.

🔳 Item Master

◯	Number	▲	Revision	State	Title (Item,CO)
▸	100-10001		-	Work In Progress	ICUVALVE.ipt
	300-10001		-	Work In Progress	ICU O-Ring Lubricant

The completed practice

1. Start Autodesk® Vault Professional. Log in using the following information:

   • For *User Name*, enter **administrator**.

   • Leave the *Password* field blank.

   • For *Vault*, select **AOTCVault**.

2. From the Go menu, select **Item Master**.

3. In the Advanced toolbar, select **All Items** from the Custom Views list.

4. From the Go menu, select **Project Explorer**.

5. From the Tools menu, select **Options**. Ensure that **Show hidden files** is selected. The DWF files display.

6. Click **OK**.

7. Expand the *Designs* folder. Click the *Clamp* folder.

8. Right-click on **Handle.ipt** and select **Assign/Update Item**.

9. In the Edit Item window, click **Save and Close**. An item icon displays next to the file name.

10. From the Go menu, select **Item Master**.

11. In the Item Master, click the *Number* column to sort the item numbers in descending order.

12. In Item Master, right-click on the new item.

Note: Your item number might differ from the illustrations shown in this practice. Your item should be the highest number. In this example, it is 100021.

13. Select **Change State**.

🖼 Item Master

○ Number	▼ Revision
▸ 100021	⋯
100020	**Open...**
100019	🖳 Update...
100018	Change Number...
100017	🖼 Change State...
100016	✖ Delete

14. In the Select Lifecycle dialog box, select **Released**.

15. Click **OK**. Note that the *Revision* is a dash (-) and the lifecycle state is changed to **Released**. A lock symbol is placed beside the item.

🖼 Item Master

○ Number	▼ Revision	State	Title (Item,CO)
▸ 🔒 100021	-	Released	Handle.ipt

16. From the Go menu, select **Project Explorer**.

17. Review the part. Note the lock symbol beside the part here as well.

🗀 Clamp

○ 🗋 Name
▸ ▼ **Entity Type:Folder**
🗀 Engineering Documents
▼ **Entity Type:File**
🔒 🖫 Handle.ipt

18. From the Go menu, select **Item Master**.

19. Right-click on the item and select **Change State**.

20. Select **Work In Progress** and click **OK**.

21. Review the status of the part. The *Revision* is now set to **A**. Note that the lock icon is removed from the item.

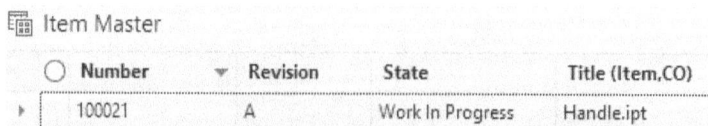

🖼 Item Master

○ Number	▼ Revision	State	Title (Item,CO)
▸ 100021	A	Work In Progress	Handle.ipt

End of practice

11.2 Change Orders

Overview

This lesson describes how to create change orders to control the release of new designs or changes to those designs.

The Change Order Editor role provides permissions to create or participate in a change order. In addition, the administrator defines appropriate change order permissions for each participant in the change order process.

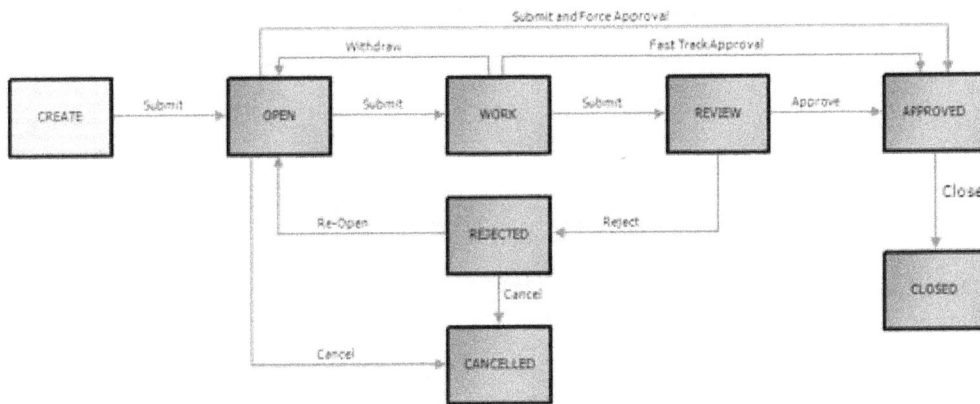

Double click on a state for summary information

Objectives

After completing this lesson, you will be able to:

- Review the Change Order dialog box.
- Create a change order.
- Attach an item to a change order.
- Review lifecycle states.
- Review change order routing.

Introduction to Change Orders

When you create a revision, design changes are made and the changes are then approved by one or more people. Using the change order process, when you (the change requestor) modify files or items, the change is routed to the correct members in the design team before being released to production. When the change order reaches the Closed state, it will display a dialog box with the associated items and files that enables the user to manually change the states.

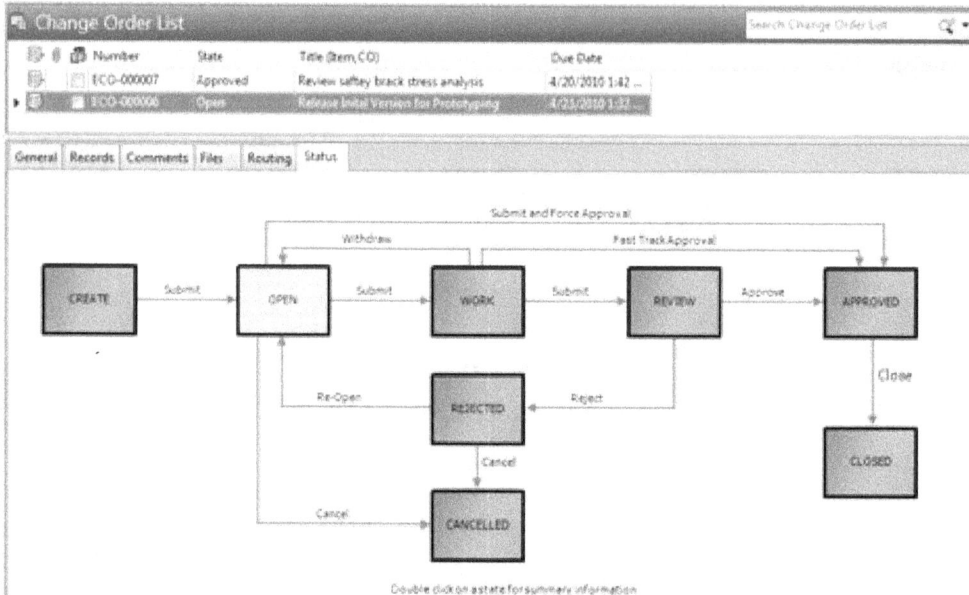

Definition of Change Orders

You can use change orders to both describe the changes made to a design and to manage the progress of those changes through review, approval, rejection, and release to production. The Change Order dialog box provides a historical record of why, how, and when changes were made.

Description of Change Order Workflow

The *Status* tab in the Change Order dialog box displays a workflow chart of all possible combinations of state progressions.

> *Note: Some companies include a Check state between Work and Review.*

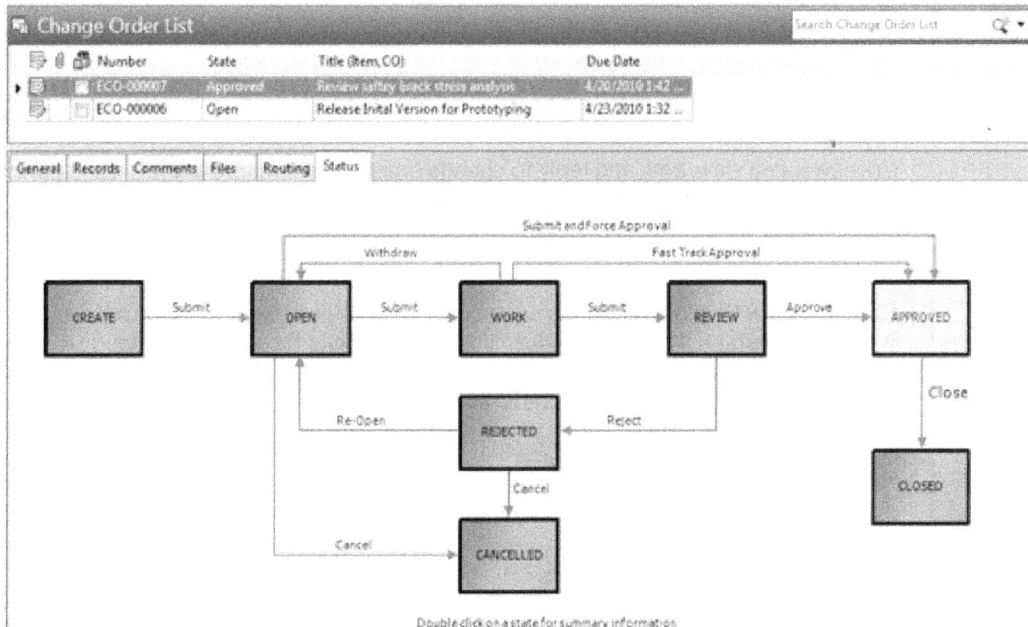

Change Order Workflow Chart

You can also visually identify the current status of the change order by clicking the *Status* tab on the respective Change Order dialog box. Double-clicking a state gives you summary information about that state.

State	Description
OPEN	After a user has created and submitted the change order, the change order enters the Open state. In the Open state, the Change Administrator can edit the title, edit the value of a user-defined property, and change the attachments. The Change Administrator can perform the same editing tasks in the open state as in the state when the change order is first being created with one exception: The specified numbering scheme cannot be changed. Change the lifecycle state of an item by using the change state command in the context menu of a selected item.
WORK	As soon as the change order enters the Work state, the Responsible Engineer is notified that there is a change order requiring attention, then the following occurs: The change order number is added to each participant's work list. An email message is sent to each person on the routing list if they have subscribed to email notification for change order events. Anyone can view the status. A reviewer can view, add, and reply to change order comments. The Responsible Engineer can edit the change order, make any required revisions, and then submit the change order for review.
REVIEW	As soon as the change order enters the Review state, routing participants are notified that there is a change order requiring attention, then the following occurs: The change order number is added to each participant's work list. An email message is sent to each person on the routing list if they have subscribed to email notification for change order events. A reviewer can view, add, and reply to change order comments. Approvers can approve or reject the changes. Unanimous approval requires that all approvers must approve the changes. Anyone can view the status.
APPROVED	A participant with approver status can approve a change order. The Approvers approve in the Review state. If the Change Administrator submits the approved change order to the Closed state, a records dialog box displays that enables the Change Administrator change the state of the attached items to release them.
REJECTED	When a participant with Approver status rejects a change order, the change order enters into the Rejected state. As a Change Administrator, you can do the following: • Cancel the change order. • Reopen the change order.

State	Description
CANCELLED	In the Cancelled state, no action can be taken by anyone.
CLOSED	In the Closed state, no action can be taken by anyone.

11.3 Creating Change Orders

Use the Change Order dialog box to create change orders. A change requestor initiates the process and adds comments, attaches files, and selects a routing template (a predefined list of participants).

Change Order Options

The tab functions in the Change Order dialog box are described in the following table.

Options	Description
General	Contains the change order attributes.
Records	Displays the list of files and items associated with the change order. The record details for each file or item include a title, description, revision, and state.
Comments	Summarizes the decisions for the change order in the form of comments. The *Comments* tab collects all actions taken on the change order or comments submitted for the change order.
Files	Lists all files for the change order. Attachments and markups are also listed.
Routing	Lists the participants involved with the current change order.
Status	Contains a graphical representation of the current status of the change order.

How To: Create a Change Order

The following steps describe how to create a change order. You must have Administrator or Change Order Editor permissions to create or participate in a change order. Note: You should not save the change order until you have selected a routing template. After the change order is saved, the change requestor cannot change the routing list, but the change administrator can change this in the Open state.

1. You can right-click on items in the Item Master or files in the Project Explorer view to display the context menu. Select **Add To Change Order>To New**.

2. The Change Order dialog box displays.

3. Click the [...] button next to *Change Order Number* to display the Change Order Numbering Schemes dialog box. Select a numbering scheme from the list and click **OK**.

Note: The numbering scheme cannot be changed by the change requestor after the change order has been saved, but the change administrator can change the number in the Open state.

4. Enter a title under *Change Order Title* and enter a detailed description. Under *Due Date*, select a date when the change order is to be completed.

Change Order Title:

Modify Pin A for tighter fit

Detailed Description:

Customer service reports that the pins are coming loose due to too much play in the assembly. Need to determine what the optimal diameter is and adjust the design.

5. Click the *Records* tab. The file selected in Step 1 displays.

ECO-000002

File Edit View Actions Help

Save ?

General   Records   Comments   Files   Routing   Status

Associated Records: Look For: All

○	Name	Revision	State (Historical)	Title		
▶	Pin_A.ipt					

Add...   Revise

- You can use **Add** to attach other files or items to the change order.

6. Select the *Comments* tab, then click **Add Comment** to add information about the required design change, etc.

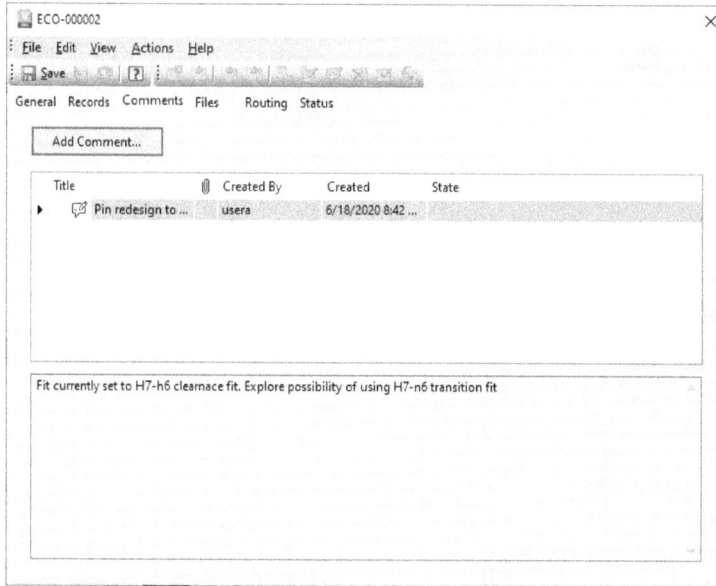

7. Click the *Routing* tab. Select a routing list.

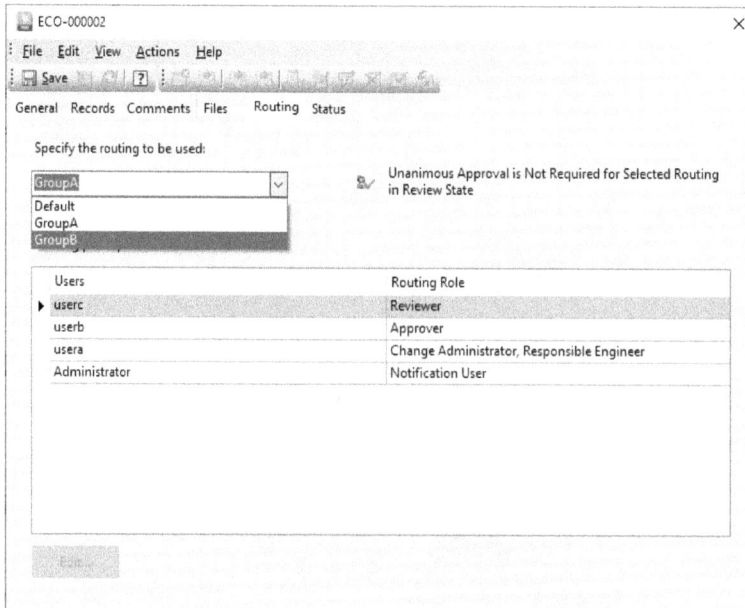

- An example of a routing list and what it represents is shown in the *Example of Change Order Routing* section.

8. Click **Save** to create the change order.

11.4 Change Orders and Revisions

The lifecycle state change generates a primary revision change to the items or files included in a change order. A qualified user can manually change the revision for any item or file.

Definition of Change Orders and Item Revisions

You can manually change an item or file revision regardless of its participation in a change order.

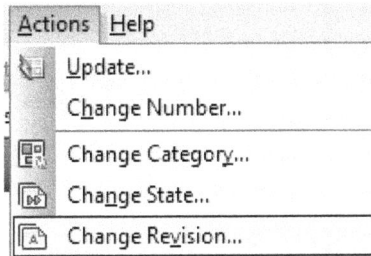

For example, if a part is currently a work in progress, a department can create a secondary revision to indicate a design change.

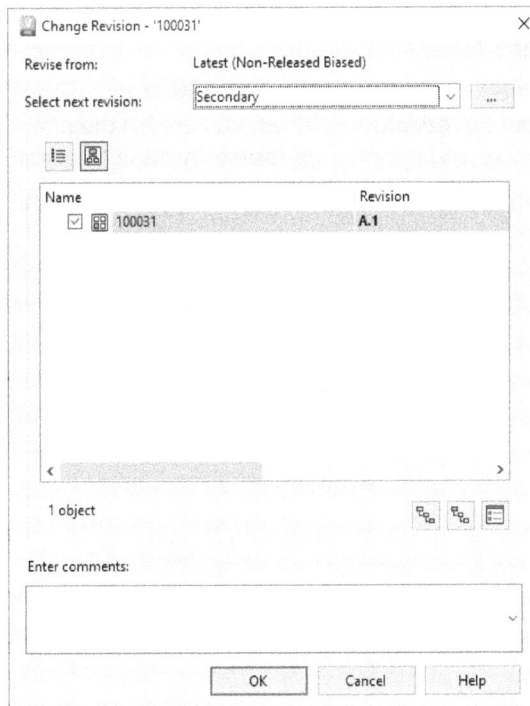

By default, items associated with a change order are locked for state changes and only the Change Administrator or Responsible Engineer can make them editable in the Open or Work states. If an item in the Released state is added to a change order and editing is enabled, the item's state changes to Work in Progress. A new revision is automatically created unless the bump revision action is set to **None** in the Lifecycle Rules dialog box.

Example of a Revision Change

In the following example, the part file Grip.ipt is released and has a revision -. When you use the **Change State** option to change the item state to Work in Progress, the revision changes from - to A and the part is now editable.

Change Orders and Lifecycle States

Example of a Change Order

Engineering has been notified that a part has had a higher-than-expected failure rate under certain conditions and must be redesigned. When you create the change order for the existing item, the part can be modified and the change routed through the design team for approval.

When the item is not included in an active change order, you can manually change the state of the item.

When an item is attached to a change order, the functionality is disabled at the item level and transferred into the change order while in the edit mode.

Rules for Using Change Orders with Files

General Rules

- Only users with Administrator or Change Order Editor security permissions can affect change orders.

- A file can only be associated with one active change order at a time. Once a change order has been closed or cancelled, the file can be associated with a new or a currently active change order.

- Change orders do not drive file state changes. However, a change order will prevent certain lifecycle state changes for the file depending on the change order's state and if linked to change order is added as a criteria in the file's lifecycle transition.

Rules for Closing a Change Order

- The change order must be in the Approved state.

Rules for Releasing Files with Relationships

- Releasing an assembly on a change order that has unreleased children (not on a change order) releases the children. Effectivity is immediate.

- If a previously unreleased child is on another change order, the change order containing the parent item cannot be closed until the change order associated with the child item is either closed or canceled.

Best Practices

- As a best practice, you should add all affected children to a change order with an assembly. Reviewers and Approvers are notified of all affected files.

- In general, you should add all files affected by a design change to the change order. For example, in Autodesk Inventor, changing a part also changes the parent assembly.

Rules for Using Change Orders with Items

Certain rules apply to using change orders with items and lifecycle states, closing a change order, or releasing items with relationships. Follow these rules and best practices for using change orders with items.

General Rules

- To alter change orders, you must have Administrator or Change Order Editor security permissions. A change order may not be editable when in a particular state where a user has no responsibilities in that state on that change order.

- An item can only be associated with one active change order at a time. Once a change order has been closed or cancelled, the item can be associated with a new or active change order.

- The Change Administrator can make an item editable in all states except Canceled and Closed. The Responsible Engineer can make an item editable in the Work state, changing the lifecycle state.

- When an item is in the Work in Progress state and associated with a change order, an Item Editor Level 2 can edit the item, but cannot use the following commands:

  - Change State
  - New Change Order

Rules for Using Change Orders with Items and Lifecycle States

- If a released item is added to a change order and the Change Administrator changes the state of the item to Work in Progress, the item changes to Work in Progress and a new revision is created according to the bump revision action specified in the Lifecycles Rules dialog box. If the bump revision action is set to **None**, a new revision is created but will display the same revision level.

- The state of an item does not change when it is attached to a change order, except at the closure of the change order. The Change Administrator is presented with a dialog box showing the attached items, which enables the Change Administrator to release the affected items.

- After a new revision is created, the Change Administrator can change the lifecycle state of the item to make the item editable or non-editable. To do this, use the **Change State** command available from the context menu.

Rules for Closing a Change Order

- In order to close a change order, it must be in the Approved state.

- When you close a change order, a Change State dialog displays asking whether you want to change the state for associated items. You can modify the item states before closing the change order, or simply close the change order without making any changes.

Rules for Releasing Items with Relationships

- Releasing an assembly on a change order that has unreleased children (not on a change order) releases the children. Effectivity is immediate.

- If a previously unreleased child is on another change order, the change order containing the parent item cannot be closed until the change order associated with the child item is either closed or cancelled.

Best Practices

- As a best practice, you should add all children to a change order with an assembly. Reviewers and Approvers are notified of all affected items.

- In general, you should add all items affected by a design change to the change order. For example, in Autodesk Inventor, changing a part also changes the parent assembly.

Roll Back the Lifecycle State of a File

Return a file to a previous lifecycle state with the **Roll Back Lifecycle State Change** command. When a file is rolled back, it:

- Returns to the file version associated with the rolled-back state.

- Returns to the security, lifecycle definition, and revisions scheme associated with the rolled-back state.

- All file properties are reset to the values of the previous version.

- Deletes the current version of the file.

Rules for Rolling Back a File Lifecycle State

The lifecycle of a file can be rolled back if:

- The file is currently checked in.

- No parent versions consume the current child version that you want to roll back.

- The previous lifecycle state has not been deleted.

- The file is not in <null> definition.

- There is no label on the current version of the file.

- The administrator has not enabled the **Restrict File and Item Lifecycle State Changes to Change Orders** option. Files should never be rolled back past the last released state. Only roll files back to Released in the Work in Progress or In Review states.

How To: Roll Back a File's Lifecycle State

You must be a Document Manager Level 2 or Administrator to roll back a file's lifecycle state.

1. Select a file in the main view and select **Actions>Roll Back Lifecycle State Change**.
2. A dialog box displays describing to which state the file will be rolled back.
3. Click **Continue** to complete the lifecycle state rollback.

Roll Back the Lifecycle State of an Item

Return an item to a previous lifecycle state with the **Roll Back Lifecycle State Change** command.

When an item is rolled back, it:

- Returns to the item version associated with the rolled-back state.
- Returns to the security, lifecycle definition, and revisions scheme associated with the rolled-back state.
- All item properties are reset to the values of the previous version.
- Deletes the current version of the item.

Rules for Rolling Back an Item Lifecycle State

You can roll back an item from any state to another state as long as:

- The rolled-back state has not been deleted.
- The current lifecycle state is not <null> and the rolled-back state is not <null>.
- The rolled-back state is not controlled by purge settings.
- There are no ECO restrictions on state change.
- The rolled-back state did not exist before the ECO was created.
- The ECO is not closed.

    Note: *If the ECO was canceled, you can still roll back to the last state in the ECO. Items should never be rolled back past the last released state. Only roll items back to Released in the Work in Progress or In Review states.*

- There are no component link restrictions. For example, if rolling back to the previous state would link the item to a component that is only permitted one link and the component is already linked to another item, then the rollback is not permitted.

Only users with Item Editor Level 2, ERP Manager, or Administrator roles can change the state on an item.

How To: Roll Back the Lifecycle State of an Item

1. Select an item in the Item Master, and then select **Actions>Roll Back Lifecycle State Change**.
2. Click **Continue** to complete the lifecycle state rollback.

Clear Item and Change Order Locks

Occasionally, it is required to remove the item and change order locks reserved to you. Use the **Clear Item and CO Locks** command to clear all of the locked items and change orders and return them to read-only mode.

Note: This command releases locks for items and change orders that are reserved to the user performing the command. Changes to the items or change orders are not saved.

How To: Clear Item and Change Order Locks

1. In the Vault Client, select **Actions>Clear Item and CO Locks**.
2. Verify that you want to clear the locks.
3. All locked items and change orders are returned to read-only state. Changes are not saved.

Identifying Change Order Participants

When you create a change order, you specify a routing list of participants with predefined roles and specific permissions and responsibilities. Participants are notified that a change order requires their attention. All roles, except the Reviewer and Notification User, control the progression of the change order (within the state that the role controls). For example, the Responsible Engineer has control over the Work state only. Change Administrators have some level of control over almost all states, but principally the Open, Rejected, and Approved states. The Reviewer role can add markups, view, add, and reply to comments.

Example of Change Order Routing

The administrator creates routing participant lists in the Global Settings dialog box (**Tools>Administration>Global Settings>***Change Orders* tab), as shown in the following illustration.

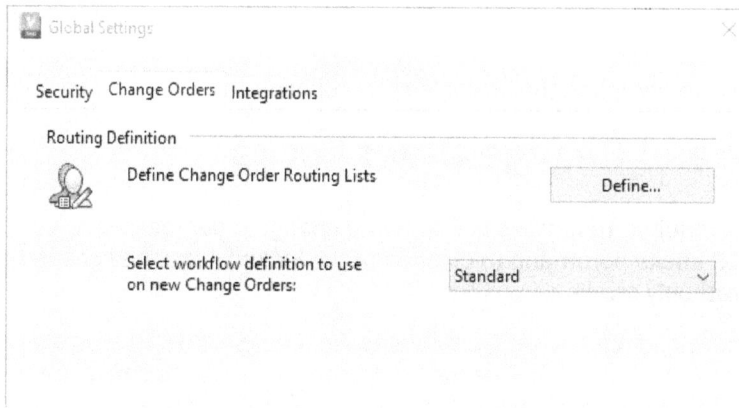

Lists can contain any number of users, but you must specify at least one Approver, one Responsible Engineer, and one Change Administrator in order to create a routing list. A Checker must also be included if the Check state is enabled.

Routing participants:

Users	Routing Role
Administrator	Reviewer, Notification User
usera	Change Administrator
userb	Approver, Responsible Engineer
userc	Approver

To set the routing, the administrator can select **Unanimous approval for Review state required** in the Routing Settings dialog box.

Routing Editing Rules

The following rules apply to editing the routing after the change order has been created:

- Depending on the state of the change order, anyone on the routing can add another reviewer, except for the Notification User.

- The Change Administrator can add or remove Approvers, Change Administrators, and Responsible Engineers. In the Work state, the Responsible Engineer can only add another user as a Responsible Engineer, Reviewer, or Notification User.

- Only the Administrator, Change Administrator, and Responsible Engineer can remove a Reviewer.

- Change order activities can only be performed by the routing participants.

Notification

A user on the routing list is notified when the change order enters a state that requires their attention. There are three notification methods:

- **My Worklist:** In the Navigation pane, when Home or Change Order List displays. The change order number and due date display on this list. Clicking on a change order in this list will change the main pane to Change Orders with that change order selected.

- **Pop-up alert:** Displays briefly in the lower right-hand corner when a change order is added to the user's work list. This pop-up message can be toggled off or on. By default, the pop-up notification is on. To change the setting, click **View>Notification Display**.

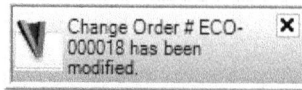

- **Email notification:** The administrator must configure Autodesk Data Management Server for email notification and Vault Professional users must have valid email addresses in their user profiles.

Routing Participants Are Notified

- The change order number displays on each routing participant's 'My Worklist' depending on the state of the change order. For example, the Responsible Engineer is notified when the change order enters the Work state, but the Approver does not get notified until it enters the Review state.

- Following the same logic, an email message is sent to each person on the routing list depending on the state of the change order. For example, the Reviewer is notified by email when the change order enters the Review state.

- Vault Professional includes a role called Notification Users in the *ECO Routing* tab. This user is notified when a change order is closed, usually indicating that a new revision of items or documents is now available.

- If Vault Professional is running but inactive, a pop-up alert displays momentarily on the user's screen in the lower-right corner when the change order is added to their work list.

Participants and Change Order Roles

The following steps describe the typical workflow for creating a change order as well as the roles of participants at each step in the process:

1. A user creates a change order. This user can be any member of the design team as long as they have a Change Order Editor role. The following actions occur:

   - They are added to the routing list as a Change Requestor.
   - The change order enters the Create state.
   - The Change Requestor adds information in the properties and can add any additional files or items to the change.
   - The Change Requestor or the Change Administrator submits to the Open state.
   - The Change Administrator is notified if the change order is submitted to the Open state.

2. In the Open state, the Change Administrator reviews the order and determines whether to add comments, markups, or additional properties. In the Open state, it is the Change Administrator's task to determine whether the change order should be processed. It can be canceled for a request that is unfulfillable.

- The Change Administrator selects the items in the *Records* tab of the change order and changes state to put them in Work In Progress. They can also add additional files or items if affected by the change.
- The Change Administrator submits the change order to the Work state.
- The Responsible Engineer is notified. Reviewers are also notified in the Work state, so that they can offer comments during the modifications.

3. If the Change Administrator did not put the items into the Work in Progress state, the Responsible Engineer can at this point. The Responsible Engineer checks out the files from the vault and modifies them with regards to the change order. The files are checked back in to the vault and the items are updated and the state is changed to In Review.

4. The Responsible Engineer submits the change order and it enters the Review state. If the Check state is enabled, the Checker is notified of the change order. They can review the changes, reject the change order back to the Work state for further changes, or approve the work to send the change order onto the Review state.

5. The Reviewers and Approvers are notified. They can review the design changes and add comments and markups. The Approvers can, at any time, approve the change order. If the administrator has selected the **Unanimous approval for Review state required** option in the Routing Settings dialog box, all Approvers must review and submit their acceptance of the change order. The change order is now set to Approved.

6. The Change Administrator is once again notified. Any Work in Progress or In Review items on the change order must be set to Released.

7. The change order is now closed. All Notification Users are notified by email (if configured), indicating new items are ready for production.

Practice 11b
Create and Approve Change Orders

In this practice, you will create two change orders. You will submit and approve the first. For the second, three routing participants must approve the change order because unanimous approval is required.

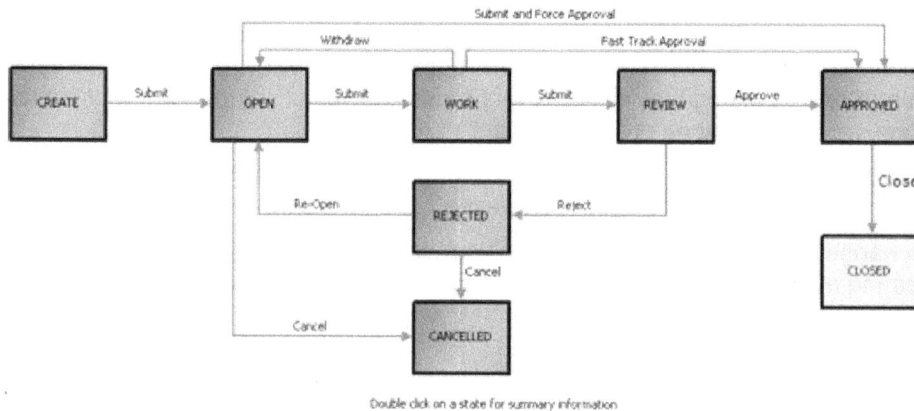

The completed practice

Task 1: Create and approve change orders.

---

1. Start Autodesk Vault Professional. Log in using the following information:

   - For *User Name*, enter **administrator**.
   - Leave the *Password* field blank.
   - For *Vault*, select **AOTCVault**.

2. In Project Explorer, expand the *Designs* folder.

3. Click the **Clamp** folder.

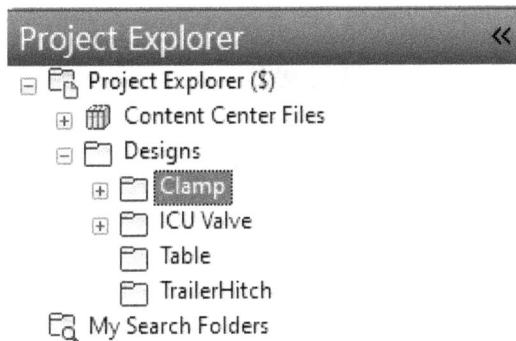

4. Right-click on **Grip.ipt** and select **Assign/Update Item**.

5. In the Edit Item window, select **Save and Close**.

    * An icon displays next to the part name and the associated drawing. After the item has been created, it is recommended to right-click on the file and select **Go To Item** to quickly change to the Item Master view with the particular item selected.

6. Switch to the Item Master. Right-click on the new item and select **Add To Change Order>To New**.

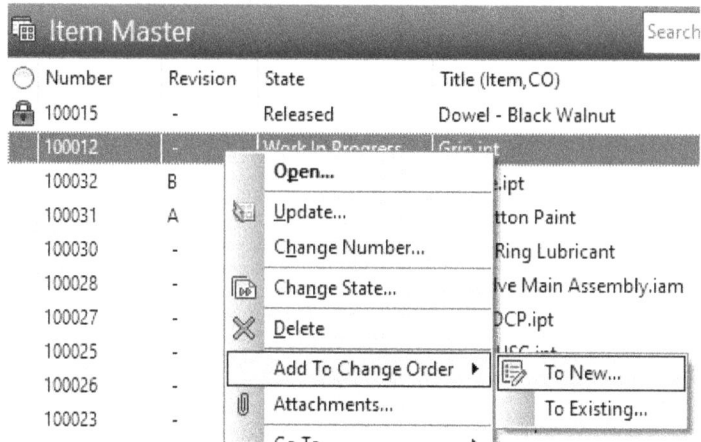

7. In the Change Order dialog box, on the *General* tab, for *Change Order Title*, enter **Modified hole diameter**.

8. For *Detailed Description*, enter **Increased hole diameter to 7.92 mm**.

9. Click **Save**. Close the Change Order dialog box.

10. An icon displays next to items controlled by a change order.

Note: Your item and change order numbers might differ from the illustrations in this practice.

11. Switch to the Change Order List by selecting **Change Order List**. It is recommended to right-click on the item and select **Go To>Go To Change Order**.

12. In the Change Order List, right-click on the new change order. Do the following:

    • Select **Respond>Submit**.

    • Click **OK** to dismiss the Submit – Add Comment dialog box.

    The status of the change order is set to **Open**.

13. Log in using the following information:

    • *User Name*: **usera**

    • *Password:* **vault**

14. In the Change Order List, right-click on the new change order. Do the following:

- Select **Respond>Submit and Force Approval**.
- Click **OK**.

Note: usera is a Change Administrator and can force the approval of a change order.

15. Log in using the following information:

- *User Name*: **userb**
- *Password*: **vault**

Note: userb is an Approver.

16. In the Change Order List, right-click on the new change order. Do the following:

- Select **Respond>Approve**.
- Click **OK**.

17. Select the change order.

18. Select the *Status* tab to display the workflow chart. Do the following:

- Double-click the **Approved** state icon to display summary information about the state.
- Close the Summary dialog box.

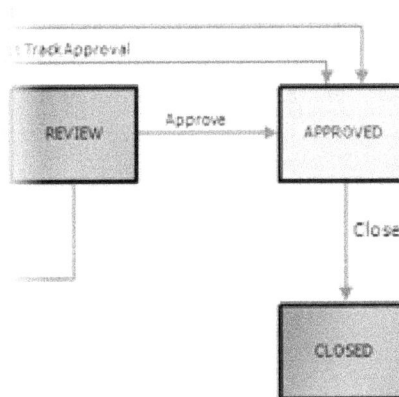

19. Log in using the following information:

- *User Name*: **usera**
- *Password*: **vault**

20. In the Change Order List, right-click on the new change order. Do the following:

   - Select **Respond>Close Change Order**.
   - Click **OK**.
   - Select **Released**.
   - Click **OK**.

21. Review the status. Because the effectivity was set to immediate, the status is now Closed.

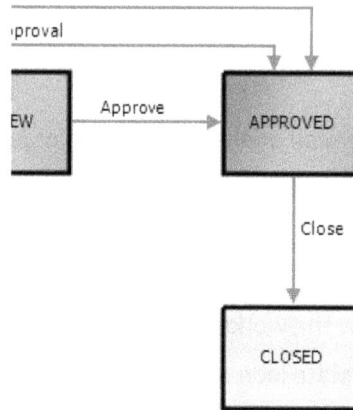

22. Switch to the Item Master.

23. Select the item.

24. In the Preview pane, note that the lifecycle state is set to **Released**.

Task 2: Create a new change order.

1. In the Item Master, right-click on the item created in the previous task. Do the following:

   - Select **Change State>Work in Progress**.
   - Click **OK**.

   A revision is created. In this example, the new revision is A.

	Number	Revision	State	Title (Item,CO)
○	100015	-	Released	Dowel - Black Walnut
🔒	100012	A	Work In Progress	Grip.ipt
	100032	B	Work In Progress	Handle.ipt

2. Right-click on the item, then select **Add to Change Order>To New**. Do the following:

   - For *Change Order Title*, enter **Increased notch depth**.
   - For *Detailed Description*, enter **Notch depth increased to 3.18 mm**.

3. Under *Properties*, in the *Value* column, click **Design**. Select **Manufacturing** from the list.

Properties:

Name	Value
Originator01	Design
	Customer Support
	Design
	Manufacturing
	Marketing

4. Select the *Files* tab. In the *Attached Files* list, select **Grip.idw**.

5. Do the following:

   - On the top view, zoom in to the notch feature.
   - In the callout drop-down list, click **Rectangle callout, revision cloud**.

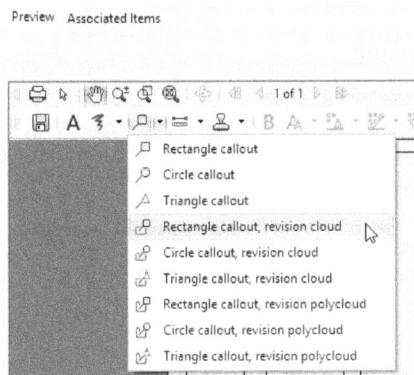

Preview   Associated Items

- Rectangle callout
- Circle callout
- Triangle callout
- Rectangle callout, revision cloud
- Circle callout, revision cloud
- Triangle callout, revision cloud
- Rectangle callout, revision polycloud
- Circle callout, revision polycloud
- Triangle callout, revision polycloud

   - Or if using Design Review, in the *Markup & Measure* tab>Callouts panel, select **Rectangle Callout with Rectangle Cloud**.

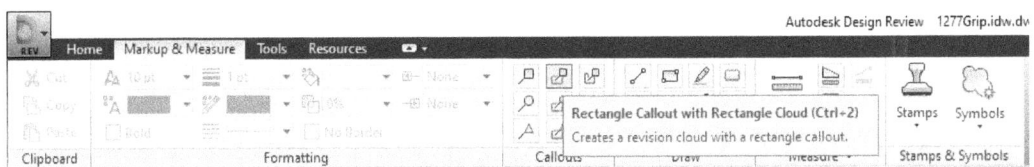

Rectangle Callout with Rectangle Cloud (Ctrl+2)
Creates a revision cloud with a rectangle callout.

6. Click and drag to create a markup around the notch.

7. In the text box, enter **Notch depth increased to 3.18 mm**.

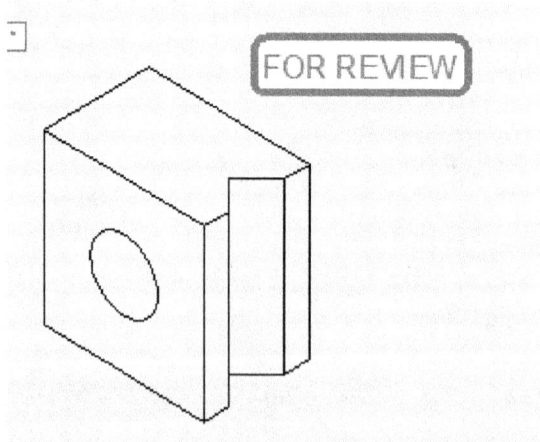

Notch depth increased to 3.18 mm

8. Click **Fit to Window**.

9. Click the down arrow next to **Stamps**. Do the following:

- Select the **For Review** stamp.

- Click in the sheet to place the stamp.

FOR REVIEW

10. Click **Save**. Do the following:

- In the Save As dialog box, navigate to the *Clamp* folder.
- Enter the filename **clamp_markup**.
- Click **Save** to add the markup file to the vault.

11. In the Add Comment dialog box, do the following:

- For *Title*, enter **Notch depth increased to 3.18 mm**.
- For *Comments*, enter **Due to a number of failures in the field, the notch depth has been increased**.
- Click **OK**.

12. Select the *Routing* tab. From the list, select **GroupB**.

13. Review the routing participants. usera, userb, and userc are part of this group.

- usera is the Change Administrator. Since usera is creating the change order, they will also be the Change Requestor for this change order.
- userb is an Approver and the Responsible Engineer.
- userc is an Approver.

The administrator created this list with unanimous approval required for a change order.

Unanimous Approval is Required for Selected Routing in Review State

14. Select the *Status* tab. The workflow chart shows that the change order is set to **Create**.

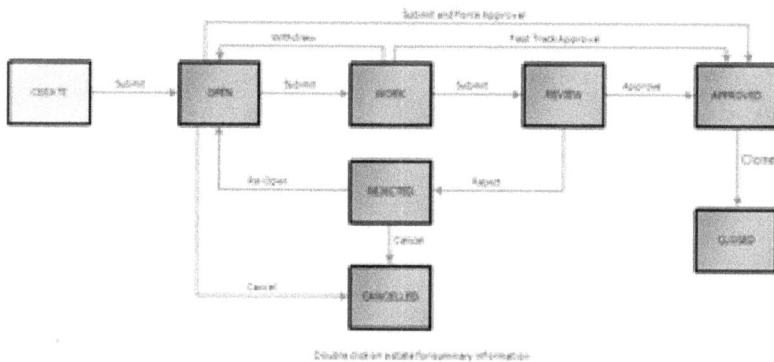

15. Click **Save**. Close the Change Order dialog box. It is recommended to NOT save the change order until this step. Saving beforehand will remove the user's ability to set the routing choice as shown in Step 12.

16. In the Change Order List, right-click on the new change order. Do the following:

- Select **Respond>Submit**.
- Click **OK** to dismiss the Submit – Add Comment dialog box. Note that by default a title is entered indicating the ECO is submitted to the **Open** state.

17. In the Change Order List, select the new change order. Select the *Status* tab to display the workflow chart.

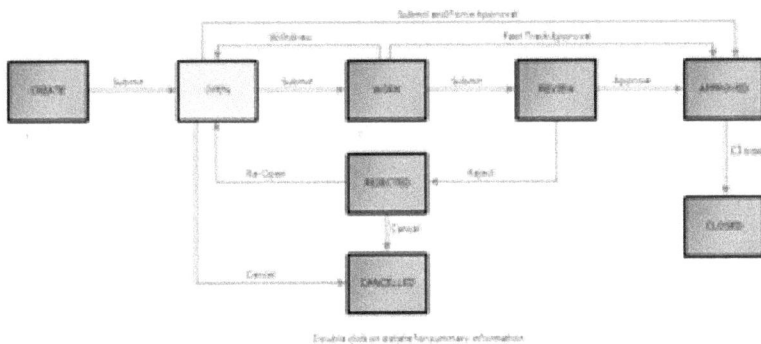

18. In the status diagram, double-click the **Open** state to display the summary information about the state. Close the Summary dialog box.

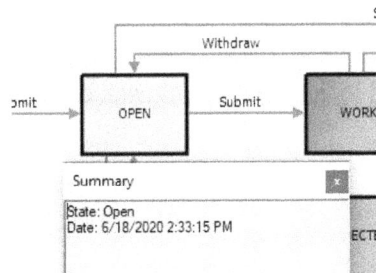

usera submits the change order again to change the status to Work.

19. In the Change Order list, right-click on the new change order. Do the following:

- Select **Respond>Submit**.
- Click **OK** in the Submit – Add Comment dialog box, again accepting the default comment.
- Note the new state of the change order in the *Status* tab.

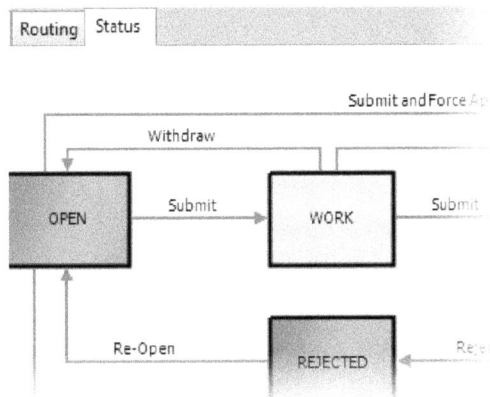

You now log in as userb, the Responsible Engineer.

20. Select **File>Log Out**.

21. Select **Log In**.

22. Log in using the following information:

    - *User Name:* **userb**
    - *Password:* **vault**
    - *Vault:* **AOTCVault**

23. Review My Worklist. The ECO is listed.

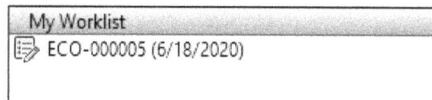

    - Clicking on the ECO in your worklist will take you directly to the Change Order List with the change order selected.

24. Select the *Comments* tab. Review the comments. Note that the details in the comment titled **Notch depth increased to 3.18mm**. Right-click on this comment and view the attachment. Close the Attachments window.

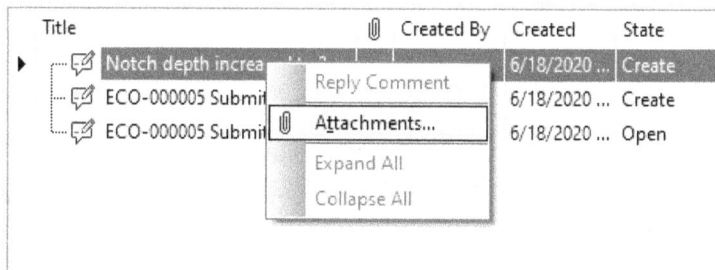

25. Select the *Files* tab and click the attached markup file **clamp_markup.dwf** in the *Attached Files* list.

26. In the Change Order List, right-click on the new change order. Do the following:

    - Select **Respond>Submit**. This will move the change order to the **Review** state.
    - The Submit – Add Comment dialog box displays. In the *Comments* field, enter **Reviewed by the responsible engineer. The new design is correct.**
    - Click **OK**.

27. Note that the change order still displays in My Worklist. The change order requires unanimous approval from all reviewers. In addition to being the Responsible Engineer, userb is also a Reviewer. userb must also approve the change order.

28. In the Change Order list, right-click on the new change order. Do the following:

- Select **Respond>Approve**.
- In the Approve – Add Comment dialog box, enter **The design has been reviewed and is correct. Ready for re-release.**
- Click **OK**.

Approve - Add Comment   ✕

⚠ Notification is not configured. Please contact administrator.

Comment   Email

Title: ECO-000005 Approve to Approved

Comment:

The design has been reviewed andis correct. Ready for re-release.

[Include original message]   [Attachments...]

[Add comment to email]

       [OK]   [Cancel]   [Help]

---

29. Select the *Status* tab. Note that the change order state is still **Review**. Double-click on the state to review the status. The change order requires unanimous approval from all reviewers.

State for summary in

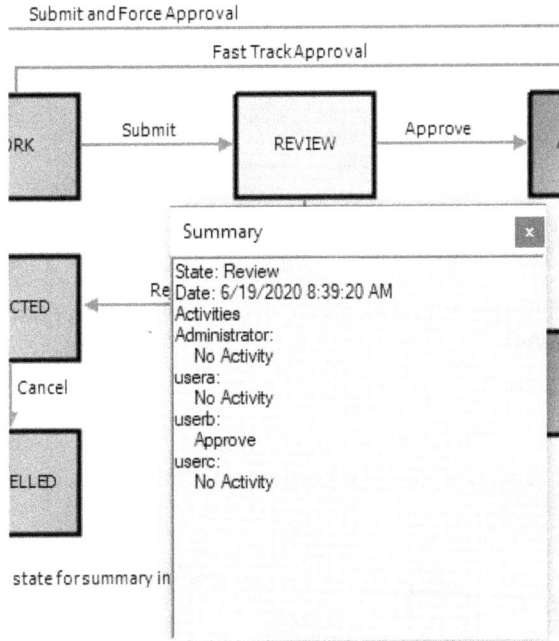

userc must also approve the change order.

30. Select **File>Log Out**.

31. Select **Log In**.

32. Log in using the following information:

- *User Name:* **userc**
- *Password:* **vault**
- *Vault:* **AOTCVault**

33. Note that the change order is in My Worklist. Select on the change order to switch to the Change Order List with the change order selected.

34. Double-click on the change order to open it for review.

35. Select the *Comments* tab and review the comments.

36. In the Respond toolbar, note that there are two possible icons enabled – **Reject** and **Approve**. Select **Approve**.

37. In the Approve – Add Comments dialog box, in the *Comment* section, enter **Agreed – ready for immediate re-release.**

38. Click **OK** to exit the dialog box.

39. Close the Change Order dialog box.

40. Select the *Status* tab. Because all three participants have approved the change, the state is set to **Approved**.

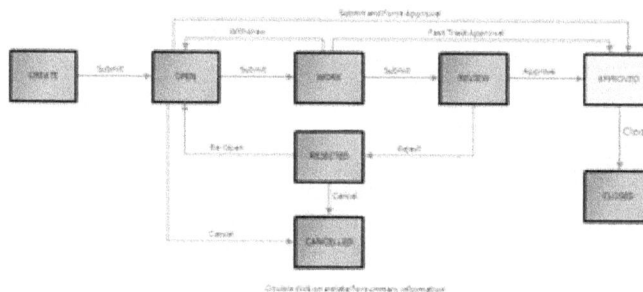

The Change Administrator is responsible for closing the change order by setting the effectivity of the items on the change order. In this scenario, usera is the Change Administrator.

41. Log in as **usera** using the data provided earlier in this practice.

42. Note once again that the change order displays in My Worklist. Select it to go to the change order.

43. In the Change Order List, right-click on the new change order. Do the following:

- Select **Respond>Close Change Order**.
- Click **OK**.
- Select **Released**.
- Click **OK**.

44. In the Change Order List, review the status of the change order. Note that it is now **Closed**.

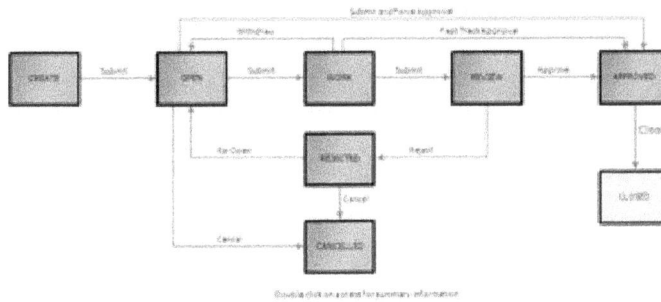

45. Select the *Records* tab and note the *Revision* and *State (Historical)* of the item. It has been now released at Revision A.

General	Records	Comments	Files	Routing	Status	

Associated Records: Look For:

	Name	Revision	State (Historical)	Title
▶	100012	A	Released	Grip.ipt

End of practice

Working with Bills of Materials

This chapter describes how to use bills of materials (BOMs) in Autodesk® Vault Professional. You learn how these BOMs are integrated with other applications, including Autodesk® Inventor® and Autodesk® Vault.

Learning Objectives

- Manage bills of materials.
- Describe the integration of Inventor, Vault, and Vault Professional and the relationship between an Inventor BOM and the associated Vault Professional item BOM.

12.1 Bills of Materials

Overview

This lesson describes how to manage and use bills of materials (BOMs).

As an essential element in the design or manufacture of products, a BOM, in its simplest form, can be a list of components and the quantity of each required. It can, however, describe much more. BOMs can indicate which parts are manufactured and which are purchased, the materials, part numbers, and stock numbers of each part, and how the parts are structured and assembled.

Use the *Bill of Materials* tab in the Edit Item Record dialog box or in the Preview pane to work with the items BOM.

Objectives

After completing this lesson, you will be able to:

- View part BOMs.

- Edit BOMs to add, delete, and reorder items, and change item quantities.

- Format, print, and export BOMs.

About Bill of Materials

You can manage and track components of an assembly by using a BOM that lists all its parts and subassemblies. When you link purchased items to an assembly, the items become part of the BOM list as well. Although you typically associate a BOM with an assembly, all items have a bill of materials. You can view the BOM for any item by clicking the *Bill of Materials* tab.

Part and Assembly Bill of Materials

A part BOM contains information related to a single item. The item can represent an Autodesk Inventor part, a purchased part, or another item added to the Item Master. If the item is linked to other items as part of a larger group, you might not be able to edit some of its properties, such as the quantity. You can add rows of other items to a part BOM. For example, you can include an existing document item that provides process or materials information on the part.

Unlike a part BOM, an assembly BOM contains multiple rows of item data that are linked directly or indirectly to the assembly item. Because these linked items are required for an assembly, some industries refer to this list as a recipe or formula. An assembly BOM does not require an actual modeled assembly. You can create a new item for non-modeled assemblies and add rows of other items to this new item's BOM.

Examples of Part Bill of Materials

The following illustration shows a BOM for an ICUSPRNG part. Standard modeled parts are usually measured in units of one (each). Note that the quantity field for this item is edited in its parent BOM.

The following illustration shows a BOM listing for a non-modeled part (lubricant). Its unit of measurement is set to milliliter.

Examples of Assembly Bill of Materials

The following illustration shows the BOM for an ICU valve main assembly, including parts, subassemblies, and non-modeled items such as paint and lubricant.

Note that when viewing the BOM in Vault Professional, the *Row Order* column indicates the order of the items. Each subassembly listed in the BOM displays its own numbering scheme, starting at 1. The parent rows increment by one and the children rows increment by tenths. For example, if a parent row is 4, then the first child starts with 4.1.

	Number	Ro...	...	Q...	Title (Item,CO)	Rev...	...	State (Historical)			Item Project
▶ ⊟	100028	-	-	-	ICU Valve Main Assembly.iam	-		Work In Progress	✎	♀	ICUV1
	1000...	6		1...	ICU O-Ring Lubricant			Work In Progress		♀	ICUV1
	1000...	1	1	1 E...	ICUHOUSG.ipt	-		Work In Progress		♀	ICUV1
	1000...	2	2	1 E...	ICUENDCP.ipt	-		Work In Progress		♀	ICUV1
⊟	1000...	3	3	1 E...	ICULBUTN.ipt	-		Work In Progress		♀	ICUV1
	1...	3.1		1...	ICU Button Paint	A		Work In Progress		♀	ICUV1
⊟	1000...	4	4	1 E...	ICURBUTN.ipt	-		Work In Progress		♀	ICUV1
	1...	4.1		1...	ICU Button Paint	A		Work In Progress		♀	ICUV1
⊟	1000...	5	5	2 E...	ICUVALVEASSY.iam	-		Work In Progress		♀	ICUV1
	1...	5.1	1	1 E...	ICUVALVE.ipt	-		Work In Progress		♀	ICUV1
	1...	5.2	2	3 E...	ICUORING.ipt	-		Work In Progress		♀	ICUV1
	1...	5.3	3	1 E...	ICUSPRNG.ipt	-		Work In Progress		♀	ICUV1

The following illustration shows the BOM for an ICU valve left button. Note that another item (button paint) is linked to the button part, making it an assembly.

	Number	✎	Row Order	Position ...	Quantity	Units	Category Name ...	Title (Item,CO)	...	...	State		
▶ ⊟	100030		-	-	-	Each	Part	ICULBUTN.ipt	-		Work In Progr...		♀
	100024		1		1	Milliliter	Purchased	ICU Button Paint	-		Work In Progr...		♀

Viewing a Bill of Materials

You can change your view of an item's bill of materials based on item revision/lifecycle state, date, BOM structure, or BOM row on/off status.

By Revision/Lifecycle State

Select the required revision/lifecycle state. Depending on the current item state, not all items will be displayed. Items in the Obsolete state only display the latest revision.

- **Latest:** The current BOM. There can be items in any state in the BOM.

- **Prior Revisions:** Past released BOMs. Views of past released BOMs are read-only, even if the item record is in edit mode.

By Date

Select a date from the Date drop-down list. The last date before a later revision was released is now displayed in the Date drop-down list. Change this date to reflect the released child item revisions for that specific date. The date selected must be on or after the date that the revision was released. The selected child revision BOM displays as of the selected date.

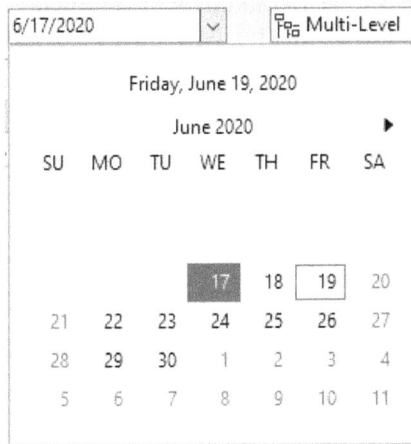

By Bill of Materials Structure

You can select from three types of BOM structures:

- **Multi-Level**: A hierarchical list of all child items in the current BOM. BOM rows can only be modified when the BOM is in **Multi-Level** view.

- **First-Level:** This displays only the top-level child items of the current item.
- **Parts Only:** Items for parts only. The BOM is flattened to a single level. No subassembly items display.

By Bill of Materials Row Display

You can filter whether all BOM rows are displayed, or only those rows that are toggled on or toggled off using the BOM Rows drop-down list.

- **All Rows:** All BOM rows display regardless of whether they are toggled on for the BOM.
- **On Rows Only:** Only rows that have been toggled on for the BOM display.
- **Off Rows Only:** Only rows that are toggled off display.

   *Note: When the **Parts Only** view is selected, the row filter is automatically set to **On Rows Only** and cannot be changed.*

Editing a Bill of Materials

You can view an item's BOM on the *Bill of Materials* tab in the Item Master. You must use the Item Editor to make changes to the BOM. The item must be in a Work in Progress state.

To edit an item, double-click it in the Item Master and select **Edit** from the toolbar. The Edit Item dialog box displays.

Click the *Bill of Materials* tab to access the BOM data.

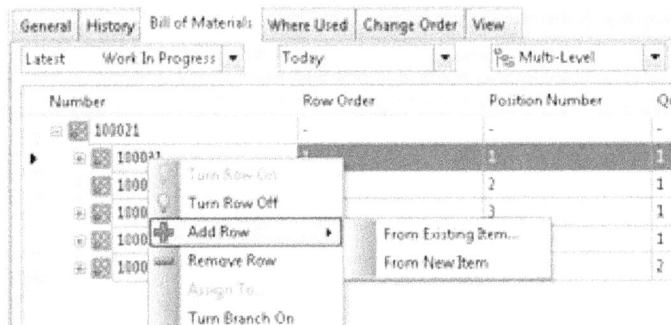

How To: Add Item Rows to an Item Bill of Materials

The following steps describe how to add item rows to an item BOM:

1. In the Item Master window, select the *Bill of Materials* tab. Right-click on the top row of the BOM.

2. Select **Add Row>From Existing Item** (or **From New Item**).

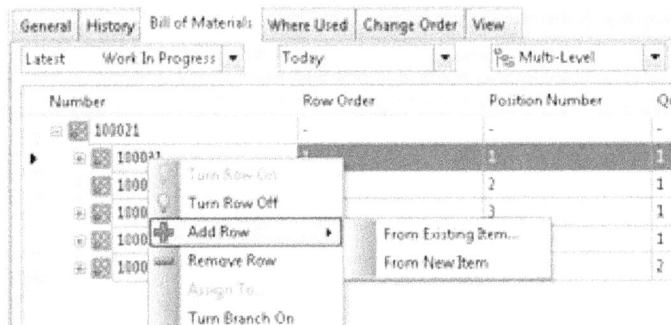

3. If you selected **From Existing Item**, enter the item number or search for the item in the list.

4. Click **OK**. The new item row displays in the BOM list.

5. If you selected **From New Item**, new items added to the BOM in Vault Professional are appended to the end of the order. New items added to the BOM from a CAD add-in are appended to the end of the order when an update is performed.

💡 Hint: Editing BOMs

You can edit a BOM only if it displays in the **Multi-Level** view (BOM tree view) that shows the relationships between the items. You cannot edit a BOM if it displays in the **First-Level** or **Parts Only** list views (the flat BOM view). Any row that you add to the top-level item becomes a first-level child item of the top-level item. To add items to a subassembly, you edit that item and add the item rows there.

How To: Delete Item Rows from an Item Bill of Materials

The following steps describe how to delete item rows from an item BOM. When you delete an item from a BOM, it is not removed from the Item Master, but rather it is removed from the Item BOM.

1. In the Item Master, select the *Bill of Materials* tab. Right-click on the item row to be removed.

2. Select **Remove Row**. The item row is removed. When an item is removed from the BOM, a gap occurs in the numbering sequence. To update the order, drag and drop rows to reset the numbers. Only the top-level children in an item's BOM can be renumbered.

How To: Reorder Item Rows in an Item Bill of Materials

Items listed in the BOM can be reordered by dragging and dropping items in the BOM. The items can be returned to the last saved order by clicking (Restore Saved Order) in the toolbar. The following steps describe how to reorder item rows in an item BOM:

1. In the Item Master, double-click the item to edit and click the *Bill of Materials* tab.

2. Click **Edit**.

3. Click on the *Row Order* column to sort by the current order. Note: The BOM must be sorted by the *Row Order* column to reorder rows.

4. Select a row and drag and drop it to the new location. Note: Rows can be dragged and dropped within the current parent. They cannot be dragged outside of the parent.

5. In the BOM Item toolbar, click **Save and Close** to save the changed order, or select **File>Exit** to close the item record without saving the new BOM order.

    Note: You can also reorder the BOM based on the values in a specific column. Click a BOM column header to sort the rows based on the values in that column. Click the same header to reverse the sort order.

6. To restore the previous saved BOM order, select **Restore Saved Order** from the Edit toolbar.

Restore Saved Order

Changing Bill of Materials Item Quantities

The correct quantities of modeled items are calculated by default. Vault Professional works with the Inventor BOM structure, uses the same units of measure, and automatically adjusts for phantom, reference, or inseparable assemblies.

The quantity of any item can be changed in the BOM. For example, you can change the quantity of items that were added to the BOM from scratch, or of parts that are modeled once but are reused throughout the design (such as bolts). When adding non-CAD items to a BOM, you must include a quantity because there is no CAD data to determine the quantity automatically. Item quantity can only be edited on the *Bill of Materials* tab in an item record.

The BOM can only be edited when it is in **Multi-Level** view.

The item quantity can be either **Static** or **Calculated**. A calculated quantity is derived from the source CAD file and updates accordingly. A static quantity overrides the quantity specified in the linked CAD file, which means that the original quantity contained in the CAD design is no longer reflected in the BOM.

A different font is used to identify whether a quantity is static or calculated. An italic font is used for static quantities.

How To: Change Item Quantites in the Bill of Materials

You can change any quantity in the BOM, including calculated numbers. The following steps describe how to change BOM item quantities:

1. In the Item record, click **Edit** and select the *Bill of Materials* tab.
2. Select a row in the BOM.
3. Click the quantity for the row.
4. Enter a new number for the quantity.
5. Press <Enter>.

    Note: When you change the quantity of an item, you override the quantity derived from the linked CAD file by default. The original quantity contained in the CAD design is no longer reflected in the BOM, and the BOM does not update if the quantity is changed in the source file.

Override the Current Quantity

Right-click on the quantity and select **Static Quantity**. The quantity no longer reflects the value in the linked CAD file and does not update when the quantity is changed in the source file.

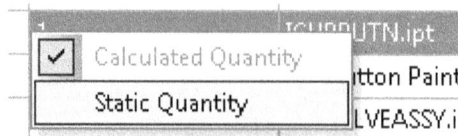

Revert the Quantity to the CAD Value

Right-click on the quantity and select **Calculated Quantity**. The quantity reflects the value in the linked CAD file.

Bill of Materials Output

You can view item BOMs in either tree or list view. Both views can be printed or exported to a Microsoft Excel spreadsheet, a tab-delimited text file, or an HTML page.

You can customize the setup for printing BOMs from the File menu or the toolbar in the Edit Item Record dialog box.

The following illustration shows the use of **Print Preview** to display the form to be printed.

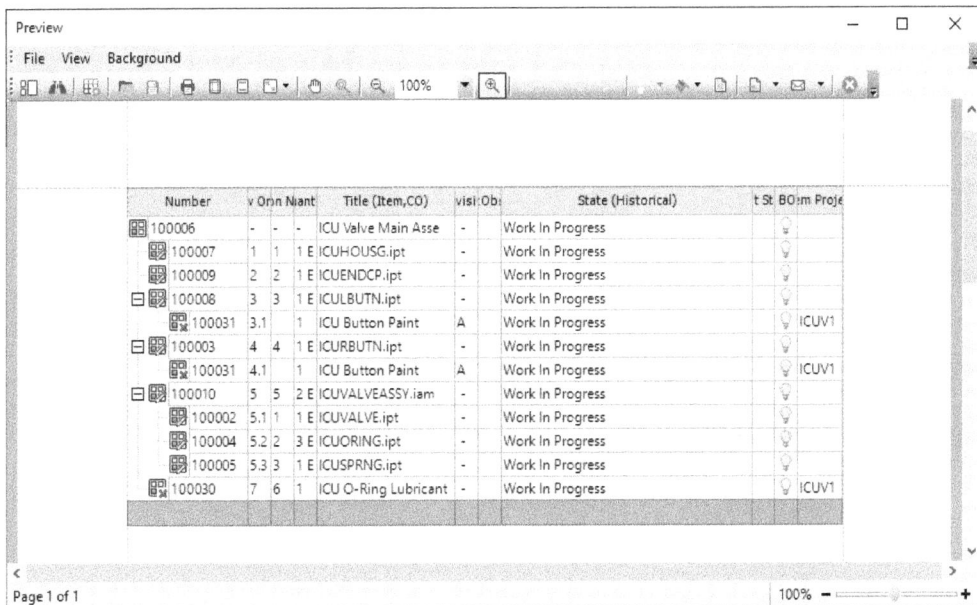

How To: Format and Print a Bill of Materials

The following steps outline how to prepare and print a bill of materials:

1. In the Open or Edit Item dialog box, or in the Preview pane, select the *Bill of Materials* tab.

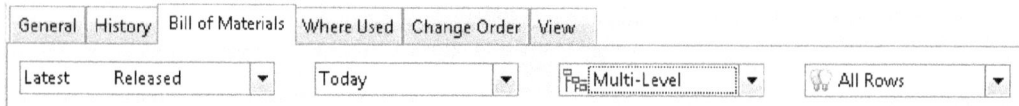

2. Select the BOM *Revision* or *Lifecycle State* for the selected item.

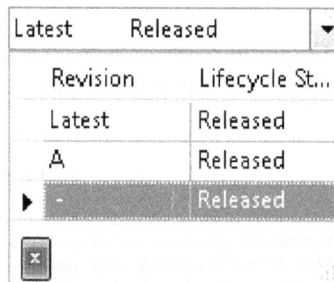

3. Select the BOM format from the Structure list.

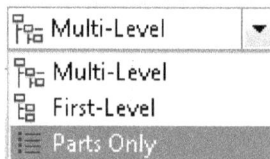

4. Click **File>Print Preview** or click the **Print Preview** icon.

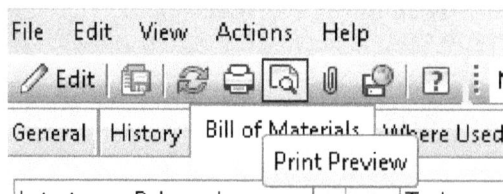

5. In the Print Preview dialog box, click **Customize**.

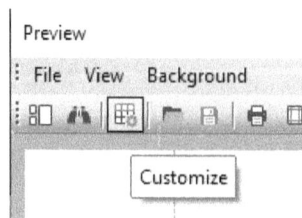

6. In the Printable Component Editor, select format and behavior settings to customize the print out. Click **OK**.

7. In the Print Preview dialog box, on the toolbar, click **Header And Footer** or **Page Setup** to further customize the report.

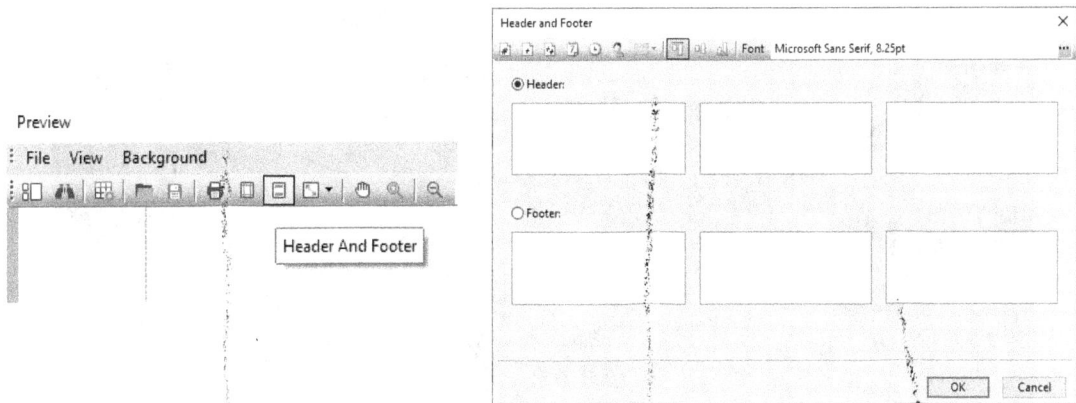

8. Click **Print** or **Print Direct**.

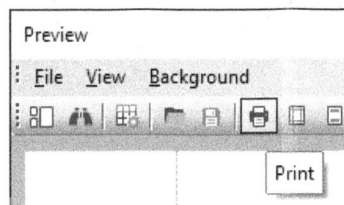

How To: Export a Bill of Materials

The following steps outline how to export a BOM in a variety of file formats:

1. In the Item Master window, right-click on an item and select **Open**.

2. In the Item Record dialog box, click **Edit** and select the *Bill of Materials* tab.

3. Select the BOM format from the Structure list. In this example, print the **Parts Only** list of the BOM.

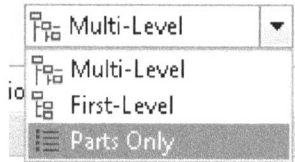

4. From the File menu, select **Save BOM View**, or click the **Save BOM View** icon in the Standard toolbar.

5. Select the file format for the export. Enter a filename. Click **Save** to save the BOM to a file.

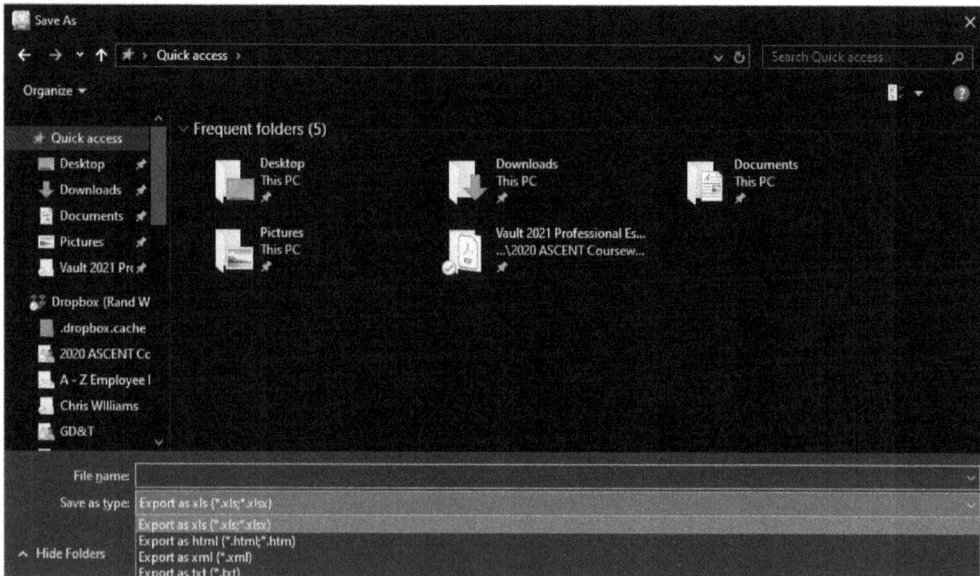

Practice 12a
Work with an Assembly Bill of Materials

In this practice, you manage and edit a product's BOM. You learn to:

- Change BOM quantities.

- Add new items and link items in the BOM.

- Reorder BOM rows.

- View BOMs.

- Redesign the Valve Assembly Packaged Product.

- Save the BOM view.

Task 1: Change BOM quantities.

1. Start Autodesk Vault Professional. Log in using the following information:

    - For *User Name*, enter **administrator**.

    - Leave the *Password* field blank.

    - For *Vault*, select **AOTCVault**.

2. In the Item Master, double-click the **ICUVALVEASSY.iam** item and select **Edit** in the toolbar. Select the *Bill of Materials* tab.

3. On the *Bill of Materials* tab, right-click on one of the column headers and select **Customize View**.

4. Click **Reset** to reset the fields to their default state.

5. In the Customize View dialog box, click **Fields**.

6. Do the following:

- For *Select available fields from*, select **Item Fields**.
- Under *Available fields*, select **Units** and **Entity Icon**. Click **Add**.
- Under *Show these fields in this order*, select **Units**.
- Click **Move Up** until it displays below **Quantity**.
- Move **Entity Icon** below **Number**.
- Click **OK**.

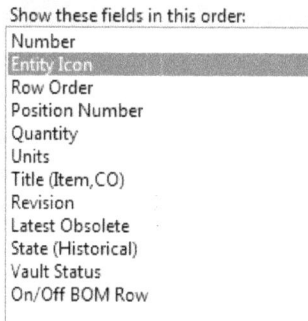

```
Show these fields in this order:
Number
Entity Icon
Row Order
Position Number
Quantity
Units
Title (Item,CO)
Revision
Latest Obsolete
State (Historical)
Vault Status
On/Off BOM Row
```

7. In the Customize View dialog box, click **Close**.

8. On the *Bill of Materials* tab, select the **ICU O-Ring Lubricant** item. Do the following:

- For *Quantity*, enter **30**.
- Press <Enter>.
- Click **Save and Close**.

General | History | Bill of Materials | Where Used | Change Order | View

Latest   Work In Progress ·   Today   Po Multi-Level   ·   All Rows   ·

Number	Row Order	Position Number	Quantity	Units	Title (Item,CO)
▼ 100025	-	-	-	Each	ICUVALVEASSY.iam
100030	1	1	1 Each	Each	ICUVALVE.ipt
100023	2	2	3 Each	Each	ICUORING.ipt
100022	3	3	1 Each	Each	ICUSPRNG.ipt
100020	4		30 Milliliter	Milliliter	ICO O-Ring Lubricant

Note: These steps can also be performed from the top-level BOM.

9. In the Item Master, double-click the **ICULBUTN.ipt** item and click **Edit** in the toolbar.

10. On the *Bill of Materials* tab, for the quantity of the **ICU Button Paint**, enter **20**.

11. Click **Save and Close**.

12. Repeat the previous two steps for the **ICURBUTN.ipt** item.

Task 2: Add new items and link items in the BOM.

1. Under Home, right-click on **Item Master** and select **New Item**.

2. For *Category*, select **Product**.

3. For *Title*, enter **Valve Assembly Packaged Product**.

4. To complete the information for the new item, do the following:

   - For *Units*, verify that **Each** is selected.

   - Under *Item Properties*, select the **Item Project** row.

   - For *Value*, enter **ICUV1**.

   - Click **Save and Close**.

5. Under Home, right-click **Item Master** and select **New Item**.

6. For *Category*, select **Purchased**.

7. Enter the following information for the new item:

   - For *Title*, enter **Valve Packaging.**

   - For *Description*, enter **Product Box**.

8. To complete the information for the new item, do the following:

   - For *Units*, verify that **Each** is selected.

   - Under *Properties*, select the **Item Project** row.

   - For *Value*, enter **ICUV1**.

   - Click **Save and Close**.

9. Under Home, right-click **Item Master** and select **New Item**.

10. For *Category*, select **Document**.

11. Enter the following information for the new item:

    - For *Title*, enter **Valve Product Specifications and Instructions Sheet**.

    - For *Description*, enter **Product Spec**.

12. To complete the information for the new item, do the following:

    - For *Units*, verify that **Each** is selected.

    - Under *Properties*, select the **Item Project** row.

    - For *Value*, enter **ICUV1**.

    - Click **Save and Close**.

13. In the Item Master, double-click the **Valve Assembly Packaged Product** item and click **Edit**. Select the *Bill of Materials* tab.

14. Right-click on **Valve Assembly Packaged Product** and select **Add Row>From Existing Item**.

15. In the Find dialog box, select the *Basic* tab if it is not selected already. Do the following:

    - Under *Search Text*, enter **valve**.

    - Click **Find Now**.

16. Select the following items in the *Found* list and click **OK**.

    - **ICU Valve Main Assembly.iam**

    - **Valve Product Specification and Instructions Sheet**

    - **Valve Packaging**

17. In the Bill of Materials, select the **ICU Valve Main Assembly** row, right-click, and select **Expand All**. Your BOM should look like the following illustration.

General | History | Bill of Materials | Where Used | Change Order | View

Latest   Work In Progress ▾   Today   Multi-Level ▾   All Rows ▾

Number	Row Order	Position Number	Quantity	Units	Title (Item,CO)
▾ 100033	-		-	Each	Valve Assembly Packaged Product
100035	1		1 Each	Each	Valve Product Specifications and Instructions Sheet
100034	2		1 Each	Each	Valve Packaging
▾ 100029	3		1 Each	Each	ICU Valve Main Assembly.iam
100028	3.1	1	1 Each	Each	ICUHOUSG.ipt
100026	3.2	2	1 Each	Each	ICUENDCP.ipt
▾ 100027	3.3	3	1 Each	Each	ICULBUTN.ipt
100021	3.3.1		20 Milliliter	Milliliter	ICU Button Paint
▾ 100024	3.4	4	1 Each	Each	ICURBUTN.ipt
100021	3.4.1		20 Milliliter	Milliliter	ICU Button Paint
▾ 100025	3.5	5	2 Each	Each	ICUVALVEASSY.iam
100030	3.5.1	1	1 Each	Each	ICUVALVE.ipt
100023	3.5.2	2	3 Each	Each	ICUORING.ipt
100022	3.5.3	3	1 Each	Each	ICUSPRNG.ipt
100020	3.5.4		30 Milliliter	Milliliter	ICO O-Ring Lubricant

Task 3: Reorder BOM rows.

1. Review the rows in the BOM. Company policy requires the packaging to be the last item in the BOM.

2. Click the (-) symbol to close the ICU Valve Main Assembly.iam tree view.

3. Drag the **Valve Packaging** row to the bottom of the list if required.

4. Drag the **Valve Product Specifications and Instructions Sheet** down to the last row.

General | History | Bill of Materials | Where Used | Change Order | View

Latest   Work In Progress ▾   Today   Multi-Level ▾   All Rows ▾

Number	Row ...	Position Num...	Quantity	Units	Title (Item,CO)
▾ 100033	-	-	-	Each	Valve Assembly Packaged Product
▸ 100029	1		1 Each	Each	ICU Valve Main Assembly.iam
100034	2		1 Each	Each	Valve Packaging
100035	3		1 Each	Each	Valve Product Specifications and Instructions Sheet

5. Click **Save and Close**. The Valve Assembly Package is complete.

6. In the Item Master, right-click on **Valve Assembly Packaged Product** and select **Change State**.

7. In the Select Lifecycle dialog box, select **Released**. Click **OK**.

- Note that all the children (the components) of the Valve Assembly Package were also released.

Task 4: View BOMs.

1. In the Item Master, select the **Valve Assembly Packaged Product** if it is not selected already.

2. In the Preview pane, select the *Bill of Materials* tab. Review the BOM rows. Note that the quantity of the O-ring lubricant is 30 milliliters in the ICUVALVEASSY item. (There are two ICUVALVEASSY items.)

⊟ 🔳 100...	🔳 1.5	5	2 Each	Ea...	ICUVALVEASSY.iam
🔳 ...	🔳 1.5.1	1	1 Each	Ea...	ICUVALVE.ipt
🔳 ...	🔳 1.5.2	2	3 Each	Ea...	ICUORING.ipt
🔳 ...	🔳 1.5.3	3	1 Each	Ea...	ICUSPRNG.ipt
🔳 ...	🔳 1.5.4		*30 Milliliter*	M...	ICU O-Ring Lubricant

3. For Structure, select **Parts Only**. Note the quantity of the ICU O-ring lubricant (60 milliliters). This value is the correct total because there are two ICUVALVEASSY items with 30 milliliters of lubricant each.

General | History | Bill of Materials | Where Used | Change Order | View

Latest   Released   -   Today   ☷ Parts Only   -   🔍 On Rows Only

	Number	Quantity	Title (Item,CO)
▸ 🔳	100020	*60 Milliliter*	ICO O-Ring Lubricant

4. For Structure, select **First Level**. The three items you linked to the Valve Assembly Packaged Product display.

General | History | Bill of Materials | Where Used | Change Order | View

Latest   Released   -   Today   ☷ First-Level   -   🔍 All Rows   -

	Number	Quantity	Title (Item,CO)
▸ 🔳	100035	*1 Each*	Valve Product Specifications and Ins...
🔳	100034	*1 Each*	Valve Packaging
🔳	100029	*1 Each*	ICU Valve Main Assembly.iam

5. For Structure, select **Multi-Level** to return to the structured BOM list.

Task 5: Redesign the valve assembly package.

1. In the Item Master, right-click on the **ICULBUTN.ipt** item and select **Change State**.

2. In the Select Lifecycle dialog box, select **Work in Progress**. Click **OK**.

3. Repeat Steps 1 and 2 to change the lifecycle state to **Work in Progress** for the **ICURBUTN.ipt, ICUVALVEASSY.iam**, and **Valve Assembly Packaged Product items**.

4. Double-click the **ICURBUTN.ipt** item and click **Edit**. On the *Bill of Materials* tab, select the **ICU Button Paint** row, right-click, and select **Remove Row**. Click **Save and Close**.

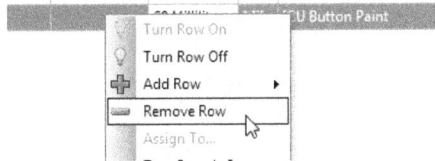

5. Repeat the previous step to remove the **ICU Button Paint** row from the **ICULBUTN.ipt** item.

6. In the Item Master, double-click the **Valve Assembly Packaged Product** item and click **Edit**. Select the *Bill of Materials* tab.

7. Select and right-click on the top row. Select **Add Row>From Existing Item**.

8. In the Find dialog box, do the following:

- Select the *Basic* tab if it is not selected already.
- Under *Search Text*, enter **ICU***.
- Click **Find Now**. A number of items are returned in the search results.
- Select the **ICUORING.ipt** row.
- Click **OK**.

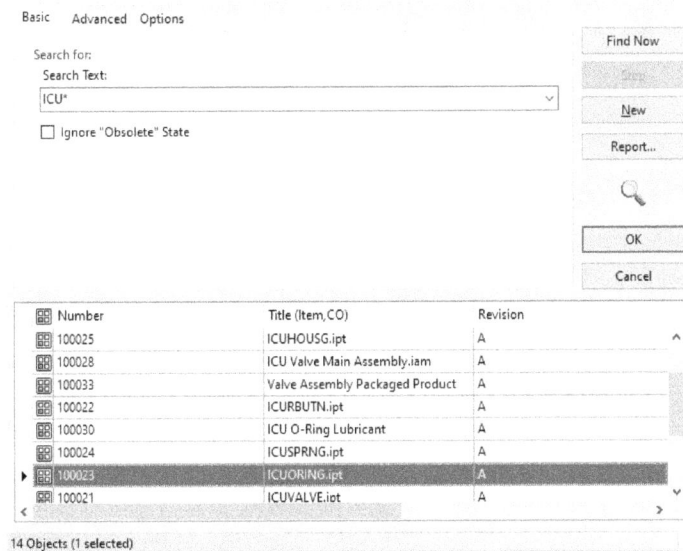

9. The ICUORING.ipt item is added to the BOM. Do the following:

   - Change its quantity to **3**.
   - Click **Save and Close**.

Row ... ▲	Position Num...	Quantity	Units	Title (Item,CO)
-	-	-	Each	Valve Assembly Packaged Product
1		1 Each	Each	ICU Valve Main Assembly.iam
2		1 Each	Each	Valve Packaging
3		1 Each	Each	Valve Product Specifications and Instructions Sheet
4		3 Each	Each	ICUORING.ipt

10. In the Item Master, change the lifecycle state of the **Valve Assembly Packaged Product** item to **Released**. If prompted to confirm the state change for children, click **Yes**.

Task 6: Save BOM view.

1. In the Item Master, double-click the **Valve Assembly Packaged Product** item. Select the *Bill of Materials* tab and select **File>Save BOM View**.

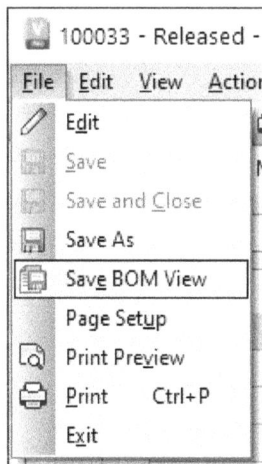

2. For *File name*, enter **ICU Product BOM - Rev B**. Click **Save**.

3. Open Microsoft Excel. Open **ICU Product BOM - Rev B.XLS**.

	A	B	C	D	E	F	G	H	I	J
1	Number	Row Order	Position Number	Quantity	Title (Item,CO)	Revision	Latest Obsolete	State (Historical)	Vault Status	On/Off BOM Row
2	100033	-	-	-	Valve Assembly Packaged Product	A		Released	No local file	On
3	100028	1		1 Each	ICU Valve Main Assembly.iam	A		Released	No local file	On
4	100025	1.1	1	1 Each	ICUHOUSG.ipt	A		Released	No local file	On
5	100027	1.2	2	1 Each	ICUENDCP.ipt	A		Released	No local file	On
6	100026	1.3	3	1 Each	ICULBUTN.ipt	A		Released	No local file	On
7	100022	1.4	4	1 Each	ICURBUTN.ipt	A		Released	No local file	On
8	100029	1.5	5	2 Each	ICUVALVEASSY.iam	A		Released	No local file	On
9	100021	1.5.1	1	1 Each	ICUVALVE.ipt	A		Released	No local file	On
10	100023	1.5.2	2	3 Each	ICUORING.ipt	A		Released	No local file	On
11	100024	1.5.3	3	1 Each	ICUSPRNG.ipt	A		Released	No local file	On
12	100030	1.5.4		30 Milliliter	ICU O-Ring Lubricant	A		Released	No local file	On
13	100035	2		1 Each	Valve Product Specifications and Instructions Sheet	A		Released	No local file	On
14	100034	3		1 Each	Valve Packaging	A		Released	No local file	On
15	100023	4		3 Each	ICUORING.ipt	A		Released	No local file	On

4. Close Vault Professional and Excel.

End of practice

12.2 Integration with Autodesk Inventor

Overview

This lesson describes how to use Autodesk Vault Professional with other applications. The primary focus is the relationship between Autodesk Inventor and Vault Professional BOMs. The lesson also covers working with Vault Professional and Autodesk Vault, AutoCAD®, AutoCAD® Mechanical, and AutoCAD® Electrical.

Objectives

After completing this lesson, you will be able to:

- Describe the integration of Inventor with Vault Professional.

- Describe the relationship between an Inventor bill of materials (BOM) and the associated Vault Professional item BOM.

- Work with Autodesk Inventor virtual components.

- Customize Content Center library components to use with Vault Professional.

- Describe how Vault and Vault Professional work with drawing files.

About Autodesk Inventor and Integration with Vault Professional

Autodesk Vault integrates with Autodesk Inventor software using an Autodesk Inventor add-in. Users can use Vault Professional to assign item numbers to vaulted parts and assemblies. You can edit assembly BOMs in both Autodesk Inventor and Vault Professional, and coordinate property information between Autodesk Inventor, Autodesk Vault, and Autodesk Vault Professional.

				Number	/	Revision	State	Title (Item,CO)	Description (Item,CO)	Category Na...
				100018		-	Work In Progress	ANSI AISC 2x2x 1/4 - 1200mm	Cross Bar	Part
				100019		-	Work In Progress	Hitch Ball	Hitch Ball	Part
				100020		-	Work In Progress	end_plate_RH.ipt	End Plate - RH	Part
				100021		-	Work In Progress	Draw Bar	Draw bar	Part
				100022		-	Work In Progress	DrawBarMountBottomPlate.ipt	Draw Bar Bottom Plate	Part
				100023		-	Work In Progress -	ANSI/ASME B18.8.1 PIN. CLEVIS. 3/4 x 1.91	Clevis Pin	Purchased
				100024		-	Work In Progress	Axle Clip.ipt	Axle Clip	Purchased
				100025		-	Work In Progress	ISO 8678 M12 x 25	Cup Head Square Neck B...	Purchased
				100026		-	Work In Progress	Hex Thick Nut - Inch 3/4 - 10	Hex Thick Nut	Purchased
				100027		-	Work In Progress	Mounting Weldment.iam	Hitch Weldment	Assembly
				100028		-	Work In Progress	Regular Helical Spring Lock Washer (Inch) ...	Helical Spring Lock Washer	Purchased
				100029		-	Work In Progress	Hitch Assembly	Hitch assembly	Assembly
				100030		-	Work In Progress	IS 3063 12	Spring Washer	Purchased

Application Overviews

Autodesk Inventor is a 3D parametric CAD application. You can combine individual part models in a hierarchy of assemblies to create a complete digital design. You supply values for intrinsic document properties and can add custom properties to any part or assembly.

Use Autodesk Vault to provide work-in-progress version control for Inventor models and other documents. A vault stores versions of documents, file relationships between documents, and property data associated with each version. You check files out of the vault to modify them in Inventor and check in the new versions to share with your design team.

When you use Autodesk Vault Professional to assign items to these files, users outside the engineering department can also access property and bill of materials data from the files stored in a vault.

Working with Autodesk Vault Professional and Autodesk Vault

Autodesk Vault Professional is an external application that adds manufacturing and release data to documents in the vault. You create an Autodesk Vault Professional item when you assign an item number to a file stored in the vault. Initial property values for the item are extracted from the property information stored in the vault. After it is created, the item is connected to the file in the vault, but property values are largely independent. You can add Autodesk Vault Professional items without associating them to a vault file.

You need to understand how actions in Autodesk Vault Professional affect the associated files in Autodesk Vault because a number of tasks can be completed only when files are checked in to the vault and lifecycle state changes can affect the state of the associated files in Autodesk Vault.

Autodesk Vault Professional and Autodesk Vault

Item Master

Number	Revision	State	Title (Item,CO)
100021	A	Released	ICUVALVE.ipt
100029	A	Released	ICUVALVEASSY.iam
100020	-	Released	Leg - Tapered
100017	-	Released	Long Rail

ICU Valve

	Name
Folder	
	Documents
File	
	ICU Valve Main Assembly.iam
	ICUENDCP.ipt
	ICUHOUSG.ipt
	ICULBUTN.ipt
	ICUORING.ipt
	ICURBUTN.ipt
	ICUSPRNG.ipt
	ICUVALVE.ipt
	ICUVALVEASSY.iam

All of the associated files of a released item in Vault Professional are locked in the vault.

Working with Autodesk Vault Professional and Autodesk Inventor

When you create an item from a part or assembly stored in a vault, Autodesk Vault Professional extracts property information from Autodesk Vault. The property values are typically assigned in Autodesk Inventor, but you can edit values for existing properties in Autodesk Vault. Item properties can be mapped back to the properties in the associated Autodesk Inventor part or assembly document. If you understand the relationship between properties in all three applications, you can effectively integrate Autodesk Vault Professional into an Autodesk Inventor design environment.

An Autodesk Inventor assembly BOM maps information to the BOM in the associated item in Autodesk Vault Professional. Your understanding of this process helps to ensure its accuracy.

Autodesk Inventor Bill of Materials

Autodesk Vault Professional Bill of Materials

Example of Application Integration

The following example shows a workflow for a change order performed on a Released item. The associated file in the vault is locked when the item is in a Released state.

1. A Vault Professional user creates a new change order for a released part or assembly item. On submittal of the change order, the Change Administrator or Responsible Engineer changes the item status to Work in Progress creating a new item revision. This action unlocks the part or assembly the vault.

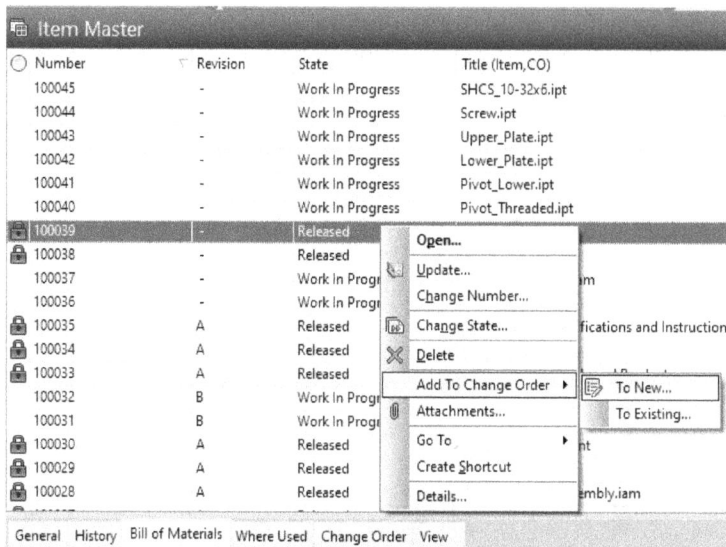

2. When the Responsible Engineer works on the change order, they can open the change order and examine the items associated with it. The items are on the *Records* tab. From here, the user can directly go to the item. Note that having an item associated to the change order on the *Records* tab causes the files associated to the item to be displayed on the *Files* tab. In the Work state, the Responsible Engineer can open a file directly from the *Files* tab and can check the file out at that time.

3. Looking at the item, the user can see which file is associated with what requires work and go directly to the vault folder containing the file.

4. Not looking at the files in the vault, the user can open and check out the file.

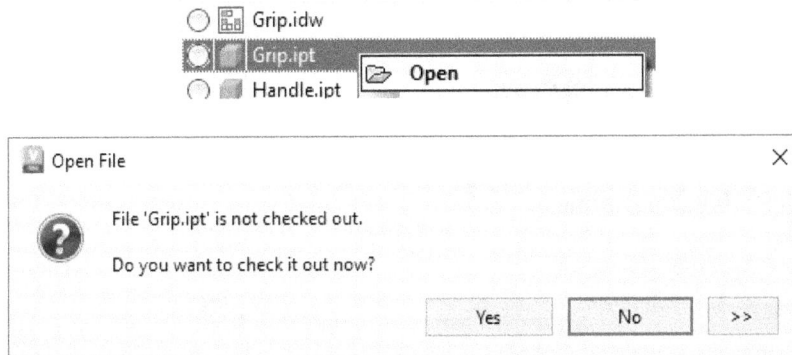

5. The Autodesk Inventor user edits the file and checks them back in to the vault.

6. The Vault Professional user then updates the item to update the link to the new file version.

7. Finally, the change order is completed, returning the item to a Released state. The files are again locked in the vault.

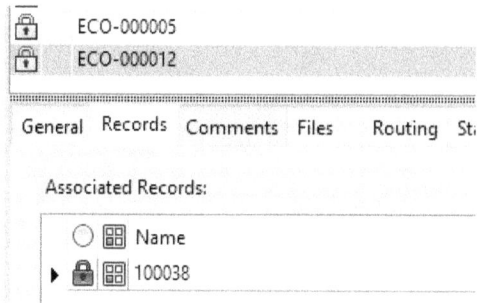

Note: When you check out, edit, and check in a component, you must update the associated item in Autodesk Vault Professional before you can change the lifecycle state of the item. Each item revision is associated with a specific version of the component in the vault. The change order cannot be completed unless the items have been updated.

Autodesk Inventor BOMs

Information in Autodesk Inventor assembly BOMs is translated into the BOMs of the associated Autodesk Vault Professional items.

Definition of Autodesk Inventor BOM

Autodesk Inventor assembly BOMs contain information about their hierarchy of parts, subassemblies, and virtual components and are usually displayed as structured lists of components, as shown in the following illustration:

Item		Δ Part Number	BOM Structure	Component...	Unit QTY	QTY	Stock Number	Description
	1	100049	$ Purchased	Part	Each	1	ANSI/ASME B18.8...	Clevis Pin
	2	100053	Normal	Part	Each	1		Draw bar
	3	100050	$ Purchased	Part	Each	1		Axle Clip
	4	100051	Inseparable	Assembly	Each	1		Hitch Weldment
	5		$ Purchased	Part	Each	1		Helical Spring Lock Washer
	6		$ Purchased	Part	Each	1		Hex Thick Nut
	7	100052	Normal	Part	Each	1		Hitch Ball
	8		$ Purchased	Part	Each	4		Cup Head Square Neck Bolt
	9		$ Purchased	Part	Each	4		Spring Washer
	10		$ Purchased	Part	Each	4		Hexagon Domed Cap Nuts

Parts Only BOM

You can select a **Parts Only** view that flattens the BOM to a single level and aggregates all parts in the assembly hierarchy, as shown in the following illustration:

Item		Part Number	BOM Structure	Unit QTY	QTY	Stock Number	Description
	1	100049	$ Purchased	Each	1	ANSI/ASME B18.8.1 PIN. CLEVIS. 3/4 x 1.91	Clevis Pin
	2	100053	Normal	Each	1		Draw bar
	3	100051	Inseparable	Each	1		Hitch Weldment
	4		$ Purchased	Each	4		Cup Head Square Neck Bol
	5		$ Purchased	Each	4		Spring Washer
	6		$ Purchased	Each	4		Hexagon Domed Cap Nuts
	7	100052	Normal	Each	1		Hitch Ball
	8		$ Purchased	Each	1		Helical Spring Lock Washer
	9		$ Purchased	Each	1		Hex Thick Nut
	10	100050	$ Purchased	Each	1		Axle Clip

BOM Structure

Each part, subassembly, and virtual component in the assembly is assigned a BOM structure that determines the status of the component in the assembly BOM.

The following table explains the display status of individual parts assigned different BOM structure types.

Part BOM Structure	Structured BOM View Status	Parts Only BOM View Status	Notes/Example
Normal	Shown as a single line	Shown as a single line	Default BOM structure for most parts Quantity can be affected by parent BOM structure
Reference	Excluded from view	Excluded from view	Typically assigned to parts that provide reference for the current design
Phantom	Excluded from view	Excluded from view	Skeleton model parts are often assigned a Phantom structure
Purchased	Shown as a single line	Shown as a single line	Assigned to components that are not fabricated
Inseparable	Not normally assigned to parts	Not normally assigned to parts	

The following table outlines the display status of a subassembly and its child components when it is assigned different BOM structure types.

Subassembly BOM Structure	Structured BOM View Status	Parts Only BOM View Status	Notes/Example
Normal	Shown as a single line Child components displayed as subcomponents in the assembly BOM	Excluded from view	Default BOM structure for most subassemblies
Reference	Components and all children excluded from view	Excluded from view	Typically assigned to parts or assemblies that provide reference for the current design

Subassembly BOM Structure	Structured BOM View Status	Parts Only BOM View Status	Notes/Example
Phantom	Excluded from view Child components promoted to Phantom subassembly level Quantity of Phantom component affects quantity of promoted children	Excluded from view	A Phantom assembly that groups a bolt, nut, and washers and can reduce model complexity
Purchased	Shown as a single line Child components displayed as subcomponents (often not shown in parts list)	Shown as a single line (treated as a part) Child components excluded from view	Assigned to assemblies that are not fabricated
Inseparable	Shown as a single line Child components displayed as subcomponents (often not shown in parts list)	Shown as a single line (treated as a part) Purchased child components promoted and shown Other child components excluded from view	Assigned to assemblies that are not easily disassembled Weldments and riveted assemblies are examples of Inseparable assemblies

A component's BOM structure also determines how the corresponding item displays in an Autodesk Vault Professional BOM.

Assigning a BOM Structure

Subassemblies retain their current BOM structure when you place them in a higher-level assembly. Parts are assigned the Normal BOM structure when placed in an assembly. The following illustration shows how you select the BOM structure in the Create In-Place Component dialog box.

Editing a BOM Structure

You can change the BOM structure of a component from its default setting to Reference by right-clicking the component in the browser and selecting **BOM Structure>Reference**. You can restore the default BOM structure using the same steps.

The following illustration shows how you can select any BOM structure for a component in the Bill of Materials dialog box. These options are not available from the browser shortcut menu.

Example of BOM Structure

You can assign the Inseparable BOM structure to the welded frame assembly, as shown in the following illustration. The assembly itself can contain a skeleton part model (Phantom BOM structure), multiple frame members (Normal BOM structure), and purchased components, such as lifting shackles (Normal or Purchased BOM structure).

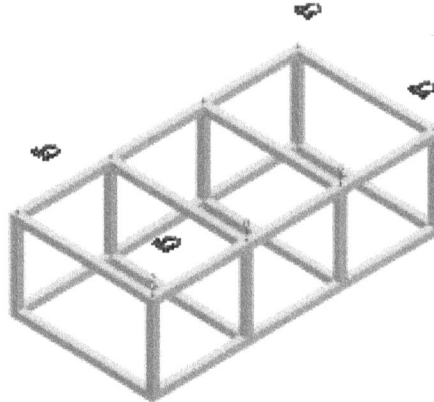

Virtual Components

You add virtual (non-geometric) components to assemblies to represent engineering components that cannot be easily modeled.

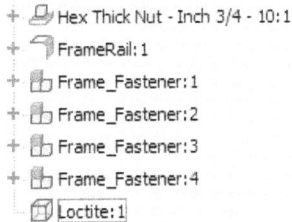

Definition of Virtual Components

You create virtual components in place in Inventor assemblies. They have no geometry and are not saved as separate files when you save the parent assemblies. Lubricants, glue, and other engineering materials are often represented by virtual parts. You can add any number of virtual components to an assembly.

Virtual Components and Autodesk Vault Professional Items

From a BOM perspective, virtual components are similar to user-created items in Vault Professional. You can add a user-created item to the BOM of another item. Similarly, when you add a virtual component to an assembly, it is automatically added to the BOM of the assembly.

When you assign item numbers to an assembly containing virtual components in Autodesk Vault Professional, each virtual component with Normal, Purchase, or Inseparable BOM structure is assigned a separate item number.

Your company's practices determine whether you should represent something as a virtual component in Inventor, or ignore it in Inventor and add a user-defined item in Vault Professional. You can add key engineering components to Inventor assemblies in the engineering environment. You can add common non-modeled components as items in Vault Professional. As with other items in a Vault Professional BOM, you can override quantity and other values for the item you create from the virtual component.

Model Data	Structured		Parts Only			
Item		Part Number	BOM Structure △	Component ...	L	
	2		Normal	Part	E	
	7		Normal	Part	E	
▶	11	Loctite	Normal	Virtual	E	
	4		Inseparable	Assembly	E	
	1		Purchased	Part	E	
	3		Purchased	Part	E	
	5		Purchased	Part	E	

Autodesk Inventor BOM with virtual component

Number		Row ...	Q...	Title (Item, CO)
⊟ 100046		-	-	Hitch Assembly
100062		11	1 ...	Loctite
100056		9	4 ...	IS 3063 12
100055		8	4 ...	ISO 8678 M12 x 25
100054		10	4 ...	IS 7790 M 12
100053		2	1 ...	Draw Bar
100052		7	1	Hitch Ball

Autodesk Vault Professional BOM with virtual component

How To: Create Virtual Components

You must create virtual components in place in an assembly. The following steps describe how to create virtual components:

1. In the Assemble panel, click **Create Component**.

2. In the Create In-Place Component dialog box, select the **Virtual Component** checkbox.

3. Under *New Component Name,* enter a name for the virtual component.

4. Under *Default BOM Structure*, select a BOM structure from the list.

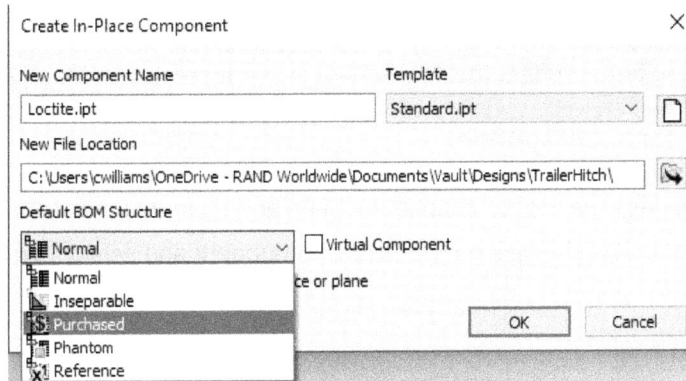

5. Click **OK**.

6. The virtual component is listed in the *Assembly* tab of the Model browser.

Editing Virtual Components

Virtual components are not separate files but they contain the same properties present in other Inventor documents. You can edit both their properties and their BOM structure. You can change this setting to better reflect the component in the assembly BOM.

How To: Edit a Virtual Component

The following steps describe how to change the units and quantity for a virtual component:

1. In the Model browser, right-click on the virtual component and select **Component Settings**.

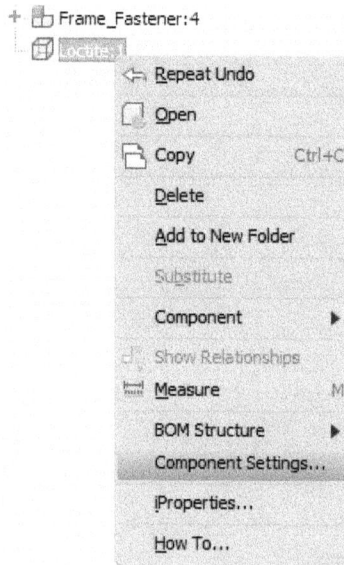

2. In the Component Settings dialog box, click the Base Quantity drop-down list and scroll until you find the appropriate value. Click **OK**.

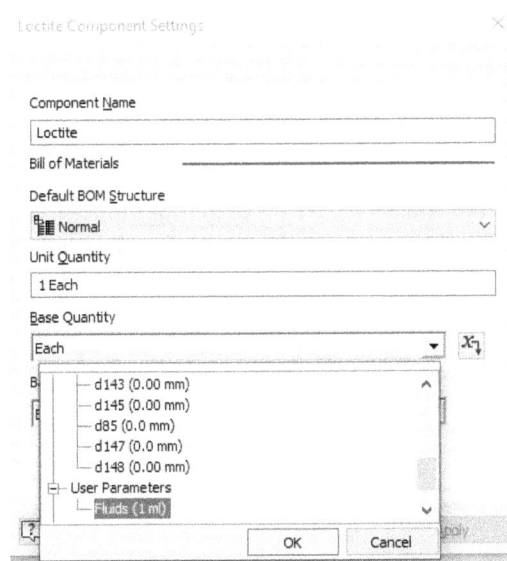

3. In the Bill of Materials dialog box, in the *Unit QTY* field, enter the appropriate value.

4. Override the quantity for the virtual part in the assembly BOM.

💡 **Hint: Base Quantity Value**

If the Base Quantity value is not in the list, it can be created by editing the Parameters table and entering a new user-defined parameter. The units associated with the user parameter are assigned to the base quantity field for virtual part.

Guidelines for Virtual Components

- Develop a company or departmental strategy for implementing virtual parts, user-created items, or combination of both.

- Virtual components are not saved as separate files, but rather are contained in assemblies.

- Virtual components with Normal, Purchased, or Inseparable BOM structures are assigned separate item numbers when their parent assemblies are assigned item numbers.

- Virtual components have the same properties as other Autodesk Inventor documents.

Modifying Content Center Component Properties

You can customize Content Center library components to integrate them into Vault Professional.

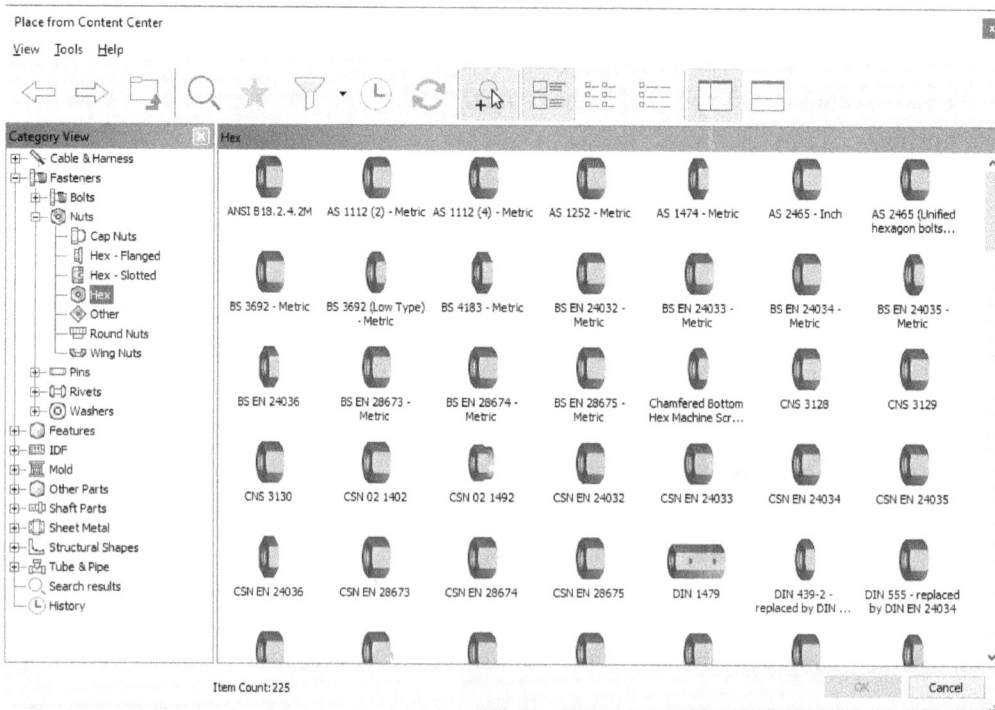

Content Center Library Components

Many Autodesk Inventor assemblies contain components from the Content Center libraries that ship with Autodesk Inventor. These libraries contain a large number of common engineering components from a variety of standards, including ANSI, ISO, JIS, and others. You copy data from the read-only default libraries to a custom read/write library where you can customize the property information in the component family. When you assign an item to an Autodesk Inventor assembly that contains library components, those components are also assigned items.

The following illustration shows a custom read-write library added to the Content Center libraries.

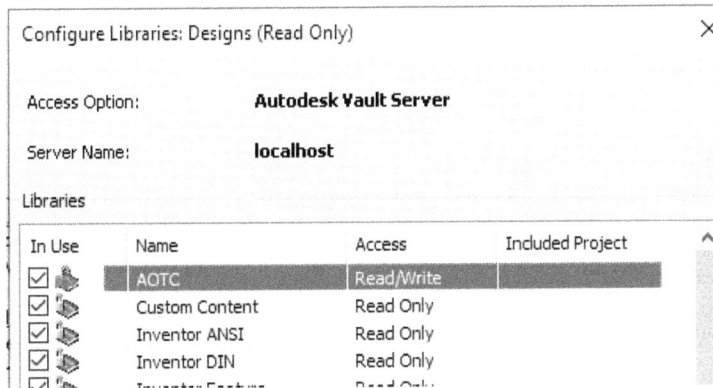

You can also publish your own components to a custom library by creating an iPart factory that includes a table to define the variations in the part. You can include model properties as columns in the table and assign default values for each variation of the part. After you publish the iPart factory to a custom Content Center library, you can place the different versions in assemblies. Each variation retains the property values defined in the original iPart table.

See "iParts" and "Content Center" in the Autodesk Inventor Help for more information on working with and publishing your own library parts.

The following illustration shows an iPart Factory part and the iPart Author table that you use to create the different iPart member definitions.

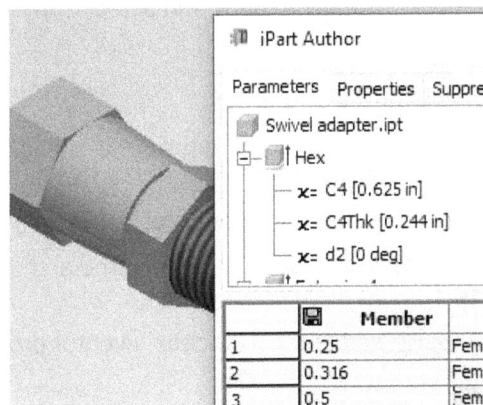

How To: Modify Properties of Content Center Components

The following steps describe how to copy data from a default read-only library to a custom read-write library and edit the properties in the library table:

1. Log in to the Autodesk Data Management Server Console as a user with at least Content Center Editor permission.

2. Expand the folders and select **Libraries**. Right-click and select **Create Library**.

3. Enter the *Display Name* and select a *Partition* based on the Inventor version you are using for the library.

4. Click **OK** to create the library.

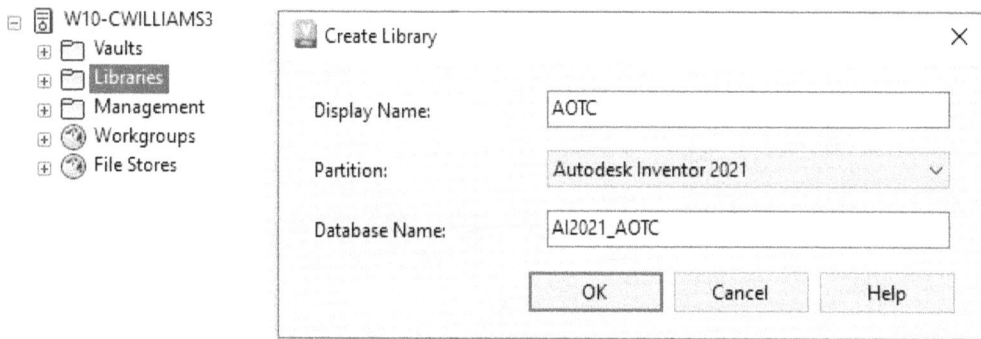

5. In Autodesk Inventor, open any assembly. On the *Manage* tab, select **Editor** in the Content Center section. User requires a Content Center Editor role.

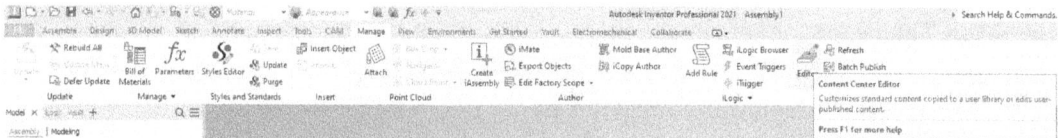

6. In the Content Center Editor dialog box, do the following:

   - Right-click on the category or family to copy and select **Copy To**.
   - Click the name of a read-write library.
   - Click **Yes** to refresh the content in the server.

7. In the read-write library, locate the part family you want to edit. On the List panel, right-click on the part family and select **Family Table** to display the Family Table dialog box.

8. In the Family Table dialog box, display the *iProperties* columns only. Add a new column.

9. In the Column Properties dialog box, enter a column name and column caption. Select a data type for the property.

10. Under *Map to Inventor Property*, select the Autodesk Inventor property to populate with the value from the new column.

11. Select the **Expression** checkbox. Enter a constant string or use a combination of strings and parameter names to populate the cells based on other values in the table. Click **OK**.

12. If required, repeat Steps 5 to 8 to add other columns.

13. Optionally, delete or suppress rows in the table that are not used in your designs. You can also add rows or edit parameter values to create custom versions of the library part.

   Note: Any component placed from the Content Center has a default Purchased BOM structure. You can edit this structure in the Bill of Materials dialog box.

When you place parts from the table into subsequent assemblies, the property values in the library part reflect the values in the columns mapped to Inventor properties.

Working with DWG Files

You can use Autodesk Vault Professional with drawing (DWG) files created in the AutoCAD software products, such as AutoCAD, AutoCAD Mechanical, AutoCAD Electrical, and Autodesk Inventor.

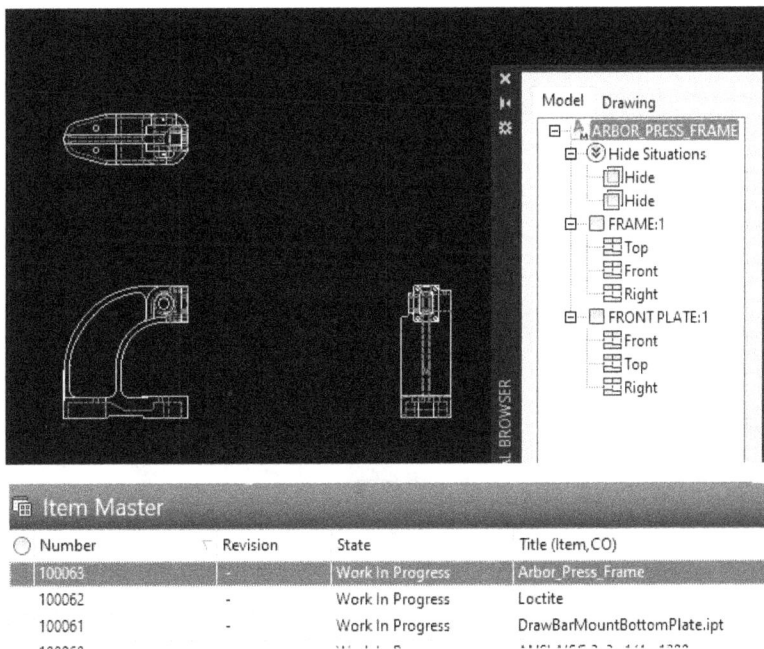

DWG Files, Autodesk Vault, and Autodesk Vault Professional

Many companies work with a variety of Autodesk CAD software applications. Although a focus of Autodesk Vault and Autodesk Vault Professional is to work with data from Autodesk Inventor, you can manage versions and assign items to drawing files in Autodesk Vault.

Always check out and check in drawing files using the Vault ARX application inside your AutoCAD-based software. AutoCAD Electrical users must check out and check in all files in a project at the same time.

When you have checked drawing files into the vault, you can assign items to them using the same technique you use to assign items to Inventor parts and assemblies. The following illustration shows an AutoCAD Mechanical file being checked in to the vault

When you work with drawing files in Autodesk Vault Professional, consider the following:

- AutoCAD Mechanical BOM data is used to determine category. Assembly drawing file BOM data is translated into the item BOM.

- When you assign an item to a drawing file, any externally referenced files (Xrefs) are added as attachments to the item in Autodesk Vault Professional. Always check in the drawing containing the Xrefs to maintain the file relationships.

- Property extraction and mapping between Autodesk Vault Professional and drawing files is not as robust as it is with Inventor documents. No provision exists for writing item property values back to the properties in a drawing file.

- You can control lifecycle status and changes to drawing files with Autodesk Vault Professional engineering change orders. If the vault is set to enforce file locking, you cannot check out a drawing file from the vault unless its lifecycle state is set to Work in Progress.

You can generate 2D drawings in Autodesk Inventor in either Autodesk Inventor's native format (IDW) or DWG format. You can assign items to both of these file formats. If a drawing file does not exist in the vault when you assign an item to its associated part or assembly, you must manually attach the drawing item to its part or assembly item when the drawing is added to vault and assigned an item.

Example of AutoCAD Files and Autodesk Vault Professional

Your design team uses AutoCAD or AutoCAD Electrical in combination with Inventor. An AutoCAD drawing contains a 2D reference layout for your Inventor assembly. AutoCAD Electrical drawing files detail electrical requirements for your design and provide pin and wire information for a harness assembly in Autodesk Inventor Professional.

You add the AutoCAD drawing file to the vault. You then attach it to your top-level Inventor assembly file and assign an item to the Inventor assembly. You add the AutoCAD Electrical drawings to the vault. You assign items to the AutoCAD Electrical drawings and use their Vault Professional bills of materials to aid the design.

Practice 12b
Work with Inventor Assemblies and BOMs

In this practice, you will examine an Inventor assembly BOM and how various BOM structure settings affect Vault Professional item creation. You will work with components having Normal, Reference, Phantom, Purchased, and Inseparable BOM structures. You will add a component to the assembly after assigning an item number to the assembly and examine how the new component is added to the Item Master.

Number	Row Order	Pos...	Quantity	Units	Title (Item,CO)
⊟ 100038	-	-	-	Each	HitchAssembly
100042	1	1	1	Each	ANSI/ASME B18.8.1 PIN.
100039	2	2	1	Each	Drawbar
⊞ 100045	3	4	1	Each	Mounting Weldment
100047	4	8	4	Each	ISO 8678 M12 x 25
100048	5	9	4	Each	IS 3063 12
100046	6	10	4	Each	IS 7790 M 12
100043	7	7	1	Each	Ball
100041	8	5	1	Each	Regular Helical Spring L
100040	9	6	1	Each	Hex Thick Nut - Inch 3/4
100044	10	3	1	Each	Axle Clip
Safety Bracket	11	11	1	Each	Safety Bracket.ipt

Task 1: Set up the vault.

1. Start Autodesk Vault Professional. Log in using the following information:
   - For *User Name*, enter **administrator**.
   - Leave the *Password* field blank.
   - For *Vault*, select **AOTCVault**.

2. Select **Go>Project Explorer**. Select **Tools>Options**. If required, clear the **Show Hidden Files** checkbox. Click **OK**.

3. Right-click on the *Project Explorer ($)* folder. Do the following:
   - Click **Details**.
   - The working folder should be set to *C:\Vault Professional Admin\VaultWorkingFolder*.
   - Click **OK**.

4. The Title property needs to be remapped in order for the item Title property to be displayed correctly. Do this:

- Select **Tools>Administration>Vault Settings**.
- Select the *Behaviors* tab and select **Properties** from the *Properties* group.
- In the *Property Name* column, find the system property **Title (Item, CO)**.
- In the Property Definitions toolbar, select **Edit**.
- Select the *Mapping* tab.
- Find the entry for **Provider: Inventor** and select the file property **Component Name**.
- Select the up arrow in the Mapping toolbar to move this entry to the top of the list.
- Click **OK** to dismiss the Edit dialog box.
- Click **Close** to dismiss the Property Definitions dialog box.

5. Start Autodesk Inventor.

6. Select **File>Manage>Projects**.

7. In the Projects dialog box, click **Browse**.

8. Do the following:

- Browse to *C:\Vault Professional Admin\VaultWorking Folder*.
- Select **Designs.ipj**.
- Click **Open**.
- Click **Done**.

9. Select the *Vault* tab, then select **Log In** from the Access group. Log in using the following information:

- *User Name:* **administrator**
- Leave *Password* field blank
- *Database:* **AOTCVault**

Note: If you have installed Inventor with separate log-ins for Vaults and Content Center libraries, select Vault Log In.

Task 2: Work with Autodesk Inventor assemblies and BOMs.

1. Select the *Vault* tab, then select **Open** from the Access group. Do the following:

- Navigate to the *Designs\TrailerHitch* folder.
- Click **HitchAssembly.iam**.
- Click **Open**.

2. If prompted to check out the assembly, click **No**. If prompted to get files from the vault, click **Yes to All**.

3. Examine the Model browser. The Model browser is a hierarchical list of the assembly components.

- The **Mounting Weldment** subassembly contains the black components that make up the welded portion of the hitch assembly.

- Each instance of the **Frame_Fastener** subassembly contains one bolt, one washer, and one nut.

4. In the Model browser, right-click on **Frame_Fastener:1**.

5. Place the cursor over BOM Structure to display the assigned structure of the Phantom assembly.

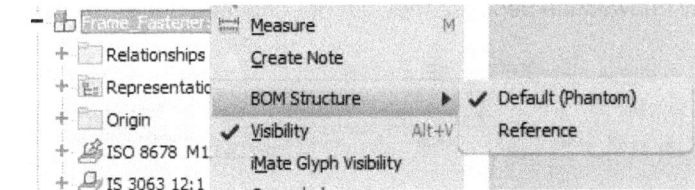

6. In the Model browser, repeat the two previous steps to examine the BOM structure of other components. (For example, the FrameRail:1 component is assigned a Reference BOM structure.)

7. On the *Assemble* tab, select **Bill of Materials** from the Manage group.

8. In the Bill of Materials dialog box, select the *Structured* tab.

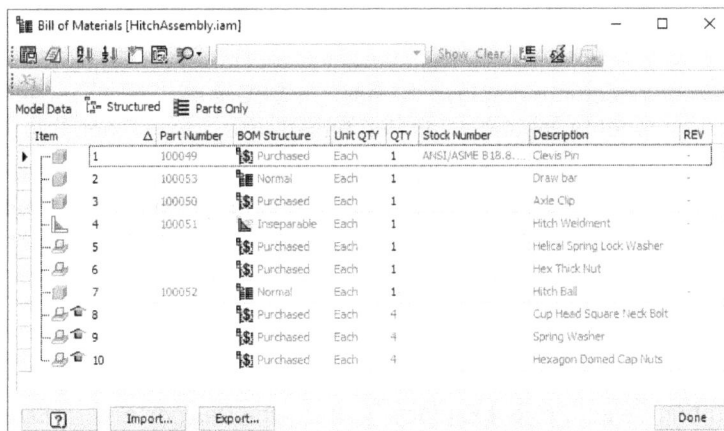

- The Phantom Frame_Fastener subassemblies are not listed in the BOM. The three child components from the Frame_Fastener subassembly display as promoted items in the BOM as items 8 - 10. The *QTY* column displays the number of components in one subassembly (1) multiplied by the number of phantom subassemblies (4).

9. If a column is not visible, do the following:

- In the BOM, right-click on a column header.
- Click **Runtime Column Customization**.
- Drag the required column from the Customization dialog box to the required location on the display.

10. Add the *Filename* column to the display if it is not visible.

11. All items display unavailable because they are not checked out of the vault.

Model Data 🔲 Structured ☰ Parts Only

Item		Δ	Part Number	Filename	BOM Structure	
▶	🗍	1	100049	Clevis Pin 3_4-1.91.ipt	$	Purchased
	🗍	2	100053	Drawbar.ipt	☰	Normal
	🗍	3	100050	Axle Clip.ipt	$	Purchased
	🗍	4	100051	Mounting Weldment.i...		Inseparable
	🗍	5		0.75.ipt	$	Purchased
	🗍	6		3_4-UNC.ipt	$	Purchased
	🗍	7	100052	Ball.ipt	☰	Normal
	🗍🏠	8		M12-25.ipt	$	Purchased
	🗍🏠	9		12.ipt	$	Purchased
	🗍🏠	10		M12.ipt	$	Purchased

- The *BOM Structure* column displays the assigned BOM structure for each component. The library components are shown as Purchased. The Drawbar and Ball components are Normal. The Mounting Weldment assembly is shown as Inseparable.

12. In the Bill of Materials dialog box, click **Done**. If you get prompted to check out the files, select **No to All**.

Task 3: Assign an item to the assembly.

1. Switch to Autodesk Vault Professional.

2. From the Go menu, select **Project Explorer**. Expand the *Designs* and *TrailerHitch* folders.

   Note: The components with the Reference and Phantom BOM structures are included in the vault. The BOM structure affects only items in Vault Professional

3. Right-click on **HitchAssembly.iam** and select **Assign/Update Item**. If the assembly is checked out, select **Undo Check Out** first.

4. In the item record window, select the *Bill of Materials* tab.

    *   The Inseparable Weldment assembly and all its child items are included in the default tree view. The Reference FrameRail part and the Phantom Frame_Fastener assembly are not included in the list. The child components in the Phantom Frame_Fastener assembly are assigned item numbers.

Number		Row Order /	Positi...	Quantity	Units	Title (Item,CO)
▶ ⊟ 100046					Each	Hitch Assembly
	100049	1	1	1 Each	Each	ANSI/ASME B18.8.1 PIN. CLEVIS. 3/4 x
	100053	2	2	1 Each	Each	Draw Bar
	100050	3	3	1 Each	Each	Axle Clip.ipt
⊟	100051	4	4	1 Each	Each	Mounting Weldment.iam
	100060	4.1	1	47.244 Inch	Inch	ANSI AISC 2x2x 1/4 - 1200mm
	100057	4.2	2	1 Each	Each	end_plate_RH.ipt
	100058	4.3	3	1 Each	Each	end_plate_LH.ipt
	100059	4.4	4	1 Each	Each	DrawBarMountTopPlate.ipt
	100061	4.5	5	1 Each	Each	DrawBarMountBottomPlate.ipt
	100048	5	5	1 Each	Each	Regular Helical Spring Lock Washer (I
	100047	6	6	1 Each	Each	Hex Thick Nut - Inch 3/4 - 10
	100052	7	7	1 Each	Each	Hitch Ball
	100055	8	8	4 Each	Each	ISO 8678 M12 x 25
	100056	9	9	4 Each	Each	IS 3063 12
	100054	10	10	4 Each	Each	IS 7790 M 12

Note: Your item numbers and column organization might not match the previous illustration.

5. Select **First-Level** from the Structure drop-down list.

    *   The child items of the Inseparable Weldment assembly are not displayed.

Latest	Work In Progress ∨	Today ∨	⧉ First-Level ∨

Number	Quantity ▽	Title (Item,CO)
100056	4 Each	IS 3063 12
100054	4 Each	IS 7790 M 12
100055	4 Each	ISO 8678 M12 x 25
100050	1 Each	Axle Clip.ipt
100053	1 Each	Draw Bar
100049	1 Each	ANSI/ASME B18.8.1 PIN. CLEVIS. 3/4 x 1.91
100048	1 Each	Regular Helical Spring Lock Washer (Inch) 3/4 Regular. Carb
100047	1 Each	Hex Thick Nut - Inch 3/4 - 10
100052	1 Each	Hitch Ball
100051	1 Each	Mounting Weldment.iam

6. For Structure, select **Multi-Level**.

7. Click **Save and Close**.

8. Switch to Autodesk Inventor.

9. On the *Vault* tab, select **Place** in the Access group.

10. In the Select File from Vault dialog box, navigate to the *$\Designs\TrailerHitch* folder. Do the following:

   - Select **Safety Bracket.ipt**.
   - Click **Open**.
   - Click in the graphics window background.

11. Right-click, then click **OK**.

Note: You typically position the bracket in the assembly with assembly constraints. You are not required to apply the constraints in this practice.

12. Save the assembly. In the Save dialog box, click **OK**.

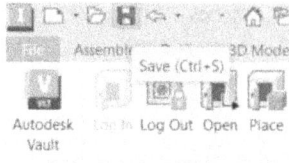

13. In the browser title bar, select **Vault**.

14. In the Vault browser, right-click on **HitchAssembly.iam** and select **Check In**.

15. In the Check In dialog box, enter **Added safety bracket** as a comment. Click **OK**.

16. Switch to Vault Professional.

17. In the Item Master, right-click on the **Hitch Assembly** row and select **Update**.

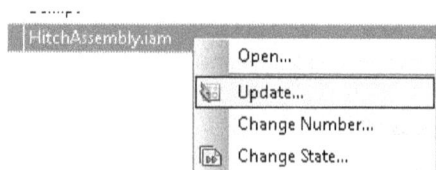

18. In the Item record window, select the *Bill of Materials* tab. Note that the safety bracket part is automatically added.

Number		Row Order /	Positi...	Quantity	Units	Title (Item,CO)
⊟ 100046	-	-	-		Each	HitchAssembly.iam
100049	1	1	1 Each		Each	ANSI/ASME B18.8.1 PIN. C
100053	2	2	1 Each		Each	Drawbar.ipt
100050	3	3	1 Each		Each	Axle Clip.ipt
⊞ 100051	4	4	1 Each		Each	Mounting Weldment.iam
100048	5	5	1 Each		Each	Regular Helical Spring Loc
100047	6	6	1 Each		Each	Hex Thick Nut - Inch 3/4 -
100052	7	7	1 Each		Each	Ball.ipt
100055	8	8	4 Each		Each	ISO 8678 M12 x 25
100056	9	9	4 Each		Each	IS 3063 12
100054	10	10	4 Each		Each	IS 7790 M 12
Safety Bracket	11	11	1 Each		Each	Safety Bracket.ipt

Note: *The item numbers do not match the item numbers in the previous illustration.*

End of practice

Administering Autodesk Vault Professional

This chapter describes how to manage the Autodesk® Vault Professional software. You will learn about configuring items, configuring and mapping item properties, and configuring change orders.

Learning Objectives

- Create units and categories, create new item numbering schemes, and create custom objects.
- Set up change orders, including routing lists, user-defined properties, and change order numbering.

13.1 Configuring Items

Overview

This lesson describes how to configure items. You learn how to create units and categories, create new item numbering schemes, and change lifecycle rules.

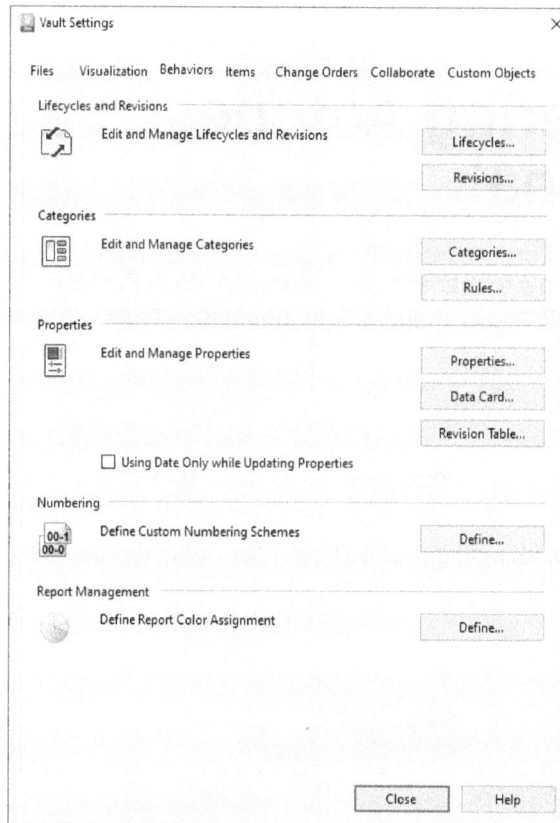

All of the workflows described in the chapter are accessed from the Vault Settings dialog box shown above. This dialog displays by selecting **Administration>Vault Settings** from the Tools menu. You will need to be logged in as an Administrator to complete these workflows.

Objectives

After completing this lesson, you will be able to:

- Describe units of measure.

- Describe item categories.

- Create item numbering schemes.

- Configure watermarking.

- Create units of measure and categories.

Units of Measure

Every item is assigned a unit type. You can create new unit types if the supplied units do not meet your company's requirements. The following illustration shows the complete set of units that ships with Vault Professional.

About Units of Measure

Unit types define the units of measure for items. You use unit types to specify the quantity of an item in a bill of materials. Many items use a special unit type, such as each, when the number of required items is countable. Other items are assigned specific unit types, such as meters or grams, when a measurable quantity is required, rather than an item count. Several predefined unit types are supplied, but if those types do not meet your requirements, you can define new ones.

Each unit type is derived from a base unit and a conversion factor. For example, centimeters are the base unit for length and all length units are defined with respect to centimeters. You can create new base units if you cannot define the new unit from the existing base units.

The following illustration shows the length units that are defined using the centimeter base unit. The conversion factor relates the unit to the base unit. For example, one inch is 2.54 centimeters and one foot is 30.48 centimeters.

✔	Name	Symbol	Base Unit	Conversion Factor
▶	Centimeter	cm	cm	1
	Each	ea	ea	1
	Foot	ft	cm	30.48
	Gallon	gal	ml	3785.41184
	Gram	g	g	1
	Inch	in	cm	2.54
	Liquid Ounce	lqd oz	ml	29.57353

How To: Create a New Unit of Measure

One of the items in your product's bill of materials is measured in kilograms. You define a new unit type to support this unit of measure. The new unit uses grams as the base unit.

1. In the Vault Settings dialog box, select the *Items* tab.

2. Select **Configure** in the *Units* group to display the Units of Measure dialog box.

3. In the Units of Measure dialog box, click **Plus sign** to display the Add Unit dialog box.

4. Enter the *Name*, *Symbol*, *Base Unit*, and *Conversion factor* information.

Add Unit	✕
Name:	Kilogram
Symbol:	kg
Base Unit:	g
Conversion factor:	1000
☐ This is a Base Unit	
OK	Cancel	Help

5. Click **OK** to close the Add Unit dialog box.

6. The Units of Measure dialog box shows the new unit.

✔	Name	Symbol	Base Unit	/	Conversion Factor
	Gram	g	g		1
	Kilogram	kg	g		1000
	Milligram	mg	g		0.001
	Ounce	oz	g		28.3495
	Pound	lb	g		453.592
	Gallon	gal	ml		3785.41184
	Liquid Ounce	lqd oz	ml		29.57353
	Liter	l	ml		1000

7. Click **OK** to close the Unit of Measure dialog box.

Item Categories

Every item has a category, such as Part, Assembly, or Product, which helps to identify the item. Some categories, such as Part, Assembly, and Purchased, are assigned automatically based on either the type of file or the CAD file's bill of materials (BOM). You assign other categories manually when you create items.

There are several predefined categories, as shown in the following illustration. If these do not match the categories you use, you can create new types to meet your requirements.

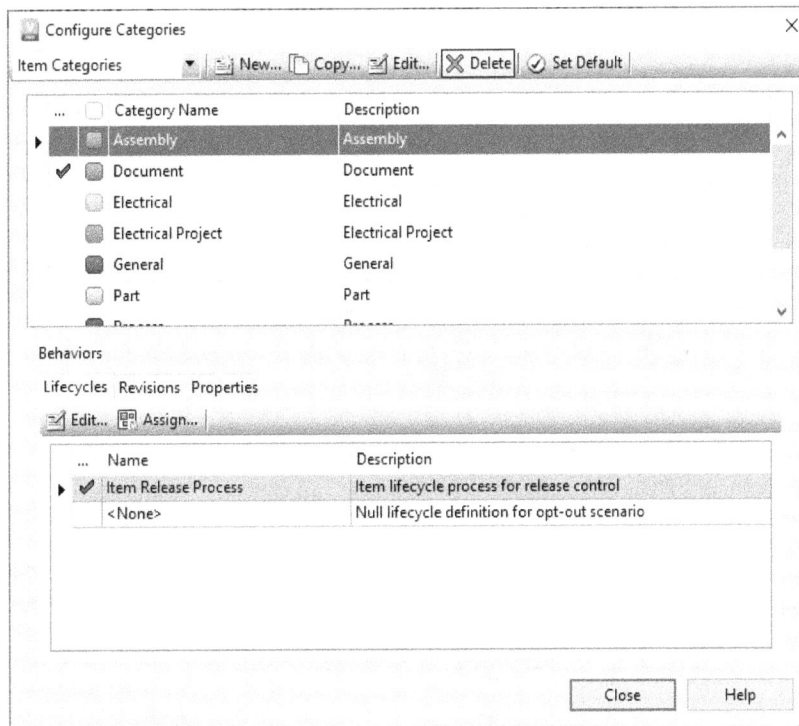

How To: Create a New Item Category

Your company manufactures industrial machinery. Frames are often built by one division of the company then brought to a central area for assembly. In your current ERP system, you identify the frame as a weldment.

1. In the Vault Settings dialog box, select the *Behaviors* tab and select **Categories** in the *Categories* group to display the Configure Categories dialog box.

2. Select **Item Categories** from the drop-down list. The Item Categories display.

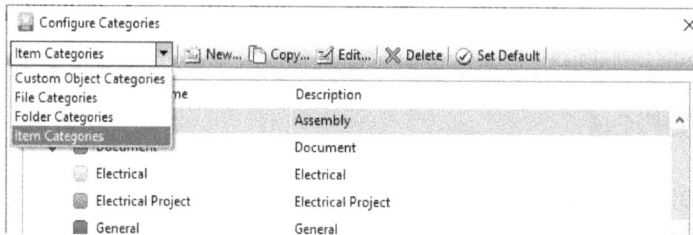

3. Select **New** from the toolbar to display the Category Edit dialog box. Enter the new item category name, pick a category glyph color, and optionally enter a description. Ensure that **Available** is selected.

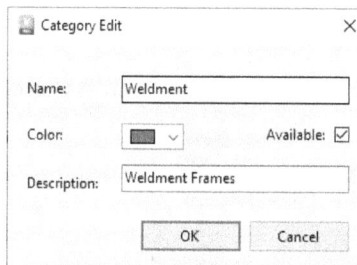

4. Click **OK** to close the Category Edit dialog box. The new item category is added to the list.

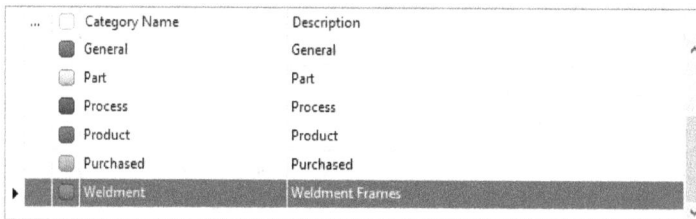

5. Optionally, assign a different lifecycle definition, a different revision scheme, and set of default properties to add to the item when it is created.

6. Click **Close** to dismiss the Configure Categories dialog box.

Item Numbering Schemes

Item numbers uniquely identify items. When you set up Vault Professional, create item-numbering schemes to match your company standards.

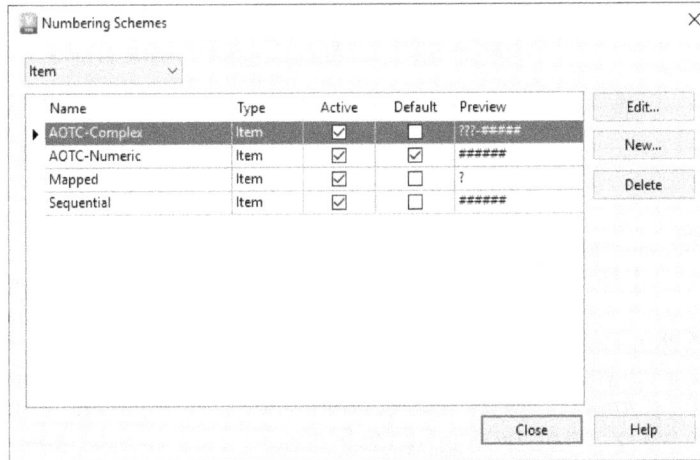

Item Number Components

Item numbering schemes can consist of one or more of the following components. For a simple numbering scheme, use a single automatically generated sequential number. For a complex scheme, combine several components together.

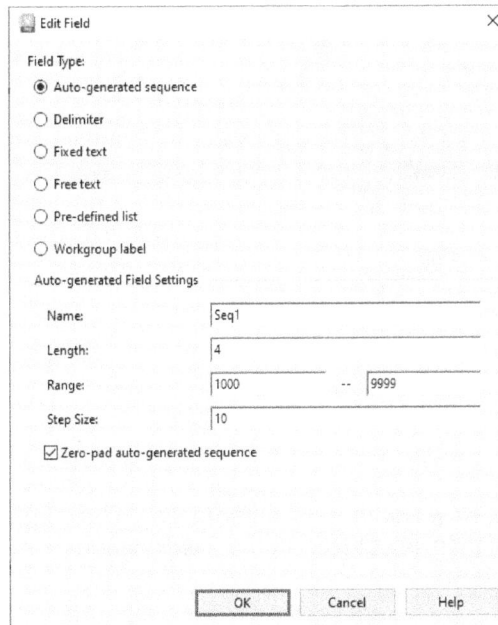

Field type	Description	Examples
Auto-generated sequence	Sequential number	100058
Delimiter	Single character	-
Fixed text	Fixed text string	ABC
Free text	User-entered text string	ANYTHING
Pre-defined list	List of choices	FAST, STRU, ELEC, OTHR 100, 200, 300, 400, 500
Workgroup label	Workgroup ID	WG1

Autodesk Vault Professional is shipped with predefined item numbering schemes named **Sequential** and **Mapped**. Neither scheme can be modified. The default **Sequential** item numbering scheme uses a single, automatically generated number that numbers items from 00000000 to 99999999. The **Mapped** item numbering scheme accepts a text string. It is automatically used when you assign an item to a file and the file contains a property that is mapped to the item's *Number* property. It is recommended that you define your own numbering scheme rather than using one of the supplied schemes.

How To: Define an Item Numbering Scheme

1. In the Vault Settings dialgo box, select the *Behaviors* tab and select **Define** from the *Numbering* group.

2. The Numbering Schemes dialog box opens. Select **Item** from the drop-down list to display the item numbering schemes.

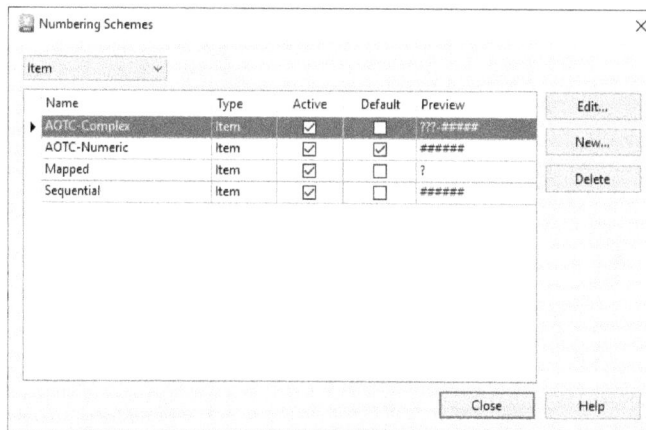

3. Click **New** to display the New Numbering Scheme dialog box. Enter a *Name* for the new numbering scheme and then select **New** in the *Fields* section.

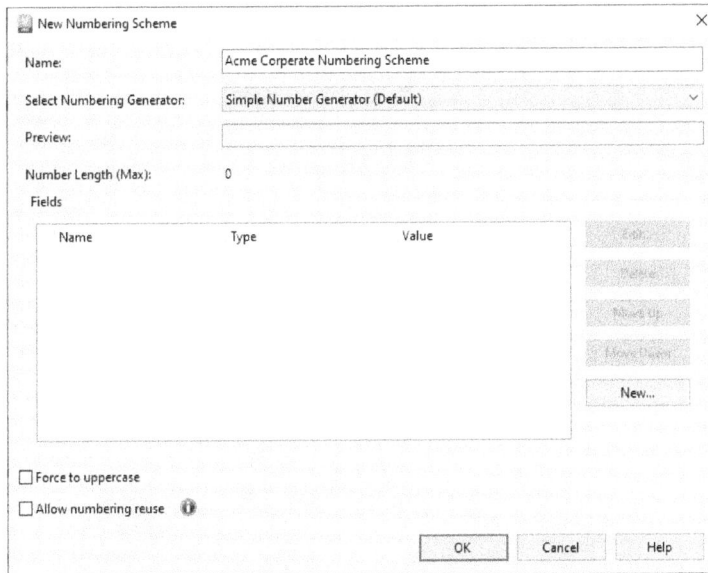

4. The Add Field dialog box opens. Create the first part of the numbering scheme. In this case, a predefined list with list values 100, 200, and 300 representing Parts, Assemblies, and Purchased items.

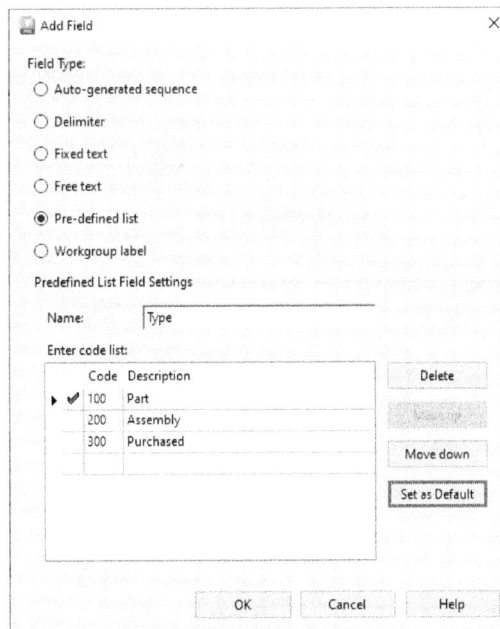

5. Click **OK** to close the Add Field dialog box. The first part of the sequence is shown in the New Numbering Scheme dialog box. Note the preview of how the number will look. Add two more parts to the sequence by repeating Step 4.

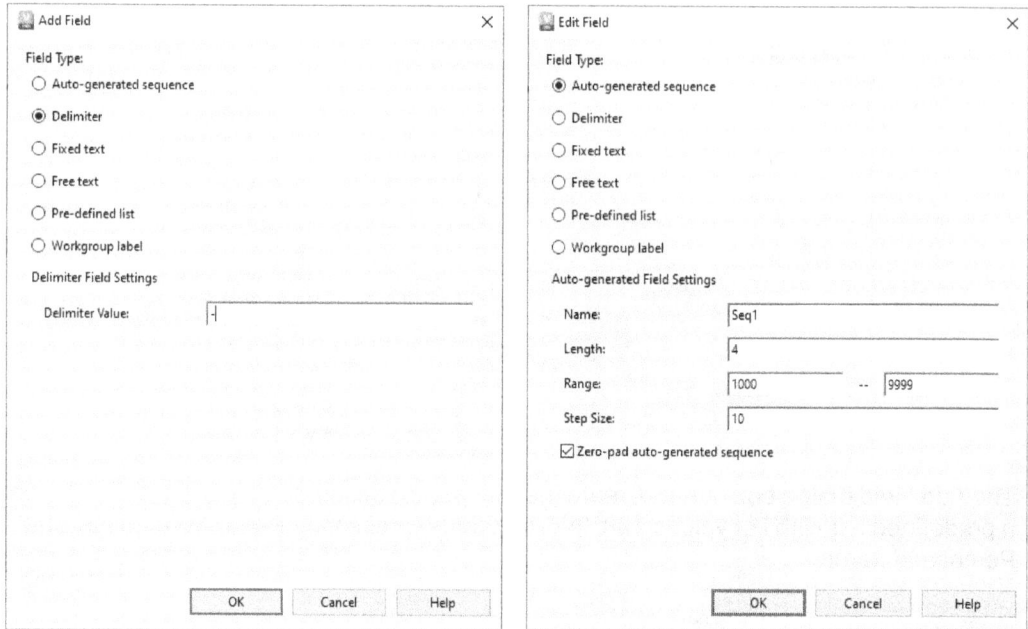

6. Return to the New Numbering Scheme dialog box to see the final sequence.

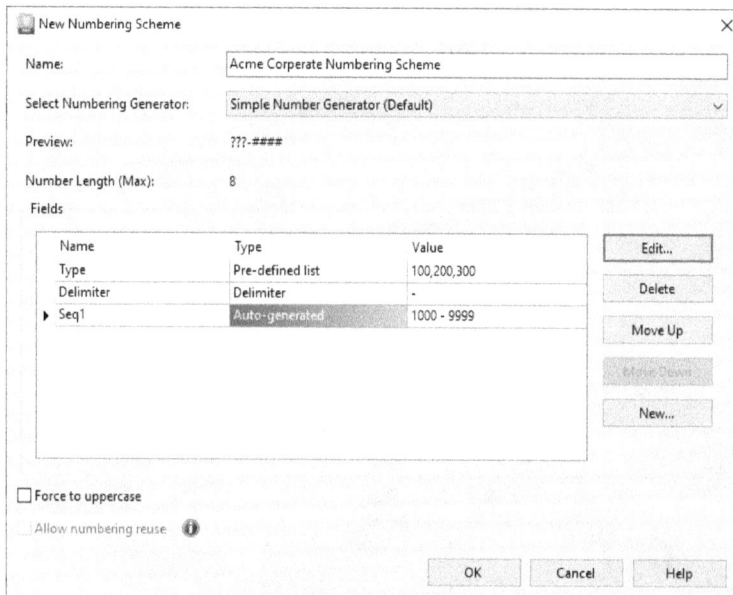

© 2024 Autodesk, Inc.

7. Click **OK** to close the New Numbering Scheme dialog box and return to the Numbering Scheme dialog box.

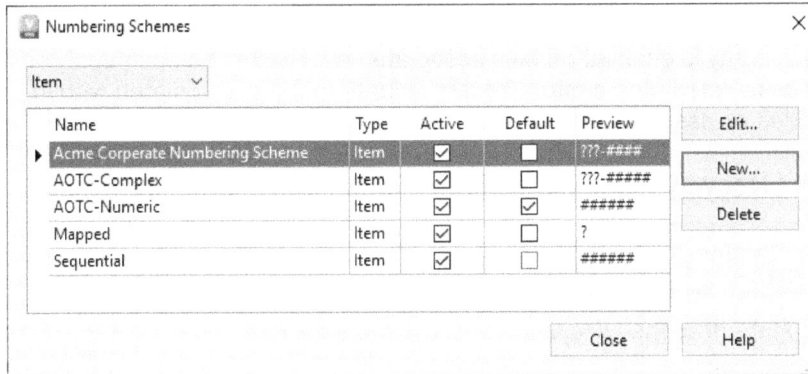

Name	Type	Active	Default	Preview
▶ Acme Corperate Numbering Scheme	Item	☑	☐	???-####
AOTC-Complex	Item	☑	☐	???-#####
AOTC-Numeric	Item	☑	☑	######
Mapped	Item	☑	☐	?
Sequential	Item	☑	☐	######

Numbering Schemes — Item

Buttons: Edit... | New... | Delete | Close | Help

8. Select the **Default** checkbox if you want this to be the default numbering scheme.

Note that numbering schemes that require user input are not good choices for the default since in automated processes like Assign Item, there is no chance to prompt for the input. In this case, the number generated will always use the default value. You will be required to go back and edit the item if you want to use a different value.

Guidelines

- Do not use one of the default numbering schemes.

  You should define your own numbering scheme rather than using the default, even if you want to use a simple sequential number. If you want to use a single sequential numbering scheme, start the first item number with a 1 rather than 0 (for example, use 1000001 rather than 0000001) because leading zeros might be suppressed when you share data with other applications.

- Create as many numbering schemes as required.

  You can create and use more than one item numbering scheme if required. For example, you might use a simple sequential numbering scheme for users who assign items. After the items are created, the ERP Manager can renumber items using a more complex scheme to make item numbers compatible with other company systems.

- Consider adding user-defined item properties to enhance searching.

  Although complex numbering schemes can be used to identify categories using fields in the item number, you can also use item properties to group and sort items. Properties are more flexible and are more easily searched than complex item numbers. For example, if you use a complex item numbering scheme such as 100-ELEC-10345-545, consider using a simple scheme. Add user-defined properties to items to include the information that is inherent in the numbering scheme. You can search on the properties to find items and new or casual users will be able to better identify and locate items.

Editing Lifecycle State Security for Files Associated with Items

By default, no security is enabled on files associated with items. You can apply an item's security to its associated files, customize the security for files associated with items, or clear security overrides on associated files.

How To: Edit Lifecycly State Security for Files Associated with Items

1. In the Vault Settings dialog box, select the *Behaviors* tab. Select **Lifecycles** to display the Lifecycle Definitions dialog box.

2. Select the state from the *Lifecycle States* list and click **Edit**.

3. Select the *Security* tab.

4. Select the **Security for associated files of items** checkbox to enable security on associated files.

5. Select **Configure**.

6. In the Security for Associated Files of Items dialog box, select one of the following actions from the drop-down list:

   - **Apply item security to associated files:** When selected, the Access Control List settings for the item for this state are also applied to the associated file.

   - **Apply custom security to associated files:** When selected, administrators can set an Access Control List that is different from the one applied to the item for that state.

   - **Clear security override from associated files:** When selected, if there is a current override Access Control List on the associated file, the security override is removed when the item enters this state.

7. If you selected **Apply custom security to associated files**, add or remove members and roles, and then configure permissions.

8. Click **OK** to save your changes and return to editing state security.

Item Revision Schemes

Autodesk Vault Professional includes several predefined revision numbering sequences. You can use one of the predefined sequences or create your own.

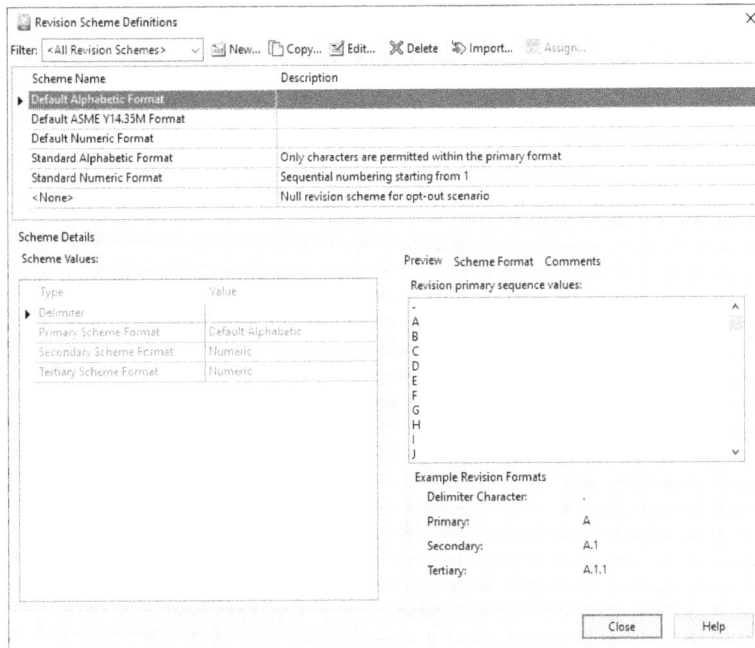

How To: Configure Revision Numbering Sequences

The following steps show how to create a revision number sequence for items:

1. Before creating a new revision sequence, you must first create a text file that contains all of the revision numbers. When you specify a new revision, you must either enable the system to choose the next character in the sequence or manually specify a character that is the imported sequence. An example is shown in the illustration below.

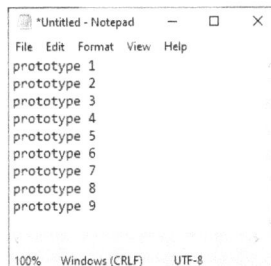

2. In the Vault Settings dialog box, select the *Behaviors* tab and click **Revisions** in the Lifecycle and Revisions section. Click **Import** to create a new revision scheme definition.

3. In the Import dialog box, specify the *Name* by browsing to the file. Enter a *Description* and select which of the item *Categories* to associate the revision scheme with.

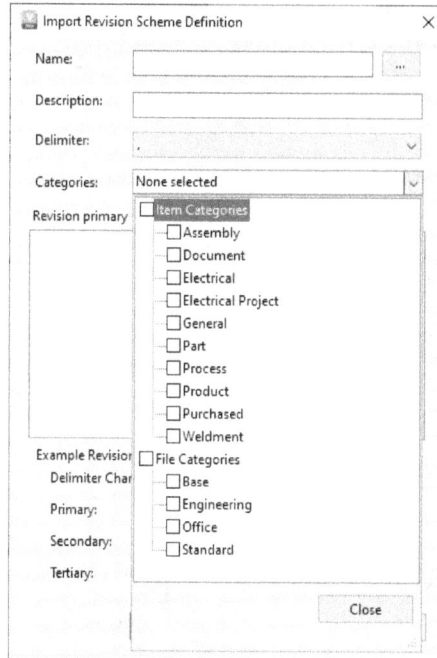

4. Click **OK** to close the Import Revision Scheme Definition dialog box and return to the Revision Schemes Definitions dialog box.

5. Click **Close** to close the Revision Scheme dialog box.

6. Close the Vault Settings dialog box.

Item Watermarking Configuration

Item watermarks can automatically be generated based on:

- an item's lifecycle state,

- a specified item property, or

- customized text.

The default watermarks are based on the system lifecycle names. Administrators can configure the watermark style and position.

> *Note: If you customize the display name for a lifecycle state, then you should also change the default watermark.*

How To: Configure an Item Lifecycle State Watermark

1. Select **Tools>Administration>Vault Settings**.

2. In the Vault Settings dialog box, select the *Items* tab.

3. In the *Watermarking* section, select **Lifecycle-based** from the drop-down list and select **Configure**.

4. In the Lifecycle Watermarks dialog box, select the lifecycle that you want to use for the state-based watermarks.

   Note: A lifecycle called Item Release Process is provided by the Autodesk Vault software.

5. Select the lifecycle state for which you want to edit the watermark.

6. Click the ellipsis (...) in the *Watermark Text* column to open the Watermark Text Entry dialog box and edit the text of the watermark.

7. Perform one of the following steps:

   • Select the **Input text for display in the watermark** option to enter text of your choice for the watermark.

   • Select a property to display as the watermark from the Insert a property from below drop-down list.

   • Create a multi-line watermark by performing one of the two steps above and clicking **Plus (+)** to add it to the *Watermark Text Display* field. Use **Plus (+)** to add additional watermarks and **Minus (-)** to remove existing watermarks. You can also use the up or down arrows to arrange the order in which the watermarks display.

8. Click **OK** to close the Watermark Text Entry dialog box.

9. In the Customize Watermarks dialog box, select a location for the watermark from the Location drop-down list. The watermark can be placed:

   • Diagonally

   • Horizontally

   • In the Border

Lifecycle State	Watermark Text	Location	Font	Color	Size
▶ Work In Progress	WORK IN PROGRE... ⋯	Diagonal	Tahoma		Medium
In Review	IN REVIEW	Diagonal	Tahoma		Medium
Released	RELEASED – EFFECTIVE	Border	Tahoma		Medium
Obsolete	OBSOLETE	Diagonal	Tahoma		Medium
Quick-Change	QUICK-CHANGE	Diagonal	Tahoma		Medium

10. Select a font for the watermark from the Font drop-down list.

11. Select a color for the watermark from the Color drop-down list.

12. Select a size for the watermark from the Size drop-down list.

13. Click **OK**.

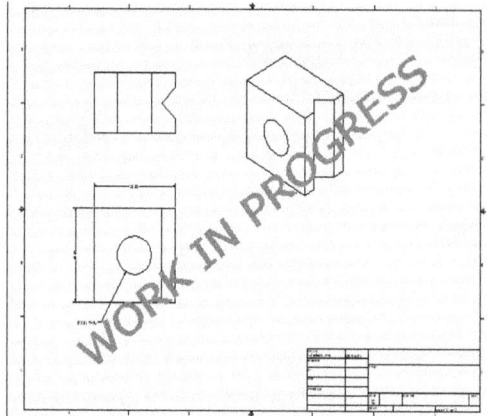

How To: Configure a Property-Based Watermark

The watermark value is based on a specific item property that you set using the Property-based Watermark Settings dialog box.

Note: You are automatically prompted to identify an item property the first time you select this option.

1. Select **Tools>Administration>Vault Settings**.
2. In the Vault Settings dialog box, select the *Items* tab.
3. In the *Watermarking* section, select **Property-based** from the drop-down list and select **Configure**.
4. In the Property-based Watermark Settings dialog box, select a property from which to draw the text for the watermark from the Property drop-down list.

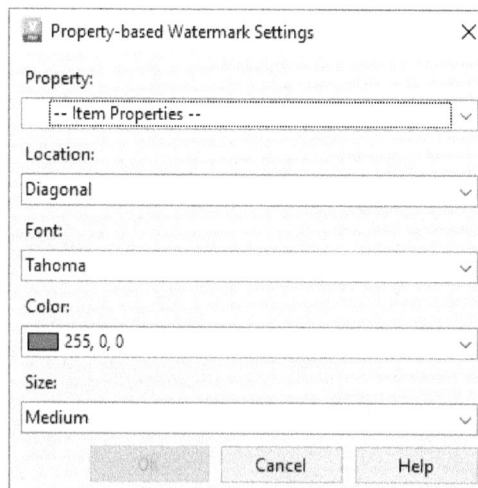

5. Select a location for the watermark from the Location drop-down list. The watermark can be placed:

   - Diagonally
   - Horizontally
   - In the border

6. Select a font for the watermark from the Font drop-down list.

7. Select a color for the watermark from the Color drop-down list.

8. Select a size for the watermark from the Size drop-down list.

9. Click **OK**.

How To: Configure a Custom Watermark

The watermark value comes from a value you enter in the Custom Watermark Settings dialog box.

Note: You are automatically prompted to identify a text value for the watermark the first time you select this option.

1. Select **Tools>Administration>Vault Settings**.

2. In the Vault Settings dialog box, select the *Items* tab.

3. In the *Watermarking* section, select **Custom** from the drop-down list and select **Configure**.

4. In the Custom Watermark Settings dialog box, enter the text for the watermark in the *Text* field.

5. Select a location for the watermark from the Location drop-down list. The watermark can be placed:

   - Diagonally
   - Horizontally
   - In the border

6. Select a font for the watermark from the Font drop-down list.

7. Select a color for the watermark from the Color drop-down list.

8. Select a size for the watermark from the Size drop-down list.

9. Click **OK**.

Assign Item Configuration

You can configure whether BOM rows are automatically displayed or hidden during item assignment.

How To: Assign Item Configuration

1. Select **Tools>Administration>Vault Settings**.

2. In the Vault Settings dialog box, select the *Items* tab.

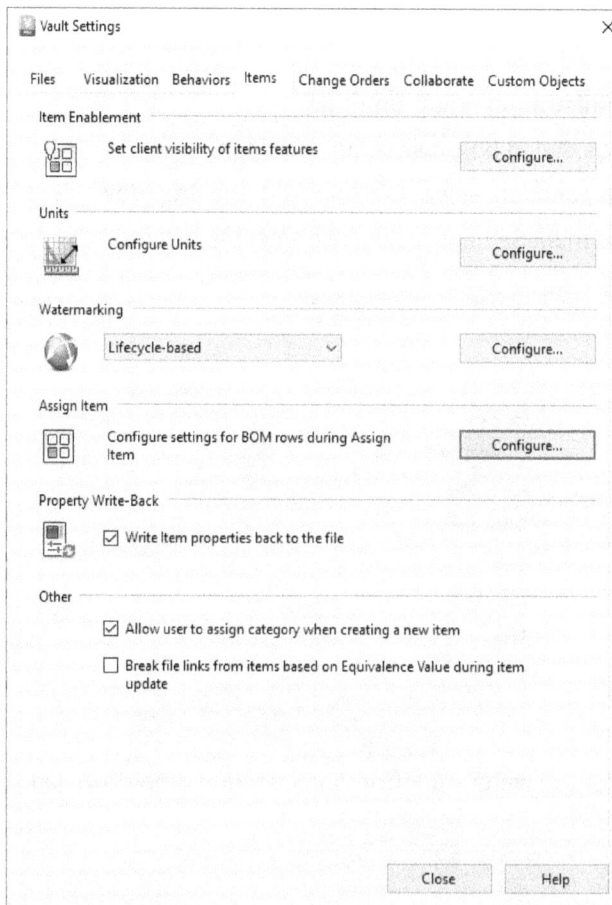

3. In the *Assign Item* section, select **Configure** to access the Configure Assign Item dialog box.

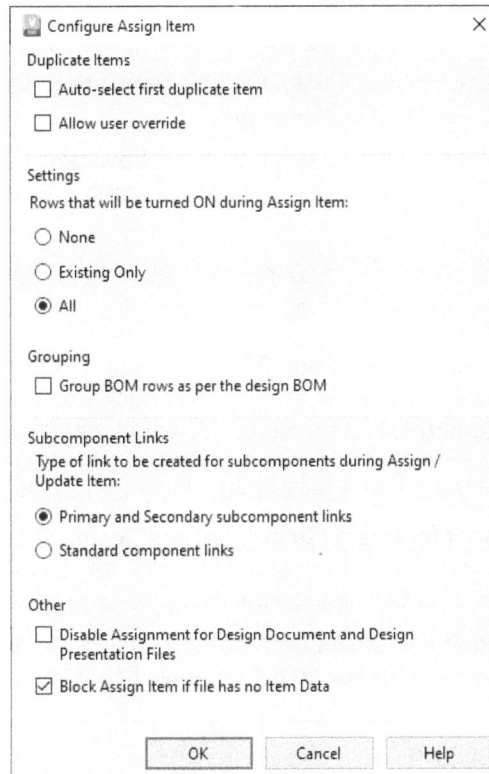

4. Select whether you want Vault to automatically select the first duplicate item in a list and assign it to the selected file. If you do not select this option, a new item is created instead. If this option is selected, child BOM components will attempt to link to an existing item using the *Equivalence Value* property.

   Note: Standard components will always attempt to link to an existing item.

5. Select the **Allow user override** checkbox if you want the user to be able to choose a duplicate item other than the one automatically selected by Vault.

6. If you want to configure how BOM rows are toggled on during item assignment, select one of the following options:

    - **None:** Components that link to existing items are not toggled on. All new item rows are toggled off. Note: This is the default setting for new vaults.

    - **Existing Only:** Components that link to existing items are toggled on. Components not linked to items remain as BOM components

    - **All:** Components that do not link to existing items have new items created for them. All new rows are toggled on. Note: This is the default setting for Vaults migrated from Vault 2014 or earlier releases.

    Note: These rules apply until a row is linked to an item. Once a row has an item identified, rows are not toggled on or off during subsequent updates.

7. Select **Group BOM rows as per the design BOM** if you want BOM rows merged or unmerged based on how the CAD application has them. If the checkbox is not selected, BOM rows are automatically merged, regardless of how the CAD application has them. For example, if Inventor has BOM rows unmerged and the checkbox is not selected, the rows are automatically merged in Vault regardless of how Inventor has them.

8. Select **Disable Assignment for Design Document and Design Presentation Files** if you want to disable the ability to assign item to design files such as .IDW files. If this option is checked, design files will only be linked to the items for which they represent.

9. Select **Block Assign Item if file has no Item Data** to prevent items from being assigned to CAD files that can have item data but do not yet have any. This option is selected by default.

10. Click **OK** to save your changes.

Property Write-Back Configuration

By default, item properties are written back to the associated file from Vault add-ins, Vault Explorer, and the Job Processor. Item properties take precedence over file properties and mappings. If the file's properties are edited and properties are synchronized, the item properties will overwrite the file properties.

> *Note: Editing and saving a property can result in an item property being written back to a file.*

You can manually synchronize properties on files associated with items.

Important: The **Write Item properties back to the file** checkbox on the *Items* tab must be selected for item properties to be written back to a file.

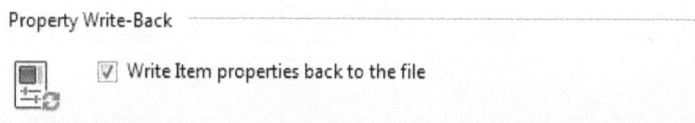

Property Write-Back

☑ Write Item properties back to the file

How To: Synchronize Associated File Properties

1. In the Item Master, select the item for which you want to synchronize file properties.
2. Select the *General* tab in the preview if it is not already selected.
3. Right-click on the *Associated Files* section and select **Synchronize Properties**.
4. Item properties are written back to the associated file.

Other Configuration

- Determine whether or not a user is able to assign a category to an item when the item is created. By default, this option is selected. Clear the **Allow user to assign category when creating a new item** option checkbox to disable this option.

- When the **Break file links from items based on Equivalence Value during item update** option is selected, Vault automatically breaks the link between an item and a file if the equivalence values do not match during an update of the item. This setting is off by default.

Other

☑ Allow user to assign category when creating a new item

☐ Break file links from items based on Equivalence Value during item update

Practice 13a
Configure Items

In this practice, you create a new unit and new category, and configure an item lifecycle state name.

Task 1: Configure units.

1. Start Autodesk Vault Professional and log in with the following information.

    *   For *User Name*, enter **administrator**.
    *   Leave the *Password* field blank.
    *   For *Vault*, select **AOTCAdminVault**.

2. From the Tools menu, select **Administration>Vault Settings** to display the Vault Settings dialog box.

3. Select the *Items* tab.
4. Select **Configure** in the *Units* section to display the Units of Measure dialog box.
5. Click the **Plus sign** to display the Add Unit dialog box. This is where you will define the new unit for microns.

6. Do the following:

    *   For *Name*, enter **Micron**.
    *   For *Symbol*, enter **um**.
    *   For *Base Unit*, select **centimeters (cm)**.
    *   For the *Conversion factor*, enter **.0001**.
    *   Ensure that **This is a Base Unit** is unchecked.
    *   Click **OK** to create the new unit.

✔	Name	Symbol	Base Unit	Conversion Factor
	Inch	in	cm	2.54 ⌃
	Kilogram	kg	g	1000
	Liquid Ounce	lqd oz	ml	29.57353
	Liter	l	ml	1000
	Meter	m	cm	100
	Micron	um	cm	0.0001
	Milligram	mg	g	0.001
	Milliliter	ml	ml	1 ⌄

7. Confirm the new unit is added. Click **Close** to dismiss the Units of Measure dialog box and return to the Vault Settings dialog box.

Task 2: Configure item category.

1. In the Vault Settings dialog box, select the *Behaviors* tab.
2. Select **Categories** in the *Categories* section to display the Configure Categories dialog box.
3. Select **Item Categories** from the drop-down list.

4. In the Configure Categories toolbar, select **New** to display the Category Edit dialog box.

5. In the Category Edit dialog box, enter the following information:

   - For *Name*, enter **Weldment**.
   - For *Color*, select a color of your choice.
   - Select the **Available** checkbox if not already enabled.
   - For *Description*, enter **Frame Weldments**.

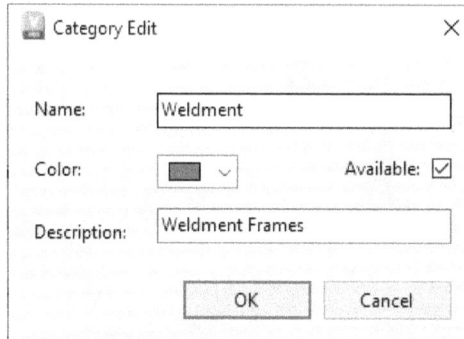

6. Click **OK** to close the Category Edit dialog box and return to the Configure Categories dialog box.

7. Click **Close** to close the Configure Categories dialog box and return to the Vault Settings dialog box.

Task 3: Check lifecycle state transition action.

1. Select the *Behaviors* tab and select **Lifecycles** to display the Lifecycle Definitions dialog box.

2. Select **Item Release Process** and click **Edit**.

3. For the lifecycle state of **Work In Progress**, select the *Transitions* tab.

4. Select the row that has a From State of **Released** and To State of **Work In Progress**.

5. Click **Edit** and then the *Actions* tab to see the **Bump primary revision** action for this lifecycle state change.

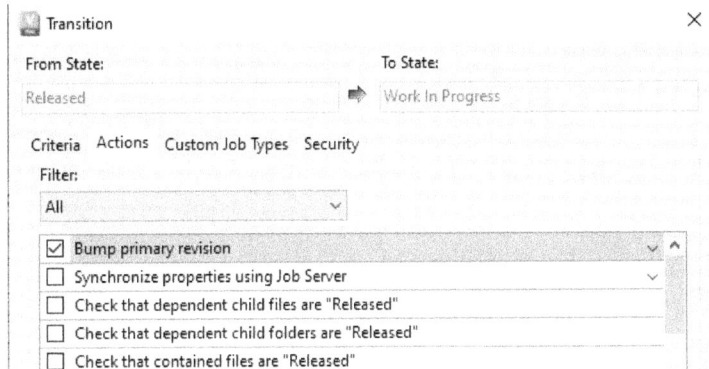

6. Click **OK**.

Task 4: Configure item lifecycle state name.

1. Select the **In Review** lifecycle state and click the *General* tab.

2. Replace **In Review** with the string **For Review**.

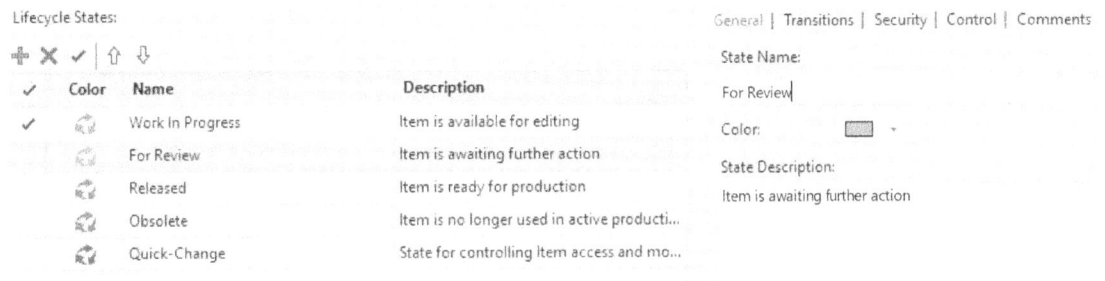

3. Click **OK**. The lifecycle state name is updated in the list.

4. Click **Close**.

Task 5: Configure watermarks.

1. Select the *Items* tab, and then in the *Watermarking* section, select **Configure** to display the Lifecycle Watermarks dialog box.

2. Select the row for the **For Review** lifecycle state.

3. Change the text to be consistent with the change. Click the button next to the *Watermark Text* **IN REVIEW** to display the Watermark Text Entry − For Review dialog box.

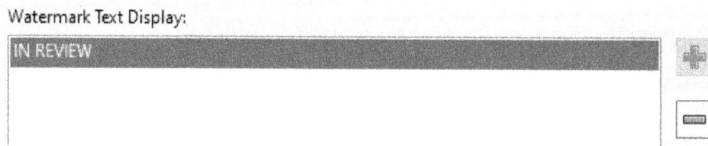

4. In the *Watermark Text Display* list, select the current text and then click the - (Remove) button to remove it.

5. Select the **Input text for display in the watermark** radio button and enter the text **For Review**.

6. Click the + (Add) button to add this text to the list.

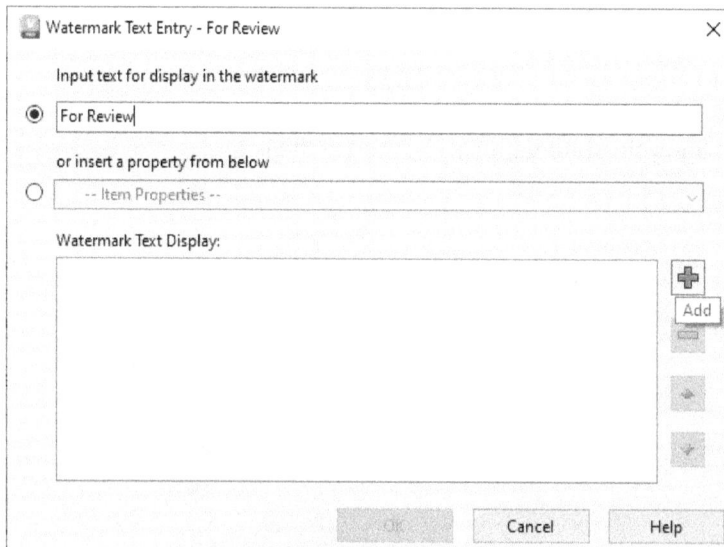

7. Click **OK** to dismiss the Watermark text Entry – For Review dialog box and return to the Lifecycle Watermarks dialog box.

8. Note the change in the *Watermark Text* for the **For Review** state.

Lifecycle State	Watermark Text	Loc
Work In Progress	WORK IN PROGRESS	Dia
I For Review	For Review [...]	Dia
Released - Effective	RELEASED – EFFECTIVE	Bor

9. Click **OK** to close the Lifecycle Watermarks dialog box and return to the Vault Settings dialog box.

10. Click **Close** to close the Vault Settings dialog box.

End of practice

Practice 13b
Create Item Numbering Schemes

In this practice, you create two item numbering schemes. One scheme consists of a simple sequential number. The other is a more complex numbering scheme, with a list, delimiter, and sequential number.

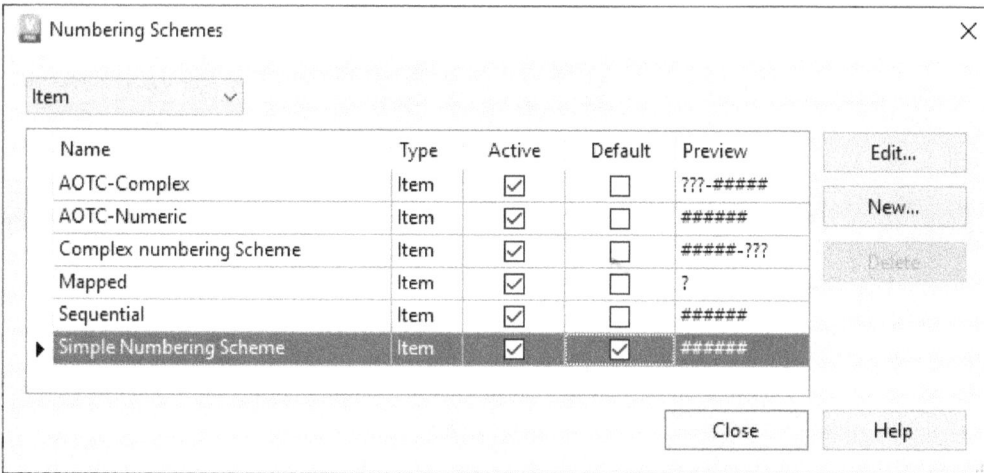

The completed practice

Task 1: Create simple item numbering scheme.

1. Select the *Behaviors* tab in the Vault Settings dialog box.

2. In the *Numbering* section, select **Define** to display the Numbering Schemes dialog box.

3. In the Numbering Schemes dialog box, in the drop-down list, select **Item** to display the item numbering schemes.

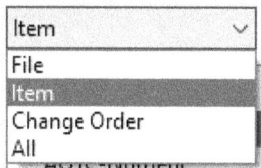

4. Click **New** to create a new item numbering scheme. The New Numbering Scheme dialog box displays.

5. In the *Name* field, enter **Simple Numbering Scheme**.

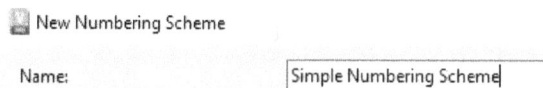

6. Click **New** to display the Add Field dialog box.

7. In the Add Field dialog box, do the following:

   - For *Field Type*, select **Auto-generated sequence**.
   - For *Name*, enter **Number**.
   - For *Length*, enter **6**.
   - For *Range*, enter **100001** for the starting number and do not change the ending number.
   - Leave *Step Size* at the default (**1**).

8. Click **OK** to return to the Numbering Schemes dialog box.

Task 2: Create complex numbering scheme.

1. Click **New** to create a new item numbering scheme.

2. The New Numbering Scheme dialog box displays. In the *Name* field, enter **Complex Numbering Scheme**.

3. Click **New** to display the Add Field dialog box.

4. In the Add Field dialog box, do the following:

   - For *Field Type*, select **Auto-generated sequence**.
   - For *Name*, enter **Number**.
   - For *Length*, enter **5**.
   - For *Range*, enter **10001** for the starting number and do not change the ending number.
   - Leave *Step Size* at the default (**1**).

5. Click **OK** to dismiss the Add Field dialog box and return to the New Numbering Scheme dialog box.

6. Click **New** to display the Add Field dialog box.

7. In the Add Field dialog box, do the following:

   - For *Field Type*, select **Delimiter**.
   - For *Delimiter Value*, enter **-** (hyphen).

8. Click **OK** to dismiss the Add Field dialog box and return to the New Numbering Scheme dialog box.

9. Click **New** to display the Add Field dialog box.

10. In the Add Field dialog box, do the following:

- For *Field Type*, select **Pre-defined list**.
- In the *Predefined List Field Settings* section, for the *Name*, enter **Type**.
- In the first row of the *Enter code list:* section, enter **100**.
- Select the *Description* field right next to it and enter **Part**.
- A second row is added to the list. In the *Code* field for this new row, enter **200**.
- Select the *Description* field right next to it and enter **Assembly**.
- A third row is added to the list. In the *Code* field for this new row, enter **300**.
- Select the *Description* field right next to it and enter **Purchased**.
- Select the first row and click **Set as Default**.

Your entries should look like the following illustration.

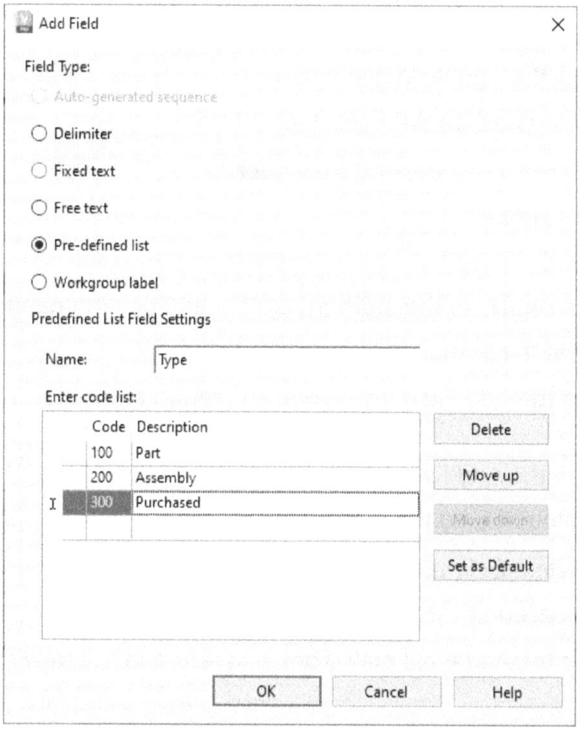

11. Click **OK** to return to the New Numbering Scheme dialog box.

12. Select the **Type** row and click **Move Up** twice to move it to the top of the list.

13. Select the **Delimiter** row and click **Move Up** once to move it between the Type and the Number. Your *Fields* list should display like the following illustration.

Fields

Name	Type	Value	
Type	Pre-defined list	100,200,300	Edit...
▶ Delimiter	Delimiter	-	Delete
Number	Auto-generated	10001 - 99999	Move Up
			Move Down
			New...

14. Click **OK** to dismiss the New Numbering Scheme dialog box and return to the Numbering Schemes dialog box.

15. In the Numbering Schemes dialog box, select the **Default** checkbox in the **Simple Numbering Scheme** row. This numbering scheme will now be applied to new items. Click **Close** to close the Numbering Schemes dialog box.

Numbering Schemes ✕

Item ⌄

Name	Type	Active	Default	Preview	
AOTC-Complex	Item	☑	☐	???-#####	Edit...
AOTC-Numeric	Item	☑	☐	######	New...
Complex numbering Scheme	Item	☑	☐	#####-???	
Mapped	Item	☑	☐	?	Delete
Sequential	Item	☑	☐	######	
▶ Simple Numbering Scheme	Item	☑	☑	######	

Close   Help

End of practice

13.2 Configuring Change Orders

Overview

This lesson describes how to set up and configure change orders to better match your company's requirements.

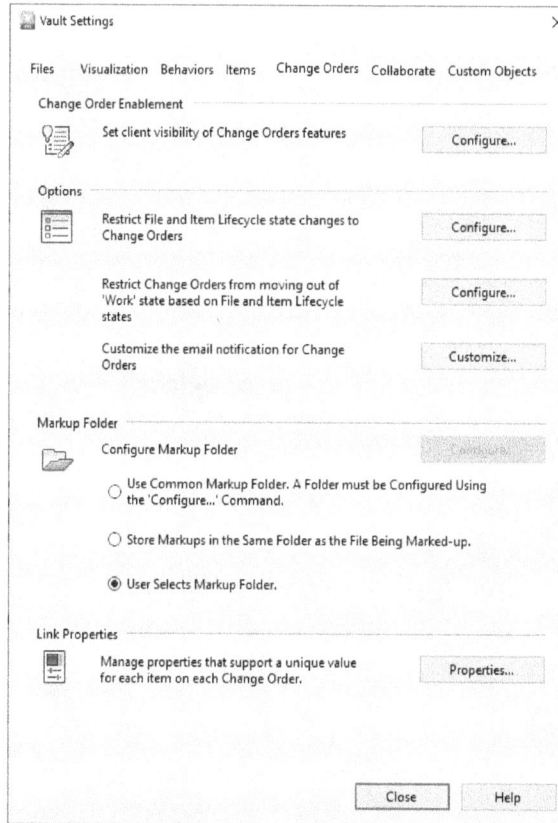

Objectives

After completing this lesson, you will be able to:

- Set change order options.
- Configure a change order markup folder.
- Add user-defined properties to change orders.
- Define change order routing lists.
- Define change order numbering schemes.
- Configure email notification.

Change Order Options

As an administrator, you can set several options for change orders that determine change order workflows. The *Change Orders* tab option settings are shown in the following illustration.

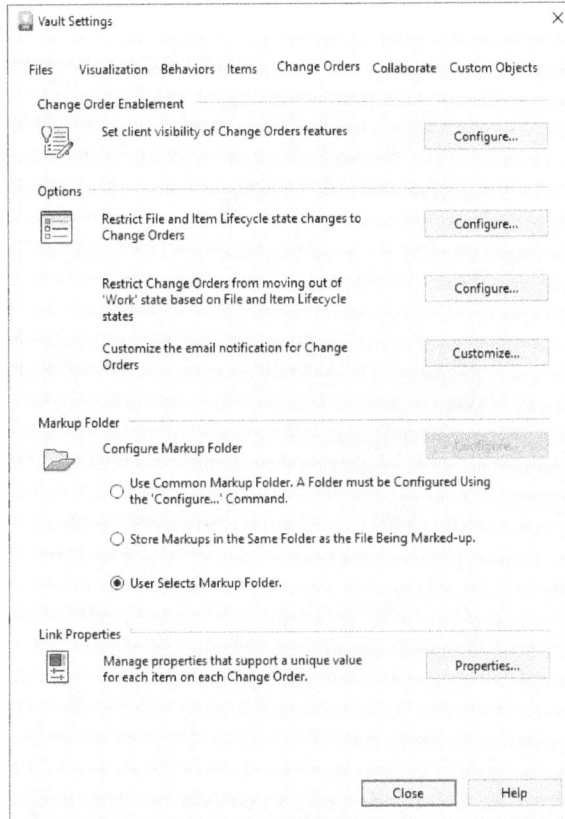

Configure Restrictions for Lifecycle State Changes Using Change Orders

Specify whether item or file lifecycle state changes are controlled only by change orders.

When the **Restrict File and Item Lifecycle state changes to Change Orders** setting is enabled, a file or item lifecycle state cannot be changed outside of a change order unless the user is an Administrator. Users must change file and items record states using the **Change State** command inside the change order.

You can select whether users with administrative permissions can override these restrictions.

How To: Configure Restrictions

1. In the Vault Client, select **Tools>Administration>Vault Settings**.
2. In the Vault Settings dialog box, select the *Change Orders* tab.
3. Select **Configure** next to **Restrict File and Item Lifecycle state changes to Change Orders**.
4. Select whether you want to restrict file and item lifecycle changes to change orders.
5. To enable users with administrative permissions to override the restriction for that entity, select **Allow Administrator Override**.
6. Click **Close** to save your changes.

How To: Prevent a Change Order from Moving Out of a Work State Based on Item and File States

Prevent a change order from leaving its work state unless its item and file records are in selected lifecycle states.

These files and items must be listed in the *Records* tab of the change order, and not the *Files* tab.

1. In the Vault Client, select **Tools>Administration >Vault Settings**.
2. In the Vault Settings dialog box, select the *Change Orders* tab.
3. Select **Configure** next to **Restrict Change Orders from moving out of 'Work' state based on File and Item Lifecycle states**.
4. Select the lifecycle states that an item or file cannot be in for the change order to move out of a Work state.
5. Click **Close**.
6. Select whether you want these settings to apply to items, files, or both.
7. Click **OK** to save your changes.

Configuring a Markup Folder

During the change order process, markups are often used to discuss changes. By default, the markup files are placed in the same folder as the associated file. As an administrator, you can enable the user to select a markup folder or you can configure a markup folder in the vault where all of the markup files are stored.

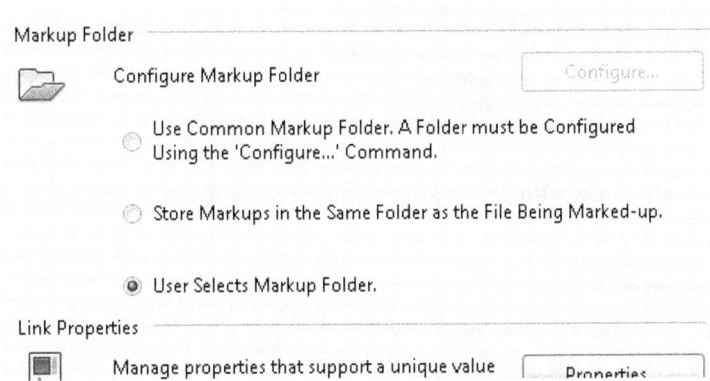

The following illustration shows a markup folder named *Markups* that was added under the root of the vault.

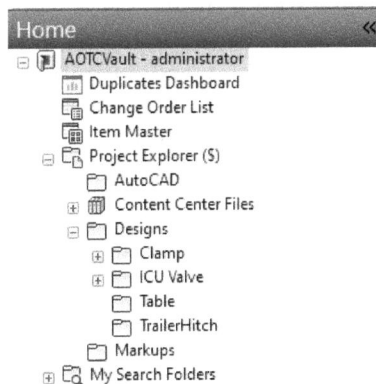

How To: Configure a Markup Folder

The following steps describe how to configure a markup folder:

1. In the Vault Settings dialog box, select the *Change Orders* tab.

2. In the *Markup Folder* section, click **Use Common Markup Folder**. The **Configure** button, in the same group, is now enabled.

3. Select **Configure** to display the Select Vault Location dialog box.

4. If the folder already exists, select it; otherwise use the **New Folder** command to create a new folder.

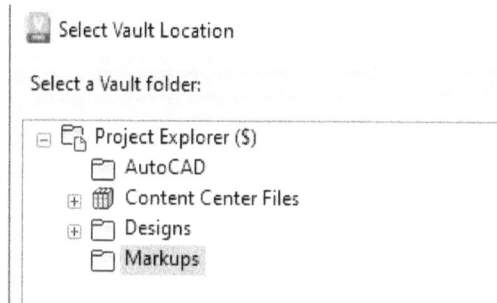

5. Click **OK** to close the Select Vault Location dialog box and return to the Vault Settings dialog box.

Link Properties

Introduction to Link Properties

Link properties are unique to change orders and enable you to support a unique value for each item on the change order. Link properties are item properties, but only in the context of the change order that they are associated with. If the item is not on a change order, it does not have this property.

Link properties are unique in the sense that they are administered in a dialog box different than file, item, and change order properties. However, they do support Property Compliance. The following change order shows the two ICU Valve Buttons on a change order to remove the paint. The cost of the change for each button is $400 to change the tooling and update the process documentation.

How To: Add a Link Property

1. In the Vault Settings dialog box, select the *Change Orders* tab. In the *Link Properties* section, click **Properties** to display the User Defined Linked Properties (Change Orders) dialog box. There are no default properties shipped with the product.

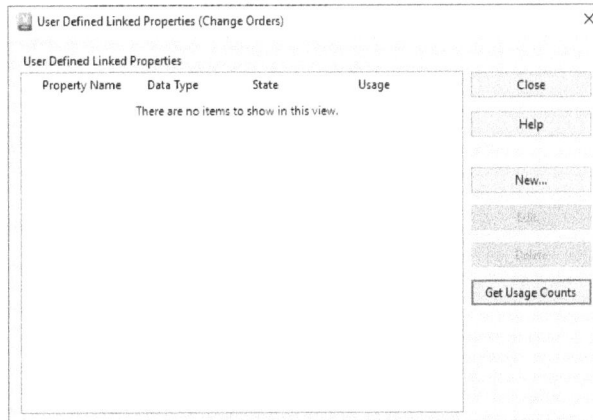

2. Click **New** to display the New Change Order Link Property dialog box. Enter the *Name* and select the *Type* from the drop-down list, then specify the *Settings* for the property. Enter *Initial Value* and *List Values* if required. Click **OK** to dismiss the dialog box and return to the User Defined Linked Properties (Change Orders) dialog box.

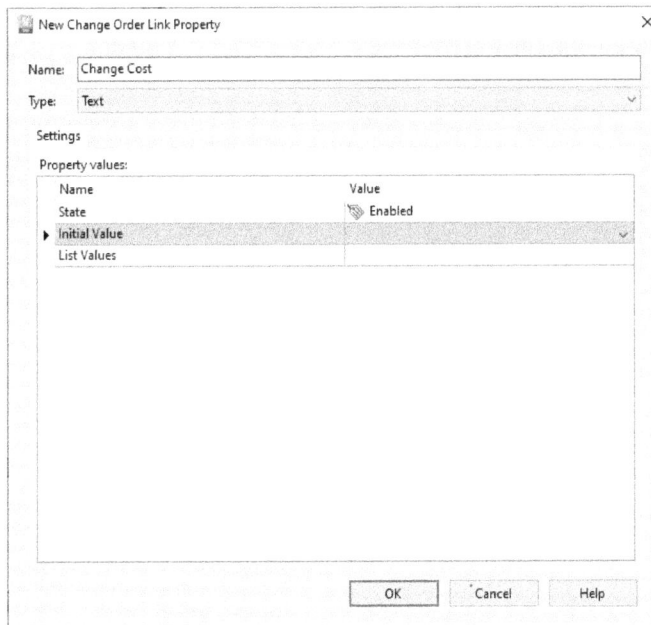

3. The new link properties display in the list. Click **Close** to return to the Vault Settings dialog box.

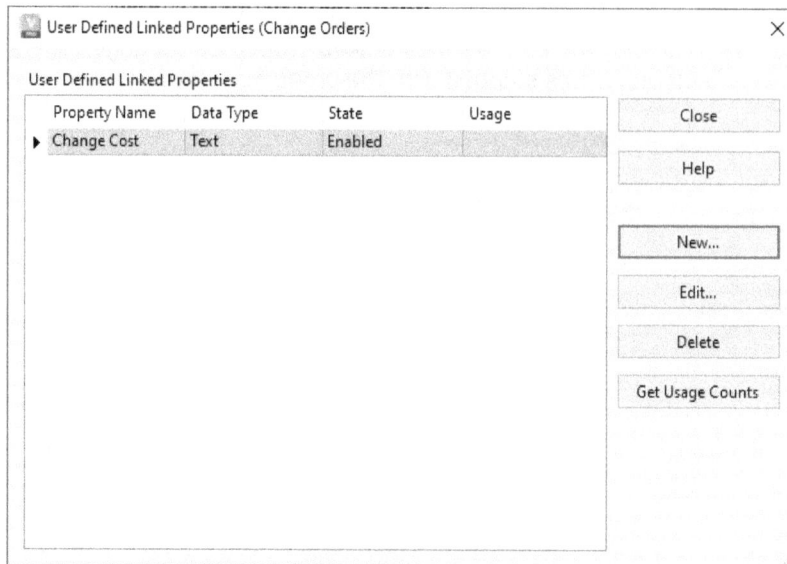

Change Order Numbering

The default change order numbering scheme uses a three-letter prefix (ECO) and an auto-generated six-digit number. If the supplied change order numbering scheme does not match your company standards or does not meet your requirements, you can create new change order numbering schemes.

If your company standards require more than one change order numbering scheme, you can create multiple numbering schemes. The person originating the change order can select the appropriate scheme when they create the change order.

How To: Define a Change Order Numbering Scheme

1. In the Vault Settings dialog box, select the *Behaviors* tab.
2. In the *Numbering* section, select **Define**.
3. In the Numbering Schemes dialog box, select **Change Order**.
4. Click **New**.
5. Enter the scheme name.
6. Click **New** to add fields for the numbering scheme.

7. In the Add Field dialog box, select one of the following field types:

   * Auto-generated

   * Delimiter

   * Fixed text – Enter a name for the fixed text field.

   * Free text – Enter a name for the free text field.

   * Predefined list – Enter a name for the free predefined list field.

   * Workgroup label

8. Click **OK**.

9. The New Numbering Scheme dialog box displays a preview of the settings defined in the Add/Edit dialog box.

10. To change the settings, click **Edit**. To delete, click **Delete**. To add another numbering scheme, click **Add**.

11. To display text in all capital letters, select the **Force to uppercase** checkbox.

12. Click **OK** to save the scheme.

13. When a new change order is created, the user selects the button next to the *Change Order Number* field to change the scheme used.

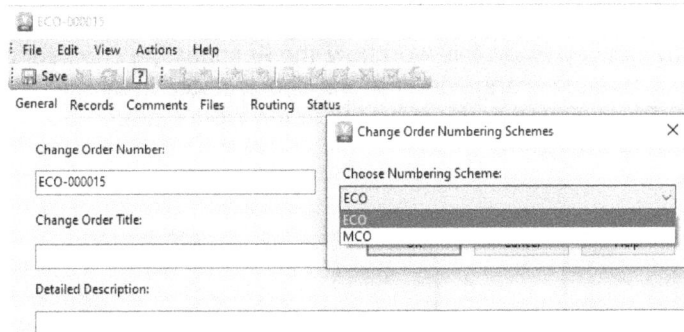

Routing Definition – Workflow Selection

There are two possible workflows available with Vault Professional:

1. **Standard:** In the workflow definition, a change order moves from the Work state to the Review state. The Responsible Engineer or Change Administrator moves the change order out of the Work state and the Approvers can either reject the change order to the Rejected state or approve it to the Approved state. This is the default workflow.

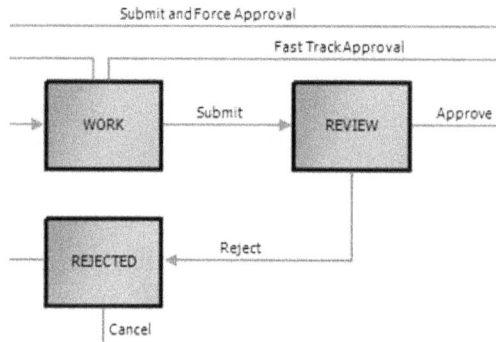

2. **Check State:** In this workflow definition, a new Check state and Checker routing participant is added to the standard workflow. This is a common workflow where someone checks the work of the Responsible Engineer to ensure adherence to company standards, etc., before it is submitted to final review. In this workflow, the Responsible Engineer or Change Administrator submits the change order to the Check state. There the Checker can either approve it to the Review state or reject it back to the Work state.

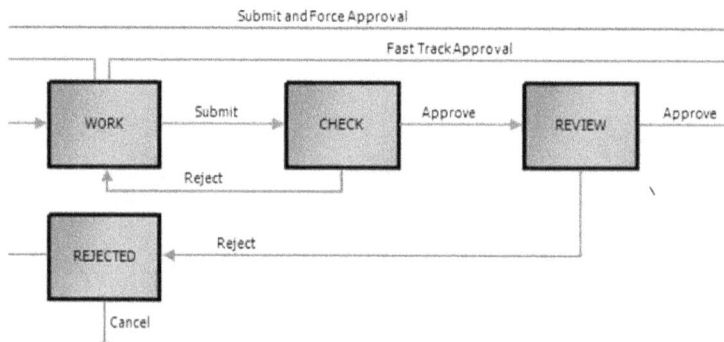

The workflow can be changed in the Global Settings dialog box by selecting **Tools> Administration>Global Settings**.

Security   Change Orders   Integrations

Routing Definition

Define Change Order Routing Lists   [Define...]

Select workflow definition to use   Standard   ⌄
on new Change Orders: Standard
                                            Check State

Routing Definition – Change Order Routing Lists

As an administrator, you define one or more routing lists to define change order participants and their roles in the change order process. When users create a change order, they select which routing list to use. Small companies might require only one routing list and large companies might require many. Because routing lists are shared across all vaults, only one set of routing lists is required regardless of the number of vaults you use.

The following illustration shows the creation of a change order routing list.

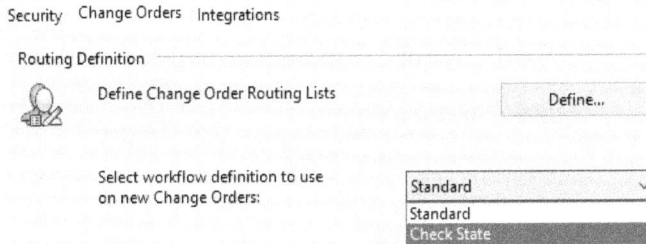

When a change order is created, you must specify a routing. A routing is a list of participants with predefined roles. Each of the different routing roles has specific permissions and responsibilities.

The Change Administrator, Responsible Engineer, and Approver roles control the progression of the change order. The Reviewer role can add markups, view, add, and reply to comments.

The person creating the change order automatically becomes the Change Requestor.

The task a routing participant can perform depends on the routing participant role.

> *Note: Only users with Administrator or Change Order Editor privileges can be assigned routing roles.*

Change Order Roles

Change order participants are assigned one or more of the following roles.

Role	Task Availability
Change Requestor	Initiated the change order.
Change Administrator	Can add or remove Approvers, Change Administrators, and Responsible Engineers. This participant can edit the title of the change order, add or remove files or items, and modify user-defined properties. Can submit the new change order to the Open state.
	The Change Administrator is also responsible for:
	• Canceling the change order or reopening a closed change order.
	• Evaluating change orders in the Open state to determine whether they should be processed or canceled, and so is responsible for submitting the Open change order to Work or canceling it.
	• Rejecting change orders to determine whether they should be canceled or can be reworked. When a change order is approved, the Change Administrator is responsible for closing the change order and releasing the associated items and files.
Responsible Engineer	Can edit the change order when in the Work state, make required revisions, and submit the change order for review.
Checker	Participates only in the Check state (when enabled). Can add comments in the Check state. Can approve to the Review State or reject back to the Work state.
Reviewer	Can only view, add, and reply to comments.
Approver	Can review, approve, and reject a change order.
Notification User	Receives notification when the change order is closed.

Example

A small company wants to track changes. They install Autodesk Vault Professional and need to set up a single change order routing list. Two engineers are responsible for all aspects of the change order process and the production manager wants to be notified of changes.

A change order routing list is created with three participants. Each of the two engineers is assigned as Change Administrator, Responsible Engineer, and Approver. The production manager is assigned as a Notification User.

How To: Create a Change Order Routing List

The following steps outline the creation of a routing list:

1. Open the Global Settings dialog box (**Tools> Administration>Global Settings**) and select the *Change Orders* tab. In the *Routing definition* section, select **Define** to display the Routing dialog box.

2. A number of routings have been defined, but only one, **Default**, is currently active and set as the default. Click **New** to display the Edit Routing dialog box.

3. Enter a *Routing Name*, then select one of the users from the *Change Order participants* list and click **Add** to display the Edit Roles dialog box.

4. Select a role from the list of *Available Roles* and click **Add** to add it to the list of *Selected Roles*.

5. Repeat the previous step to add any additional roles.

6. Click **OK** to return to the Edit Routing dialog box. Note the *Routing Roles* assigned to the first selected user.

7. Repeat Steps 3 to 5 to add the rest of the *Change Order participants* and define their *Routing Roles*.

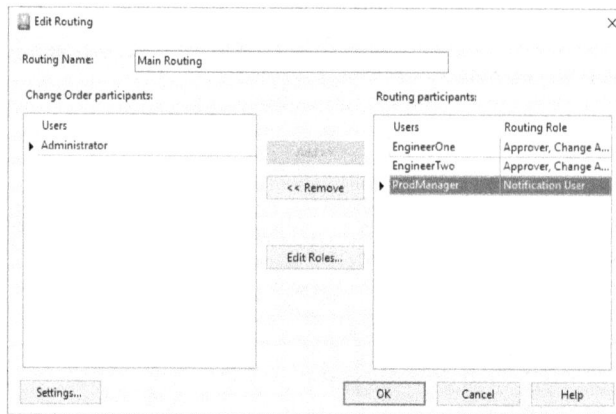

Note: You must add users in the Change Administrator, Responsible Engineer, and Approver role. If you are using the optional Check state, a Checker must also be added.

8. If you have more than one approver, use **Settings** to display and select the approval type required.

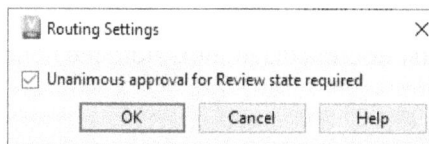

9. Click **OK** to close the Edit Routing dialog box and return to the Routing dialog box.

10. In the Routing dialog box, select the new routing and drag it from the *All routings* list to the *Active routings* list.

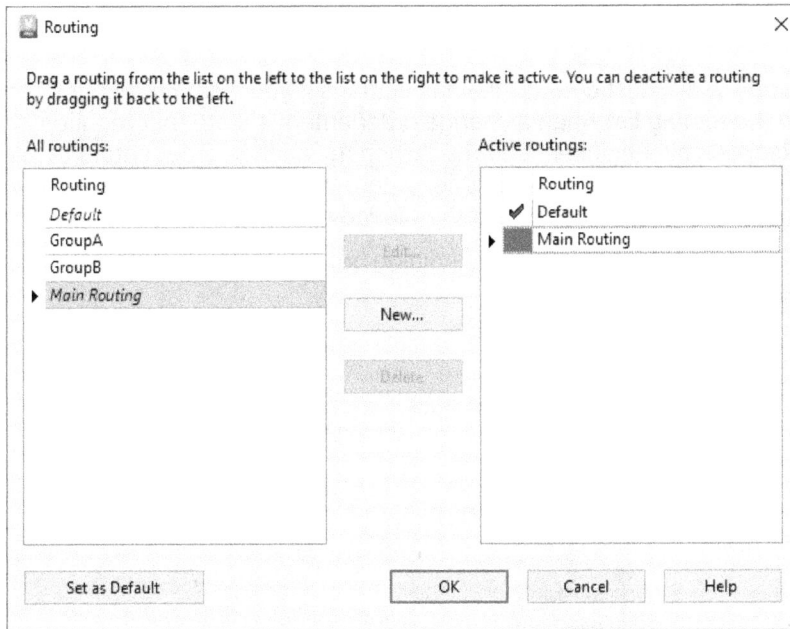

11. In the Routing dialog box, select the new routing. If this is to be the new default routing, click **Set as Default**.

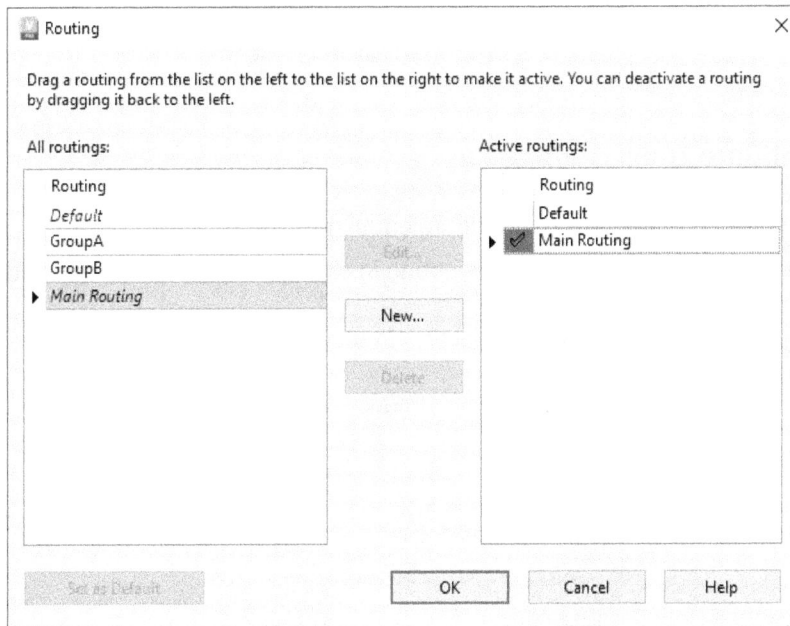

12. Click **OK** to close the Routing dialog box and return to the Global Settings dialog box.

Configure Email Notification

As an administrator, you must configure email settings if you want notifications emailed to participants on the routing list when a change order enters a state that requires attention. For example, the Responsible Engineer is notified when the change order enters the Work state, Approvers are notified when the change order enters the Review state, and Notification Users are notified when the change order enters the Closed state.

The following illustration displays the Email dialog box in which you enable email notification and enter the email server information.

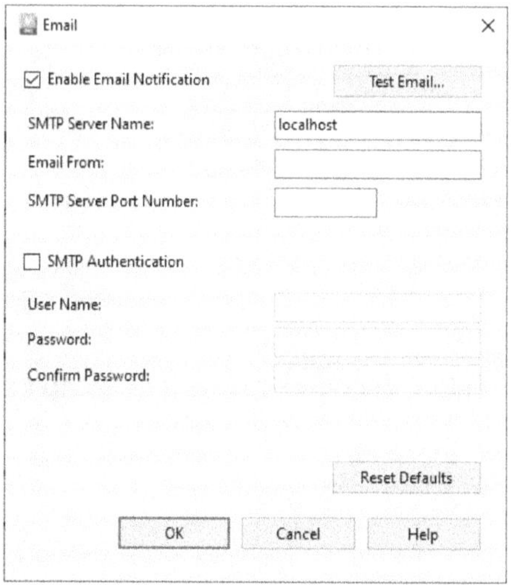

How To: Configure Email Notification

The following steps describe how to configure email notification:

1. Ensure that all users that will be participating in change orders have email addresses.

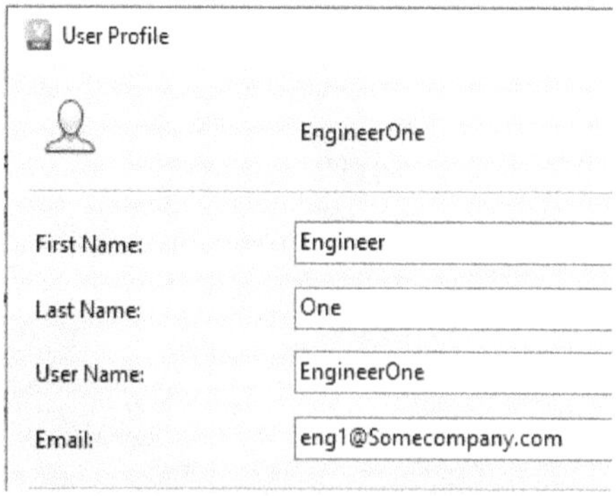

2. Log in to the Autodesk Data Management Server console as an Administrator.

3. From the Tools menu, select **Administration**.

4. Select the *Advanced Settings* tab. In the *Email* section, click **Email** to display the Email dialog box.

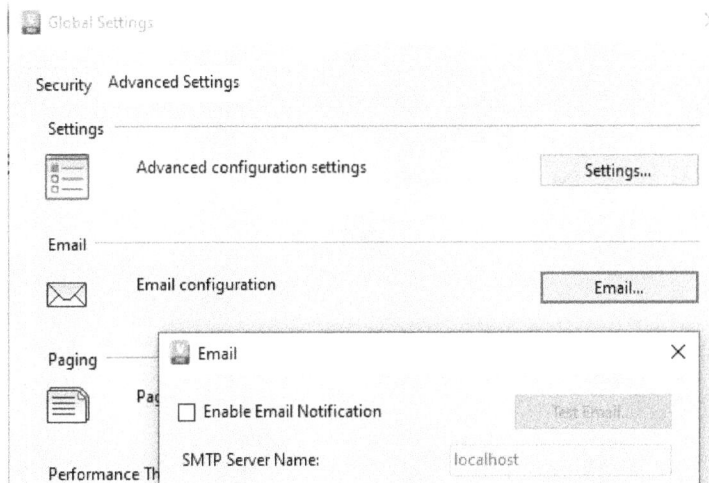

5. Select **Enable Email Notification**, then enter the appropriate *SMTP Server Name*, the *Email From* address that will show up as the from address in the email, and the *SMTP Server Port Number*. If your company requires authentication, check the box to enable **SMTP Authentication** and provide the user credentials.

6. Use **Test Email** to verify that the configuration is correct.

7. Click **OK** to dismiss the Email dialog box and return to the Global Settings dialog box.

8. Click **Close** to dismiss the Global Settings dialog box and log out of the Autodesk Data Management Server console.

Practice 13c
Set Up Change Orders

In this practice, you set up a markup folder, add a user-defined change order property, create a new change order numbering scheme, and add a new change order routing list.

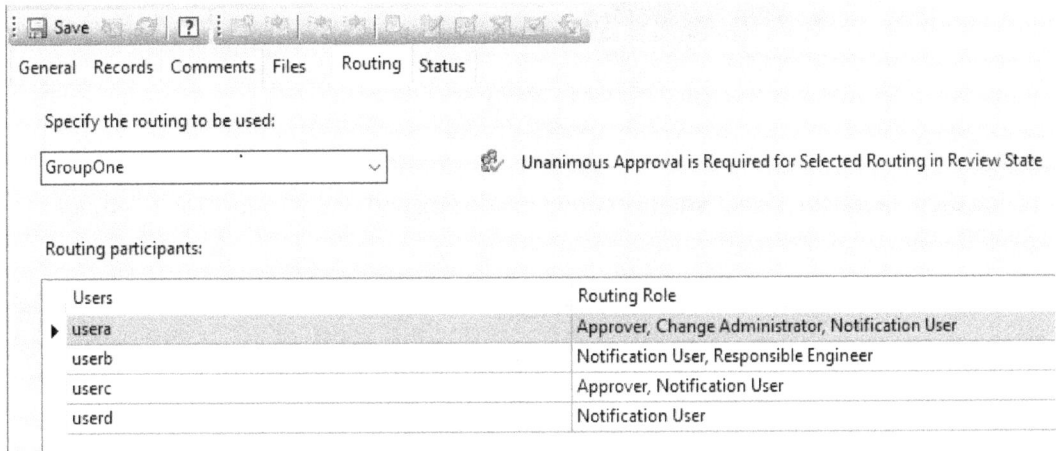

The completed practice

Task 1: Configure change orders.

1. Start Autodesk Vault Professional and log in with the following information:
    *   For *User Name*, enter **administrator**.
    *   Leave the *Password* field blank.
    *   For *Vault*, select **AOTCAdminVault**.
2. Open the Vault Settings dialog box by selecting **Tools>Administration>Vault Settings**.
3. Select the *Change Orders* tab and review the default options.

Task 2: Set up a markup folder.

1. In the *Markup Folder* section, select **Use Common Markup Folder**. The **Configure** button, in the same section, is now enabled.

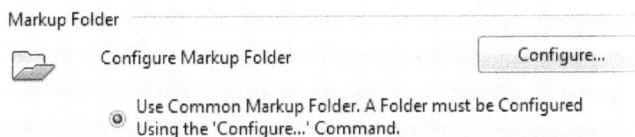

2. Select **Configure** to display the Select Vault Location dialog box.

3. Select **New Folder** to create a new folder named *Markups* in the *Project Explorer ($)* root folder.

4. Enter **Markups** in the New Folder dialog box and click **OK**.

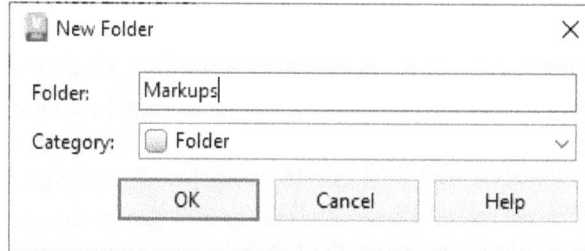

5. Click **OK** to close the Select Vault Location dialog box and return to the Vault Settings dialog box.

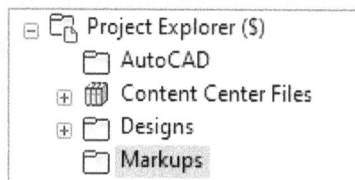

Task 3: Add link properties.

1. In the Vault Settings dialog box, select **Properties** in the *Link Properties* section to display the Link Properties dialog box.

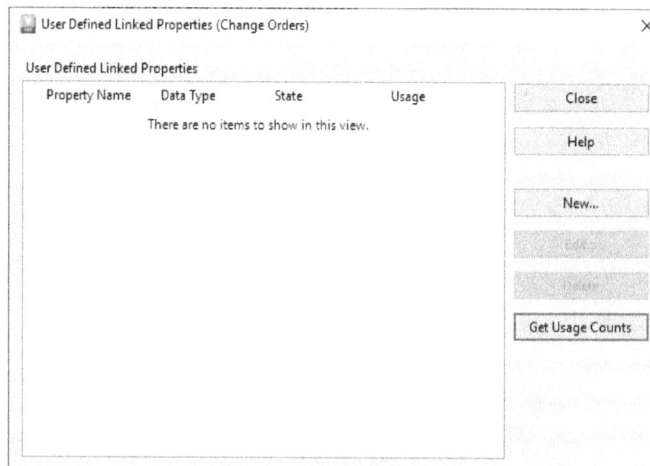

- Note that unlike other properties, there are no default link properties.

2. Click **New** to display the New Change Order Link Property dialog box.

3. Enter the following information for a new *Disposition* link property:

   * For the *Name*, enter **Disposition**.
   * Keep the default *Type* as **Text**.

4. In the List Values dialog box, do the following:

   * In the *Click here to add a new row* section, enter **Revise** and press <Enter>.
   * Enter **Substitute** and press <Enter>.
   * Enter **Obsolete** and press <Enter>.

5. Select the entry for **Revise** and select **Set Initial Value** to make this the default value.

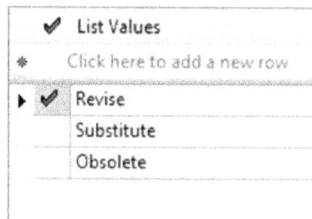

6. Click **Close** to close this dialog box and return to the New Change Order Link Property dialog box.

7. Review the entries. They should look like the following list:

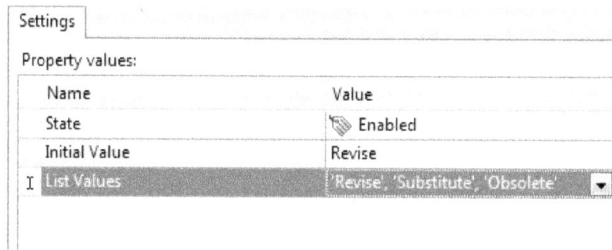

8. Click **OK** to return to the User Defined Linked Properties (Change Orders) dialog box and then **Close** to return to the Vault Settings dialog box.

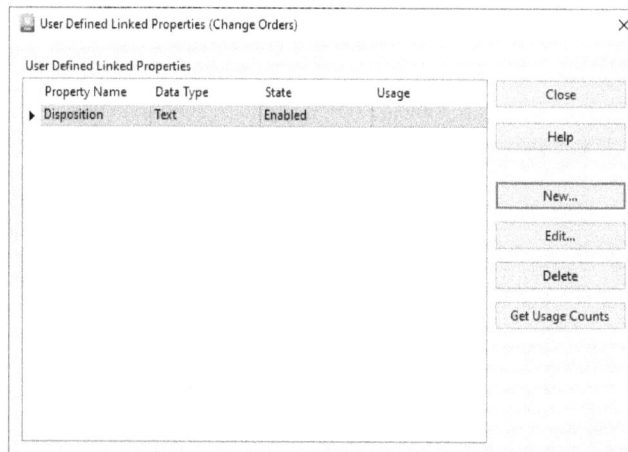

Task 4: Change order numbering.

1. In the Vault Settings dialog box, in the *Behaviors* tab, in the *Numbering* section, select **Define** to display the Numbering Schemes dialog box.

2. Select **Change Order** from the drop-down list.

3. Click **New** to create a new change order numbering scheme with name of **AOTC ECO**.

4. Add the following three fields and the results display as shown in the image below:

    *   Select the **Fixed Text** field type with values of *Name:* **Fixed Text**, *Fixed Text:* **AOTC ECO**.
    *   Select the **Delimiter** field type with *Delimiter Value: -*.
    *   Select the **Auto-generated sequence** field type with values of *Name:* **Auto-generated**, *Length:* **3**, *Range:* **1-999**.

5. Click **OK** to return to the Numbering Schemes dialog box.

6. Select the new numbering scheme and then click the **Default** checkbox to set it as the default.

7. Click **Close** to close this dialog box and return to the Vault Settings dialog box.

Task 5: Create routing list.

1. Click **Close** to close the Vault Settings dialog box.

2. From the Tools menu, select **Administration>Global Settings** to display the Global Settings dialog box.

3. In the Global Settings dialog box, select the *Change Orders* tab.

4. Select **Define** to display the Routing dialog box.

5. Click **New** to display the Edit Routing dialog box.

6. Do the following:

   - For *Routing Name*, enter **GroupOne**.

   - Press <Shift> and select **usera**, **userb**, **userc**, and **userd** from the *Change Order Participants* list and click **Add** to add them to the *Routing participants* list.

   - In the Edit Roles dialog box that opens, select **Notification User** from the *Available Roles* list, then click **Add** to add that to the *Selected Roles* list.

   - Click **OK** to close the dialog box and return to the Edit Routing dialog box.

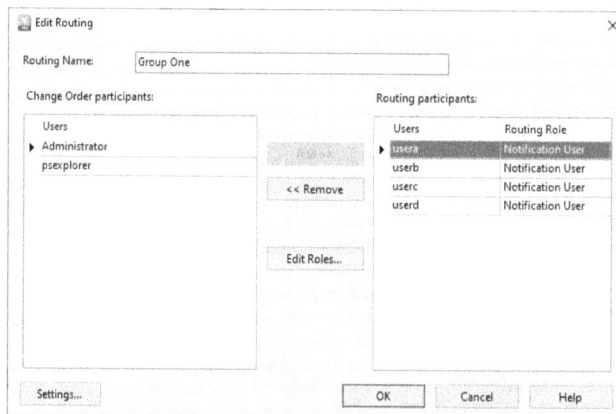

7. In the *Routing participants* list, select **usera** and click **Edit Roles** to display the Edit Roles dialog box.

8. Hold <Ctrl> and select **Change Administrator** and **Approver** from the list.

Available Roles:

Role Name
Change Requestor
Change Administrator
Reviewer
▶ Approver
Responsible Engineer
Notification User

Add ->

<- Remove

9. Click **Add** to add these roles to the *Selected Roles* list.

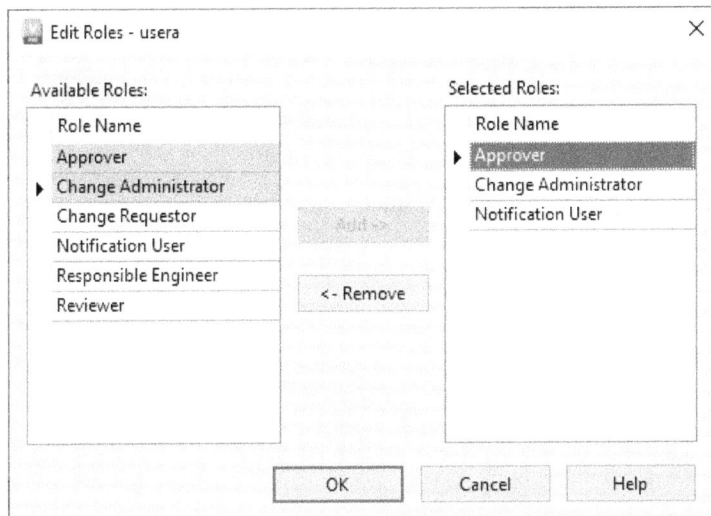

Edit Roles - usera   ✕

Available Roles:

Role Name
Approver
▶ Change Administrator
Change Requestor
Notification User
Responsible Engineer
Reviewer

Add ->

<- Remove

Selected Roles:

Role Name
▶ Approver
Change Administrator
Notification User

OK   Cancel   Help

10. Click **OK** to close this dialog box and return to the Edit Routing dialog box.

11. Do the following:

- Select **userb** in the *Routing participants* list.
- Click **Edit Roles**.
- In the Edit Roles dialog box, select **Responsible Engineer** from the *Available Roles* list.
- Click **Add** to add this role in the *Selected Roles* list.
- Click **OK** to close the dialog box and return to the Edit Routing dialog box.

12. Do the following:

- Select **userc** in the *Routing participants* list.
- Click **Edit Roles**.
- In the Edit Roles dialog box, select **Approver** from the *Available Roles* list.
- Click **Add** to add this role in the *Selected Roles* list.
- Click **OK** to close the dialog box and return to the Edit Routing dialog box.

13. Examine the Edit Routing dialog box to see the *Routing participants* and their roles that you set up.

Routing participants:

Users	Routing Role
usera	Approver, Change Administrator, Notification User
userb	Notification User, Responsible Engineer
▶ userc	Approver, Notification User
userd	Notification User

14. Click **Settings** in the lower-left part of the dialog box.

15. Select **Unanimous approval for Review state required**.

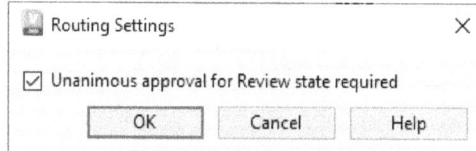

Routing Settings   ✕

☑ Unanimous approval for Review state required

    OK   Cancel   Help

16. Click **OK** to close this dialog box and return to the Edit Routing dialog box.

17. Click **OK** to close the Edit Routing dialog box.

18. In the Routing dialog box, select the new routing **GroupOne** and drag it to the *Active routings* list.

19. In the lower-left corner of the dialog box, click **Set as Default**.

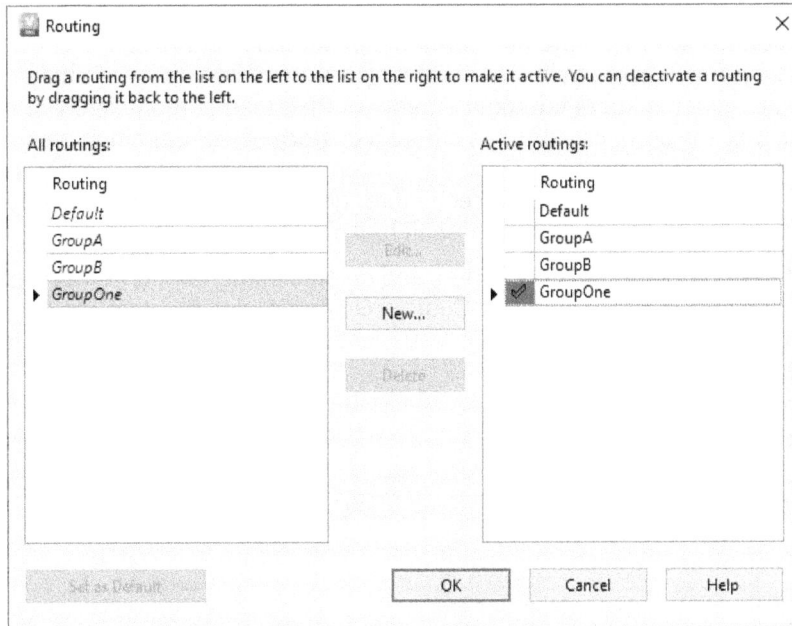

20. Click **OK** to close this dialog box and return to the Global Settings dialog box.

21. Click **Close** to close this dialog box.

22. Exit Vault Professional.

End of practice

13.3 Custom Objects Definition Administration

Overview

This lesson describes how to create and configure custom objects to suit your company's requirements. Custom objects enable Vault administrators to use an extensible system to create new Vault entities to meet the requirements of their team, organization, or company. Right out of the box, the administrator can create a custom object definition and assign it categories, lifecycles, and properties. Once the custom object definition is created, users can create instances of that custom object directly through the user interface. As with files and folders, users can perform many common Vault tasks with custom objects.

Custom object definitions are created, edited, and deleted in the Configure Custom Objects dialog box. You can access the Configure Custom Objects dialog box through the *Custom Objects* tab in the Vault Settings dialog box. You must be an administrator to create and modify custom object definitions.

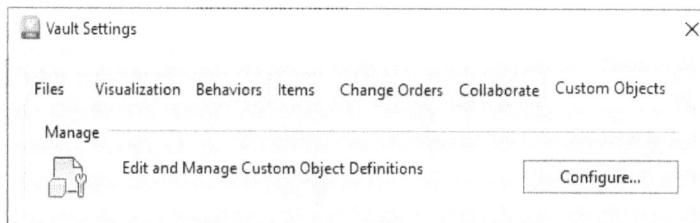

Objectives

After completing this lesson, you will be able to:

- Create a custom object definition.
- Edit a custom object definition.
- Delete a custom object definition.

Create a Custom Object Definition

The custom object definition is the type of entity that is being created. For example, an administrator can create a custom object definition called Contacts or Tasks.

When the user creates a new custom object based on a definition, it is considered an instance. For example, an administrator creates a custom object definition called Contact. A user could then create an instance of that custom object called Bob Smith.

Users can attach files, folders, and other Vault entities to a custom object with a link. For example, if a custom object definition has been created called Tasks and a user has created a task called Review John's Design, the task (Review John's Design) can be linked to John's design in the vault.

Custom object instances can be checked in or checked out, undergo a change state, and be managed with many common Vault commands. Similarly, linked objects are also affected, depending on the user's settings for the Vault function.

For example, if a user wants to check out a custom object and the custom object has links to files, folders, items, or change orders, the files associated with that linked data are gathered and checked out as well.

How To: Create a New Custom Object Definition

Follow these steps to create a new custom object definition:

1. In Autodesk Vault Professional, select **Tools>Administration>Vault Settings**.

2. In the Vault Settings dialog box, select the *Custom Objects* tab and select **Configure**.

3. In the Configure Custom Objects dialog box, click **New**.

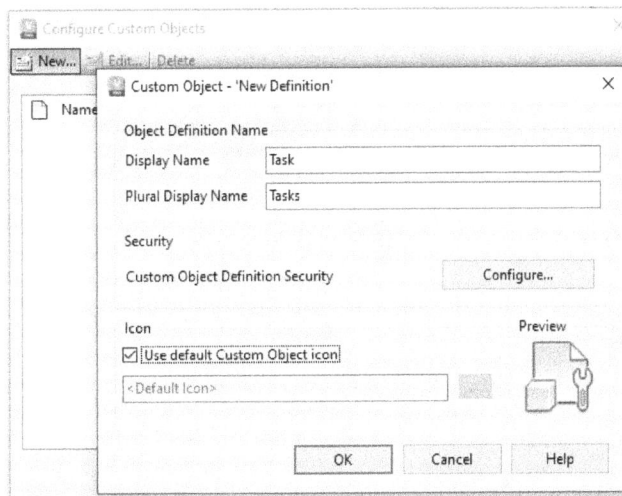

4. Enter a new *Display Name* for the custom object. This name is used in the Vault user interface when the new custom object displays.

   Note: A display name and plural display name are required because Vault uses both contexts throughout the interface. Since there is no universal way to make a name plural, the administrator requirements are to insert the value upon creation.

5. By default, new custom objects use object-based security. This can be customized by configuring different permissions for individual users and groups.

6. New custom objects can use any icon file (*.ICO). Defining four different sizes of the icon, provides the best-looking icons throughout the Vault interface (16x16, 32x32, 64x64, or 128x128). If only one size is defined, it is stretched or compressed to fit each size. If no icon is available, the **Use default Custom Object icon** option should be selected.

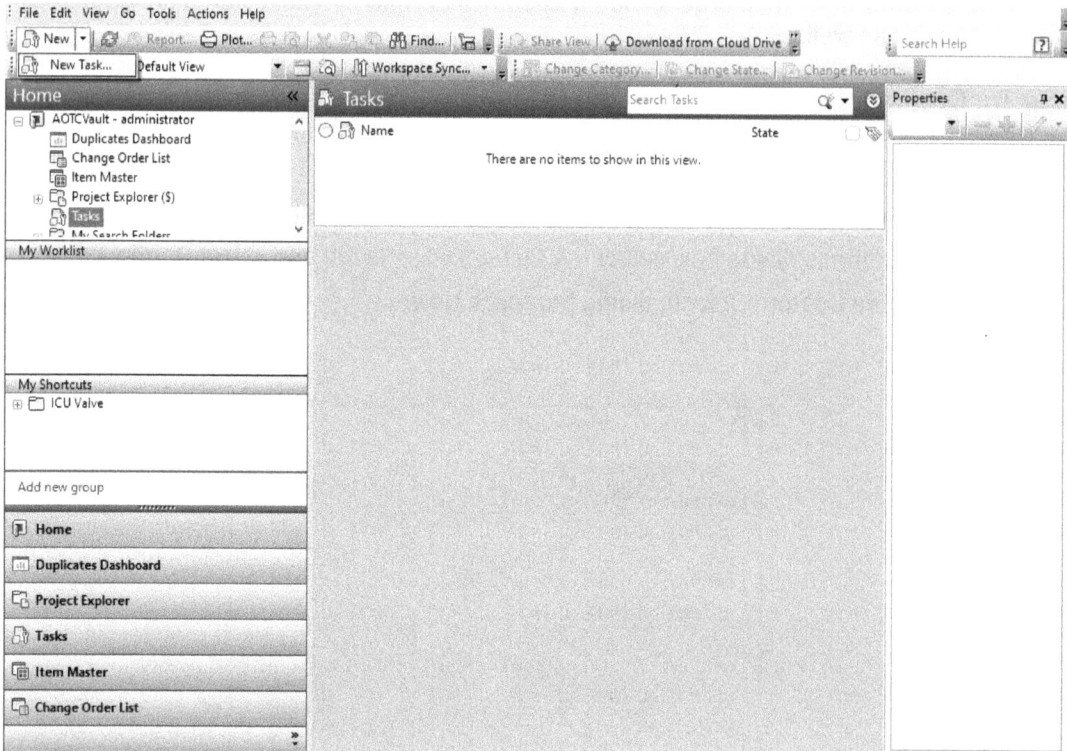

Note: New custom objects do not display in the user interface until the user logs out and logs back in after the custom object is created.

Edit a Custom Object Definition

Once a custom object definition is created, the administrator can navigate back to the Configure Custom Objects dialog box and modify the existing settings.

How To: Edit Custom Object Definition Name

1. In Autodesk Vault Professional, select **Tools>Administration>Vault Settings**.
2. In the Vault Settings dialog box, select the *Custom Objects* tab and select **Configure**.
3. Select a custom object definition and click **Edit**.

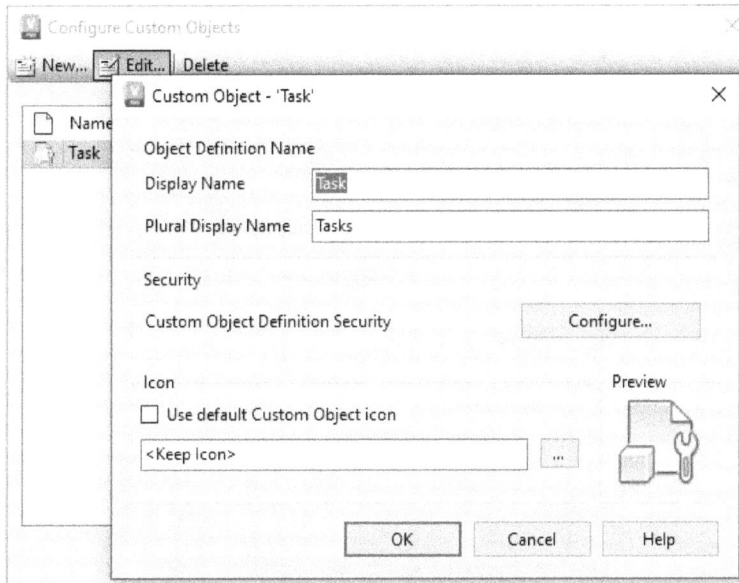

4. Modify the value in the *Display Name* and *Plural Display Name* fields.
5. Click **OK**.

    Note: The changes made to the custom object name are seen after logging out and logging back in to the Vault client.

How To: Edit Custom Object Definition Security

1. In Autodesk Vault Professional, select **Tools>Administration>Vault Settings**.

2. In the Vault Settings dialog box, select the *Custom Objects* tab and select **Configure**.

3. Select a custom object definition and click **Edit**.

4. Select **Configure** under the *Security* section.

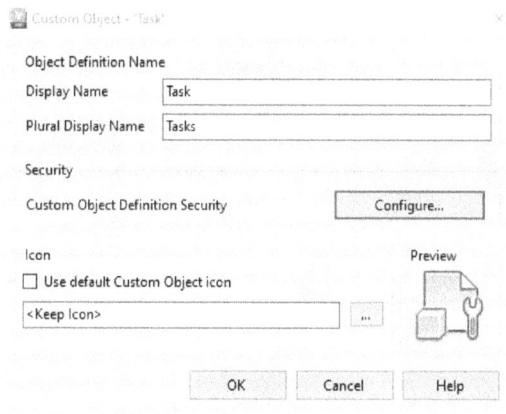

5. Make edits to the existing access control list.

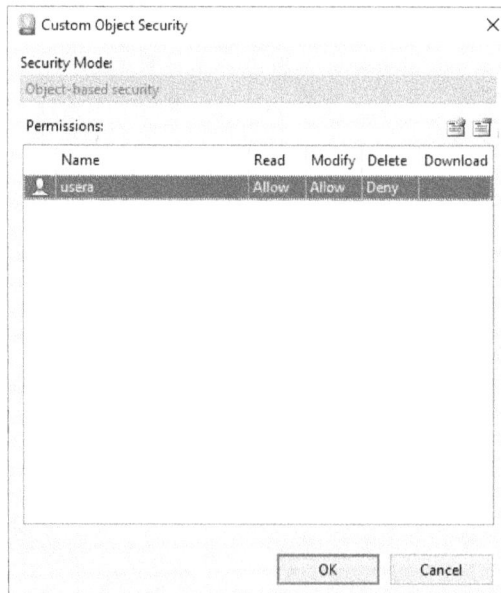

6. Click **OK**.

   • Edits to the security are made immediately to all instances of the custom object definition.

How To: Edit Custom Object Definition Icon

The icon associated with a custom object definition can be changed after the definition is created.

1. In Autodesk Vault Professional, select **Tools>Administration>Vault Settings**.

2. In the Vault Settings dialog box, select the *Custom Objects* tab and select **Configure**.

3. Select a custom object definition and click **Edit**.

4. Change the icon by either choosing to use the default custom object icon or browsing to a new .ICO file.

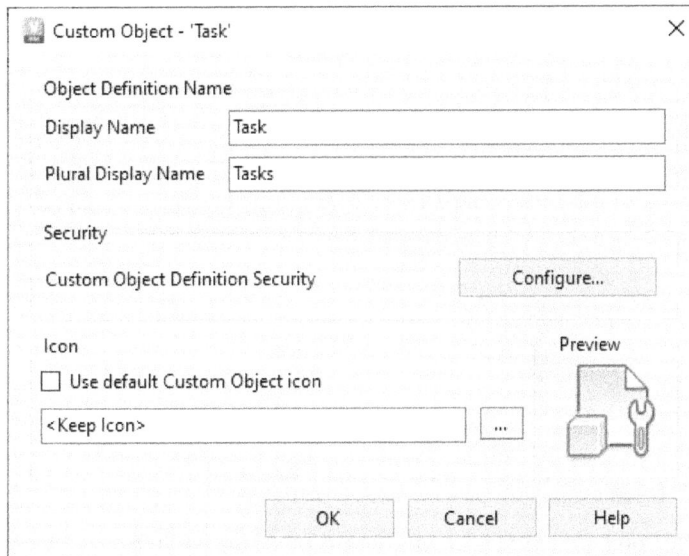

5. Click **OK**.

   Note: The changes made to the custom object icon are seen after logging out and logging back in to the Vault client.

Delete a Custom Object Definition

A user can delete an existing custom object at any time using the Configure Custom Objects dialog box. As long as the custom object is not in use, the definition can be deleted from the Vault.

Once an instance of a custom object definition has been created, the definition cannot be deleted.

Note: All instances of a custom object definition have to be removed from the vault before the definition can be deleted.

How To: Delete a Custom Object Definition

1. In Autodesk Vault Professional, select **Tools>Administration>Vault Settings**.
2. In the Vault Settings dialog box, select the *Custom Objects* tab and select **Configure**.
3. In the Configure Custom Objects dialog box, select the custom object to delete.
4. Click **Delete**.

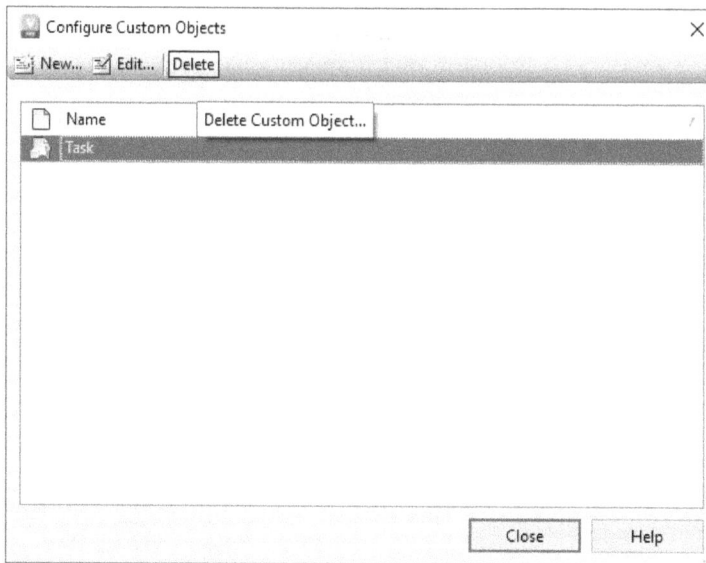

5. Perform one of these tasks:

- If no instances of the custom object were created in the Vault, click **Yes** in the Confirm Deletion dialog box.

- If there are instances of the custom object in the Vault:

  - Click **OK** in the dialog box that confirms the definition is in use.
  - Search the Vault for the custom object instances.
  - Delete the instances.
  - Navigate back to the Custom Object Configuration dialog box and select the definition.
  - Click **Delete**.
  - Click **Yes** in the Confirm Deletion dialog box.

  The custom object definition is deleted. A new definition can be created using the same name, if required.

  Note: If there are properties associated with the custom object definition, the administrator is restricted from deleting it.

Job Server, Vault Revision Tables, and Backups

Topics covered in this chapter include the Job Server, revision tables, and backups. The process of creating and checking in visualization files manually can be time-intensive for some users, especially those responsible for managing large assemblies. The Job Server utility enables users to automatically create and check-in visualization files from their local workstation. The Vault Revision Table feature enables you to automatically update a drawing's revision table with Vault data when properties are synchronized through the Job Server. To prevent data loss, you can use the Backup and Restore functionality.

Learning Objectives

- Differentiate between the Job Server and Job Processor.
- Enable the Job Server.
- Administrate the Job Server.
- Log in to the Job Processor to view jobs.
- Enable the Vault Revision Table functionality.
- Understand the Vault revision table settings.
- Backup and restore your Autodesk Vault machine.

14.1 Enabling the Job Server

Overview

With Autodesk® Vault Professional, you can use the Job Server utility to automate specific jobs like DWF or PDF generation when changing the state from Work in Progress to Released.

Objectives

After completing this lesson, you will be able to:

- Differentiate between the meaning of Job Server and Job Processor.
- Enable the Job Server in the Global Settings dialog box.
- Initiate a job.
- Work with the job queue.

Job Server vs. Job Processor

Administrators can manage the Job Server by tracking jobs, resubmitting stalled jobs, and deleting unnecessary jobs. However, the Job Server must be enabled by an administrator.

Users assign their publishing jobs to a job queue where they are stored until certain parameters are met. The Job Processor then creates the visualization files and checks them into the Vault based on the publishing properties defined in the Global Settings dialog box.

How To: Enable the Job Server

Note: You must be an administrator to enable the Job Server.

1. Select **Tools>Administration>Global Settings**.
2. In the Global Settings dialog box, click the *Integrations* tab.
3. Select the **Enable Job Server** checkbox to activate the Job Server.

Note: The Job Server permits for publishing jobs to be queued and processed at a later time. You must activate the Job Server prior to sending any jobs to it for publishing.

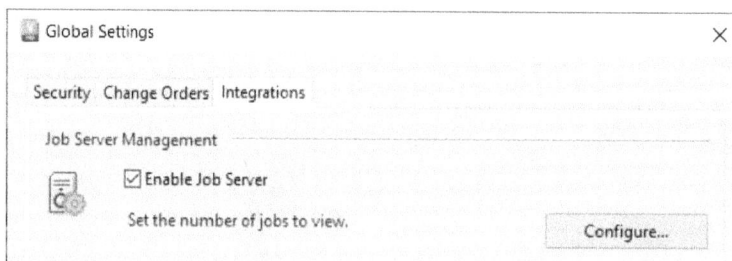

Job Processor

The Job Processor is installed at the same time as the Vault Client. As of the 2019 software release, the Job Processor has all of the required CAD applications included with it, so that it can be installed on a computer that does not otherwise have CAD tools installed.

> *Note: You must have the Job Server enabled to set up jobs. Having a Job Processor running is not required to submit jobs. The jobs will enter a queue until a Job Processor comes online to request jobs.*

As already explained in the section before, the Job Processor is the engine that controls and completes the jobs.

The first time you access the Job Processor, you must specify the user name, password, and server name. The Job Processor will remember these login credentials each time you log in until changed through the Administration menu.

How To: Install the Job Processor

1. On the workstation where you want jobs to be processed, select **Start menu>All Programs>Autodesk Data Management>Autodesk Job Processor [Edition] for Vault** to launch the Job Processor application.

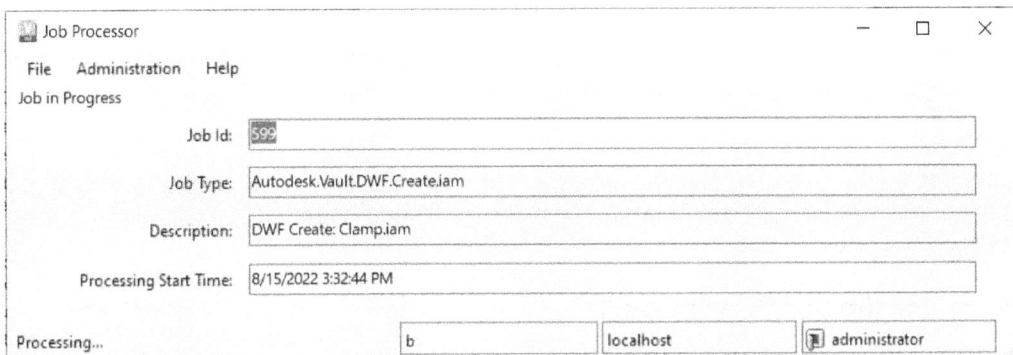

> *Note: Select File>Pause at any time to halt the Job Processor and prevent it from processing any new jobs. If the Job Processor is in the middle of processing a job, it will finish the job first. The Administration>Settings are not accessible unless the Job Processor is paused.*

2. Select **Administration>Settings** to display the Settings dialog box.

3. Enter the *User Name* and *Password* of the user for this workstation.

4. Specify the server from which you want the Job Processor to pull jobs for publishing.

5. Click **OK** to save your changes and close the Settings dialog box.

6. Select **File>Resume** to log in to the specified server.

You can find the Job Processor in your taskbar. Click on the arrow-up symbol to see the Job Processor symbol.

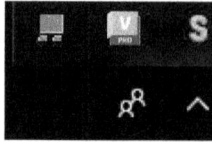

You do not have to start the Job Processor each time you are starting your machine. There is a mechanism to automate this start procedure by configuration. This is handled in the *Configure Job Server* lesson.

Job Processor Details

See the following table for an explanation of all fields in Job Processor:

Detail	Description
Job ID	Displays the number of the job currently being processed.
Job Type	Displays a description of the job being processed.
Description	Displays more information about the job in the queue.
Status	Displays the current state of the Job Processor.
Processing Start Time	Time at which the Job Processor began working on a job.

Job Server Queue

The Job Server Queue dialog box lists all active jobs and displays the status whether the jobs were executed successfully (job is gone from list), is still pending (*Status* = **Pending**) or an error has occurred (*Status* = **Error**).

How To: Use the Job Server Queue

1. Select **Tools>Job Queue**.

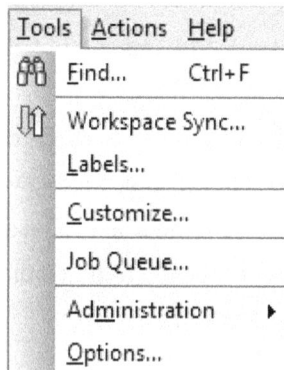

2. In the Job Server Queue dialog box, you can sort the jobs by *ID*, *Priority*, *Status*, *Description*, *Submitted Date*, or by whom they were submitted.

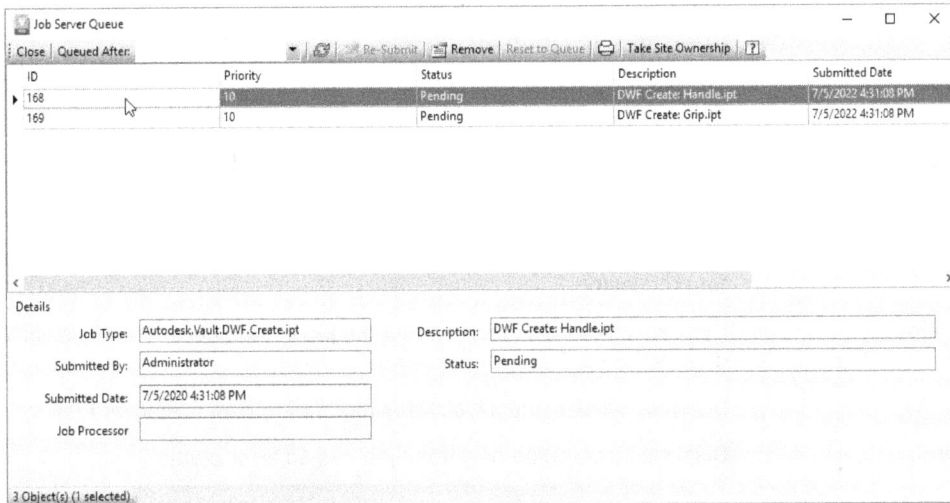

Note: The Job Server Queue dialog box displays up to 1,000 jobs. A warning will display to inform the user if there are more than 1,000 jobs in the queue.

3. Right-click on the column heading to customize the layout and view of the queue.

   • If you want to filter the list so that it only displays the jobs queued after a specific date and time, click the Queued After drop-down list and specify when.

4. Select a job that you want to modify and perform one of the following actions:

   • If you want to delete the job from the queue, click **Remove**.

   • If the job has an error status, click **Re-Submit** to reprocess the job.

   • If you want to remove the Job Processor from the task and leave the job in the queue, click **Reset to Queue**.

   • If you want to assign the task to the Job Processor on your workstation, click **Take Ownership**.

5. Click **Print** to send a copy of the grid to the default printer.

6. Click **Refresh** at any time to update the queue.

Job Server Details

This table describes the details of the Job Server Queue dialog box.

Detail	Description
Job Type	The type of job that was submitted for processing. Visualization jobs display as Autodesk.Vault.DWF.Create {0} where {0} is the file extension.
Submitted By	Displays the name of the user who submitted the job to the queue.
Submitted Date	Displays the date and time the job was submitted to the queue.
Job Processor	Displays the name of the computer that has taken the job from the queue for processing.
Description	Displays more information about the job in the queue. This field will also display the DWF Create: filename.
Status	Displays whether the job's status is Pending, Processing, or Error.
Results	Displays information only if the job has an error status.

Job Server Commands

This table describes the commands in the Job Server Queue dialog box.

Command	Description
Close	Closes the Job Server Queue dialog box.
Queued After	Filters the list by showing the first 1,000 jobs queued after the specified date and time.
Refresh	Refreshes the queue.
Re-Submit	Reprocesses a job that has encountered an error. This button is only enabled when a job has been placed in an error state.
Remove	Removes any job with the status of Error or Pending.
Reset to Queue	Removes the reservation of a job by the Job Processor. **Note:** This command is not in the toolbar by default. To add the command, click the toolbar list and select **Add or Remove Buttons**.
Take Site Ownership	Transfers ownership of the job's reservation to the current user's Job Processor. When a site that has reserved jobs is deleted, or a backup is performed but the information is restored to a different site, the pending jobs are deleted from the queue. This feature enables administrators to claim ownership for processing the job before it is deleted.
Print	Prints the current queue grid to the default printer.

Initiating a Job

In your default Autodesk Vault installation, there is already a job integrated, which starts to automatically generate and save DWF files to selected elements.

How To: Initiate a Job

Use the following steps to view the current queue status:

1. Select one or more CAD files from the list in the main grid.

2. Select **Actions>Update View>Queue Update** to set up a DWF generation job in the Job Server Queue.

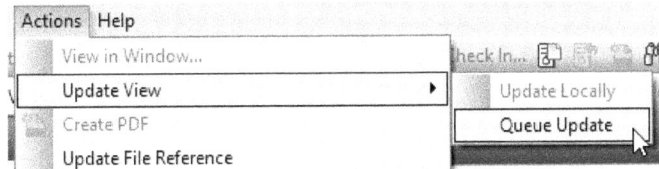

3. Go to the Job Server Queue by selecting **Tools>Job Queue**.

4. You should see the new DWF job listed as **Pending**.

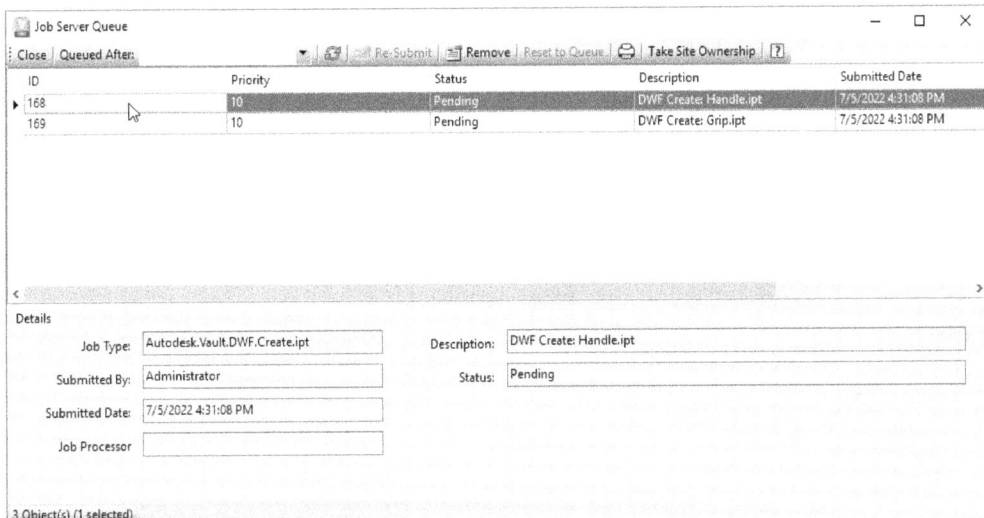

5. As soon as the DWF is generated successfully, the job will disappear from the queue.

6. Click (Refresh) from time to time to check whether the job is already done.

7. Have a look back to your component list and find the new generated DWF.

In case the job is still hanging in the queue, ensure that your Job Processor is running and completing your job. You can easily check whether your Job Processor is running or not by having a look to the task bar.

Practice 14a
Run Some Jobs and Watch Them in the Job Queue

In this practice, you will first enable the Job Server and get the Job Processor running, then you will select multiple CAD files and run the predefined DWF job.

Task 1: Enable the job server and get the job processor running.

1. Log in to Autodesk Vault as an Administrator. Ensure that **Designs.ipj** is set as the Inventor project file.

2. Go to **Tools>Administration>Global Settings**.

3. Select **Enable Job Server** in the *Integrations* tab.

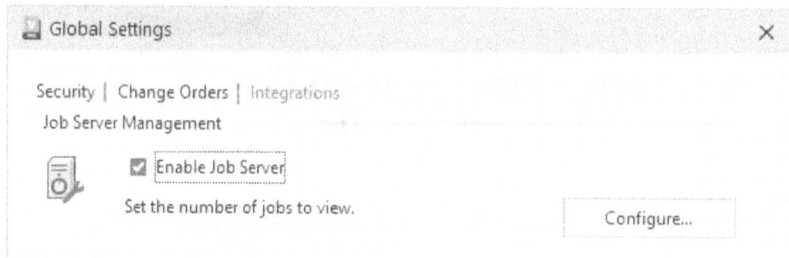

4. Open your File Explorer.

5. Browse to the *Program Files>Autodesk>Vault Client [Edition]>Explorer* folder and start the **JobProcessor.exe** file.

    *   Alternatively, use your Windows Start menu and select **All Programs>Autodesk Data Management>Autodesk Job Processor [Edition] for Vault**.

6. If required, enter your name, password, and server to log on.

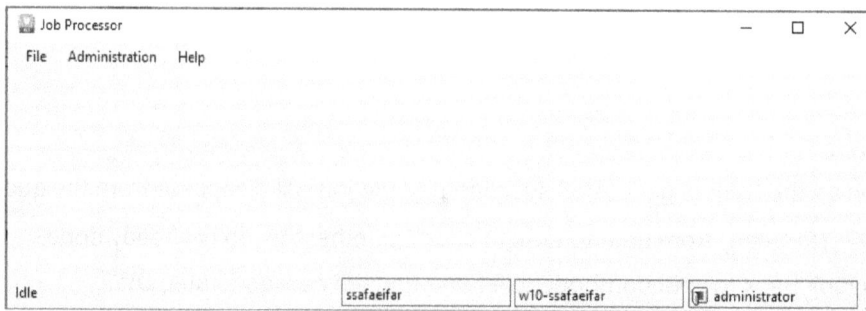

    *   Ensure that the required CAD Applications are installed on the same machine the Job Processor is installed.

Task 2: Multi-select some CAD files and start the automatic DWF generation.

1. Select CAD files from the main Vault grid.
2. Select **Actions>Update View>Queue Update**.

3. Select **Tools>Job Queue** to open the Job Server Queue to watch the newly created DWF jobs and their status.
4. Select one pending job from the list and remove it by clicking **Remove** in the Job Server Queue dialog box.

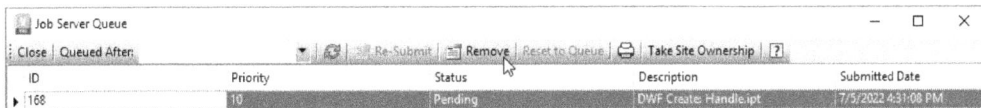

5. Wait a few seconds and refresh your list by clicking **Refresh** in Job Server Queue dialog box. If no error occurred and the list is empty, exit the Job Server Queue. If the Job Processor is idle, it can take up to 10 minutes to evoke again.

   - **Tip:** To facilitate the job processing, pause the Job Processor and resume it by selecting **File>Pause** and then selecting **File>Resume**.

6. Double-check with your list in Vault whether all DWF's were generated, besides the one you removed from the Job Server Queue.

End of practice

14.2 Configuring the Job Server

Overview

From the administrative point of view, there are several tools that help you to configure and administrate the jobs and events in Vault. The Job Processor can be configured to automatically start each time your machine is started.

Objectives

After completing this lesson, you will be able to:

* Configure the Job Server/Job Processor via UI.

* Understand settings in the configuration file.

* Use the Job Server log files for analyses.

Configuration via Job Processor UI

There are several options and commands in the Job Processor dialog box that are explained in the following table:

Command	Definition
Pause	On **Pause**, the Job Processor will pause and the jobs remain in the queue. It prevents it from processing any new jobs. If the Job Processor is in the middle of processing a job, it will finish the job first.
Resume	After you have set the Job Processor to **Pause**, you can click **Resume** to go on completing the jobs in the queue.
Exit	On **Exit**, the Job Processor will exit and close.
Start on Windows Logon	Here you can set whether the Job Processor is started automatically on Windows Logon.
Settings	In the Settings dialog box, you can enter your name, password, and server.
Job Types	Displays the Job Types dialog box, which contains all available job types to use. If the workstation does not have the required information to process the particular type of job, that type of file is unchecked.
About Job Processor/Help	Here you can find useful Help files for handling and administrating the Job Processor.

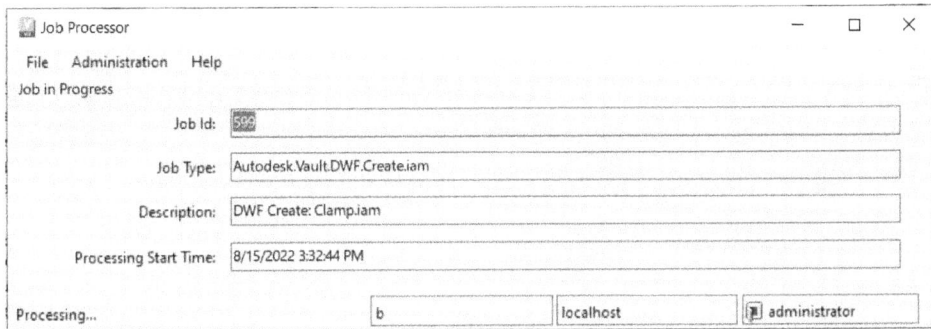

The Configuration File

In the Job Processor configuration file, you can add, edit, and delete your custom jobs and set some global settings for the job services.

*   Name of configuration file: **JobProcessor.exe.config**.

Location of the Configuration File

The configuration file can be found in the *Explorer* folder.

*   Path to the configuration file: *Program Files>Autodesk>Vault Client [Edition]>Explorer*.

Settings in the Configuration File

To add a new job to the configuration file, go to the jobHandler section in the configuration file.

<jobHandler>	Add your custom jobs here. As soon as they are implemented correctly in this configuration file, you should check whether the job is available and listed in the Job Processor. Open the Job Processor and select **Administration>Job Types**. The new job should be listed here and is ready to use.

Log File

For analyses and control, you can have a look to the Job Processor log file, which can be found in the same *Explorer* folder as the configuration file.

- Path to the log file: *Program Files>Autodesk>Vault Client [Edition]>Explorer*.

Here you can find useful information why your job could not be completed successfully or why the Job Processor or Job Server does not work.

Practice 14b
Change Settings in the Job Processor

In this practice, you will change the configuration of the Job Processor to start it each time your machine is started. You will then set up some jobs in Vault and pause them in the Job Processor. Finally, you will resume and look at the Job Processor log file to see whether or not all processes were successful.

Task 1: Configure the Job Processor.

1. Start the Job Processor if it is not started yet.

    * Browse to the *Program Files>Autodesk>Vault Client [Edition]>Explorer* folder and start the **JobProcessor.exe** file or use your Windows Start menu and select **All Programs>Autodesk Data Management>Autodesk Job Processor [Edition] for Vault**.

2. From the Administration menu, activate the automatic start by selecting **Start on Windows Logon**.

3. For your information, select **Administration>Job Types** and get an overview of which jobs are available in this Vault installation.

Task 2: Pause and resume the job process.

1. Select several components and create the DWF job, explained in the first lesson (go to **Actions>Update View>Queue Update**).

2. Go to the Job Server Queue and watch the progress.

3. When only a few jobs are left and still pending, go to the Job Processor and select **File>Pause**.

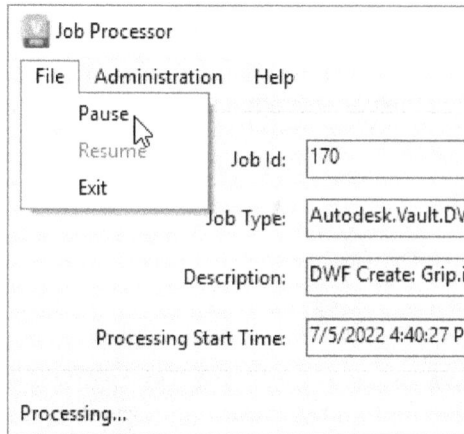

4. The progress of job execution is paused. The job which was currently in progress will be finished. All jobs queued after this current job are paused and will not be handled as long as the Job Processor is "stopped" (paused).

5. After a while, click **File>Resume** in the Job Processor dialog box to go on with job execution.

6. Double-check with your Job Server Queue whether all files were generated successfully. Exit the Job Server Queue and the Job Processor (**File>Exit**).

7. Have a look to the Job Processor log file, which is stored in the *Explorer* directory of your Vault installation, and analyze the content.

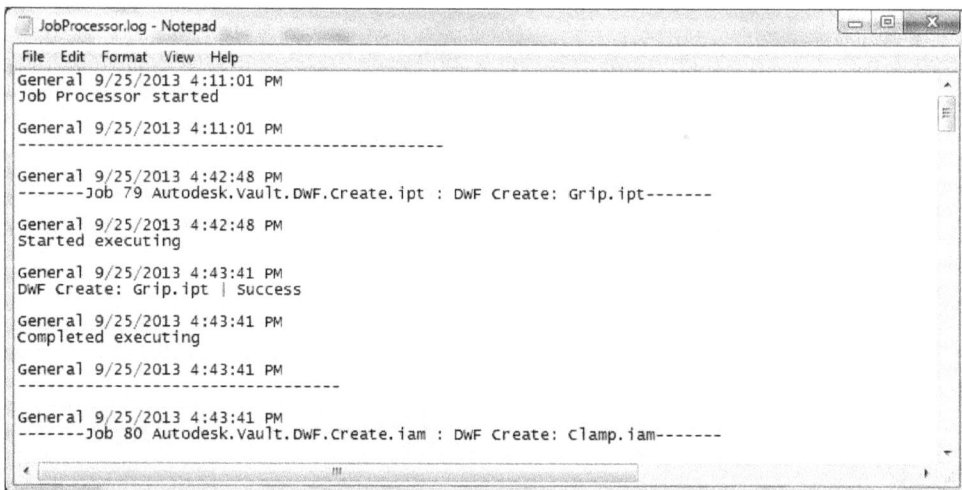

End of practice

14.3 PDF Publishing

You can automatically publish and manage 2D PDF files from CAD files as documentation in the design release process at any lifecycle state.

How To: Configure PDF Publishing Options

Use the following steps to select the required settings for 2D AutoCAD and 2D Inventor PDF printing (you must have administrative access to peform these tasks):

1. Create a user with access to Released files. See *Assign Roles to Users* for more information.
2. Configure lifecycle definitions.
   a. Select **Tools>Administration>Vault Settings**.
   b. In the Vault Settings dialog box, select the *Behaviors* tab and select **Lifecycles**.
   c. Select the definition to be modified and click **Edit**.
   d. In the Lifecycle Definition dialog box, select the *Transitions* tab, then (as an example) select **Work in Progress to Released>Edit**.
   e. In the Transitions dialog box, select the *Actions* tab.
   f. From the drop-down list, select one of the following options:
      * **Synchronize properties, update view and PDF using Job Server**
      * **Synchronize properties and update PDF using Job Server**

   Note: Selecting one of these options from the list does not automatically select the checkbox as well. Make sure to select the checkbox beside the option, too.

   g. Select the *Security* tab, add the user created in Step 1, and allow **Modify** access under the **Released** state.
   h. In the Lifecycle Definition dialog box, select **Design Representation Process>Edit**.
   i. In the Lifecycle Definition dialog box, select the **Released** state.
   j. Select the *Security* tab, add the user created in Step 1, and assign it **Modify** access. See *Edit Lifecycle State Security* for more information.

   Note: You can create PDFs at any lifecycle state.

3. The sync state job fails if you do not have adequate permission for a particular state to be set on a PDF file, for example, you do not have the Modify access on the Released state.
4. To enable the Job Server, select **Tools>Administration>Global Settings** and on the *Integrations* tab, select **Enable Job Server**.

   Note: For Job Processor to generate DWF and 2D PDF files, launch AutoCAD DWG Trueview at least once on the Job Processor.

2D AutoCAD PDF Publishing Options	Details
Add As An Attachment	Shows the published PDF file as an attachment to the file.
Upload to Source File Location	Automatically stores the published PDF file to the selected file location.
Upload To Selected Vault Path	Defines a specific location (using Browse) to store the published PDF file.
Sync Lifecycle State and Revision As Source	Allows both the published PDF and its source file to have the same lifecycle state and a revision value.
Use Page Settings From User DWG	Eliminates the need to reconfigure page settings in Vault if previously done in the native application. Checked and cannot be unchecked.
Include Model Space	Enables the published PDF file to contain model space view.
Include Layouts	Enables the published PDF file to contain model space view only.
Include Layer Info	Enables the published PDF to contain layer information.
Initialize Layouts	Enables support for legacy files.
Include Font Handling	Enables publishing a PDF file with font styles.

2D Inventor PDF Publishing Options	Details
Add As An Attachment	Shows the published PDF file as an attachment to the file.
Upload to Source File Location	Automatically stores the published PDF file to the selected file location.
Sync Lifecycle State and Revision As Source	Allows both the published PDF and its source file to have the same lifecycle state and a revision value.
Upload To Selected Vault Path	Defines a specific location (using Browse) to store the published PDF file.
Vector Resolution	Set as 400 DPI for managing large PDF file size and appropriate details.
Plot Object Lineweights	Enables the published PDF file to display a consistent lineweight for object and consistent lineweight for linetypes.
All Sheets	Prints all the sheets in the drawing. To print sheets for which the Exclude from Printing option is checked in the Edit Sheet dialog box, select Print Excluded Sheets.
All Colors As Black	Prints the drawing in black and white. Embedded images and shaded views are still printed in color.

How To: Publish PDFs from 2D CAD Files

Use the following steps to configure lifecycle definitions and PDF options to publish PDFs from 2D CAD files (you must have administrative access to peform these tasks):

1. Create a user with access to Released files. For more information, see *Assign Roles to Users*.

2. Configure lifecycle definitions.

   a. Select **Tools>Administration>Vault Settings**.

   b. In the Vault Settings dialog box, select the *Behaviors* tab and select **Lifecycles**.

   c. Select the definition to be modified and click **Edit**.

   d. In the Lifecycle Definition dialog box, select the *Transitions* tab, then (as an example) select **Work in Progress to Released>Edit**.

   e. In the Transitions dialog box, select the *Actions* tab.

   f. From the drop-down list, select one of the following options.

      - **Synchronize properties, update view and PDF using Job Server**
      - **Synchronize properties and update PDF using Job Server**

   Note: Selecting one of these options from the list does not automatically select the checkbox as well. Ensure that the checkbox beside the option is also selected.

   g. In the *Security* tab, add the user created in Step 1 and enable the **Modify** access under the **Released** state.

   h. In the Lifecycle Definition dialog box, select **Design Representation Process>Edit**.

   i. In the Lifecycle Definition dialog box, select the **Released** state.

   j. Select the *Security* tab, add the user created in Step 1, and assign it **Modify** access.

   Note: You can create PDFs at any lifecycle state.

3. The sync state job fails if you do not have adequate permission for a particular state to be set on a PDF file, for example, you do not have the modify access on the Released state.

4. To enable the Job Server, select **Tools>Administration>Global Settings** and on the *Integrations* tab, select **Enable Job Server**.

   Note: For the Job Processor to generate DWF and 2D PDF files, launch AutoCAD DWG Trueview at least once on the Job Processor.

5. Select **Tools>Administration>Vault Settings** and in the *PDF Options* section, select **Options** to launch the PDF Publish Options dialog box and configure the PDF publishing options.

6. Publish a PDF from a CAD file.

   a. Select any AutoCAD DWG file or Inventor 2D CAD file.

   b. Select **Change Category**. In the Change Category dialog box, select the **Engineering** category. Click **OK**.

c. Select **Change State**. In the Change State dialog box, select **Released** from the lifecycle state drop-down list. Click **OK**.

This generates a PDF as an attachment to the selected file. Additionally, a thumbnail for the PDF displays in the *Preview* tab.

Note: To synchronize the revisions of the drawing file and 2D PDF file, set each file's lifecycle revision to be the same.

Note: To verify the Design Representation classification, click Tools>Administration> Vault Settings>Behaviors>Rules. In the Assignment Rules dialog box, view the Rule Criteria for Design Representation.

How To: Create a PDF from 2D CAD Files

When using this command, a PDF can be created without going through a lifecycle state change for a 2D file. As an Administrator, you must enable the **Enable Manual PDF Creation** checkbox in the *PDF Options* section of the Settings dialog in order to use the **Create PDF** capability.

Note: You must have appropriate access given by your administrator to access the Create PDF command in the different access points.

Use the following steps to create a copy of a PDF file using a 2D CAD file:

1. Select the 2D CAD file for which you want to manually create a PDF.

2. Right-click and select **Create PDF**, or select the command from the Actions menu.

   * **IMPORTANT:** The **Create PDF** command is available only for the latest version of the file and not for any historical version/revision of the 2D CAD files.

How To: Specify the PDF Publish Location

Use the following steps to specify a desired location outside of Vault Client for PDFs (you must have administrative access to perform these tasks):

1. Select **Tools>Administration>Vault Settings**.

2. In the Vault Settings dialog box, select the *Files* tab.

3. Select **Define** next to *Specify PDF Publish Location*.

4. In the PDF Publish Location dialog box, select the desired option:

   * **Save in Vault** (local copies will not be created)

   * **Save on a local drive in one folder**

   * **Save on a local drive using the Vault folder structure**

5. Click **OK**.

Note: By default, automatically generated PDF files are hidden in the file list. Select Tools>Options to enable to Show hidden files.

14.4 Vault Revision Table Administration

Overview

The process of manually updating the revision tables on drawings can be time-consuming, especially for changes that require simple property updates throughout a design's lifecycle. The Vault Revision Table feature enables you to automatically update a drawing's revision table with Vault data when properties are synchronized through the Job Server. This functionality eliminates the need to open each drawing in its native CAD application for updates.

Important: You must be an administrator with appropriate ownership privileges to enable the Vault Revision Table.

Objectives

After completing this lesson, you will be able to:

*   Understand Vault revision table supported drawings and prerequisites.

*   Enable the Vault Revision Table functionality.

*   Understand the Vault revision table settings.

*   Create a Vault revision table.

Vault Revision Table Supported Drawings and Prerequisites

Supported Drawings

*   AutoCAD® drawings (.DWG)

*   AutoCAD Mechanical drawings (.DWG)

*   Autodesk® Inventor® drawings (.IDW)

*   Autodesk Inventor drawings (.DWG)

Prerequisites

*   Autodesk Inventor is installed so that Inventor IDW and DWG drawings can be updated.

*   Revision Table functionality is enabled.

*   The Job Server is enabled with the **synchronize properties** option selected for the required state transition(s).

- Suitable column headers are created and their property mappings established between the drawings' revision table columns and the Vault properties.

  Note: The system property 'Revision' is a key mapping and must be mapped to at least one of the column headers.

Once all the prerequisites are met, the revision tables for the supported drawings are automatically updated with specified Vault data whenever properties are synchronized with the Job Server. This way, you can be sure that the revision table in your drawing is always up to date with the appropriate information from the vault.

Vault Revision Table Administration

Administrators can configure the information to be displayed in the revision table of the drawings for standardization across vault through the Revision Table Settings.

The Vault Revision Table feature must be enabled before you can configure revision table settings or use the Revision Table feature in the Autodesk Inventor and AutoCAD Vault add-ins.

How To: Enable the Vault Revision Table

1. Select **Tools>Administration>Vault Settings**.

2. In the Vault Settings dialog box, select the *Behaviors* tab and select **Revision Table**.

   *Note: You can also open this dialog box from within the add-in by selecting **Vault Options** in the Vault ribbon and clicking **Settings** next to Configure Revision Table.*

3. In the Revision Table Settings dialog box, select the **Enable Revision Table control** checkbox to enable the Vault Revision Table functionality across Vault.

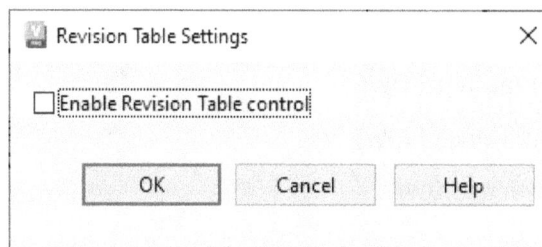

- When this checkbox is selected, the full view for the Revision Table Settings displays.

Revision Table Settings Dialog Box

In the Revision Table Settings dialog box, you can configure how data displays, which Vault properties are mapped to the revision table, and the type of content displayed. You can also incorporate filters so that only the information you need displays in the revision tables.

Feature	Details
⬚	Loads suggested settings.
⬚	Loads the default settings for the dialog box.
⬚	Restores all changes in the Revision Table Settings dialog box to the settings used the last time the dialog box was opened.
Mappings Tab	On the *Mappings* tab, you can map Vault properties to the revision table columns.

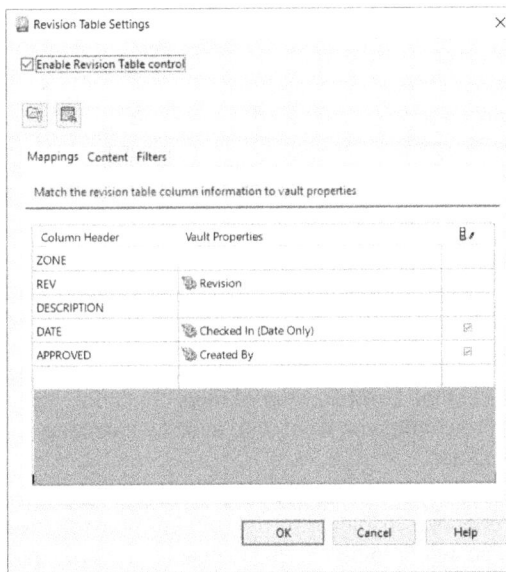

Column Header	Column name that displays in the revision table.
Vault Properties	The name of the Vault property that you have mapped to the associated revision table column.
	The value for this property will automatically display in the column field of the revision table for the drawing.
⬚	Released vs. non-released bias control.
	Select the checkbox for any row where you want the system to update the revision table only with released information. If the checkbox for a row is not selected, then the latest information from the vault is used.

Feature	Details
Content Tab	In the *Content* tab, you can enforce the type of information that displays in the revision table.

Populate information using	Select version control.
	Select the version and the released state that you want to apply to revision history records.
Limit number of rows checkbox	If you want to limit the number of rows displayed in the revision table, select the **Limit number of rows** checkbox. Specify the limit for the number of rows that you want displayed by selecting a value from the value spinner.
	Note: When the **Limit number of rows** option is toggled ON, the exceeding records are deleted by default. In Autodesk Inventor drawings, you can also select to hide these exceeding records instead of deleting them.
Hide exceeding records for Inventor drawings checkbox	Select this checkbox to hide, instead of delete, the additional Autodesk Inventor drawing records.
Update latest revision only	Select this checkbox to update the mapped values only for the latest revision row in the revision table. All other mapped values in previous historical revision rows do not get updated even if the data is non-equivalent in the vault.
	Note: Even with the **Update latest revision only** option enabled, the Vault Revision Table feature continues to remove revision rows that are not found in the Vault.

Feature	Details
Detect revision scheme change and remove previous revision history	If you are using multiple revision schemes, select this checkbox to ensure that the current revision scheme is used. Historical revision rows of an older revision scheme are replaced with the current revision scheme.
Filters Tab	In the *Filters* tab, you can further refine the data displayed in the revision table by applying revision level filters.

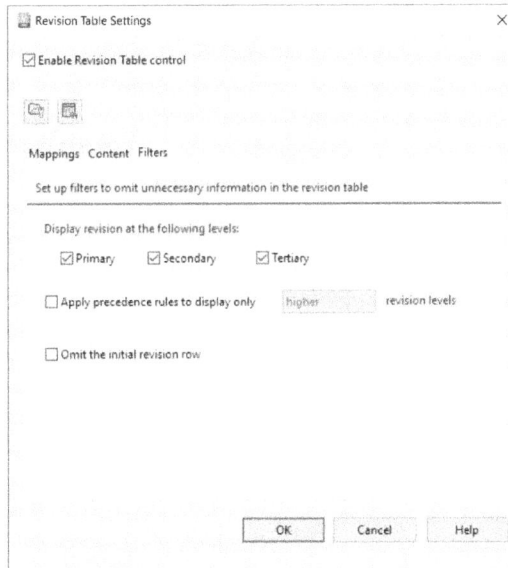

Feature	Details
Display revision at the following levels	Select the checkbox for each revision level that you want displayed in the revision table. For example, if you have a drawing marked as revision B.2.1, and you only select the **Primary** and **Secondary** checkboxes, then only B.2 displays in the revision table.
	Refer to *Revision Schemes* for more information about the Primary, Secondary, and Tertiary revision levels.
Apply precedence rules to display only X revision levels	When multiple revision levels exist in a revision group, it is important to identify the level of revision that you want to be displayed. Enable this checkbox and select whether you want the highest or lowest revision levels displayed in the revision table.
	This selection takes precedence over the *Display revision at the following levels* option.
Omit the initial revision row	Select this checkbox to omit the initial revision row from the revision table.
	Some users find that if the initial revision value (e.g., A) is already in the title block for the revision table, having it repeated as the first revision row is unnecessary. By selecting this checkbox, the first revision row in the revision table becomes the next revision value (e.g., A.1).

Practice 14c
Use Vault Revision Tables

In this practice, you will create a Vault revision table in Grip.idw. Grip.idw is a drawing of Grip.ipt. These files are managed by the Flexible Release Process lifecycle definition. To permit the Job Server to run in the Released state, the default settings for Security for the Released state in the Flexible Release Process needs to be modified. For the Released state, change Modify and Delete for Everyone to Allow, as shown in the image below.

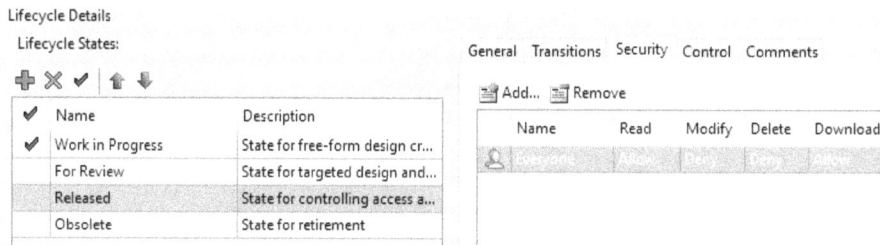

Also, ensure that the properties get synchronized using the Job Server for the transition of Work in Progress to Released, as shown in the image below.

Task 1: Enable the Vault Revision Table functionality and map the Description property.

1.   Start the Autodesk Vault. Log in using the information below and ensure that **Designs.ipj** is set as the Inventor project file.

 * For *User Name*, enter **administrator**.

 * Leave the *Password* field blank.

 * For *Vault*, select **AOTCVault**.

2.   Select **Tools>Administration>Vault Settings**.

3.   In the Vault Settings dialog box, select the *Behaviors* tab and select **Revision Table**.

4. In the Revision Table Settings dialog box, select the **Enable Revision Table control** checkbox to enable the Vault Revision Table functionality.

5. Click **Yes** to load recommended settings. The Revision Table Settings dialog box updates as shown below.

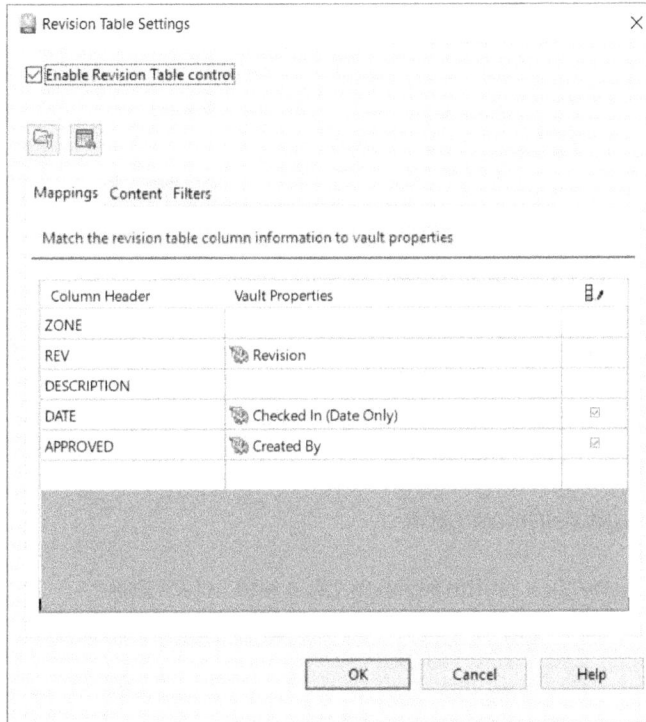

6. For the Inventor property *DESCRIPTION*, select the Vault system property **Comment**. Note that by default, the *APPROVED* property maps to the **Created By** Vault property. Click **OK**, then click **Close** to close the Vault Settings dialog box.

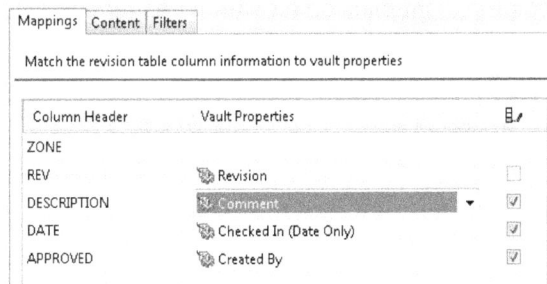

Task 2: Add a Vault revision table to the drawing.

1. In Inventor, log in to Vault and from the *Vault* tab, select **Open**. In the *Designs/Clamp* folder, select **Grip.idw**.

2. In the *Annotate* tab, select **Vault Revision**.

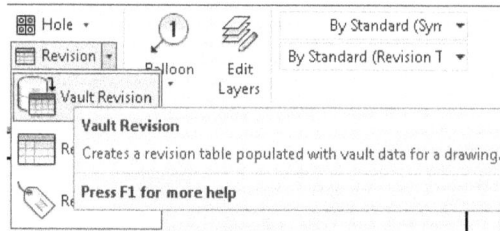

3. Insert the table in the top-right corner of the drawing.

Task 3: Edit the Vault revision table.

1. To edit the table, right-click on the revision table and select **Edit**.

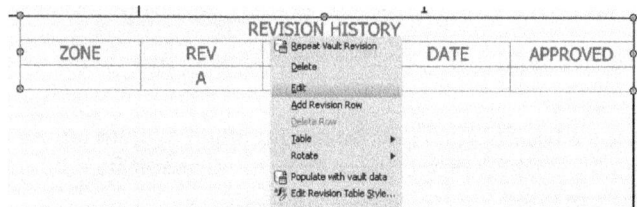

2. To remove the *Zone* column, right-click on a column header and select **Column Chooser**.

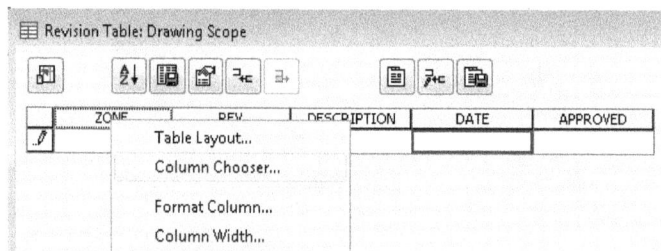

3. Select **Zone** in the *Selected Properties* list and click **Remove**, then click **OK**.

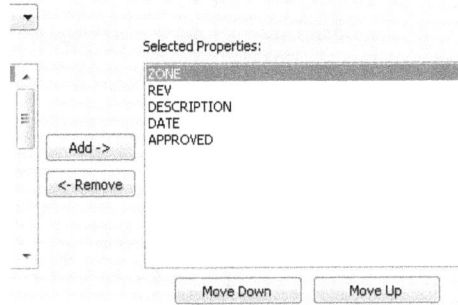

4. Click **OK**. The revision table in the drawing updates without the *Zone* column.

REVISION HISTORY			
REV	DESCRIPTION	DATE	APPROVED
A			

5. Save the drawing and check it in to the vault using the **Close files and delete working copies** option.

Task 4: Release the drawing.

1. In Vault, select **Grip.idw**, right-click, and select **Change State**. You can also perform a Change State in Inventor.

2. Select **Released** from the new lifecycle state drop-down list.

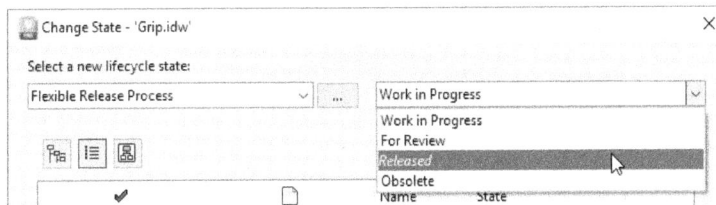

3. Update the comment to say **Initial Release** and click **OK**. The state updates to **Released** in the main table.

4. Now the Job Server will create the visualization files. To force the jobs, open Job Processor and select **File>Pause** then **File>Resume**.

Task 5: Create a new revision.

1. Now you will create a new revision to make a change to the Grip.ipt. In Vault, select **Grip.idw**, right-click, and select **Change State**.

2. Select **Work in Progress**.

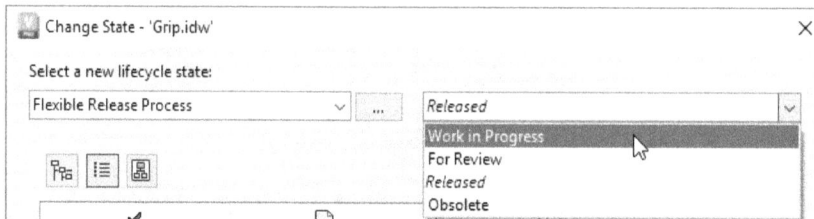

3. Click **OK**. In the main table, the state updates to **Work in Progress** and the revision changes to **B**.

| Grip.idw | Work in Progress | B |
| Grip.ipt | Work in Progress | B |

4. In Inventor, open **Grip.idw** from the vault using **Open (Check Out All)**. Click **Yes to All** to update properties. Note the change to the Vault revision table.

REVISION HISTORY			
REV	DESCRIPTION	DATE	APPROVED
A	Initial Release	5/10/2016	Administrator
B			

5. In the Vault browser, open **Grip.ipt** and make a change to the length. Save and close Grip.ipt.

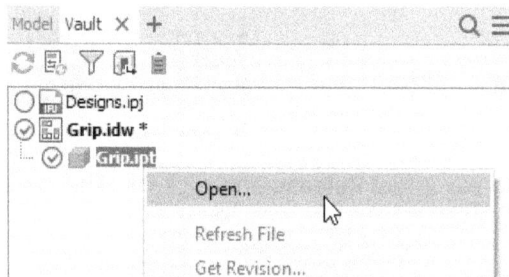

6. In the Vault browser of **Grip.idw**, save and check in both the drawing and the part. Select the **Close files and delete the working copies** option.

7. In Vault, change the state of the drawing to **Released** again. For the comments, enter **Rev B - Changed Length**.

8. Once again, the Job Server will create the visualization files upon release. To force the jobs, open Job Processor and select **File>Pause** then **File>Resume**.

Task 6: View the Vault revision table.

1. In Vault, right-click on **Grip.idw** and select **Open** to open the drawing in Inventor.

2. The Vault revision table is updated.

REVISION HISTORY			
REV	DESCRIPTION	DATE	APPROVED
A	Initial Release	5/10/2016	Administrator
B	Rev B - Changed Length	5/10/2016	Administrator

3. The **Update Properties** feature is integrated with the Vault revision table feature so that the revision block data is synchronized with the vault released information. The manual ways of updating properties if mapped properties are edited include using **Update Properties** in the Vault browser or *Vault* tab, or right-clicking on the Vault revision table and selecting **Populate with vault data**.

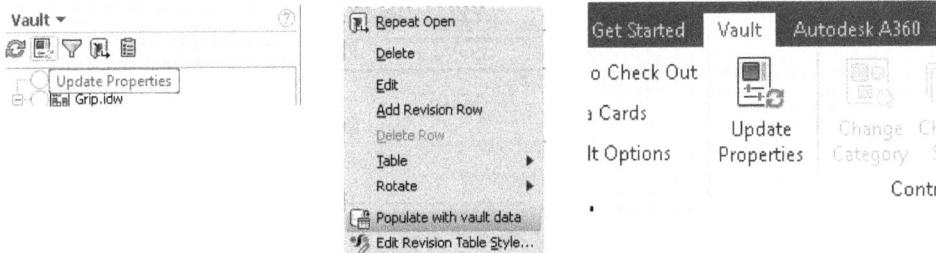

4. (Optional) If you would like to change the files back to a previous lifecycle state, in Vault, select the files, select **Actions>Roll Back Lifecycle State Change**, and follow the prompts.

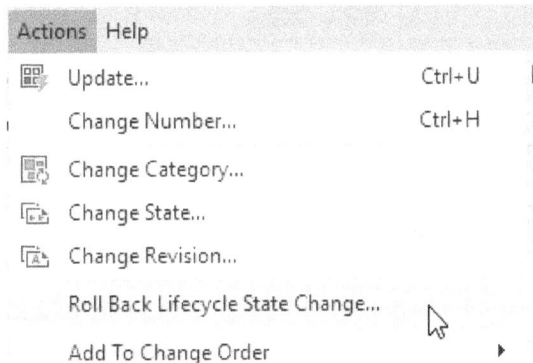

End of practice

14.5 Backup and Restore

Overview

To prevent data loss, you can select **Backup and Restore** for your Vault.

Objectives

After completing this lesson, you will be able to:

* Backup and restore your Vault machine.

How To: Back Up the Vault

1. Log in to Autodesk Data Management Server Console.

2. From the Tools menu, select **Backup and Restore**.

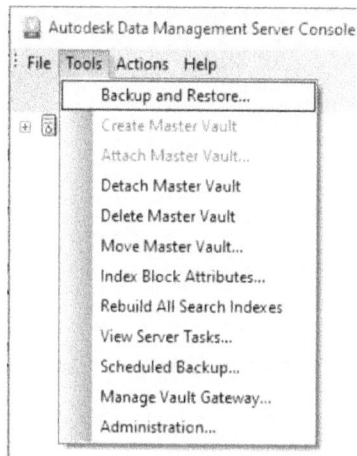

3. Select **Backup** in the wizard. Before backing up the data, the server console validates the data to ensure that the file store and databases are synchronized. If the database is out of sync, a dialog box displays listing the files that are mismatched. You can cancel the backup to correct the files.

4. Select **Full Backup** or **Incremental Backup**. The Incremental Backup option will not be available if no changes have occurred since the last full or incremental backup.

5. Specify the location to store the backed up data. To browse for a location, click the ellipsis (...) and then locate a directory using the file browser.

6. Toggle on the **Validate** checkbox to verify the archive is good once it is created.

7. By default, standard Content Center libraries are included in the backup process. To exclude standard Content Center libraries from the backup, toggle off the **Backup Standard Content Center Libraries** checkbox.

8. By default, a backup will wait until all files that need to be replicated are replicated before starting. Check the **Ignore non-replicated files** checkbox to start the backup without waiting for these files to replicate.

9. Click **OK**.

Restoring a Vault

How To: Restore the Entire Vault

Note: Access to the vault database is blocked during this task. Data management clients cannot access the database until the task is complete.

1. From the Tools menu, select **Backup and Restore**.

2. Select **Restore** in the wizard.

3. Restoring a vault deletes the data sets and file store. You are prompted for confirmation before proceeding. Click **Yes**.

4. Select **Full Restore** or **Incremental Restore**.

   Note: Access to the Incremental Restore option is available when no changes have occurred since the restore of the previous increment

5. Specify the location of the backed-up data. To browse for a location, click the ellipsis (...) and then locate a directory using the file browser.

6. Select whether the database is to be restored to the default location or a different location. If you choose **Select Restore Location**, specify a target directory for database

7. Select whether the file store is to be restored to the default location or a different location. If you choose **Select Restore Location**, specify a target directory for the file store.

8. Click **OK**.

The vault data is automatically migrated when it is restored using the server console. If you are restoring the data using the command line, you must migrate the data after it is restored.

Caution: If you have another vault on your machine where you want to restore a vault, you need to detach these existing vaults prior to restoring the required vault to avoid any overwriting! When you have finished the restore of the vault, you can attach the other vaults.

How To: Manually Restore Only the File Store

The file store can be manually restored by itself from a backup package to a remote location in a multi-site environment. This process should only be done by experienced vault administrators.

1. In the selected backup package, open the *FileStores* folder. The *FileStores* folder contains one folder for each vault in the backup. Each folder is named according to the vault to which it belongs.

2. Locate the appropriate file store folder and copy it to the remote location.

Backing Up Vault Data

Backing up vault data is essential. The following are recommendations for backing up Autodesk® Vault.

Use the Supplied Backup and Restore Utility

Use the server console to back up all data required to restore a server if a failure occurs. Vault Professional provides a 'hot backup' process, enabling users to continue to access the vault during the procedure. In addition, server console backs up or restores all vaults on the server. There is no way to select individual vaults to back up or restore.

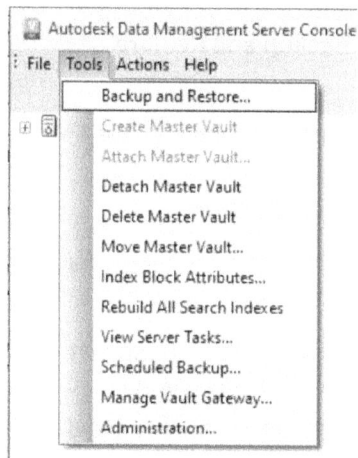

Develop a Backup Schedule

The next step is to automate the process. Two common methods are:

- Use **Tools>Scheduled Backup**. This process uses the backup tools included with the server console to create the backup script and task automatically.

- Include the backup as part of a tape backup set. This process uses a tape backup system to back up the vault directly.

The preferred and most reliable method for backing up a vault is to integrate the server console backup tools into your tape backup plan.

How To: Schedule Backups

1. From the Tools menu, select **Scheduled Backup**.

2. In the Backup Configuration dialog box, specify the location of the backed up data. To browse for a location, click the ellipsis (...) and then locate the directory using the file browser.

3. In the *Vault Credentials* tab, if using a Vault user account, for the Vault account name, specify **administrator**.

4. Select the *Full Backup* tab or *Incremental Backup* tab depending on what type of backup is being scheduled.

5. Select the checkbox for **Schedule a full backup** or **Schedule an incremental backup** depending on which tab was selected in Step 4.

6. Specify the schedule name, start date, time, and days for the backup.

7. Click **OK**.

The batch file is created and a task automatically created in the Windows Task Scheduler.

How To: Restore Vaults from Backups

1. From the Tools menu, select **Backup and Restore**.

2. Select **Restore**.

3. Restoring a vault deletes the current data sets and file store. This action cannot be undone. You are prompted for confirmation before proceeding. Click **Yes**.

4. In the *Restore from directory* field, specify the location of the backed-up data. To browse for a location, click the ellipsis (...) and locate a directory using the file browser.

5. Select whether to restore the database to the original location or to a different location. If you choose **Select Restore Location**, specify a target directory for the database. This selection is sometimes required when restoring data to a different machine that does not have the same drive letters or locations available.

6. Select whether to restore the file to the original location or to a different location. If you choose **Select Restore Location**, specify a target directory for the file store.

7. Click **OK**.

The vault data is automatically migrated when it is restored using Autodesk Vault server console. If you are restoring the data using the command line, migrate the data after it is restored.

Practice 14d
Back Up Your Vault

1. Back up your Vault using **Backup and Restore** as described above.

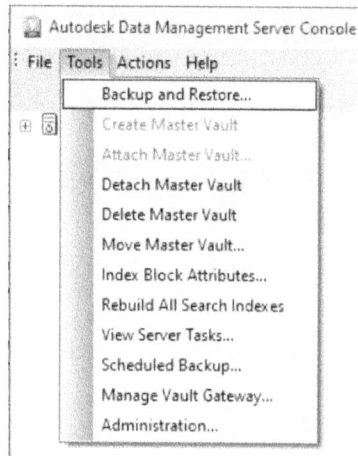

End of practice

Active Directory, Vault Gateway, and Replication

There are several options to configure and manage your Autodesk® Vault for your needs. User and group and security options make Autodesk Vault highly flexible. The Autodesk Vault Professional software has replication solutions available, such as the ADMS full replication (Connected Workgroups) and Autodesk File Server (AVFS), a file store replication solution. This chapter introduces these replication solutions and their associated components and configuration procedures.

Learning Objectives

- Manage user accounts regarding the Active Directory.
- Manage groups in Autodesk Vault.
- View and manage Vault gateways.
- Enable and disable workgroup replication.
- Add and delete workgroups.
- Enable and disable a vault for a multi-site environment.
- Replicate a vault, files, and folders.
- Export, import, and configure replication priorities.
- Schedule replication for a multi-site environment.
- Describe the benefits of Autodesk Vault File Server (AVFS).

15.1 Active Directory

Overview

An administrator can create a vault server account with credentials unique to the vault server or import a Windows Active Directory account. By using an Active Directory account, users can log in to Autodesk data management clients using their Windows account credentials. Users and groups can then be managed using Windows permissions.

Objectives

After completing this lesson, you will be able to:

*   Understand the advantages of Active Directory.

*   Manage user accounts.

Managing Groups

Individual users have roles and permissions assigned to them that define what actions they can take and to which vaults they have access. You can create groups of users and assign roles and permissions to the group. As a member of a group, a user has all the permissions and roles assigned to the group. By default, every new user is added to a group called **Everyone**. The Everyone group is only available on Access Control Lists. It does not display in the Groups dialog box. If the Everyone group is granted membership to a folder, all new users have access to that folder

Groups can be comprised of users or other groups. Groups can be disabled, toggling off all permissions assigned to the group. The permissions and roles assigned to a group are independent of individual user roles and permissions. Groups can also be restricted to specific folders in a vault, so you can keep projects and other data secure between groups.

By assigning users to groups and then granting folder membership to those groups, you can easily manage users and their access to vault folders. This is the best practice for creating a vault security model.

> **Note:** *Folder membership is only available with the vault server that is installed with Autodesk Vault.*

How To: Manage Groups

You must be assigned the role of Administrator to perform this operation.

1. Select **Tools>Administration>Global Settings**.

2. In the Global Settings dialog box, select the *Security* tab

3. Select **Manage Access**, then select the *Groups* tab.

4. In the User and Group Management dialog box, you can list groups three different ways:

    *   Select **View>List** to view the groups in a flat list.
    *   Select **View>By Effective Vault** to view the groups as a list grouped by the vaults to which they are assigned.
    *   Select **View>By Effective Role** to view the groups as a list grouped by roles.

How To: Create a Group

1. Click **New** in the *Groups* tab.
2. In the New Group Profile dialog box, specify the group settings and click **OK**.

How To: Edit an Existing Group

1. Select a group from the list.
2. Click **Actions>Edit**.
3. In the Group Profile dialog box, specify the group settings and click **OK**.

Import an Active Directory Domain User Account

Domain user accounts and domain user groups can be imported to the Autodesk vault server. This enables accounts to be created using Active Directory information and enables users to log in to a data management client without requiring a new account. If a user account or group already exists on the server, it can be promoted to an Active Directory account or group. Likewise, an account or group created by importing an Active Directory account can be disconnected or demoted from the Active Directory domain, making the account or group unique to the server.

> *Note: The Active Directory feature is only available with Autodesk Vault Professional and you must be assigned the role of Administrator to perform this operation.*

You cannot manage Active Directory accounts through the server console. You can only import Active Directory accounts, promote server accounts to the Active Directory accounts, or demote Active Directory accounts to standard server user accounts. To manage Active Directory user accounts and Active Directory group membership, you must use the **User Accounts** controls in the Windows Control Panel.

How To: Import Users

1. Select **Tools>Administration>Global Settings**.

2. In the Global Settings dialog box, select the *Security* tab.

3. Select **Manage Access**.

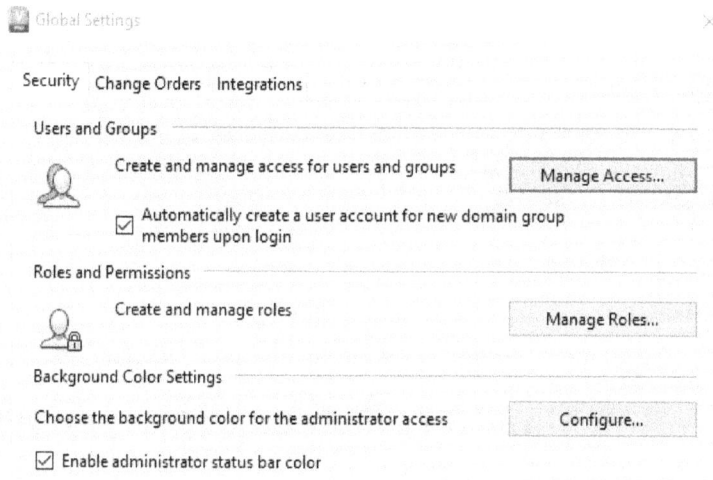

4. In the User and Group Management dialog box, select the *Users* tab.

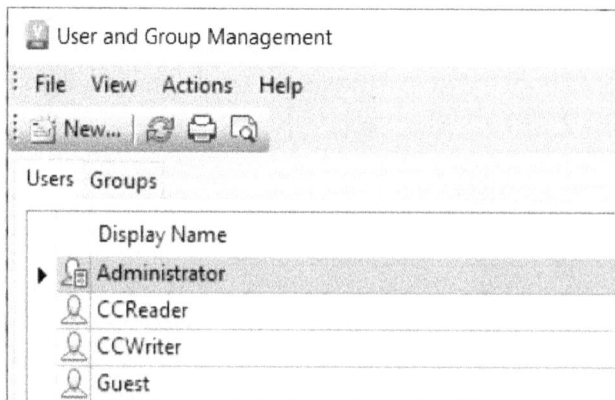

5. In the User and Group Management dialog box, you can list user accounts three different ways:

    *   Select **View>List** to view the user profiles in a flat list.

    *   Select **View>By Effective Vault** to view the user profiles as a list grouped by the vaults to which they are assigned.

    *   Select **View>By Effective Role** to view the user profiles as a list grouped by roles.

6.   In the User and Group Management dialog box, select **Actions>Import Domain User**.

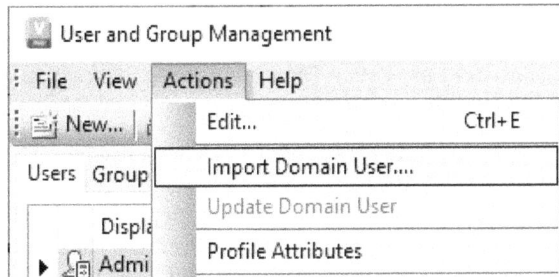

7.   In the Select User dialog box, click **Locations** to specify the domain containing the Active Directory accounts to import. In the Locations dialog box, select the domain to use and click **OK**.

8.   In the Select User dialog box, enter the names of the users to add from the Active Directory domain or click **Advanced** to search for the users.

9.   Once the uses accounts have been specified, click **OK** in the Select Users dialog box. The selected Active Directory domain user accounts are added to the User Management list.

Note: Imported users are not automatically assigned to a group, role, or vault unless they are members of a linked Active Directory group.

Vault server user accounts imported from an Active Directory domain use the first name, last name, user name, email address, and password associated with the Active Directory account and cannot be edited. The domain name displays in front of the user name. Changes made to the Active Directory user account are updated in the vault server user account automatically.

How To: Update Domain Users

If users have been added or removed from the Active Directory domain, the Vault server can be updated to reflect the changes to the user account.

Note: You must be assigned the role of Administrator to perform this operation.

1.   Select **Tools>Administration>Global Settings**.

2.   In the Global Settings dialog box, select the *Security* tab.

3.   Select **Manage Access**.

4.   In the User and Group Management dialog box, select the *Users* tab.

5.   Select a user or multiple users and select **Actions>Update Domain User**.

Import an Active Directory Domain Group

An administrator can create a group of users on the Autodesk vault server or Active Directory groups can be imported. Importing an Active Directory group imports all members of the group, as well as sub-groups.

This enables accounts to be created using Active Directory information and enables users to log into a data management client without requiring a new account. If a user account or group already exists on the vault server, it can be promoted to an Active Directory account or group. Likewise, an account or group created by importing an Active Directory account can be disconnected or demoted from the Active Directory domain, making the account or group unique to the vault server.

How To: Import Groups

1. In the User and Group Management dialog box, select the *Groups* tab and select **Actions>Import Domain Group**.

   Note: Only Security groups can be imported. Distribution groups cannot be imported.

2. In the Select Groups dialog box, click **Locations** to specify the domain containing the Active Directory groups to import. In the Locations dialog box, select the domain to use and click **OK**.

3. In the Select Groups dialog box, enter the names of the groups to add from the Active Directory domain or click **Advanced** to search for the groups.

4. Once the groups have been specified, click **OK** in the Select Groups dialog box. The selected Active Directory domain groups are added to the Group Management list.

All members of the group as well as sub-groups are imported. Groups imported from an Active Directory domain retain the group name and email address from Active Directory. The domain name displays in front of the group name.

How To: Update Domain Groups

If members have been added or removed from the Active Directory domain group, the Vault server group can be updated to reflect the changes to the group.

Note: You must be assigned the role of Administrator to perform this operation.

1. Select **Tools>Administration>Global Settings**.
2. In the Global Settings dialog box, select the *Security* tab.
3. Select **Manage Access**.
4. In the User and Group Management dialog box, select the *Groups* tab.
5. Select a group and select **Actions>Update Domain Group**.

   Note: One advantage to using groups is when you are adding users to a vault or vaults. First, create a group and add members to the group. Once members have been added to the group, assign a vault to the group.

Practice 15a
Create and Edit Groups

In this practice, you will manage your groups by creating and editing them in the Group Management dialog box. You will add roles, databases, and members to the groups.

Task 1: Create a new group in Vault.

1. Select **Tools>Administration>Global Settings**.
2. Select the *Security* tab and select **Manage Access**.
3. The User and Group Management dialog box opens. Select the *Groups* tab, then click **New** to open the New Group Profile dialog box.
4. In the *Group Name* field, enter a name for your new group.
5. Enter an email address in the *Email* field to add contact data to this group.
6. Select **Linked to** to link to an Active Directory group.
7. Click the **Roles** button to add roles to the group. Repeat with **Vaults** and **Groups**.

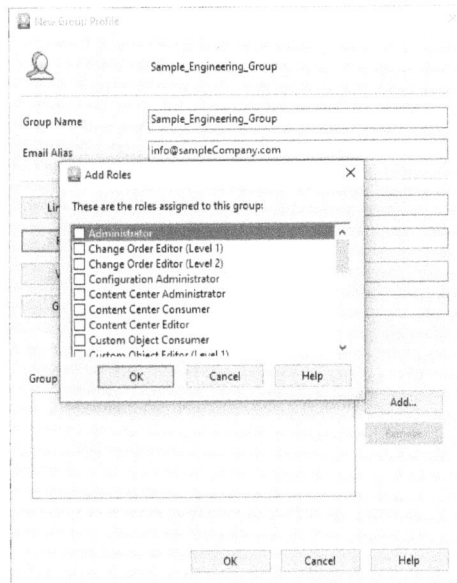

8. Add or remove *Group Members* to the group by clicking **Add** or **Remove**.
9. Confirm your settings and click **OK** to save the new group in Vault.

Task 2: Edit the new group.

1. To editing an existing group, select the group you want to edit, right-click, and select **Edit**.

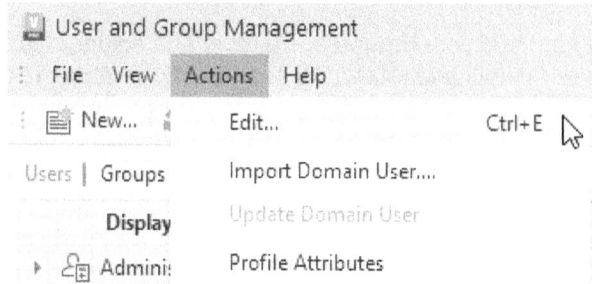

2. Make the required changes, then click **OK** to save the edited group in Vault.

End of practice

Practice 15b
Import User/Group via Active Directory

In this practice, you will import users and groups to use the Active Directory functionality in Vault.

Task 1: Import a user.

1. Select **Tools>Administration>Global Settings**.
2. In the Global Settings dialog box, select the *Security* tab.
3. Select **Manage Access**.

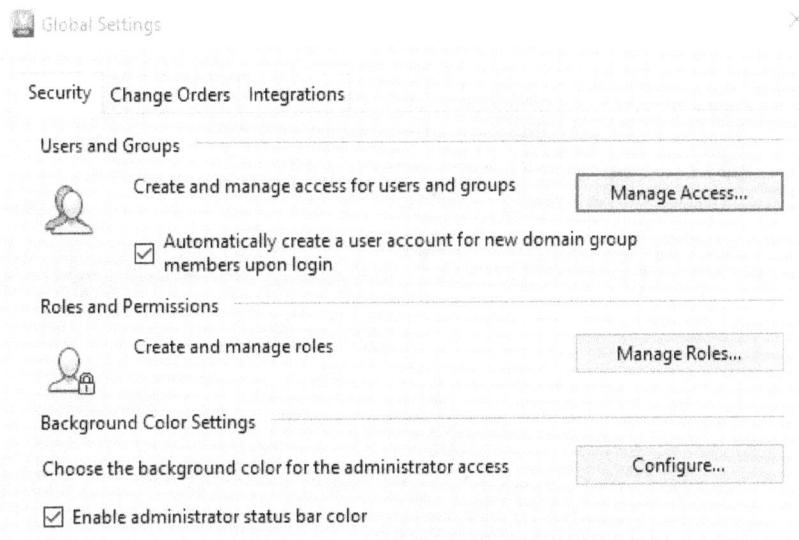

4. In the User and Group Management dialog box, select the *Users* tab and select **Actions>Import Domain User.**

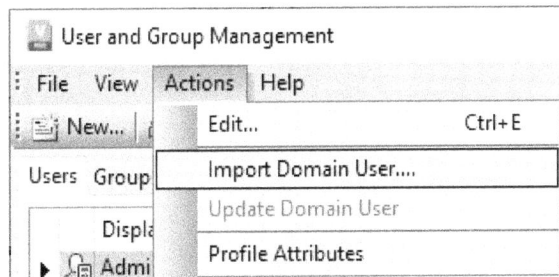

5. In the Select Users dialog box, click **Locations** to specify the domain containing the Active Directory accounts to import. In the Locations dialog box, select the domain to use and click **OK**.

6. In the Select Users dialog box, enter the names of the users to add from the Active Directory domain or click **Advanced** to search for the users.

7. Once the users accounts have been specified, click **OK** in the Select Users dialog box. The selected Active Directory domain user accounts are added to the User Management list.

Task 2: Import a group.

1. In the User and Group Management dialog box, select **Actions>Import Domain Group**.

   Note: Only Security groups can be imported. Distribution groups cannot be imported.

2. In the Select Groups dialog box, click **Locations** to specify the domain containing the Active Directory groups to import. In the Locations dialog box, select the domain to use and click **OK**.

3. In the Select Groups dialog box, enter the names of the groups to add from the Active Directory domain or click **Advanced** to search for the groups.

4. Once the groups have been specified, click **OK** in the Select Groups dialog box. The selected Active Directory domain groups are added to the Group Management list.

End of practice

15.2 Vault Gateway

Overview

Vault Gateway enables members of a team to remotely connect to the vault. Vault Gateway technology securely connects remote devices to Vault servers through a cloud service. The Vault Gateway service generates a URL used in place of the Vault server name when logging in to the Vault client software (e.g., Vault Client, Add-ins, etc.). The cloud service interfaces with the Vault server, exchanging data between the client and server in real time.

*   Configuring and using Vault Gateway does not require any of the following network resources:
    *   Connection to an on-premise network
    *   Connection to a VPN
    *   Opened inbound network ports

Objective

After completing this lesson, you will be able to:

*   View and manage gateways in the ADMS Console.

Managing Vault Gateways

Administrators configure gateways for individual Autodesk Account teams. A Vault administrator must manage at least one Autodesk Account team to configure a gateway.

How To: Manage a Vault Gateway

To manage your team's gateway:

1. In the ADMS Console, select the **Tools** option in the menu bar.
2. Select **Manage Vault Gateway**. If you are not signed in, you will be prompted to sign in to an administrator account.
3. The Autodesk Account Teams window displays if you manage more than one team. Select a team and click **OK**.

    Note: When a gateway is already configured, the Autodesk Account Teams window does not display.

4. The Vault Gateways window displays. The Vault Gateways window is the primary dashboard for your team's gateways. It shows information for the local gateway that you manage and other gateways for your team.

How To: Add a Vault Gateway

Administrators create gateways and share gateway URLs with their team.

To add a new gateway:

1. In the ADMS Console, select the **Tools** option in the menu bar.

2. Select **Manage Vault Gateway**. If you are not signed in, you will be prompted to sign in to an administrator account.

3. If you manage more than one Autodesk Account team, the Autodesk Account Teams window displays. Select a team and click **OK**. The Vault Gateways window displays.

4. The *Local Gateway* section is blank when a team does not have a gateway configured. Select **Configure** in the Vault Gateways window.

5. Complete the following fields in the Configure Local Gateway window:

   - *Region:* Select the region closest to the physical location of your Vault server. Note: A gateway's region cannot be edited after the gateway is configured.

   - *Service Account:* This is the Autodesk ID associated with the gateway. Click **Service Account** to sign in to an account.

   Note: *The service account must have a Vault Professional license and be part of the team selected in Step 3 above. Additionally, a service account can only be associated with a single gateway.*

6. Click **OK**. The Vault Gateways window displays. Information on the new gateway is updated in the *Local Gateway* section.

Connecting to a Vault Gateway

After Vault Gateway is configured by your administrator, team members can use the gateway URL to connect to their vault remotely.

Logging in to a gateway follows the same procedure as logging in to a vault through a direct server connection. The Server field takes an HTTPS URL to the gateway (a gateway's host name, displayed when an administrator manages a gateway) instead of a server name. Vault clients cannot connect to the gateway if https:// is omitted from the URL.

   Note: *Vault Gateway does not support logging in with Windows authentication.*

Deleting a Vault Gateway

Administrators can permanently delete a gateway and its gateway URL. After deleting a gateway, your team can no longer use the gateway URL. Deleting a gateway is irreversible.

- Team members cannot use the URL to connect to the vault.

- Administrators cannot reuse the URL when configuring a new gateway.

How To: Delete a Vault Gateway

To delete a gateway:

1. In the ADMS Console, select the **Tools** option in the menu bar.
2. Select **Manage Vault Gateway**. If you are not signed in, you will be prompted to sign in to an administrator account.
3. Select a team and click **OK**.
4. Click **Delete** to delete the local gateway. To delete a gateway in the *Other Gateways* section, select the X icon in the *Action* column to delete the corresponding gateway.

15.3 Replication

Overview

Replication is the process of copying data from one server to another server usually located in two different physical locations. This process enables the setup of a Vault environment which has two different locations and users will not have to spend time downloading large CAD files across their Wide Area Network (WAN) connection. The replication solutions for Vault Professional include ADMS full replication (Connected Workgroups) for both file store and SQL database replication, and Autodesk Vault File Server (AVFS), which is an alternative file store replication solution.

Objectives

After completing this lesson, you will be able to:

- Enable and disable workgroup replication.

- Add and delete workgroups.

- Enable and disable a vault for a multi-site environment.

- Replicate a vault, files, and folders.

- Export, import, and configure replication priorities.

- Schedule replication for a multi-site environment.

- Describe the benefits of Autodesk Vault File Server (AVFS).

Replication Solutions Overview

Data replication is only available in a multi-site environment. A multi-site environment consists of multiple remote sites that can be configured to access the same vault data. A site is comprised of a dedicated Autodesk data management server and a file store. Each site accesses a shared AUTODESKVAULT SQL instance. The SQL database tracks which files and versions are at each site in a multi-site environment. Each site can be synchronized so that newer files and newer versions are shared across sites. Individual vaults can be replicated, or all of the enabled vaults on a site can be replicated. Replication can also be scheduled. By default, replication is set for 12:00 AM (midnight) each weekday when a vault is enabled. During the day, if a user finds that a file is not located on their site, they can replicate the file on demand. Companies that have multiple design organizations that work on the same projects need the ability to collaborate and share files.

Full replication, or Connected Workgroups, is an architecture suited for multiple sites that are distributed over great distances or poor networks. With this architecture, SQL databases are replicated across the multiple locations, as well as the file store.

The Autodesk Vault File Server (AVFS) is an alternative file store replication solution.

Full Replication (Connected Workgroups)

To enable sites to have their own database server to increase SQL performance, the Autodesk Vault software uses Connected Workgroups. The following illustration shows a workgroup with two different sites connected to a second workgroup with a single site. Note that in this illustration, site B in Workgroup 1 would be an AVFS server.

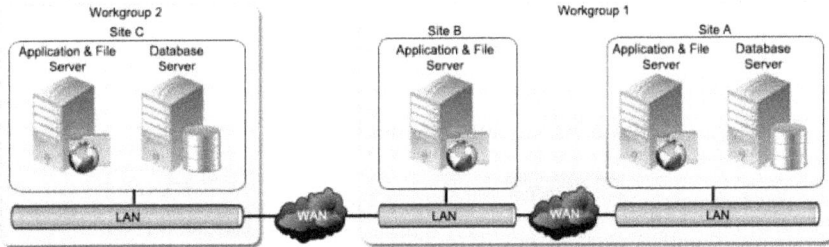

The Connected Workgroup feature, or full replication, supports the use of multiple database servers using Microsoft SQL Publisher/Subscriber technology. This technology enables the replication of the SQL database at multiple locations.

The terminology used for a Connected Workgroup (i.e., full replication) environment includes:

- **Site:** A location where the Vault server software is installed to which users connect using the client application.

- **Workgroup:** A group of sites connecting to the same SQL database.

- **Publisher:** The first SQL server configured in a full replicated environment.

- **Subscriber:** SQL servers replicating to the publisher in a full replicated environment.

Autodesk Vault File Server (AVFS)

The Autodesk Vault File Server is a simple file store management system that enables you to move and configure a file store.

Sometimes in multi-site environments, a latency can occur when the Autodesk Data Management Server (ADMS) communicates with SQL. To reduce this latency, the File Server talks directly to the ADMS instead. Similarly, the Vault client(s) communicate directly with the ADMS for metadata and the File Server for file upload/download events, reducing the time it takes to update the file store.

Important: The File Server machine must be able to access the machine where the ADMS Console is installed.

> *Note: Although the File Server supports a multi-site environment, all file replication must be scheduled from the ADMS Console.*

Managing Workgroup Replication

To create a Connected Workgroup environment, workgroup replication must be enabled. Workgroup replication must be enabled from the publisher site before installing the subscriber sites.

How To: Enable Workgroup Replication

1. Use File Explorer to create a shared network folder.

2. In the Navigation pane, select **Workgroups**.

3. Right-click and select **Enable Workgroup Replication**.

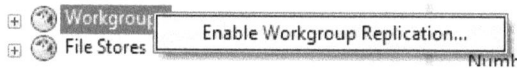

4. Enter the path to the shared network folder.

5. Enter the user account setup to run replication. This account should have access to the shared network folder.

6. Enter and confirm the password for the replication account.

7. Click **OK**.

How To: Disable Workgroup Replication

To discontinue the use of a Connected Workgroup environment, workgroup replication must be disabled. Before disabling workgroup replication, all workgroups must be deleted.

1. In the Navigation pane, select **Workgroups**.

2. Right-click and select **Disable Workgroup Replication**.

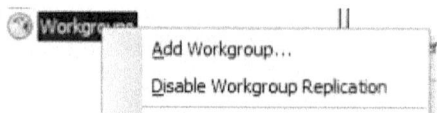

3. If the subscribing sites have not been deleted, check the box to delete the subscribing sites.

4. Click **OK**.

How To: Configure Workgroup Replication

Once a workgroup has been added to the Connected Workgroup environment, each vault in the new workgroup has to be configured to replicate. Only vaults selected to replicate from one workgroup will be accessible from a different workgroup.

1. In the Navigation pane, select the workgroup of the vault to be replicated.

2. In the right pane, right-click on the vault to replicate and select **Manage Replication**.

3. Use **Add (>>)** and **Remove (<<)** to select which workgroups to replicate the vault.

4. Click **OK**.

Adding and Deleting Workgroups

Before adding a subscribing workgroup, a supported version of Microsoft SQL Server must be installed on the subscribing server (the same version as is installed on the publishing server). Vault does not support Connected Workgroups on Microsoft SQL Express.

> *Note: Do not install the Vault server on the subscribing server.*

How To: Add a Workgroup

1. Install Microsoft SQL with an instance named **AUTODESKVAULT** on the subscribing server.

2. Launch the Vault server console from the publishing server.

3. Right-click on the **Workgroups** node and select **Add Workgroup**.

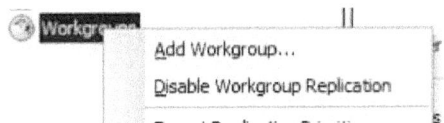

4. In the Add Workgroup dialog box, enter the required information.

    *   **Workgroup Name:** The name of the new workgroup.
    *   **Workgroup Label:** The unique name for the new workgroup. This name will be tied to all schemes created for this workgroup.
    *   **Subscriber Server Name:** The name of the server with SQL installed for the new workgroup.
    *   **Remote SQL Credentials:** The login credentials for the new SQL server being used for the new workgroup.
    *   **Remote Replication Credentials:** The credentials set up for replication when defined when configuring the publishing server.

5. Click **OK**.

How To: Delete a Workgroup

A workgroup that is no longer required can be deleted. A workgroup can be deleted using the server console from the publisher workgroup.

1. In the Navigation pane, select **Workgroups**.
2. Right-click a workgroup in the list and select **Delete Workgroup**.
3. When prompted for confirmation to delete the workgroup, click yes.
4. If an error occurs where the subscriber database cannot be cleaned up, repeat the process but select Unconditional delete.

Replicating Vaults, Files, and Folders

How To: Replicate a Vault

Use the following steps to replicate a vault from the Autodesk Data Management Server console:

1. In the Navigation pane, expand the **Workgroups** node.
2. Expand the correct workgroup node.
3. Expand the correct site node.
4. Select a vault located on the current site from the list.
5. Right-click on the site and select the replication option:

    *   **Replicate Now:** Synchronize all of the vaults on the current site immediately.
    *   **Replicated Folders:** Select which folders and files to replicate.
    *   **Replication Schedule:** Establish a synchronization schedule, or toggle off scheduled synchronization.

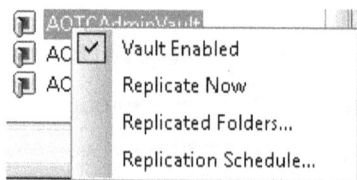

Replicating Files and Folders

Folder and file replication can be accessed from the Autodesk Data Management Server console's Navigation pane.

Note: You can also replicate files and folders from the Replication Schedule dialog box by clicking Replicated Folders.

How To: Replicate Files and Folders

Use the following steps to access the Folder and File Replication dialog box from the Autodesk Data Management Server console:

1. In the Navigation pane, select the workgroup of the vault to be replicated.

2. In the right pane, right-click on the vault to replicate and select **Replicated Folders**.

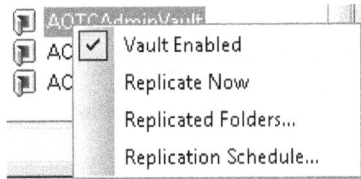

3. By default all folders will be checked. Uncheck any folders which do not need to be replicated. Check folders which need to be replicated.

    Note: This feature only controls which files will be replicated from the file store and not the metadata about the files. Regardless of what is selected, all metadata is replicated to the subscriber sites. If you want to limit visibility of metadata, you need to apply the correct security on the folders and files.

Enabling or Disabling a Vault for a Multi-Site Environment

To make a vault accessible to other sites, it must be enabled. When a vault is enabled, it is available to all sites in a multi-site environment. A replicated vault must be enabled on the replicated site. This applies to the subscriber and to the AVFS server. This is not done from the publisher, but rather from the remote site.

How To: Enable a Vault

To enable a vault:

1. In the Navigation pane, expand the **Workgroups** node.

2. Select the site to work with.

3. Select a vault located on the current site from the list.

4. Right-click on the vault name and select **Vault Enabled**.

5. If the file store path for the selected vault is not set or is invalid, you are prompted to specify the file store path for the selected vault. Specify the location of the file store and click **OK**.

6. You are prompted to select whether the vault data is synchronized now or at the next scheduled replication. By default, replication is set for 12:00 AM (midnight) each weekday.

How To: Disable a Vault

To restrict any other site from accessing a vault, it must be disabled. When a vault is disabled, it is no longer available to any other site in a multi-site environment. A disabled vault is available only to the site where the vault is located. Only vaults at the site from which the server console is running can be disabled.

To disable a vault:

1. In the Navigation pane, select **Sites**.
2. Select the line containing the current site and the vault to enable at this site.
3. Right-click on the vault name and select **Vault Enabled** to toggle it off.

How To: View Site Details

To view site details:

1. In the ADMS console's Navigation pane, select **Workgroups**.
2. Select the site that you want to manage.

Each site is listed along with a summary of site statistics, including:

- Server Name
- Description
- Location of File Store
- Vault Name
- Vault Status
- Replication Type
- Last Replication
- Next Replication
- Site Status

Replication Priorities

Replication Priority (Site Affinity) enables administrators to gain control of how multi-site and database replication files are handled from site to site. Replication priority enables you to set up a preferred list of sites or a selected site for file replication. With replication priority, you can prioritize sites in the *Preferred Sites* list. Once replication priority has been set up for a site, any subsequent file replication (both on-demand and scheduled) uses the preferred list of sites. Replication priorities for all sites can be exported to an XML file, which can then be edited in a text editor and imported back into Vault.

How To: Configure Replication Priority

1. On the Server Console, select a site by expanding the **Workgroups** node and then expanding the site's workgroup.
2. Right-click on the site and select **Manage Replication Priority**.
3. In the Manage Replication Priority dialog box, add sites to the *Prioritized* section by using **Add**.
4. Prioritize sites in the *Prioritized* section by using **Move Up** and **Move Down**.
5. Click **OK** to save your changes.

How To: Export Replication Priorities

1. In the Server Console, right-click on the **Workgroups** node and select **Export Replication Priorities**.

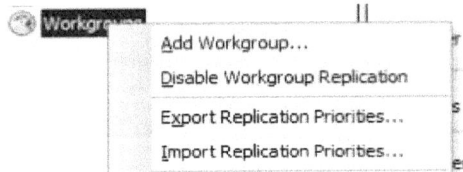

2. Select a location, enter a name in the Save dialog box, and click **Save**.
3. Click **OK** in the confirmation dialog box.
4. Open the XML file in a text editor.
5. Set up replication priority by editing the XML file and saving your changes.

How To: Import Replication Priorities

1. In the Server Console, right-click on the **Workgroups** node and select **Import Replication Priorities**.

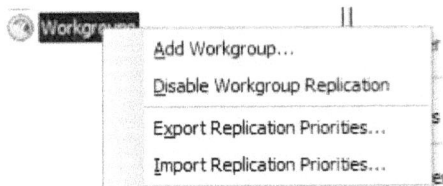

2. Browse to where the XML file with the replication priority is located.
3. Select the file and click **Open**.
4. Click **OK** in the confirmation dialog box.
5. Validate the import by selecting each site under the **Workgroups** node and viewing the site's Replication Priority table.

Scheduling Replication for a Multi-Site Environment

How To: Schedule Replication

Data replication can be scheduled to occur daily, or at a specified intervals. By default, replication is set for 12:00 AM (midnight) each weekday when a vault is enabled.

1. In the Navigation pane, expand the **Workgroups** node.

2. Select the workgroup you want to work with.

3. Select the appropriate site.

4. Right-click on the vault and select **Replication Schedule**.

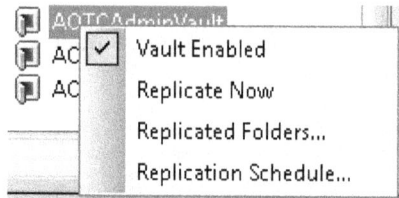

5. In the Scheduled Replication dialog box, select the **Enable scheduled replication** checkbox.

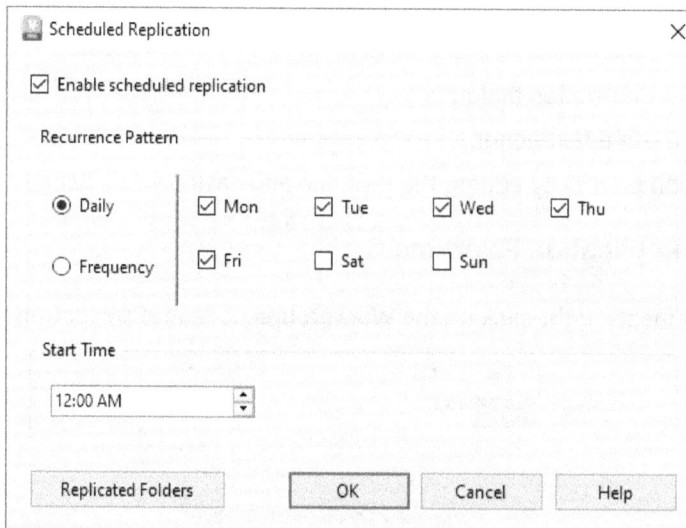

6. Choose either a daily schedule or a replication frequency.

   - **Daily:** The default daily replication schedule is weekdays at midnight. Specify a start time and select which days to perform the replication.

   - **Frequency:** Specify a start time and then select how often the replication is performed.

7. Click **OK**.

Autodesk Vault File Server (AVFS) Configuration

Once the Autodesk Vault File Server is installed, ideally you would copy the file store to the AVFS server so that it is not replicating all files from scratch. After configuring the connection between the AVFS server and the primary ADMS server, you need to enable the vault on the AVFS server. This prompts you to specify where the file store folder resides.

Thin Client

With Autodesk® Vault Thin Client, you are able to access files and items in a vault via the web. Employees or groups can view, search, and print details of items and files. This chapter covers how to access and view files and items in the vault.

Learning Objectives

- Explain requirements for Vault Thin Client.
- Confirm browser compatibility.
- Sign in and out of Thin Client.
- Navigate the folders and files in the Thin Client.
- Search files and items using the Thin Client.
- Configure view display settings.
- Print using the Thin Client.
- Access and identify the panes in the File Details page for a selected file.
- Navigate between the *History*, *Uses*, and *Where Used* tabs for a selected file.
- Preview a selected file.
- Access the Actions menu to download files from the vault.
- Access the Item Master list in the Thin Client.
- Access and identify the panes in the Item Details page for a selected item.
- Navigate between the *Bill of Materials*, *History*, *Where Used*, and *Associated Files* tabs for a selected item.
- Preview a selected item.

16.1 Getting Started with the Thin Client

Overview

In this lesson, you will review the requirements for Vault Thin Client on various browsers and learn how to sign in and out of the vault using the web-browser interface. Once in the Thin Client, you will navigate the vault, locate files using search tools, configure view displays, and preview and print files.

Objectives

After completing this lesson, you will be able to:

- View data associated with individual vault objects.

- Preview Autodesk Inventor files and other supported file types in the Viewer.

- View records and attachments in change orders.

- Switch between vaults in the Thin Client.

- Share links you can open in the Vault Client on desktop or in the Thin Client.

- Download copies of files directly to your computer.

    Note: The Thin Client is compatible with Vault Professional only. There is no subscription or license requirement for Thin Client.

Requirements

The Autodesk Vault Thin Client is supported by the following web browsers:

- Apple Safari

- Google Chrome

- Microsoft Edge

- Mozilla Firefox

Make sure that your browser meets the Thin Client's requirements before signing in. Consult the system requirements for Autodesk Vault products to learn more about Thin Client browser compatibility.

Sign In and Sign Out of the Thin Client

You must sign in using a unique user name and password assigned by the vault administrator. If an account has not been set up for you, contact your vault administrator.

   Note: Your administrator can also import a Windows Active Directory account. With an Active Directory account, you can sign in using your Windows account credentials.

How To: Sign In to the Thin Client

1. In the browser address field, enter the URL for the Thin Client application. For example, **http://<servername>/ AutodeskTC/<vaultname>**, where server name is either the IP address or the name of the computer hosting the Autodesk Data Management Server (for this class, it is '**localhost**'). Note: After signing in to the Thin Client, you can change vaults in the Thin Client interface, if required.

2. On the Sign in page, enter your user credentials, depending on the authentication method:

    *   **Sign in to Vault (Autodesk Vault Account):** Enter the username and password for the Autodesk Data Management Server account assigned to you by your system administrator and click **Sign in to Vault**.

    *   **Windows Account (Windows Authentication):** Click **Windows Account**, enter your Active Directory username and password in the window that appears, and click **OK**.

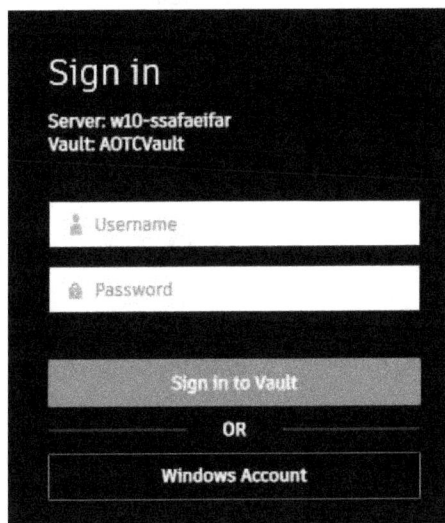

3. The Thin Client interface displays.

How To: Sign Out of the Thin Client

1. To sign out of the session, click **Sign Out** in the Profile menu in the upper-right corner of the page.

Navigation Bar

- The navigation bar contains several icons at the top of the window. It also contains a search bar.

- **Vault2** ⌄ **Vault Selector**: Displays a list of available vaults.

  - To switch to a different vault:

  a. Click the Vault Selector, indicated by the current server/vault name.

  b. Select one of the vaults displayed.

  c. Click **Confirm** to change vaults. You must sign in again before you can access the selected vault.

- **Help Icon**: Displays a menu containing the following options:

  - **Help and Support:** Opens the Autodesk Knowledge Network help for Autodesk Vault.

  - **About:** Displays the current version information for the Thin Client.

  - **Contact Us:** Opens the Vault Products Feedback Forum, where you can communicate directly with Autodesk about Autodesk Vault software.

- **Notification Icon**: Displays unread notifications. When you have a new notification, a badge appears on the icon.

- **Profile Icon**: Displays the following options:

  - **Settings:** Displays settings for viewing data in the Thin Client.

  - **Sign Out:** Ends your session in the Thin Client and signs out the current account.

Workspace Navigation

The workspace navigation pane, to the left of the Thin Client interface, contains three icons. Each icon represents one of the Vault object types that you can work with in the Thin Client: **Files**, **Items**, and **Change Orders**.

Click a workspace icon to display that workspace. If a workspace contains folders, you can navigate the folder tree by clicking folder names in the workspace navigation pane.

Search Bar

The search bar searches in the current workspace.

Data Tables

Click an object or a folder in the data table of a workspace to display its contents and to view more details.

A checkbox displays to the left of the items in a data table. Select a checkbox to display icons at the top of the table. Each icon represents an action available for that type of object.

Properties Panel

The properties panel shows the properties associated with an object in the vault.

Click the (Properties Panel) icon to open the panel. Select an object to display its properties. An object is selected when its checkbox is marked.

Details View

Every object in the vault has specific data and relationships associated with it.

The Viewer

The Thin Client displays files with viewable geometry in an integrated viewer.

16.2 Working with Files

Overview

This lesson covers how to view details of the files in the Vault using Thin Client. You will learn how to access the File Details page and how the panes on this page can be used to get information on the active file. This includes viewing its system and user-defined properties, File *History*, *Uses*, and *Where Used* information. Additionally, you will learn to view the file and access the options in the Actions menu.

Objectives

After completing this lesson, you will be able to:

- Access and identify the panes in the File Details page for a selected file.

- Navigate between the *History*, *Uses*, and *Where Used* tabs for a selected file.

- View a selected file.

- Access the Actions menu to download files from the vault.

The Files Workspace

The **Files** workspace displays files and documents in your vault. Folders in the Files workspace organize data in nested levels. A breadcrumb trail, displayed above the data table, represents the location of the current folder. Click a folder name in the breadcrumb trail to view its contents.

Files are listed in a data table. Click the (Configure Columns) icon to modify the column headers in the Files workspace. You can reorder or add user- and system-defined headers to the data table in the Configure Columns drop-down list. The default order contains headers for the following data:

- Name (required)
- State
- Revision
- Category Name
- Checked Out By
- Vault Status

Viewing File Details

From the Files list page, click the filename to view detailed information about the selected file on the File Details page. The file details view contains several tabs that display file information and viewing functions. The following tabs are available in the details view of a file:

- *Properties* tab
- *History* tab
- *Uses* tab
- *Where Used* tab
- *Item* tab
- *Change Order* tab
- *View* tab

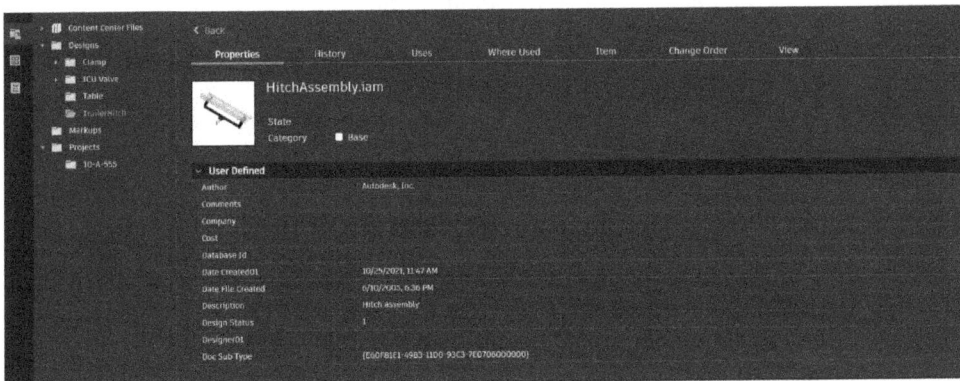

How To: View the Details of a File

1. Select the **Files** workspace in the navigation panel.
2. Navigate the folder tree to find your file. You can click folders in the workspace navigation pane or in the data table. Alternatively, you can search the vault to find the file with the search bar.
3. Click the filename in the data table.

16.3 Working with Items

Overview

This lesson covers how to view the details of items in the Vault using the Thin Client. You will learn how to access the Item Master list and the Item Details page for a selected item. Similar to working with files, you will learn how the panes on the Item Details page can be used to view information on the active item. This includes viewing its system and user-defined properties and its *Bill of Materials*, *History*, *Where Used*, *Associated Files*, and *Change Order* tabs.

Objectives

After completing this lesson, you will be able to:

- Access the Item Master list in the Thin Client.

- Access and identify the panes in the Item Details page for a selected item.

- Navigate between the *History*, *Bill of Materials*, *Where Used*, *Associated Files*, and *Change Order* tabs for a selected item.

The Items Workspace

The **Items** workspace displays items in your vault. Items are listed in a data table. Click the
(Configure Columns) icon to modify the column headers in the Items workspace. You can reorder or add user- and system-defined headers to the data table in the Configure Columns drop-down list. The default order contains headers for the following data:

- Name (required)
- State
- Revision
- Vault Status
- Category Name
- Title (Item, CO)

Viewing Item Details

The Item Details page contains several tabs that display item information. The following tabs are available in the details view of an item:

- *Properties* tab
- *History* tab
- *Bill of Materials* tab
    - The BOM view supports Multi-Level and Parts Only views.
    - To change the BOM view, click the view icon (either or , depending on the current view) in the upper-right corner of the table.
    - If **Show released files only** is toggled on in Administrator Settings, non-released versions of the item don't display.
- *Where Used* tab
- *Associated Files* tab
- *Change Order* tab

How To: View the Details of an Item

1. Select the **Items** workspace in the navigation panel.
2. Scroll through the Items list to find your item. Alternatively, you can search the vault to find the item using the search bar.

3. Click the item name in the data table.

16.4 Change Orders

Overview

This lesson covers how to view the details of change orders in the Vault using the Thin Client. You will learn how to access the Change Orders list and the Change Orders workspace for a selected change order. Similar to working with files, you will learn how the panes on the Change Order Details page can be used to get information on the active change order. This includes viewing its system and user-defined properties, records, and attachments.

Objectives

After completing this lesson, you will be able to:

- Access the Change Orders list in the Thin Client.

- Access and identify the panes in the Change Orders page for selected change orders.

- Navigate between the *Properties*, *Records*, and *Attachments* tabs.

The Change Orders Workspace

The **Change Orders** workspace displays change orders in your vault. Change orders are listed in a data table. Click the ⚙ (Configure Columns) icon to modify the column headers in the Change Orders workspace. You can reorder or add user- and system-defined headers to the data table in the Configure Columns drop-down list. The default order contains headers for the following data:

- Number (required)
- State
- Due Date
- Vault Status
- Title (Item, CO)
- Number of File Attachments

Viewing Change Order Details

The Change Order Details page contains several tabs that display change order information. The following tabs are available in the details view of a change order:

- *Properties* tab
- *Records* tab
- *Attachments* tab

How To: View the Details of a Change Order

1. Select the **Change Orders** workspace in the navigation panel.
2. Scroll through the Change Orders list to find your change order. Alternatively, you can search the vault to find the change order using the search bar.
3. Click the change order number in the data table.

16.5 Viewer

The Thin Client includes a browser version of the viewer, Autodesk's tool for exploring, examining, and reviewing the contents of CAD files.

The Thin Client viewer implements the same controls and features as the viewer available in the Vault Client.

How To: Open the Viewer in the Thin Client

1. Select the **Files** workspace in the navigation panel.
2. Navigate the folder tree to find your file. You can click folders in the workspace navigation pane or in the data table. Alternatively, you can search the vault to find the file with the search bar.
3. Select the file by clicking, or tapping on touchscreen devices, the checkbox to the left of the file name. The file is selected when its checkbox is marked.

   Note: You can select multiple files to open at once.

4. Select the (View) icon above the data table.

   • Alternatively, you can view a file's details and select the *View* tab to open the viewer.

16.6 Working with Vault Data

The Thin Client enables you to share links to vaulted data, download files, view file contents, and more to effectively work with your vault data.

Downloading a File

When downloading multiple files at once, the Thin Client limits the download to 500mb. Downloading files individually doesn't have a maximum limit.

How To: Download a Local Copy of a File from the Vault

1. Select the **Files** workspace in the navigation pane.
2. Navigate the folder tree to find your file. Select folders in the navigation pane or in the data table to view their contents. Alternatively, you can search the vault to find the file using the search bar.
3. Select the file name to view its details or select the checkbox to the left of the file name.

   Note: You can select multiple files to download at once.

4. Select the (Download) icon to display a drop-down list with the following options:
   - Select **Download File** to download a local copy of the file.
   - Select **Download Visualization File** to download a local DWF of the file.

Sharing Links

How To: Generate a Link That You or Others Can Open in the Vault Client or Thin Client

1. Select a workspace in the navigation pane.
2. Navigate the data table to find the object to share. Alternatively, you can search the vault using the search bar.
3. Select the object name to view its details or select the checkbox to the left of the object name.

   Note: You can select multiple files to share at once.

4. Select the (Share) icon.
5. Select the *Desktop Client* tab or the *Web Client* tab in the Share window.

   Note: Links for the Vault Client and the Thin Client are not interchangeable. The type of link that you select can only be viewed in the specified client.

6. To share the link, use either of the following methods:

   - Enter an email address in the open field and select **Send**. An email is automatically generated by your computer's default email client.
   - Select **Copy Link** to copy the link to your clipboard.

Update File Visualization

Visualization files can be updated so that the latest DWF of a CAD file is available. When a visualization file is updated, the job is sent to the job server for processing. The **Update Visualization** command is only available if the Job Server is enabled and turned on.

How To: Update Visualization Files

1. Select the **Files** workspace in the navigation pane.

2. Hover over a row and select the ⬛ icon of the file to update.

   Note: On touch screen devices, tap a row to the right of the file name to reveal this icon.

3. Select **Update Visualization** to send the job to the Job Processor.

Sort Data Tables

Select a header in a data table to sort the table. Number-based fields sort numerically in ascending or descending order. Text-based fields sort alphabetically from A-Z or Z-A. Date-based fields sort from older to newer or newer to older.

View Historical Versions and Revisions

In object details, select the **Latest / Latest Released** drop-down list to browse and select historical versions or revisions. You can also select past versions in the *History* tab.

Version and revision apply when you share a link to the Thin Client. Links redirect to the version and revision selected in the drop-down list or *History* tab.

Filter Data in the History Tab

When you're viewing file or item details, the *History* tab can be filtered. Select the **Filter** icon to the far right of the table header to display filter options. Filter options include **Show Latest Versions Only** and **Show All Versions**.

Modify Data Table Headers

Data tables display in a default header configuration that can be modified. You can rearrange the display order of headers and also add system-generated or user-generated properties to the header.

How To: Modify Table Headers

1. Select the (Configure Columns) icon to the far-right of the table header.
2. Click, or tap and hold on touchscreen devices, to drag a header and rearrange the display order.
3. To hide a header, unselect its checkbox.

16.7 Searching

Use the Thin Client to search for specific data in your vault.

Search Bar

The current workspace, indicated by the drop-down list to the left of the search field, is automatically selected when you click the search bar. Click the menu to select a different workspace.

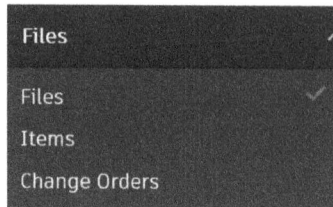

How To: Search in the Thin Client

1. Click **Search** in the navigation bar to expand the search field.
2. Enter your search term(s) and press <Enter> to search in the selected workspace.

16.8 Settings

Administrators can customize display settings in the Thin Client.

File and Item Display Settings

You can modify which files and items are displayed on the page by selecting **Settings** in the Profile menu.

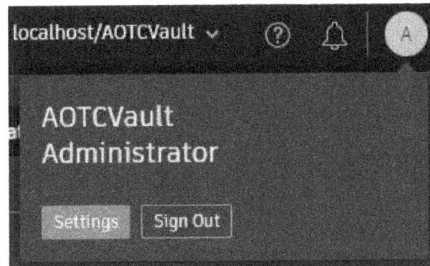

Files

- Show released files only
- Show latest version of file only

Items

- Show released items only
- Show latest version of item only

16.9 Printing

You can print data tables and object details in the Thin Client.

How To: Print a Page from the Thin Client

1. Select a workspace (**Files**, **Items**, or **Change Orders**). Alternatively, you can search the vault using the search bar.
2. To print the data table in your current workspace:
   a. Modify the table as necessary. The page will print as it appears in your browser.
   b. Select the (Print) icon in the upper-right corner of the page.
   c. Follow your browser's instructions to print the page.
3. To print the details of a specific object:
   a. Select the object name to view its details.
   b. Select the tab you want to print (e.g., *History*, *Bill of Materials*, etc).
   c. Modify the table as necessary. The page will print as it appears in your browser.
   d. Select the (Print) icon in the upper-right corner of the page.
   e. Follow your browser's instructions to print the page.

Practice 16a
Get Started with the Thin Client

In this practice, you will sign in to the vault using the Thin Client, navigate the vault, change the layout and configuration of the properties displayed in a view, and search the vault.

1. Open a browser to access the Autodesk Vault Thin Client.

2. Type in the URL to access the Thin Client Login page (**http://localhost/AutodeskTC/ AOTCVault** for this class).

3. Enter your user name (**administrator**) and password (leave blank) and press <Enter> or click **Sign in to Vault**.

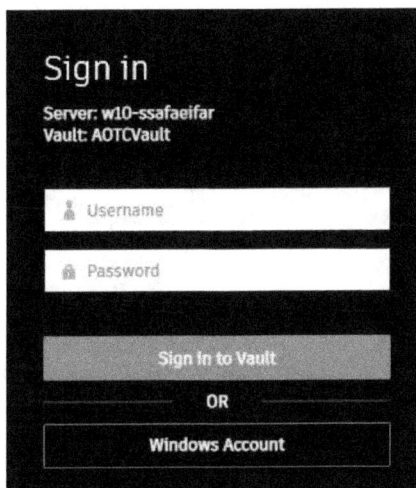

4. Select the **Files** icon on the left side on the Thin Client page.

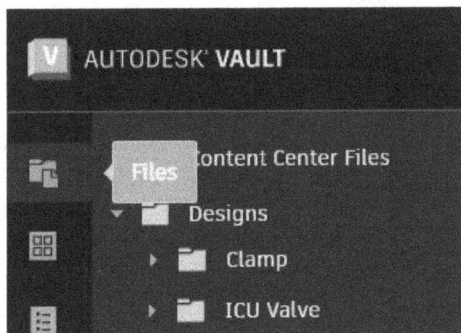

5. Navigate to the *Designs>TrailerHitch* folder. Note that there are no files displayed in the folder. This is because the default setting for the Thin Client is to only show released items and files. Currently there are no released items or files in this folder.

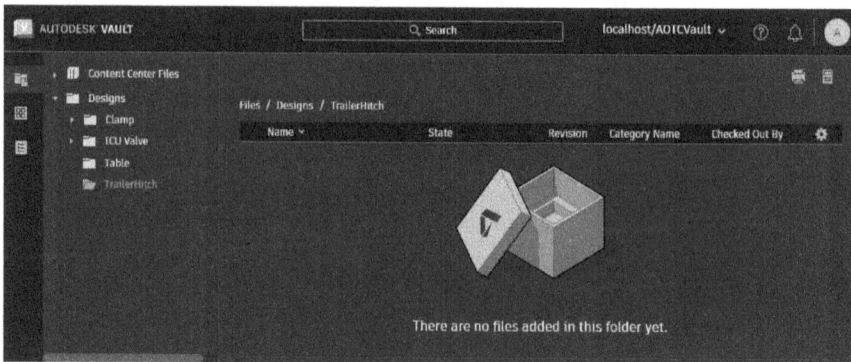

6. Click the **Profile** icon and select **Settings**.

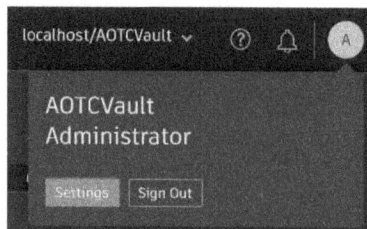

7. In the Administrator Settings window, disable the options for **Show released files only** and **Show released items only**.

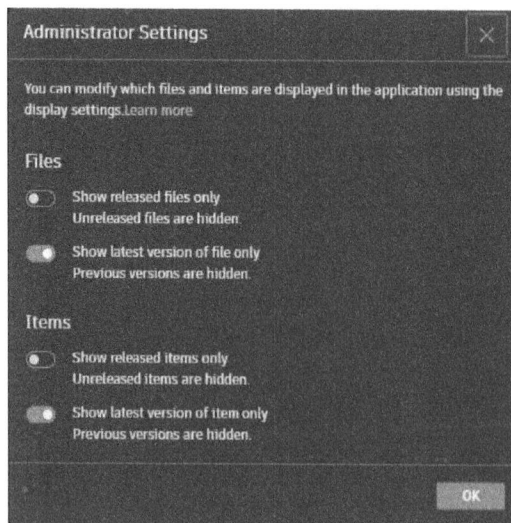

8. Click **OK** to close the window. Note how all the files are now displayed in the view in the Thin Client.

9. Select the arrow beside the *Name* column header to change the sort order for the names.

10. Select the ⚙ (Configure Columns) icon.

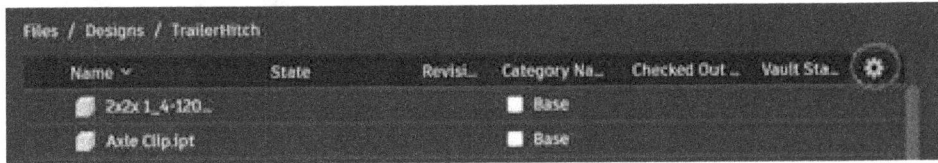

11. Select **Vault Status** in the *SELECTED HEADERS* section and drag it up until it is listed under **Name**.

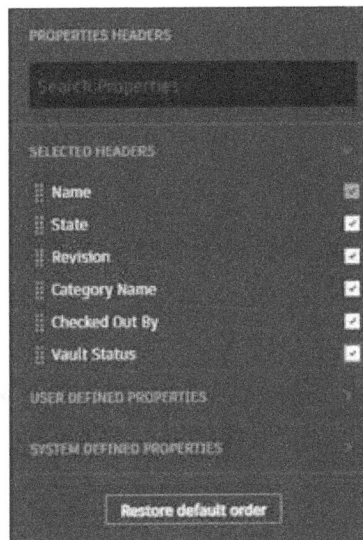

12. Select **Category Glyph** in *SYSTEM DEFINED PROPERTIES* section. It will be added to the *SELECTED HEADERS* section.

13. Note that the display for the current folder has changed. Switch to other folders and note that the column properties displayed have also changed.

14. Select ⚙ (Configure Columns). Select **Restore default order** to return to the default column display.

15. In the search field, click on the drop-down list to expand the search options. Select **Files**. Enter **ICU*** in search bar and press <Enter>.

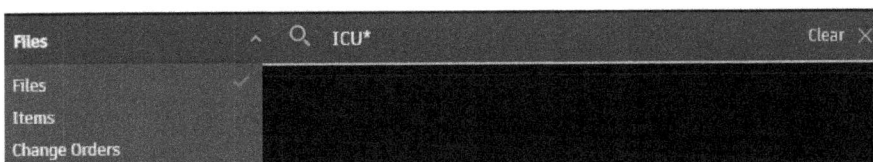

End of practice

Practice 16b
Work with Files

In this practice, you will navigate through the file structure to locate a file. Once located, you will access the File Details page and view the details of the file using the *History*, *Uses*, and *Where Used* tabs. You will also open the DWF preview of the file.

1. In the Project Explorer, navigate to the *Designs>TrailerHitch* folder or conduct a search for **Hitch**.

2. In the Files list, select **HitchAssembly.iam** to view the detailed information about the file on the File Details page.

3. The thumbnail for the selected file displays in the left pane of the File Details page. Below the thumbnail is the detailed summary of the *User Defined* and *System Defined* properties. Scroll through the list to review the details.

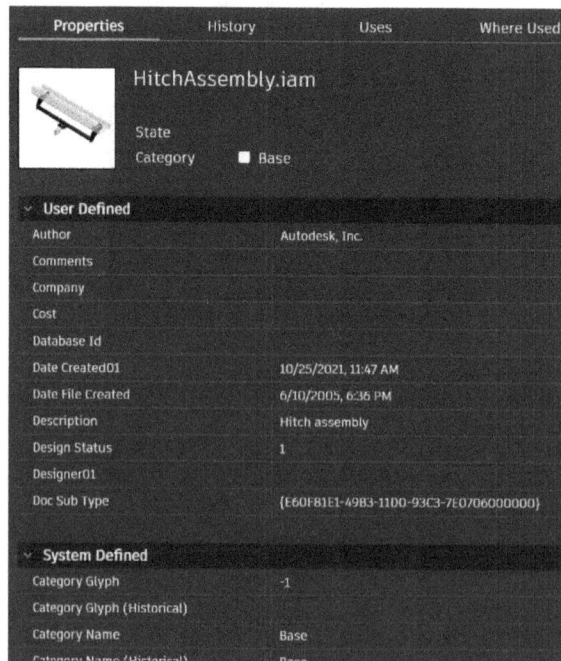

4. In the right pane, select the *History* tab.

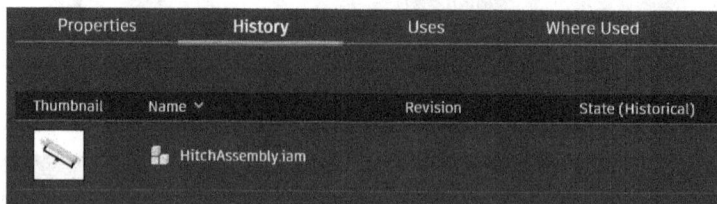

5. Select the *Uses* tab to display all the files that are used in the HitchAssembly.iam file.

6. Select **Axle Clip.ipt** in the *Uses* tab. This is now the active file listed on the File Details page.

7. Select the *Where Used* tab to display where the Axle Clip is used. This part is only used in the HitchAssembly.

8. Select the **HitchAssembly** in the *Where Used* tab to make it the active file.

9. Select the *View* tab.

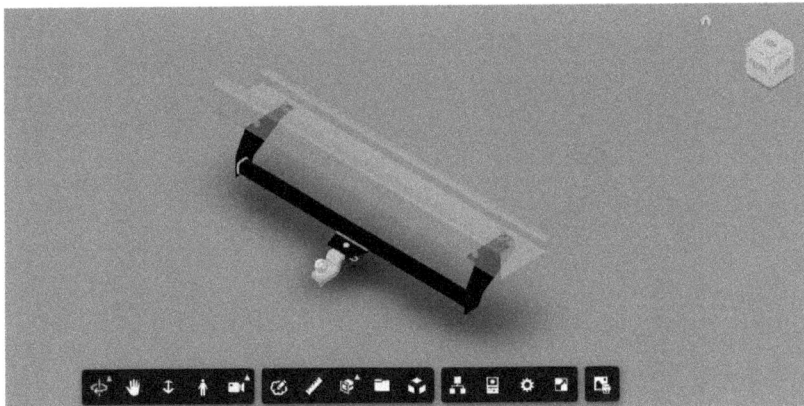

- When viewing a visualization file in the viewer, you can use markup to superimpose annotations on the 2D or 3D representation of the file. Markup tools in the viewer include freehand drawing, text, and callouts, among others.

- The **Save Snapshot** function downloads a local copy of the current markup in the viewer as a PNG. **Print Snapshot** automatically launches your browser's print function.

10. Use the toolbar and the ViewCube to navigate the assembly. Select the **Home** icon to return the model to its default orientation.

11. In the Viewer toolbar, select **Explode Model** and separate the model's geometry to see individual parts of the design. Select **Markup** and select the **Callout** icon.

12. Enter **Please Review** in the text box to add this markup to the file.

13. Select the text and using the font options in the *Markup & Measure* tab, change the size of the font and its bold setting. Press <Enter>.

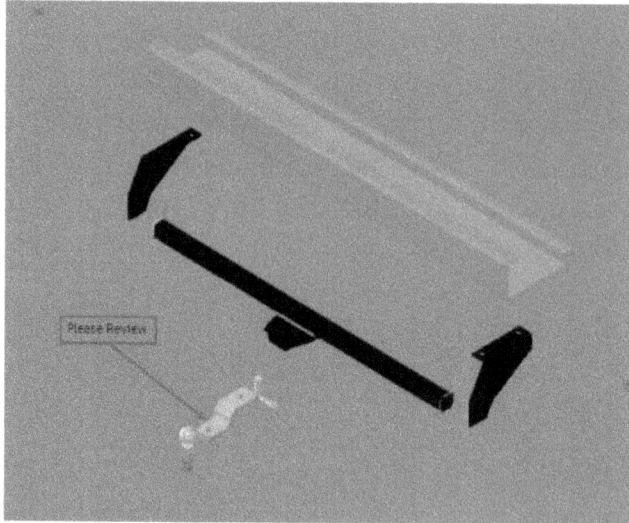

14. In the Viewer toolbar, select **Measure**. Select the overall length by selecting two vertices on parallel edges at the extent of the model.

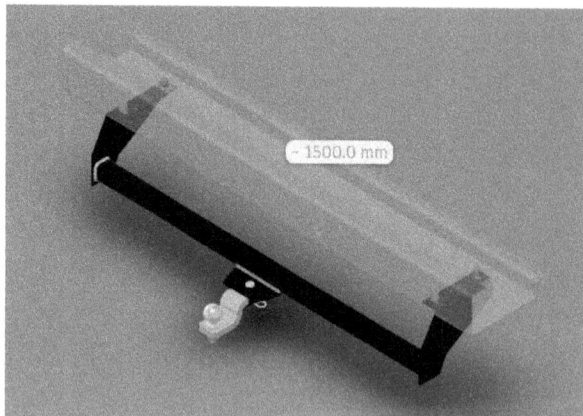

15. Select **Download Visualization File** from *Download* tab at the top-right of the toolbar to save a local copy of the DWF file.

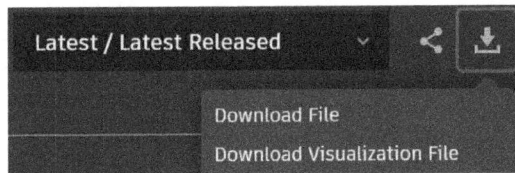

End of practice

Practice 16c
Work with Items

In this practice, you will activate the **Items** view and review the information and tabs available on the Item Details page for a selected item.

1. To display the list of items in the vault, select **Items** in the menu on the left side of the Thin Client browser. All items that exist in the vault display in the Items list.

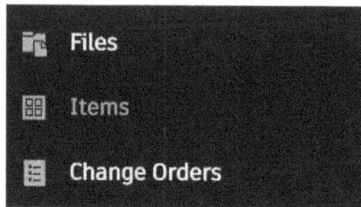

> *Note: If no items are listed in the Item view, check the settings for the Thin Client and ensure that the **Show released items only** option is disabled.*

2. Select the arrow beside the *Name* property header to change the sort order for the items.

3. Select ⚙ (Configure Columns) and click **Restore default order** to return to the default property display.

4. With the Items view still active, use the search field to search for **Work in Progress** items. The results of the search are returned in the Items view showing only those items identified in this view as Work in Progress. If no files have been assigned this state, search the Items list another way.

5. Select **Clear** in the search field to clear the filtering of the list. Select **Back** to return to the Items view.

6. Select the **100038** item (**HitchAssembly.iam**) to open the Item Details page. Note that your item name may be different.

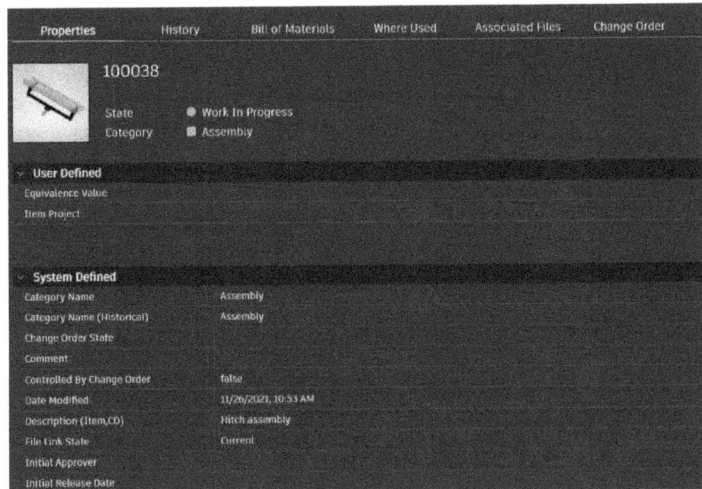

7. Select the *History* tab and note the history of this item.

8. Select the *Bill of Materials* tab. The default display option for the *Bill of Materials* tab is **Multi-Level**.

9. Change the display to **Parts Only**.

10. Note the **Print, Share**, and **Open Properties Panel** icons available in the top-right corner.

End of practice

Additional Resources

A variety of resources are available to help you get the most from your Autodesk® software. Whether you prefer instructor-led, self-paced, or online training, Autodesk has you covered.

- Learning Tools from Autodesk
- Autodesk Certification
- Autodesk Authorized Training Centers (ATC®)
- Autodesk Subscription
- Autodesk Communities

Learning Tools from Autodesk

Use your Autodesk software to its full potential. Whether you are a novice or an advanced user, Autodesk offers a robust portfolio of learning tools to help you perform ahead of the curve.

- Get hands-on experience with job-related practices based on industry scenarios from Autodesk Official Training Guides, e-books, self-paced learning, and training videos.

- All materials are developed by Autodesk subject matter experts.

- Get exactly the training you need with learning tools designed to fit a wide range of skill levels and subject matter—from basic essentials to specialized in-depth training on the capabilities of the latest Autodesk products.

- Access the most comprehensive set of Autodesk learning tools available anywhere: from your authorized partner, online, or at your local bookstore.

- To find out more, visit http://www.autodesk.com/learning.

Autodesk Certification

Demonstrate your experience with Autodesk software. Autodesk certifications are a reliable validation of your skills and knowledge. Demonstrate your software skills to prospective employers, accelerate your professional development, and enhance your reputation in your field.

Certification Benefits

- Rapid diagnostic feedback to assess your strengths and identify areas for improvement.

- An electronic certificate with a unique serial number.

- The right to use an official Autodesk Certification logo.

- The option to display your certification status in the Autodesk Certified Professionals database.

For more information:

Visit www.autodesk.com/certification to learn more and to take the next steps to get certified.

Autodesk Authorized Training Centers

Enhance your productivity and learn how to realize your ideas faster with Autodesk software. Get trained at an Autodesk Authorized Training Center (ATC) with hands-on, instructor-led classes to help you get the most from your Autodesk products. Autodesk has a global network of Authorized Training Centers that are carefully selected and monitored to ensure you receive high-quality results- oriented learning. ATCs provide the best way for beginners and experts alike to get up to speed. The training helps you get the greatest return on your investment, faster, by building your knowledge in the areas you need the most. Many organizations provide training on our software, but only the educational institutions and private training providers recognized as ATC sites have met Autodesk's rigorous standards of excellence.

Find an Authorized Training Center

With over 2,000 ATCs in more than 90 countries around the world, there is probably one close to you. Visit the ATC locator at www.autodesk.com/atc to find an Autodesk Authorized Training Center near you. Look for ATC courses offered at www.autodesk.com/atcevents.

Many ATCs also offer end-user Certification testing. Locate a testing center near you at www.autodesk.starttest.com.

Autodesk Subscription

Autodesk® Subscription helps you minimize costs, increase productivity, and make the most of your Autodesk software investment. With monthly, quarterly, annual, and multi-year options, you can get the exact software you require for as long as you need it. For a fee based on the term length, you receive upgrades released during your contract term. Subscribers can also get licensed software that they can use on their home computer.

- For more information, visit www.autodesk.com/subscription.

Autodesk User Communities

Autodesk customers can take advantage of free Autodesk software, self-paced tutorials, worldwide discussion groups and forums, job postings, and more. Become a member of an Autodesk Community today!

> *Note: Free products are subject to the terms and conditions of the end-user license agreement that accompanies download of the software.*

Feedback

Autodesk understands the importance of offering you the best learning experience possible. If you have comments, suggestions, or general inquiries about Autodesk Learning, please contact us at learningtools@autodesk.com.

As a result of the feedback we receive from you, we hope to validate and append to our current research on how to create a better learning experience for our customers.

Useful Links

- Learning Tools: www.autodesk.com/learning
- Certification: www.autodesk.com/certification
- Find an Authorized Training Center: www.autodesk.com/atc
- Find an Authorized Training Center Course: www.autodesk.com/atcevents
- Autodesk Store: store.autodesk.com
- Communities: www.autodesk.com/community
- Student Community: students.autodesk.com
- Blogs: www.autodesk.com/blogs
- Discussion Groups: forums.autodesk.com

www.ingramcontent.com/pod-product-compliance
Lightning Source LLC
Chambersburg PA
CBHW060944210326
41598CB00031B/4710